THE MAVERICK GUIDE TO THAILAND

mav·er·ick (mav'er-ik), *n* 1. an unbranded steer. Hence [colloq.] 2. a person not labeled as belonging to any one faction, group, etc., who acts independently. 3. one who moves in a different direction than the rest of the herd—often a nonconformist. 4. a person using individual judgment, even when it runs against majority opinion.

The Maverick Guide Series
The Maverick Guide to Australia
The Maverick Guide to Hawaii
The Maverick Guide to New Zealand
The Maverick Guide to Thailand

In preparation:
The Maverick Guide to Bali and Java
The Maverick Guide to the Philippines

MAVERICK GUIDE TO THAILAND

Len Rutledge

1991 EDITION

PELICAN PUBLISHING COMPANY
GRETNA 1991

Copyright © 1991
By Pelican Publishing Company
All rights reserved

ISBN: 0-88289-792-6

Information in this guidebook is based on authoritative data available at the time of printing. Prices and hours of operation of businesses listed are subject to change without notice. Readers are asked to take this into account when consulting this guide.

Maps by Len Rutledge

Photos courtesy of Tourism Authority of Thailand, Thai Airways International, and Len Rutledge

Manufactured in the United States of America
Published by Pelican Publishing Company, Inc.
1101 Monroe Street, Gretna, Louisiana 70053

Contents

Acknowledgments	9
1. Why Go to Thailand?	13
2. Happy Landings	
How to Get There	23
Transportation within Thailand	27
Local Transportation	36
Travel Facts and Figures	36
Metrics and Electrics	39
Money and Prices	40
Governmental Fiddle-Faddle	41
Travellers' Guide	43
Travel Tips	50
Visit the Region	52
3. The Land and Life of Thailand	
Religion	58
The Modern Monarchy	62
The Thai Language	64
Thai Food	69
Rural Life	74
The Economy	83
Leisure Time	86
4. Who Are the Thais?	
Early Settlers	92
Sukhothai: "The Dawn of Happiness"	93
The Rise of Ayutthaya	95
The Rise Again	97
Bangkok, the New Capital	99
New Directions	102
5. Bangkok	
1. The General Picture	105
2. Getting There	106
3. Local Transportation	108
4. The Hotel Scene	110
5. Dining and Restaurants	122
6. Sightseeing	127
7. Guided Tours	155
8. Culture	157
9. Sports	161
10. Shopping	164

11. Entertainment and Nightlife	168
12. The Bangkok Address List	171

6. Chiang Mai and the North
1. The General Picture	173
2. Getting There	175
3. Local Transportation	176
4. The Hotel Scene	178
5. Dining and Restaurants	180
6. Sightseeing	182
7. Guided Tours	209
8. Culture	214
9. Sports	217
10. Shopping	219
11. Entertainment and Nightlife	220
12. The Chiang Mai Address List	221

7. Phuket and the South
1. The General Picture	223
2. Getting There	225
3. Local Transportation	227
4. The Hotel Scene	228
5. Dining and Restaurants	235
6. Sightseeing	238
7. Guided Tours	253
8. Culture	257
9. Sports	259
10. Shopping	261
11. Entertainment and Nightlife	263
12. The Phuket Address List	264

8. Pattaya and the East
1. The General Picture	265
2. Getting There	267
3. Local Transportation	267
4. The Hotel Scene	268
5. Dining and Restaurants	273
6. Sightseeing	277
7. Guided Tours	287
8. Culture	287
9. Sports	288
10. Shopping	291
11. Entertainment and Nightlife	291
12. The Pattaya Address List	293

9. The Northeast
1. The General Picture	295
2. Getting There	297

CONTENTS

3. Local Transportation	298
4. The Hotel Scene	298
5. Dining and Restaurants	301
6. Sightseeing	303
7. Guided Tours	315
8. Culture	317
9. Sports	320
10. Shopping	320
11. Entertainment and Nightlife	321
12. The Northeast Address List	322
Index	323

LIST OF MAPS

Thailand	12
The Region	15
Major Tourist Interest	17
How to Reach Thailand—Map 1	24
How to Reach Thailand—Map 2	26
Domestic Routes	28
Rail	30
Road	34
Thai Asian Routes	53
Bangkok—Map 1	104
Bangkok—Map 2	107
Hotels and AC.Bus Routes	111
Bangkok Environs	132
Around Bangkok	136
Lop Buri	138
Ayutthaya	140
Phetchaburi	142
Hua Hin	146
Nakhon Pathom	148
Kanchanaburi	152
Chiang Mai	174
Central Chiang Mai	177
Go West	186
Mae Hong Son	189
Go North	192

LIST OF MAPS

Chiang Rai	194
Go South	198
Sukhothai Historic Park	202
Phitsanulok	204
Central Plains	206
Phuket	224
Phuket Town	226
Phuket Beaches	232
Go North	240
Koh Samui	242
Go South	248
Hat Yai	250
Pattaya	266
Pattaya—The East	278
Chantaburi	284
Central Northeast	296
Nakhon Ratchasima (Korat)	302
Khon Kaen	306
North-Northeast	308
Udon Thani	310
The Far Northeast	312
Ubon Ratchathani	314
East-Northeast	316

ACKNOWLEDGMENTS

During the preparation of this book, I met a wide cross-section of people who were unfailingly helpful and friendly. I would like particularly to acknowledge the following:

Pensri Athisumongkol, Chalermlap Ganachara Na Ayudhaya, Opas Netraumpai, S. Winij, Punduhwat Komarakul Na Nakorn, Janet Collingwood, Bart Duykers, Ken Trifford.

THE MAVERICK GUIDE TO THAILAND

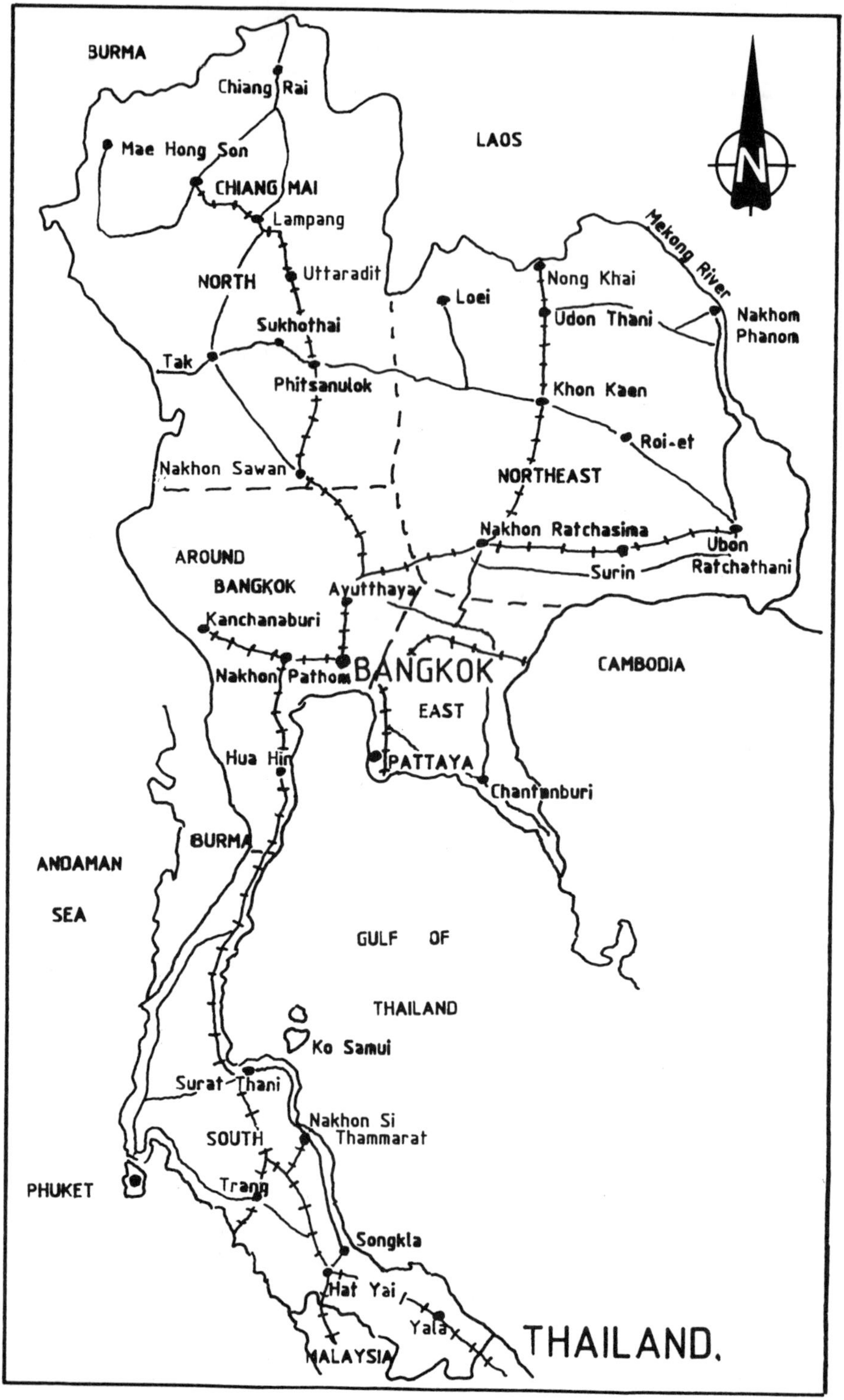

L.R. Copyright.

1

Why Go to Thailand?

I am in the midst of a love affair with Thailand. This book is written from that perspective but I make no apologies for that.

Like most love affairs, it has happened almost unexpectedly. A brief visit in 1974 showed me the pretty, picturesque side of Thailand and subsequent visits introduced me to the "Land of Smiles." Then during two periods in 1980 and 1981, when I was a consultant to the Tourism Authority of Thailand, I found a surprising diversity within a country that I thought I knew.

By the mid-1980s I was almost hooked, and now in the 1990s, I no longer try to hide it. I know of no country in the world that has a more appealing mix of diverse scenery, ancient culture, modern infrastructure, and charming people.

As a vacation destination, Thailand has almost everything you could want. The early Europeon writers created an image, an aura of romance and adventure that much of the East has had difficulty in living up to, but Thailand has succeeded without even trying. If you crave sun, sand, and sea, they are all here. So are mountains, national parks, forests, stately rivers, and rushing waterfalls. There are castles, walled cities, and ancient ruins. You can find peace and solitude or areas of adventure.

This is a land of golden-roofed temples, of saffron-robed monks gliding silently through the misty dawn, of colorful markets throbbing with life, of classical Thai dancing dripping of sensuality. The descriptions are almost erotic, too unreal, and yet they are an accurate reflection of what Thailand has to offer.

Consider this. If your major interest is history, you can visit excavations which reveal a civilization 5,000 years old; walk through huge stone castles left by the Khmers, who controlled Thailand 1,000 years ago; visit the original Thai capital of Sukhothai, where majestic temples and huge Buddhas reflect a life that is still lived in Thailand today; then finally explore Ayutthaya, where the Thai civilization flourished for over 400 years, creating what many regarded as the most beautiful city in the world.

If history has no appeal but the sun and sea are your idea of paradise, you can stay in luxurious hotels while being pampered with attentive service on some of the best beaches in Asia. Or you can find an island hideaway where the sand is pure white, the sea is crystal clear, and the modern world is only a memory, far away.

Perhaps you are a city person. You will find that Bangkok has shopping opportunities that border on the unbelievable. There are restaurants rating among the best in the world, museums and art galleries, parks for relaxing, and a nightlife scene that has become almost legendary.

If what you need is to get away from cities, there are national parks for bush walking, fine rivers for rafting, jungles for elephant riding, undeveloped wilderness for trekking, and deserted beaches for camping. You will find it all in Thailand. This book will point you in the right direction.

The wonder of Thailand is that all this enormous diversity is jammed into a relatively small area and, despite an influx of over five million visitors a year, it will remain accessible to everyone, at an affordable price.

Literally translated, Thailand means "Land of the Free," a particularly appropriate title since it is the only southeast Asian nation that escaped nineteenth-century European colonial domination. The Thais cherish their independence and are proud of their distinctive culture, language, cuisine, customs, traditions, beliefs, and approach to life. They are also one of the most hospitable people on earth and every visitor is given a warm and friendly welcome. It is through the people of a country that a visitor obtains the sharpest and longest-lasting images. In Thailand it can be simply a matter of absorbing the good vibes that abound everywhere.

The people are diverse. About 75 percent are ethnic Thais, 15 percent are Chinese, and the remainder include Malays, Khmers, Laotians, Vietnamese, Mons, hilltribe people, and a few Westerners. You will meet sophisticated city dwellers who have studied abroad and speak perfect English, simpler village folk, farmers and fishermen, and colorful hilltribe people who keep their own traditions and distinct identity.

To meet them all, you will need to visit Bangkok and some of the other major tourist centers, but also get off the beaten track to some of the more

THE REGION.

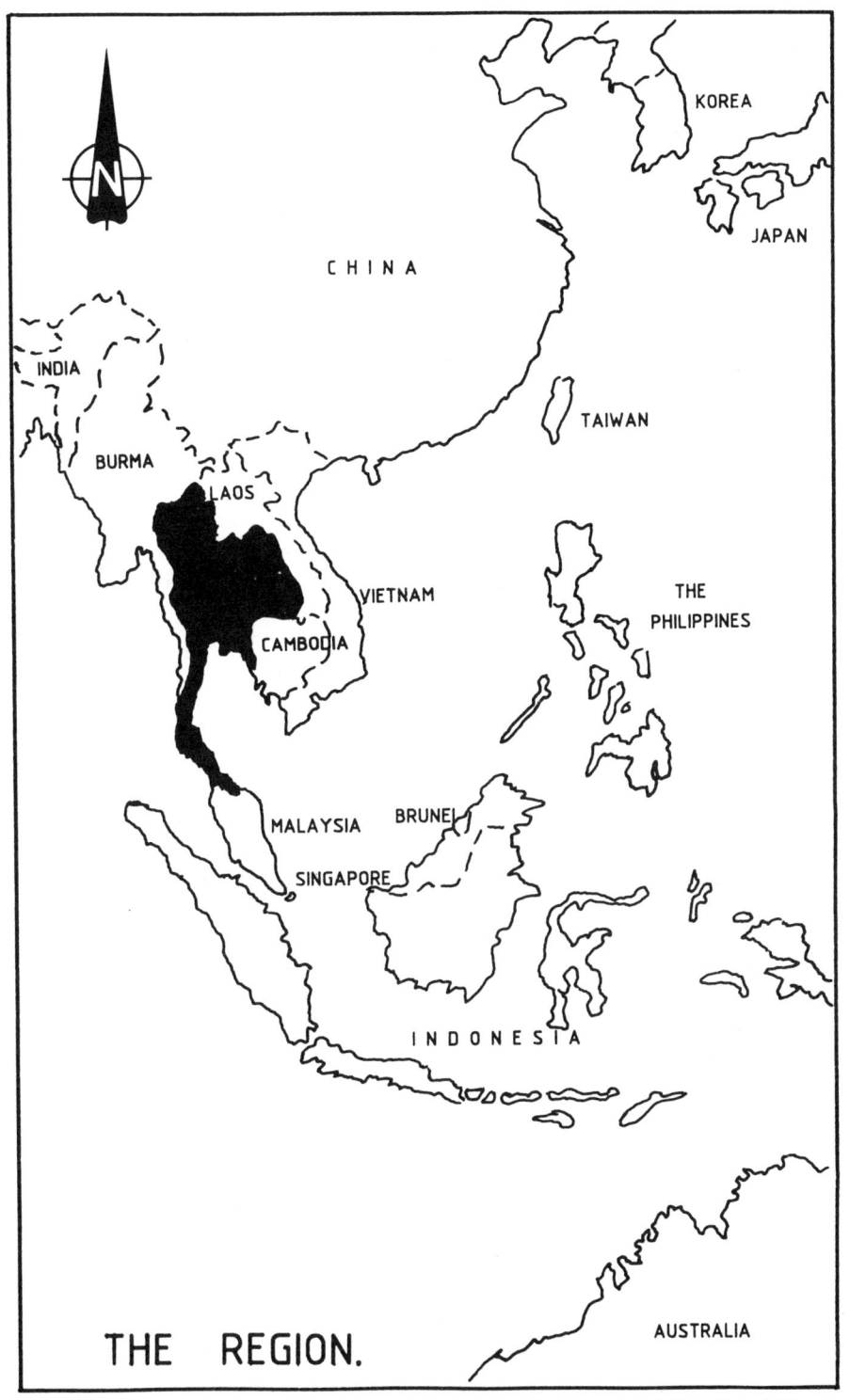

L.R. Copyright.

remote attractions. In Thailand that's easy because wherever you go throughout the country you will find that there is reliable transport, reasonable hotel and restaurant facilities, and a warm welcome. A long time ago, someone, obviously from a more uptight society, called Thailand "The Land of a Thousand Smiles." You'll see at least that many every day you are in the country. When later you are describing your experience with Thai service, Thai hospitality, and the people's eagerness to please, it's a safe bet you will be saying it with a smile. It really is contagious.

As a travel writer writing for a 1990s readership, I have to be realistic. Most readers will already have their own impressions of Thailand, molded by press stories, films, or television documentaries. Our grandfathers learned of Asia from great writers such as Joseph Conrad or Somerset Maugham. They wrote in flowery phrases that no one questioned, yet many of their descriptions remain true even today.

Joseph Conrad described the scene from his steamer as he anchored in Bangkok in the 1880s, but his strong thoughts and brilliant words could almost be used to portray the scene 100 years later: "Here and there in the distance, above the crowded mob of low, brown roof ridges, towered great piles of masonry, King's palaces, temples, gorgeous and dilapidated, crumbling under the vertical sunlight, tremendous, overpowering, almost palpable, which seemed to enter one's breast with no breath of one's nostrils and soak into one's limbs through every pore of one's skin." Were Conrad to return to Bangkok today he would first shake his head in disbelief, but once the initial shock wore off he would recognize landmarks and feelings that he knew so well.

For while Bangkok is jammed with traffic and hopelessly polluted—the skyline constantly changing with booming high-rise office blocks, apartments and luxurious hotels, and countless restaurants, clubs, discos and shops competing for business—much of the old remains. Visitors who explore back lanes in the city's riverside sections will come across the memorably unexpected: garlanded spirit houses, Buddhist "wats" that flash in the sunlight, women poling lotus-filled sampans through narrow waterways, somnolent temple courtyards where only tinkling windchimes and chirping birds disturb the air.

Thailand is unlike any other country on earth. The memories and photographs that you carry home will be unique and you will find that you will be the envy of all your neighbors and friends. It seems the whole world suddenly wants to go to Thailand. Most of the five million or so lucky ones that will make it this year will have the vacation of a lifetime.

Tourist Thailand in Summary

- Thailand is the most interesting and varied of all Asian countries.

Major Tourist Interest

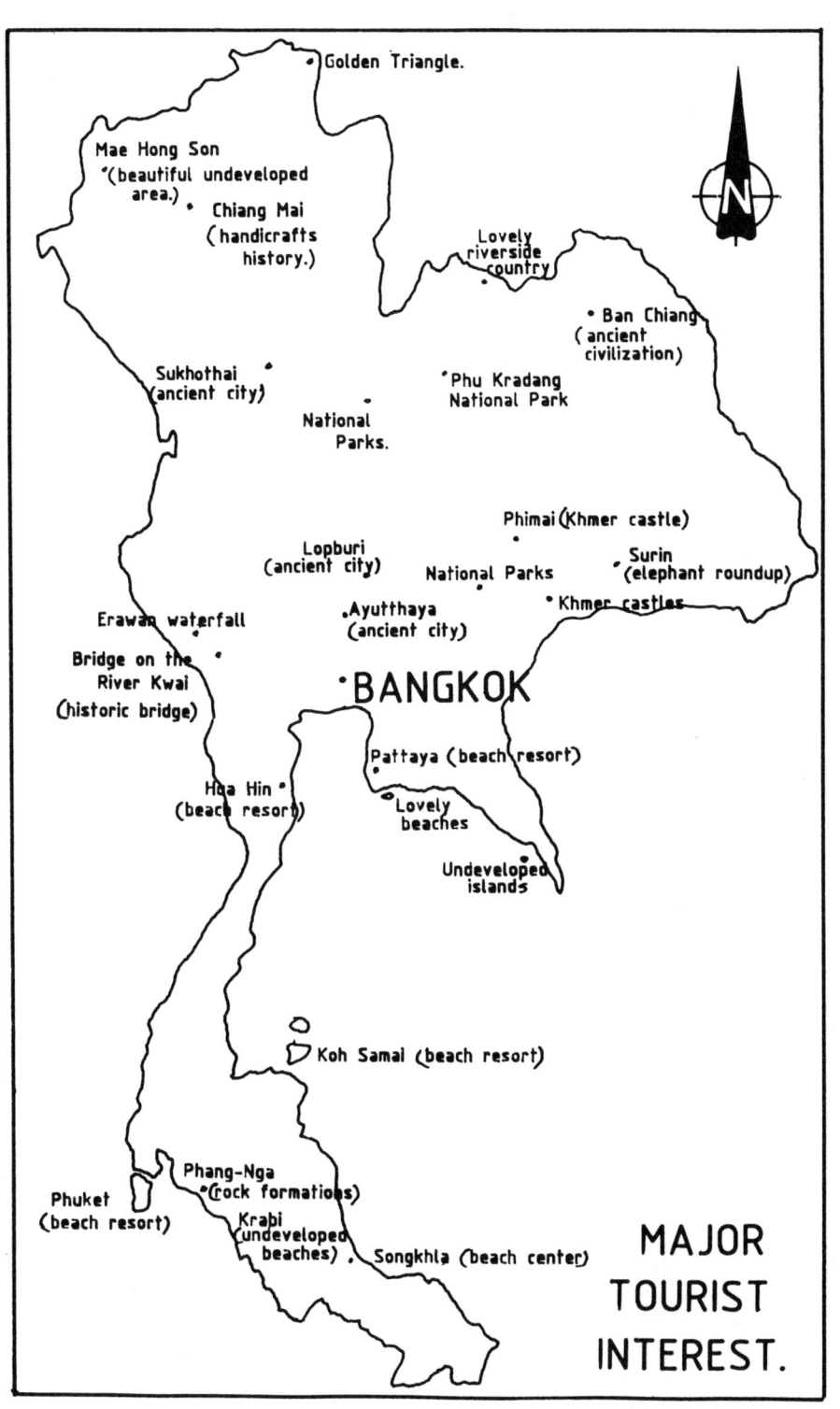

- Golden Triangle
- Mae Hong Son (beautiful undeveloped area.)
- Chiang Mai (handicrafts history.)
- Lovely riverside country
- Ban Chiang (ancient civilization)
- Sukhothai (ancient city)
- Phu Kradang National Park
- National Parks.
- Phimai (Khmer castle)
- Lopburi (ancient city)
- National Parks
- Surin (elephant roundup)
- Erawan waterfall
- Ayutthaya (ancient city)
- Khmer castles
- Bridge on the River Kwai (historic bridge)
- BANGKOK
- Pattaya (beach resort)
- Hua Hin (beach resort)
- Lovely beaches
- Undeveloped islands
- Koh Samai (beach resort)
- Phang-Nga (rock formations)
- Phuket (beach resort)
- Krabi (undeveloped beaches)
- Songkhla (beach center)

L.R. Copyright.

- The 58 million Thais are among the most friendly people on earth.
- Many costs in Thailand are cheap compared to most other tourist destinations.
- *Bangkok* is a throbbing city of over six million people built on a river floodplain. It is exciting, overcrowded, a shopper's paradise, polluted, hot, a nighttime dream, traffic plagued, and fascinating.
- Beach resorts are a great feature of the country. *Pattaya* is the most developed resort, much loved by Europeans, but *Phuket* is growing at an enormous rate and is set to become a total vacation destination in its own right. *Hua Hin* is quieter but the accommodation choice is good, while *Ko Samui* has grown from a backpacker's escape island into almost a mainstream destination.
- *Chiang Mai* is the center of north Thailand. It is a charming old city of temples, great handicrafts, and trekking opportunities.
- North Thailand is home to remote mountain settlements such as *Mae Hong Son,* with its surrounding hilltribe people, and to the infamous *Golden Triangle* region, which in reality is an overdeveloped riverside tourist destination.
- *Ban Chiang* has changed our thoughts on ancient history. Here in northeast Thailand a bronze age civilization existed 5,000 years ago.
- Further ancient remains exist throughout the northeast. These are primarily the remnants of the Khmer civilization that developed world-famous Ankor Wat in Cambodia. Major restoration has been undertaken at *Phimai* and at *Praset Phanom Rung* where huge stone castles provide a great reminder of a lost civilization.
- The ancient cities of *Sukhothai* and *Ayutthaya* show glimpses of the wonderful early development of the Thai nation. In their time they were world leaders in modern development.
- Modern Thailand has an excellent and extensive infrastructure to cope with five million visitors annually. The hotels in most centers are superior, sightseeing is well organized and efficient, and transportation facilities are oustanding.
- Thai food is varied, interesting, and usually hot. You can enjoy a meal for less than a dollar at a market food stall or you can dine in some of the finest restaurants in the world.
- Thai culture has survived the pressures of modern society and is thriving. You see it in the music, drama, and literature that is part of everyday life for the Thais.
- The Thai calendar is littered with festivals that beg the visitor's attendance. Go, look, listen, and enjoy.
- The best time to visit Thailand is October to March.

The Confessional

Anyone can visit Thailand without a guidebook. As the tourist industry has grown, so too has the amount of information available to the visitor. The Thais are friendly and will offer to point you towards the things they think will interest you. Some make a living from steering you into shops, restaurants, and night spots which pay a fee for such customers. In Bangkok, Pattaya, and Chiang Mai there are "free" publications which are paid for by advertisements. All this is valuable, but by necessity it only provides a small part of the total picture.

Unlike many guidebooks, this one contains no advertising, either overt or covert. The opinions expressed, and there are many, are those of myself. As with other books in the series, no one can use friendship or favors to influence the coverage of their commercial interests. You may not agree with my opinion but you will know it is based on my personal experience, told honestly and openly.

The Maverick Guide to Thailand has been written without any economic assistance from any organization. I would have it no other way. At the same time I appreciate the help that was provided by the Tourism Authority of Thailand and others in making suggestions for my travels and in honestly answering questions I put to them. I have been visiting Bangkok since 1974 and have built up a well of useful knowledge on the country. It was not sufficient to write this book, however, and since I began to produce this volume, I made five visits specifically to obtain the latest information. During these visits I deliberately stayed in a wide variety of accommodation, often changing hotels each night, to sample as many options as possible.

It has not been possible to stay in every hotel that a visitor may use, but the book covers a good range, from luxury to basic. Likewise with restaurants—you will end up eating at some places not mentioned in this book. If they are particularly good, cheap, or friendly, please let me know and I will visit them before completing the next edition of the guide.

For over twenty years I have worked as a travel writer, a career started when I was owner and editor of a brand new newspaper in Australia in 1969. Since then I have travelled throughout the world and hopefully have allowed my travel experiences to make me a more tolerant, aware, and appreciative person. I ask the same from you. Don't visit Thailand expecting it to be a duplication of your home country. Please don't complain because the salad you ordered doesn't come exactly as you expected or because the television programs are not in English. See these things as a broadening of your experience and as an insight into a new culture that may just have as many pluses as your own.

Getting the Most out of This Book

This guide is arranged in a similar pattern to the other Maverick Guides. It is a format that enables you to get a good feel for the country and the people while at the same time getting specifics that are so necessary for a successful vacation.

After a chapter on how to reach Thailand and travel around, there are two chapters on the land and the people. Following these, there are five "area chapters" which cover all the major areas of interest within the country.

The chapters need not be read in that sequence, of course. In fact, those areas that you will not be visiting need not be read at all, except that I have tried not to repeat similar information in all five area chapters. You should at least skim through them all to see if there is some specific information you need. If you are using the book to plan your trip, you need to read all sections so that you can decide which areas you will and will not be able to visit.

Each of the area chapters is divided into twelve numbered sections, and after you become familiar with them in one chapter you should know where to look for these same subjects in each of the others. The categories are as follows:

1. **The General Picture**
2. **Getting There**
3. **Local Transportation**
4. **The Hotel Scene**
5. **Dining and Restaurants**
6. **Sightseeing**
7. **Guided Tours**
8. **Culture**
9. **Sports**
10. **Shopping**
11. **Entertainment and Nightlife**
12. **The Address List**

The book has been set up to be used two ways. First, you should look it over before you leave home, to help you plan your trip. Remember that while travel agents are well qualified to advise on airfares and some package tours, it is unrealistic to expect them to be familiar with details of all destinations around the world. A good agent will appreciate you making informed suggestions, and will benefit from contact names and telephone numbers found inside this guide.

Next, the book is also designed to be used on the scene—to help solve those day to day concerns that put tension into independent travel. The recommendations on sightseeing tours, hotels, restaurants, and shopping will help your quest for smooth, fun travelling and will also help you save time and money as you travel through Thailand.

I have included many maps in this volume because it seems to me that a guidebook without good maps is somewhat of a misnomer. The city maps will help you orient yourself quickly and will help to show you where hotels and attractions are situated. The regional maps are designed for the traveller who has his own transportation, but they are also useful in planning itineraries and even to follow as you pass through an area on the train or bus.

Some Quick Comments

I hope you find this book a good read. It has been written so you can pick it up and put it down as time permits. Even if you have no immediate plans to visit Thailand you should gain a good appreciation of the country and culture by reading the descriptive chapters. They are not intended as a comprehensive guide for the serious student, but after reading them you will know more about Thai life and the Thai people than many tourists who have briefly visited Thailand on a fully escorted package tour.

If you are serious about planning a great vacation to Thailand, be sure to take advantage of the good literature available from the Tourism Authority of Thailand or Thai Airways International. Telephone or write the offices most convenient to you. The addresses are listed under "Tourist Information" in the next chapter.

Write also to other addresses you'll find throughout this book and tell them you are planning a visit. I like to think that if you tell them you are using the Maverick Guide, they will recognize you as a good potential customer and will respond with a useful amount of up-to-date literature and information.

If you have a well-stocked public library in town, you'll find that there will be some large picture books on Thailand or southeast Asia. They can provide something that we cannot—magnificent full-color photographs by professionals—which will help you decide what sightseeing attractions you just cannot afford to miss.

Most of all, after you've made your trip, would you please write to me (care of the publisher) and tell me about it? The travelling experiences of persons such as you will help me tremendously in preparing the next edition of this guidebook. Use either the enclosed letter/envelope form, or if that's not enough space, copy the address onto your own envelope and include as many pages as you like. Your reactions to both the book and the country are earnestly solicited and will be warmly appreciated.

Prices in the book are all quoted in the Thai currency, called baht. B200 means 200 baht. It is a good idea to become familiar with its value before you arrive in Thailand because all prices, except tariffs of luxury hotels, will be quoted in baht. If you are a serious shopper you should check out home prices, convert them to baht, then write them down in a notebook you take with you. You will then know instantly which are the true bargains.

Because the Thais use a completely different alphabet to us, all place names have had to be translated into English. There is no universally accepted method for doing that, so you end up with several different spellings of the same word. This can be very confusing to the visitor. A good system is to assume that words that look similar are probably the same: Korat is the same as Khorat, and Koh is the same as Ko. I have tried to standardize in this book but inevitably some discrepancies will occur. Please understand the problem and assist me with your comments.

"Sawardee!"
LEN RUTLEDGE

2

Happy Landings

How to Get There

Thailand is served by dozens of the world's airlines and it can be conveniently reached from almost every part of the globe. These days there are nonstop flights from many places in Europe to Bangkok and, even from North America, many flights are one-stop affairs. Thailand, of course, hasn't moved any closer to these places, it's just that the newer aircraft (747-400's, MD 11's, and so on) have a longer range than the planes of ten years ago. Thailand is still a long way from the North American, European, and South Pacific markets.

A long way usually means big cost and Thailand is certainly not a cheap short-haul flight away. Yet the cost can be surprisingly low if you go at the "off-season" time of year and your travel agent keeps abreast of the various "offers" that come on to the market. It pays to consider all the options, though, as the lowest airfare is not necessarily the cheapest in the long run. Consider the stop-overs and decide if you wish to combine several destinations in the one vacation. Take convenience into account. Ask if you have to change aircraft and what is the time delay between flights.

Airlines give you the option of flying first class, business class, or economy class. The service deteriorates as you move down-market, but so does the price. Your perception of what is the best fare level will be determined by your finances at home. Some travellers insist that first class is the only way to

EUROPE TO BANGKOK.

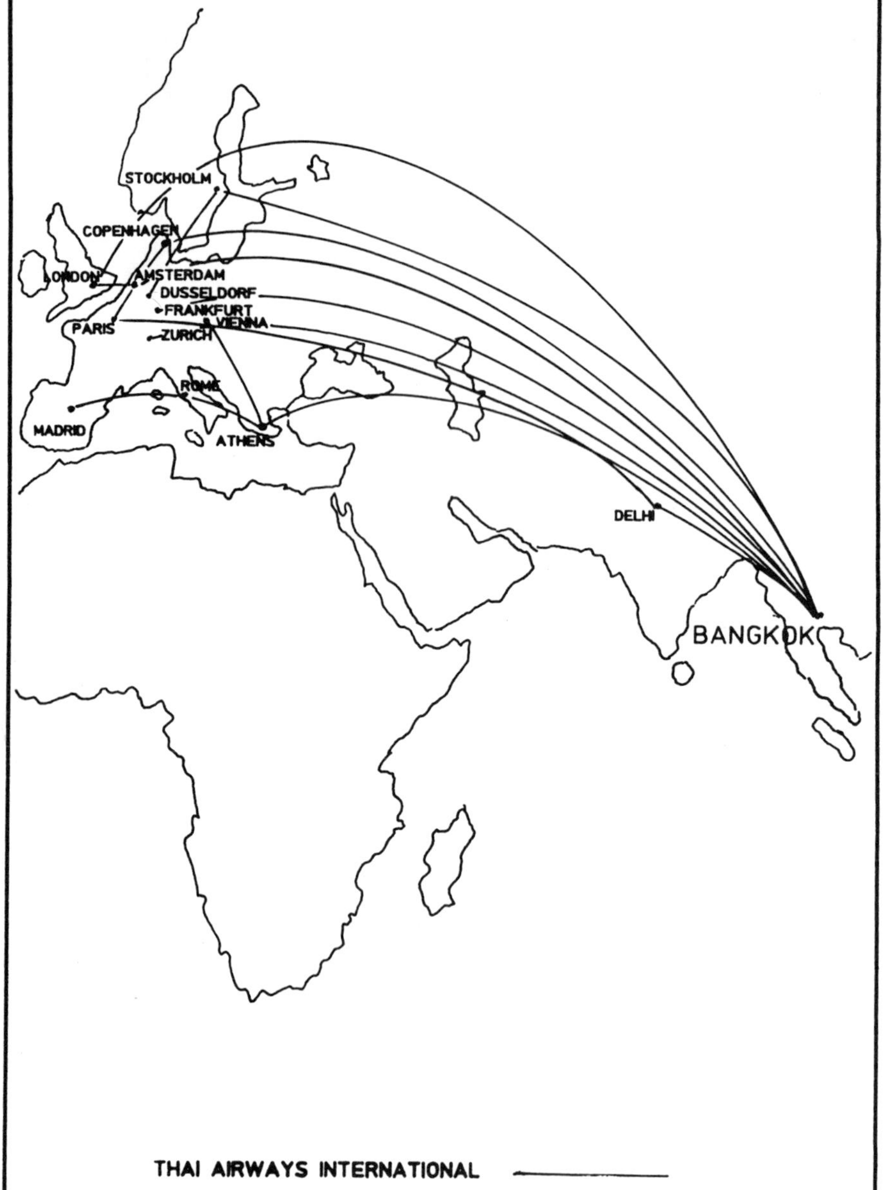

HOW TO REACH THAILAND MAP 1.

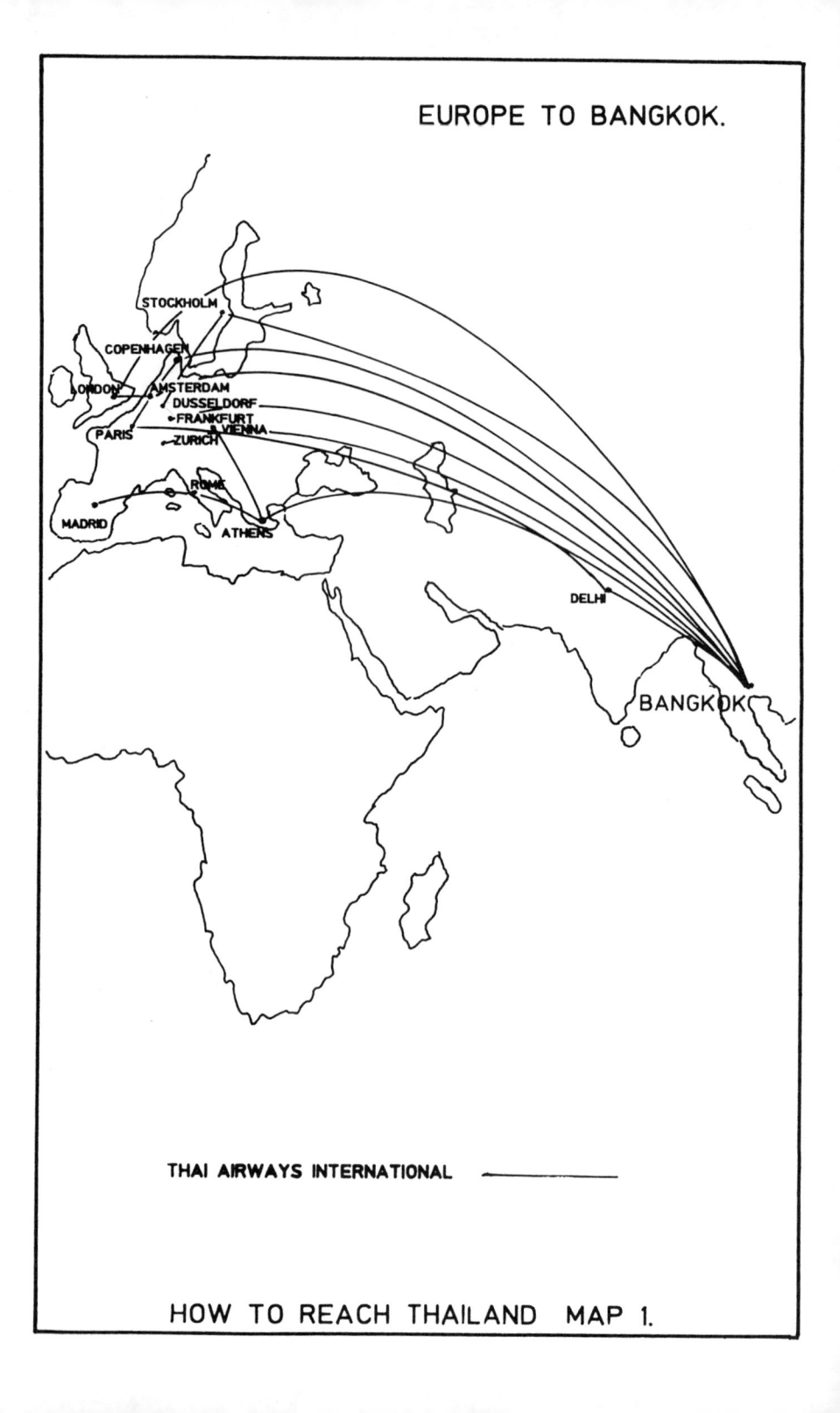

avoid jet lag and some of the other problems associated with modern travel. Others determine that the large savings from travelling economy are better spent at the destination. That decision is a very personal one and I will have no part of that.

I do have advice, however, on what airlines you should consider. I have a strong preference for using the airline of the destination country if I can be assured that its service and safety record are as good as the competition. This is because you get an introduction to the country as soon as you step aboard the aircraft. In the case of **Thai Airways International,** I personally rate this airline within the top five in the world, so I have no hesitation in recommending it to you.

Thai Airways International has one of the most comprehensive Asian and European networks around, but it has more limited access to the North American market. At present the airline serves Seattle and Dallas/Fort Worth in the U.S. and Toronto in Canada, but more ports are set to come on-line shortly. There are good services from Australia (Sydney, Melbourne, Brisbane, Perth, and Cairns) and from New Zealand (Auckland, Christchurch). European ports are London, Paris, Amsterdam, Copenhagen, Stockholm, Helsinki, Munich, Dusseldorf, Frankfurt, Zurich, Madrid, Rome, Athens, and Vienna. In all, the airline flies to seventy-three cities on four continents and it has grown to be the largest airline in southeast Asia.

Thai Airways International was founded in 1959 as a joint venture between Thailand's domestic carrier, Thai Airways Company, and Scandinavian Airlines System (SAS). The airline developed rapidly and, in 1977, the Thai government bought out SAS's remaining shareholding and the airline became entirely Thai owned. In 1988 Thai Internationl merged with Thai Airways Company to become Thailand's only national carrier.

The airline uses Boeing 747's, McDonnell Douglas DC-10's, and Airbus aircraft on international routes, and it carries over five million passengers a year. It has achieved profitability every year since 1965. Since the merger, it has increased the frequency of many domestic flights and has added capacity by purchasing new aircraft and transferring aircraft between domestic and international regional routes as necessary.

For passengers, one of the big benefits has been the ability to make international and domestic bookings at the same time and on the same ticket. Agents like it too, because they receive commission for the domestic sectors as well.

It's nice to know that an airline is reliable, safety conscious, and financially viable, but it is its airport and cabin service that influences most passengers. This is an area where Thai excels. As you enter the aircraft, a hostess greets you with a warm "Sawardee." Hands clasped, she is welcoming you aboard in the traditional way a Thai would welcome a good friend into his home.

NORTH AMERICA AND THE SOUTH PACIFIC TO BANGKOK.

HOW TO REACH THAILAND   MAP 2.

Other components are fresh orchids which are given to passengers, a gift to help you remember your flight, excellent food including some taste-tingling Thai delicacies, free drinks, free stereo headsets, and first run movies.

The Thai people consider friendliness, good manners, courtesy, and hospitality essential to their daily lives. It is no surprise to find these characteristics on display in the national airline.

Several North American carriers fly to Thailand. Services are changing very rapidly at present so it is best to check with your travel agent on the current level and origin of flights. At the time of writing, **Northwest Airlines** has a daily service from San Francisco to Bangkok via Tokyo, **United** flies from Los Angeles via Hong Kong, **Delta** has a service via Taipei, while **Canadian International** flies four times a week from Vancouver via Hong Kong.

From the South Pacific, **Qantas** has services from most capital cities plus Townsville and Cairns to Bangkok, while **Air New Zealand** flies from Auckland.

The occasional cruise liner visits Thailand as part of a world, Pacific, or Asian cruise but this is not normally a viable way to visit the country.

It is possible to reach Thailand by road or rail but at present the only land border always open to foreigners is the one in the south between Thailand and Malaysia. The road system from Singapore, through Malaysia to Thailand, is good and the train service is the best in the region. There is an international express from Singapore to Malaysia several times a day and one from Malaysia to Thailand (Bangkok) most days of the week. The trip from Singapore can be made in several stages and is popular. Travel time is about forty hours.

Transportation within Thailand

Thailand is not a large country by many standards, yet the distances are deceiving. A visitor hoping to see Bangkok, Phuket, Pattaya, Chiang Mai, and some of the countryside, all within a short period, really has to travel some sectors by air. That is no hardship because the internal service is excellent. But I would also urge you to try and do some surface sectors because this is the only way you really see and appreciate the rural areas.

Air. Thai Airways International has an extensive network which covers almost all of Thailand. It is centered on Bangkok with flights departing to points north, south, and northeast. There is a secondary network based on Chiang Mai in the north and some local flights from Phuket go to other centers in the south. The system is operated by A300 airbuses, Boeing 737's, British Aerospace BAC 146, and Shorts 360 and 330 aircraft. The Shorts aircraft are used on feeder services while jets operate on all the major routes. Frequency is excellent. There are at least seven daily services on the Bangkok-Chiang Mai route, six on the Bangkok-Hat Yai route, two on the Bangkok-Khon Kaen route, and three on the Bangkok-Phitsanulok route and the Bangkok-Surat Thani route.

DOMESTIC ROUTE NET

INTERNAL AIR.

The system is constantly being expanded—not in the number of ports being served but in the new connections between existing ports. In 1989 a daily Bangkok-Chiang Rai service was established. There is a new Chiang Mai-Khon Kaen-Sakon Nakhon service linking the north and northeast. Of major benefit to tourists are the new services linking Chiang Mai with Phuket, and Chiang Mai with U-Tapao (an airport near Pattaya). Anyone contemplating a visit to these centers should try and use these flights to avoid the inconvenience and congestion of changing flights in Bangkok.

Thai Airways International has released for the first time a "Discover Thailand" ticket, to be sold only outside Thailand, which allows visitors to fly any four sectors of Thai's domestic network of twenty-four destinations within Thailand. The cost of this is currently US$200 and additional sectors can be added for US$40 each to an overall total of eight flight sectors. The tickets are valid for sixty days from the first domestic flight.

As well as Thai Airways International, there are a few small airlines which operate limited services within the country. The only service likely to be of interest to visitors is the flight from Bangkok to Ko Samui, operated three times a day by **Bangkok Airways** (Tel. 2530414).

Rail. The rail network in Thailand is owned and operated by the Thai government through the State Railway of Thailand. The system is good. Given a choice between road and rail public transportation for long-distance travel, I would always take rail. It may take that little bit longer but it is more comfortable, safer, and it seems easier to meet and talk with the locals when travelling on a train.

There are four main rail lines—the Northern, Southern, Eastern, and Northeastern routes—and several side routes as well. Most of the major population centers in Thailand are served by train but some major tourist centers, notably Pattaya, Phuket, and Chiang Rai, are not.

There are three classes of travel in Thailand, although not all trains have all classes. Third class is used by most locals for most journeys. It can be fun for visitors to use third class for short journeys but I don't recommend it for long-distance travel. The seats are harder than second class and it can be very crowded. The exception to this is the Eastern line, where only third class is available.

Second class is available on all services except the Eastern line. On day trains, this is the top class and you pay double the third-class fare. On night trains you can buy second-class sleeper berths. You usually have the option of airconditioned or non-airconditioned carriages.

First class is available on certain express trains. These long-distance trains all have first-class airconditioned sleeping cars. They are comfortable and convenient for international visitors, although they are not cheap.

RAIL.

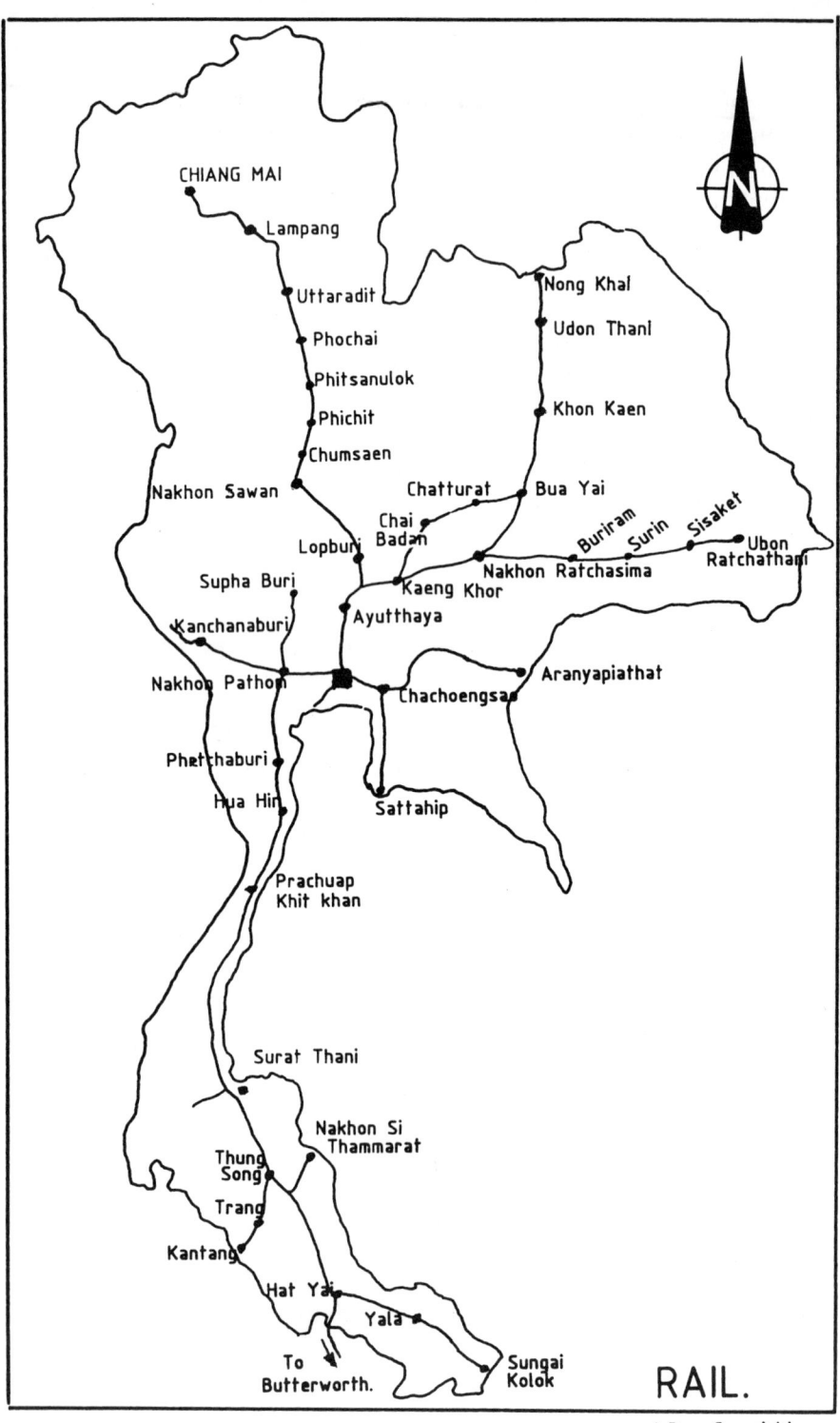

L.R. Copyright

Working out rail fares is not just a straightforward exercise. The basic fare is easy but there are supplementary charges which then have to be added. Take the one-way Bangkok-Chiang Mai fare as an example. The basic fare at the moment is first US$21, second US$10, third US$5. There is, in fact, no train available that will get you there for that cost. For a rapid train, there is a US$0.80 extra charge (there are two of these each way but neither offer first-class travel). For an express train there is a US$1.20 extra charge and for a special express train there is a US$2 extra charge. But that's only the start.

If you wanted an airconditioned sitting-coach seat in second or third class you would pay an extra US$1.20. If, however, you wanted a sleeping berth you would pay an extra US$14 for a first-class airconditioned single cabin, US$10 per person for a first-class airconditioned double cabin, US$6 for an upper berth in a second-class airconditioned cabin, US$8 for a lower berth in a second-class airconditioned cabin, US$3 for an upper berth in a second class non-airconditioned cabin, US$4 for a lower berth in a second-class non-airconditioned cabin, and so on. Are you confused yet?

There are five trains a day to Chiang Mai, each with different facilities, so you really have to study a timetable to see what combination is right for you. To other destinations, for example, Nakhon Ratchasima, the problem is compounded because there are at least twelve trains a day from which to choose.

Some of this problem is eliminated by purchasing a **Visit Thailand Rail Pass.** These passes are only available to tourists with international passports and they can be an excellent value, if you plan to use the trains frequently during your stay. There are two passes—a Blue Pass and a Red Pass—both giving unlimited second- or third-class rail travel for twenty days. The Blue Pass costs US$60 for adults, and US$30 for children (under twelve years old). Supplementary charges are *not* included. The Red Pass costs US$120 adults and US$60 children and includes all supplementary charges. Further details of these passes can be obtained from Bangkok railway station (Tel. 2237010 or Fax 2256068).

Ordinary tickets on trains from Bangkok can be difficult to book. Particularly at festival times, seats are in great demand so advance planning is the key to success. If possible, you should book a week or more ahead. Tickets can be bought at the main station (Hualamphong Station on Rama IV Road) or at some travel agents. I have never used an agent for rail tickets in Bangkok so I don't know how effective they are. I do know that going to the station can be frustrating, particularly in the hot season, but at least you know you have a ticket and seat after you have been through the rather complicated process. Look for the "Advance Booking" sign in English and you will be told what to do. It is much easier to book a ticket to Bangkok from a country station. At Bangkok's station, there is also a baggage storage service and a travellers' aid counter.

The advance ticket office in Bangkok is open daily from 8:30 to 6:00 weekdays and 8:30 to noon on weekends and public holidays. One good thing about this office, however, is that you can book a ticket between any stations in Thailand, so you can finalize all your arrangements in one visit.

Even if you do not plan extensive rail travel, you may wish to do a one- or two-day trip to the River Kwai. These operate every Saturday, Sunday, and public holiday and are very popular with visitors. The one-day trip offers several alternatives but I believe the trip which includes a visit to the River Kwai Jungle House is an excellent value at US$8 per person. The train leaves Bangkok at 6:35 A.M., stops at Nakhon Pathom to visit Phra Pathom Chedi (the world's tallest Buddhist monument), stops at the River Kwai Bridge, then journeys along Death Railway to Tha Kilen. From here you visit Prasat Muang Singh Ruin, have lunch at the Jungle House, visit Krasae Cave Bridge, then return to Bangkok via Kanchanaburi and the Allied War Cemetery. It is a long day but it is extremely enjoyable. For further details of this trip, telephone Bangkok 2230341 Extension 4217.

Bus. Buses operate all over Thailand and are by far the most popular form of transportation for most Thais. There are both government-run buses and private buses but these days they are all licensed by the government company and there seems to be at least some general control over their operation.

The most common buses are the ordinary government-run ones. These are non-airconditioned, are often very crowded, and are sometimes poorly maintained and dirty. The one thing going for them is that they are cheap. For most international visitors they will have little appeal for long-distance travel but if you are travelling around the countryside between small towns, these will be your only choice.

For long-distance travel, the government also operates an airconditioned coach service. The standard varies considerably between vehicles but they are faster and more comfortable than the ordinary buses so they will have more appeal to most foreigners. In Bangkok these buses leave from the same terminals as the ordinary buses, but in some country cities there are separate airconditioned and non-airconditioned bus terminals.

As well as government buses there are long-distance private buses. In some cases these have similar fares while in other instances they are considerably higher. These are often referred to as "tour buses" although there is no tour involved—they are simply transportation between two points. Recent years have seen an "up-market" version of these buses introduced with no smoking, video systems, more room between seats, and a better standard of comfort. You really need to make local inquiries to see what is available on the route in which you are particularly interested.

Unfortunately this information is not readily forthcoming in Bangkok. If you telephone the bus terminal, you will get half a story or no story at all depending on your luck with the operator. If you ask a travel agent you will be steered towards the particular company which offers the highest commission, and if you ask your hotel, you will usually only be told about the company that regularly provides transportation to that particular establishment. When you get to the country it is much easier to discover the true picture, so I suggest that you only make the one initial booking in Bangkok, then follow up with new bookings as you travel around the countryside.

Bus safety is an on-going problem in some areas and after a few bus trips you will understand why. Fares are often sold on a reputation for speed, and when this is added to doubtful maintenance, inexperienced drivers, and a concept of bigger-has-right-of-way, it is sometimes a fatal combination. Head-on collisions and overturning at sharp bends are not uncommon. Fortunately, considering the number of buses on the roads, the statistics are still on your side, so most trips end safely, on time.

In the past, particularly in border areas, bus robberies were a fairly frequent event. That sort of activity has almost ceased now, but it's still wise to keep your eye on your bags and belongings when travelling by bus because petty theft still occurs. Thailand is no worse than most countries and certainly much safer than some, but it's better to be warned than to be sorry afterwards because you didn't take a few elementary precautions.

Car rental. If you are limited to a week or so in Thailand, car rental is probably not a good option. If, on the other hand, you are planning a long visit and hope to see many different areas of the country, having your own transportation can open up some possibilities.

I did not rent a car or motorcycle on my first half a dozen trips to Thailand but increasingly it has become my first choice for transportation. Many people will find Bangkok driving a problem, though in the rest of the country it really is quite easy. The rural roads are good, they are not heavily used, and there are a growing number of English-language signs appearing. Traffic drives on the left.

Rental rates vary considerably between operators so it is wise to check around. It is usually possible to "do a deal" with the smaller agencies on rentals longer than four or five days. Some companies offer "low-priced" cars but I am not sure if they are worth the risk. I recently had one of these "specials" for three days and while it was cheap (US$24 a day) it caused me considerable worry each time I tried to start it. I doubt the mental anguish was worthwhile.

Many of the smaller companies don't have fueling facilities so the car will be almost out of fuel when you get it. You are expected to bring it back in the same condition. When you take the car, ask where the nearest filling facility is, because it is not always obvious.

ROAD.

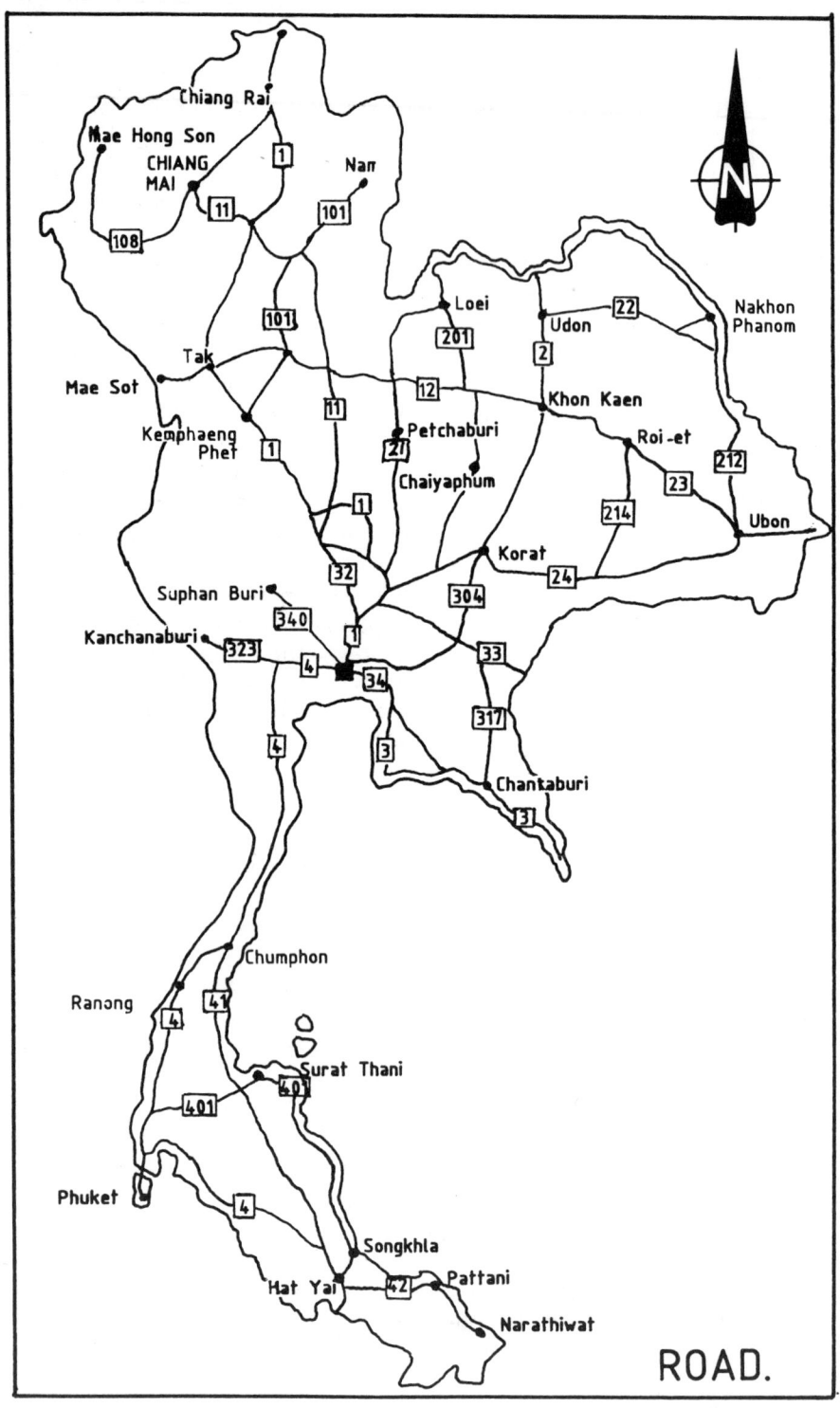

L.R.Copyright.

Here are some suggested car-rental companies in Bangkok.
Avis—10/1 Sathon Nua Rd., 233-0397
Central Car Rent—24 Soi Ton-Son, Phloenchit, 251-2778
Dollar Car Rent—272 Soi Chinda-Thawin, Si Phraya Rd., 234-9770
Hertz—987 Phloenchit Rd., 252-4903
Highway Car Rent—6/2 Rama IV Rd., 235-7746
Inter Car Rent—45 Sukhumvit Rd., 252-9223
King Car Rent—18/1 Sathon Nua Rd., 233-4514
Klong Toey Car Rent—1921 Rama IV Rd., 250-1141
National Car Rental—518/2 Phloenchit Rd., 251-1393
Phetchaburi Car Rent—2371 New Phetchaburi Rd., 318-1753
Silver International—Esso Station, Sukhumvit 22, 259-6867

Some of these organizations are also prepared to rent you a car and a driver. While this will cost more, you may well recoup this by having a Thai-speaking person with you to negotiate with hotels and suggest cheap meal stops. My limited experience with these drivers, however, is that they are not particularly good guides, they may not be able to read maps, and they may not have ever visited the area where you wish to go. As you can tell, I'm not a real fan of car-driver rental.

Hydrofoils. The introduction of several hydrofoil services is set to revolutionize transportation on several important tourist routes. The Thai Intertransport Company has announced the purchase of four 155-seat and two 74-seat gas-turbine hydrofoils. Services will operate from Bangkok to Hua Hin (two trips daily), Bangkok to Pattaya to Hua Hin (two trips daily), and Bangkok to Ko Samui (daily). The hydrofoils will be based at the Menam Hotel pier on the Chao Phraya River.

Two hydrofoils will operate other services to and from Ko Samui. There will be a daily Samui to Songkhla trip and several Samui to Surat Thani trips each day. The other very interesting trip is a new service which will link Phuket in southern Thailand with Langkawi, a resort island in northern Malaysia. This service could have considerable appeal to international visitors who are planning a more extensive tour through southeast Asia.

At the time of writing these services had not yet commenced nor had booking facilities been announced. I would recommend that you contact the Tourist Authority of Thailand (Tel. 2821143) to find out more about these services.

Cruises. Cruise vacations are fast gaining in popularity in Thailand. The **Siam Cruise Company** operates the 450-passenger *Andaman Princess* in the Gulf of Thailand from June to September, and in the Andaman Sea from October to May. Departure details can be obtained by telephoning the company at 2554563.

The *Seatran Queen,* which can accommodate 120 passengers in forty cabins, operates in the Gulf of Thailand from April to September and in the Andaman Sea from October to March. Contact **Seatran Travel** for further details (Tel. 2535307)

Local Transportation

This is covered in more detail in each section but it is wise to learn a few names for local transportation.

Buses operate in most larger cities and generally their costs are low.

Taxis are also common. They do not have meters, so fares must be negotiated before you board.

Samlors are three-wheeled vehicles which can be bicycle rickshaws or motorized versions.

Tuk-tuks are motorized samlors.

Songthaews are converted pickup trucks with bench seats down the side—something like an undecorated Philippine Jeepney.

Long-tail boats are narrow riverboats with a long propeller shaft attached to the engine.

Travel Facts and Figures

Here are some essential facts to make planning your trip a little easier and to make visiting Thailand a breeze. Frequent travellers may think all this is mundane, but we all have to learn about these things at some time in our travels. Frankly I wish someone had listed them for me in a logical sequence, before I made my first overseas sortie.

Weather and Climate. Thailand is situated within the tropics so day temperatures vary from hot to very hot depending on where you are and the time of the year. The central plains, the North, and the Northeast share the same seasonal weather patterns. The South has only subtle seasonal variations.

For most of Thailand there are three distinct seasons. The "hot season" is from March to May, the "rainy season" is from June to mid-October, and the "cool season" is from mid-October to the end of February. In the hot season, daytime temperatures in Bangkok can reach the high 30s Celsius (90-100 degrees F). In the cool season they will be in the high 20s Celsius (70-80 degrees F) but at night they may drop to 5-10 degrees Celsius (40-50 degrees F). In the north they may even go lower on occasions.

The temperature during the wet season depends on the amount of rain and cloud cover. At this time of the year the humidity is higher but it may go for a week or more without raining. Some days are bright and sunny, others overcast with storms, while at times it will rain almost continuously for two or three days.

The cool season is generally regarded as the best time to visit Thailand. In November and December facilities for tourists are stretched to the limit.

Packing and Wearing. If you're an experienced traveller there is no need to tell you to travel light. If you can't conveniently carry your bags without a trolley, you have too much. The other thing to remember is that Thailand is one of the best and cheapest places in the world to buy clothes, so you are sure to be tempted to buy up big while you are there.

There are two absolute essentials: cool cottons rather than synthetics, and comfortable footwear. For the hot season, pack clothes that give you protection from the sun, such as loose-fitting long-sleeved shirts or blouses, a foldable hat, and sunglasses. For the rainy season, you need clothes that dry quickly, an umbrella, and shoes that can stand being saturated. If you plan to visit the north during the cool season, a sweater and warm socks would be good insurance against the chilly evenings.

Bangkok and most "nonbeach" centers are surprisingly formal. You will rarely see a Thai in shorts, and for most business and social occasions, a long-sleeved shirt and tie are considered necessary. It is not uncommon to see Thais in business suits even in the hot season. However, a vacationer will not require a suit under normal circumstances. Many executives travel to work in chauffeur-driven airconditioned cars and they spend their days in airconditioned offices. You on the other hand will probably be outdoors most of the time. Very few restaurants require a tie and jacket.

Even at the beach resorts, short-shorts and skimpy tops are not considered appropriate away from the beach. There are a few beaches frequented by Western tourists where topless bathing is tolerated but you will rarely see a Thai like this. If your idea of Thailand is colored by stories of topless nightlife, you need to think again. The average Thai is far more conservative and demure than most Westerners, and you should take this into account when dressing.

Public Holidays. Traditional Thai holidays are usually occasions for celebration. Some are on fixed dates. Others are determined by the Thai lunar calendar, and hence the dates vary from year to year.

Government offices and many business offices observe all public holidays but most retail stores do not. Tourists may wish to incorporate a public holiday into their visit so that they will be able to join or watch the celebrations. Business travellers on a short visit will need to be aware that no business will be discussed on a public holiday. In fact it is often worse than that. If public holidays fall on a Tuesday or Thursday, most of the work force takes the extra day to form a long weekend so they can return to family or friends in the country areas. The old Thai New Year period (April 13-15) and the King's Birthday (December 5) are particular times that business people should avoid. The following are the major holidays:

January 1—New Year's Day; mid-February—Chinese New Year (government offices usually do not shut down completely but some private businesses do); mid- to late February—Makha Puja, a Buddhist religious holiday; April 6—Chakri Day, commemorating the founding of the Chakri (the present) royal dynasty; April 13—Songkran, the Thai traditional New Year; May 5—Coronation Day, commemorating King Bhumipol's coronation in 1950 with military parades and religious pageants; May—Visakhaa Bucha, celebrating the birth, enlightenment, and death of the Buddha; July—Asalaha Puja, marking the commencement of the annual three-month Rains Retreat; August 12—Queen's Birthday; October 23—Chulalongkorn Day; and December 5—King's Birthday.

Mail and Telephone Service. Thailand has a reliable mail service and there are modern telecommunication services to most areas. Cable, telex, and fax services are available.

The main Bangkok post office is on New Road, reasonably close to the Oriental Hotel. Letters addressed to a person c/o Poste Restante Bangkok will end up here. They can be collected from 8 A.M. to 8 P.M. on weekdays and on Saturdays and Sunday mornings. The Telegraph Office is open twenty-four hours a day.

Mail to and from Thailand seems to take at least a week from the U.S.A., Canada, or Australia. Whether that is a reflection of the Thai postal system or your home country service is hard to say. All towns in Thailand have a postcode and this may help speed things up, if it is included in the address.

The telephone system is improving all the time and I believe it is now in the good category. Domestic and overseas calls can be dialed direct from a growing number of locations.

Telephone numbers in this book have been listed without area codes because most will be made locally. However, if you are making long-distance calls within the country, you must dial the area code before the local number. All area codes start with zero. If you are dialing Thailand from overseas, you first dial the country code (66), then the area code minus the zero (38 for Pattaya), then the local number. These are the area codes inside Thailand:

Bangkok—02
Chiang Mai—053
Pattaya—038
Phuket—076
Hat Yai—074
Nakhon Ratchasima—044

Central Region
Phetchaburi, Ratchaburi, Hua Hin—032
Kanchanaburi, Samut Sakhon—034
Ayutthaya, Suphanburi—035

Lop Buri, Saraburi, Sing Buri—036
Nakhon Pathom, Prachinburi—037

Eastern Region
Chonburi, Rayong—038
Chantaburi, Trat—039
Ko Samet—01

Northeast Region
Loei, Nakon Phanom, Nong Khai, Sakon Nakhon, Udon Thani—042
Kalasin, Khon Kaen, Mahasarakham, Roi-Et—043
Buri Ram, Chaiyaphum—044
Si Sa Ket, Surin, Ubon Ratchathani, Yasothon—045

Northern Region
Lamphun, Mae Hong Son—053
Chiang Rai, Lampang, Phrae—054
Kamphaeng Phet, Phitsanulok, Sukhothai, Tak, Uttaradit—055
Nakhon Sawan, Phichit, Uthai Thani—056

Southern Region
Pattani, Yala—073
Songkhla—074
Krabi, Nakhon Si Thammarat, Trang—075
Phangnga—076
Chumphon, Ranong, Surat Thani, Koh Samui—077

Metrics and Electrics

Thailand uses the metric system for most weights and measures so you will have to learn quickly a few key conversions if you are not familiar with this system. The important measures are temperature, distance, and volume.

Temperature. Let's assume that you are not really interested in knowing if the temperature is 77 degrees F. or 78 degrees F. Your real concern is whether it is hot or cold. To do this you have to remember three Celsius numbers—10 degrees Celsius equals 50 degrees Fahrenheit, 20 degrees C. = 68 degrees F., and 30 degrees C. = 86 degrees F. That's not too difficult. It's also handy to know that the freezing point of water is 0 degrees C. and the boiling point is 100 degrees C.

Distance. With distance, it is much the same thing. A kilometer is 0.621 of a mile but no one is going to start multiplying that figure to determine a distance. What you should remember is 5 kilometers equals 3 miles, 10km = 6 miles, and 100km = 60 miles. For small distances, remember 5 centimeters equals 2 inches, 30cm equals 1 foot, and a meter and a yard are roughly equal.

Volume, Weight, and Thai Measure. Volumes are important because gasoline and milk are sold in litres. It's close enough to equate a litre to an American quart so there are roughly 4 litres in a gallon. Weight is also easy. A kilogram is 2.21 pounds, which to me means that 1 kilogram approximates 2 pounds. If you think in pounds, remember that is half a kilogram.

Land measure is one place where Thais seem to deviate from the metric system and use their own peculiar measure. This will not concern 99.9 percent of visitors but perhaps it is worth knowing that 1 Rai (the Thai measure) equals 1,600 square meters, which in turn equals 0.4 acres.

Electricity. The important thing to remember about Thai electric current is that it's supplied at 220 volts, 50 cycles. European and Australian appliances will work on this current, but American and Canadian ones will fry.

Fortunately most of the major hotels have 110 volt outlets in the bathroom for light-duty appliances such as razors. Don't try plugging a hair dryer or iron into these outlets because you will quickly blow the circuit. The Thais realize this problem, so major hotels usually have locally wired hair dryers and irons available for those who need them.

The best solution to this problem is to leave your own appliances at home and make do with what you can find in Thailand.

Money and Prices

The Thai currency, known as *baht*, comes in notes of 500 (purple), 100 (red), 20 (green), and 10 (brown) denominations. Coins are 5 baht and 1 baht (silver) and you will occasionally see brown 50-stang and 25-stang coins. There are 100 stang to 1 baht. That sounds easy, but because there are "new" and "old" coins of different sizes, it is not difficult to confuse a new 5 baht with an old 1 baht. The best way to tell the difference is by looking for a copper-colored rim on the 5-baht coin.

Exchange rates vary from time to time, but at the time of writing, one U.S. dollar was worth about 25 baht—i.e., a 100-baht note is equivalent to US$4. An Australian dollar would buy you about 20 baht, a Canadian dollar 22 baht, and a New Zealand dollar 15 baht.

It's a good idea to pick up a little Thai money before you leave home, to become familiar with it and also to find out the current exchange rate. If you don't do this, there are several banks at the arrival terminal of Bangkok Airport and they will give you a fair exchange rate.

Most internationally recognized credit cards are widely accepted in Bangkok, Pattaya, Chiang Mai, and parts of Phuket but there is much less acceptance of them outside these tourist centers. The use of cards is growing, however, and new signs are appearing all the time. When paying with a credit card, particularly American Express and Diners Club, you may be asked to pay a surcharge which is intended to cover the fee charged by the card company. This surcharge on the customer is illegal and you should refuse to pay it. I am told by American Express, however, that should you be forced to pay it, mark it clearly on the form and the card company will subtract it from the amount that they will bill you.

Traveller's checks are widely accepted and you will find that the exchange rate is slightly better for these than for cash. The best place to change cash or traveller's checks is at a bank. In the major tourist centers, banks operate money exchange booths for about twelve hours a day. These are scattered throughout the major cities and tourist areas. In other areas, most banks can change common currencies quickly and efficiently. All banks appear to use the same exchange rates. Normal banking hours are Monday through Friday, 8:30 to 3:30.

Thailand prices, until the late eighties, were a delight. The huge increase in tourism, however, has helped cause considerable price rises in those services specifically for tourists, such as five-star hotels, airport transfers, Western meals, and so forth. In some cases these have now risen to international level.

The trick is to avoid "touristy" things whenever you can, and use the facilities provided for the locals. With some local people only earning US$1-2 a day, these facilities have to be cheap. Bangkok buses and ferries, street restaurants, and markets are all still great bargains. Rural areas are often significantly cheaper than Bangkok but of course the choice available to you is usually less.

After paying for your hotel, it is easy to eat and sightsee on US$20 a day, if you need to. Lunch with a cola can cost $1-2 and dinner maybe $2-4. Add a beer and it's still only $6. A taxi anywhere within Bangkok city should be less than $4, so you still have some to spend on admissions, souvenirs, and so forth.

A friend of mine claims he can travel the rural areas by public bus, eating at small stalls and staying at basic accommodation, for B150 a day. That's about US$6. No one could claim that this was expensive.

Governmental Fiddle-Faddle

Passports and Visas. You'll need a passport to enter Thailand and get back into your own country. You should ask your travel agent, passport office, or post office for information about obtaining a passport. The procedure is not difficult but don't leave it until the last minute because it's a bureaucratic process which is hard to hurry. Visitors of most nationalities (including Americans, Canadians, Australians) do not require a visa for tourist visits of up to fifteen days.

If you think your stay may be longer than fifteen days, you should apply for a "tourist visa" from any Thai consulate or embassy. These are valid for a stay of up to sixty days and a thirty-day extension may be possible if you apply to an immigration office while you are in Thailand. The validity of a tourist visa is three months, meaning a visitor must enter Thailand within three months of a visa being issued. There is a fee for a tourist visa which is currently B500.

If you are going to Thailand on business, you can apply for a "Non-Immigrant Visa," which is valid for ninety days. A letter from your home company or organization saying you will be returning within this period is necessary with your application, and a tax clearance is needed before you leave Thailand at the end of your stay.

Thai embassies are situated in many Asian, North American, European, and Oceania countries including Canada (Ottawa), the U.S. (Washington), United Nations (New York), Australia (Canberra), and New Zealand (Wellington). Consulates are located in many cities including Montreal, Toronto, and Vancouver in Canada; Boston, Chicago, Detroit, Honolulu, Los Angeles, New Orleans, Kansas City, Philadelphia, El Paso, Montgomery, Richmond, in the U.S.; and Melbourne and Sydney in Australia.

Health. No health certificates are required unless you have recently been to a yellow fever area or other declared infected zone. Within the major tourist areas, no abnormal health risks exist. In the more remote areas, including parts of the north and east, malaria can be a problem, so if you are trekking in these areas or plan to camp on a beach, you should take appropriate precautions. Bangkok and most other major cities have excellent medical facilities and hospitals. Many doctors have studied overseas and almost all can speak good English.

Tap water is not recommended. Drink bottled water. Most ice is okay, but I personally avoid the bulk cool drinks available from mobile vendors or street stalls. Cola, beer, and other bottled drinks are quite safe.

The Thais are hygiene-conscious. Despite the pungent smell of stagnant canals and sidewalk drains, and the noxious exhaust of cars and buses on city streets, Thai cities are not health risks to most people. Travel does, however, play havoc with most people's systems and minor diarrhea is common. This is partly induced by the tropical weather, the different water, and the hotter-than-normal food. A doctor will prescribe either a Western (tablets) or Thai (charcoal pills) remedy.

The tropical sun can be a hazard to those unaware of its strength. Do not sunbathe between the hours of 11 and 3 even on a cloudy day, as you can burn in fifteen minutes. Even when you are touring, it pays to wear a hat and drink more than normal. Some Thais and visitors take salt tablets during the hot season.

Be aware that tropical temperatures and insanitation are a potentially dangerous combination. Thailand is one of the safest of the tropical countries but you should be conscious of the possibility of prickly heat, an itchy rash that often occurs on the buttocks; heat stroke, which is a serious condition caused when the body's heat-regulating mechanism breaks down; fungal infections, such as athlete's foot; and typhoid fever, cholera, and hepatitis, which are rare but extremely dangerous if not treated. Your local physician is best able to recommend precautions.

Then there are sexually transmitted diseases. The situation with these in Thailand is somewhat cloudy. There is an active homosexual community and a thriving sex industry but official statistics do not indicate that Thailand has a high incidence of sexually transmitted disease. Certainly in recent years there have been active campaigns to bring AIDS and other diseases to the attention of the public and the use of condoms has been encouraged. Despite the relatively good news in the official figures, abstinence seems to be a wise choice.

Customs. Most visitors will complete a customs form which allows you to pass through the "Nothing to Declare" gates at Bangkok Airport. You should be aware of the following, however, because there are spot checks made, and a false declaration is regarded seriously by the officials.

It is forbidden to take narcotics, obscene literature or pictures, and firearms and ammunition into Thailand. Avoid doing so at all cost. There are also some money restrictions. Foreign visitors can only take in B2000 and take out B500 in Thai currency. You may take unlimited amounts of foreign currency with you into Thailand, but you need to declare the amount if it exceeds US$10,000. On leaving the country, any amount over US$10,000 must again be declared and you will only be allowed to take out a sum equivalent to that which you brought in.

Visitors are permitted to take 200 cigarettes and one litre of wine or spirits into Thailand, duty free.

Airport and Departure Tax. Every time you use an airport in Thailand you pay a tax. For domestic travel, the cost is only B20 per trip. But on departure from the international airport you will be levied a fee of B200, which is paid at the airline check-in counter.

Travellers' Guide

Safety. Thailand is a relatively safe country, but you should be aware that what might be a few unimportant dollars to you may be a month's savings to a local. Don't put this temptation in front of hotel room staff or others. All hotels have security boxes or a safe for guests' valuables, so use them.

Bag snatching is not common but you should be aware that snatchers do operate. Again take normal precautions. The same goes for pickpockets. It is foolish to flash bank rolls or have a bulging wallet. In the same way, you should avoid wearing expensive jewelry during the day. You are on vacation and don't need it, so why put temptation in someone's way?

I have never been concerned for my safety anywhere in Thailand and under normal circumstances you will not either. The streets are much safer at night than many U.S. or European cities and women can safely walk alone in most areas at any time of the day or night. I recommend that you ask the hotel receptionist for any precautions you should take in that particular area. For those needing assistance relating to safety, security, unethical practices, or other matters, call the Tourist Assistance Center at 281-5051 or 282-8129 in Bangkok.

Business Hours. Government offices mostly open Monday through Friday from 8:30 to 4:30, with a noon to 1:00 break for lunch.

Private business offices tend to work longer. Monday through Friday from 8:30 to 5:00 are typical hours. Some work a half-day on Saturday.

Retail stores work hours to suit their location. The bigger department stores open around 10 daily and close at 7 or 8. Many smaller stores, particularly in areas such as Sukhumvit Road in Bangkok, will remain open until 9 or later.

Tipping. Most establishments charge a 10 percent service fee so there is no need to leave anything additional. Tipping, in fact, is much less a way of life than it is in the U.S. and visitors are encouraged not to popularize this practice. My personal rule is that where a service charge is added to the bill in a restaurant, I will leave the small coins in the change *if* I have received good service. In hotels, I will tip the porter a small amount if he provides some extra service above the normal.

Airport porters charge a fixed fee for helping with baggage and expect no extra. Taxi drivers are not tipped on top of the negotiated fare.

Tourist Information. The Tourism Authority of Thailand (TAT) is a government agency established to serve the needs of visitors. The main offices keep government hours but most branches (including the Bangkok head office) have a Tourist Information Service which remains open on Saturdays, Sundays, and holidays. Here are the main offices within Thailand:

Bangkok—Ratchadamnoen Nok Rd. (Tel. 02-282-1143 or Fax 02-280-1744).

Chiang Mai—105/1 Lampang Rd. (Tel. 053-248-604 or Fax 053-252-812).

Hat Yai—Soi 2, Niphet Uthit 3 Rd. (Tel. 074-243-747 or Fax 074-245-986).

Kanchanaburi—Saeng Chuto Rd. (Tel. 034-511-200).

Nakhon Ratchasima—2102 Mittraphap Rd. (Tel. 044-243-427 or Fax 044-243-427).

Pattaya—382/1 Chaihat Rd. (Tel. 038-428-750 or Fax 038-429-113).

Phitsanulok—209 Boromtrailokanet Rd. (Tel. 055-252-742).
Phuket—73 Phuket Rd. (Tel. 076-212-213 or Fax 076-213-582).
Surat Thani—5 Talat Mai Rd. (Tel. 077-282-828 or Fax 077-282-828).
Ubon Ratchathani—Si Narong Rd. (Tel. 045-243-770 or Fax 045-243-771).

TAT also has a number of offices worldwide which will provide much useful information on touring Thailand. These are the main offices in North America, Europe, and the South Pacific:

Frankfurt—Bethmann St., 58/IV (Tel. 069-295-704 or Fax 069-281-468).
London—49 Albemarle St. (Tel. 01-499-7679 or Fax 01-629-5519).
Los Angeles—3440 Wilshire Blvd. (Tel. 213-382-2353 or Fax 213-380-6476).
New York—5 World Trade Center (Tel. 212-432-0433 or Fax 212-912-0920).
Paris—90 Ave. des Champs Elysees (Tel. 45-628-658 or Fax 45-637-888).
Rome—Via Barberini, 50 (Tel. 06-474-7410 or Fax 06-474-7660).
Sydney—56 Pitt St. (Tel. 02-247-7549 or Fax 02-251-2465).

News Media. Thailand has a thriving press, radio, television, and film industry but a large part of it is in Thai rather than English.

There are two major English language daily newspapers: the Bangkok *Post,* and the *Nation.* Both have excellent local and world news coverage and you will even be able to keep up with major sporting events in your own country. The *International Herald Tribune* and the *Asian Wall Street Journal* are also available in Bangkok and the major tourist centers on the afternoon of publication day. Most major hotels provide one local and one international paper to all English-speaking guests.

Thailand has a wide range of AM and FM radio stations. Bangkok and surrounding areas have an astonishing choice but of course most broadcasts and music are in Thai. There are some English broadcasts on some stations and English-language music is now appearing more often than in the past. Radio Thailand broadcasts in English for several hours a day (including news) and the Chulalongkorn University FM station has two hours of Western classical music most evenings. Current English-language broadcasts, times, and frequencies are in the English-language newspapers.

Major English-language programs are on the FM band. FM 107 has a nonstop music program with English news at 7:00-8:00 A.M., 12:30-1:00 P.M., and 7:00-8:00 P.M. FM 107.75 Radio Thailand presents "International Community Radio" from Bangkok Studios from 5:00 A.M. till 6:00 P.M., then from Pattaya until 2:00 A.M. Service FM 97 operates for various times each day between 6:00 A.M. and midnight. FM 95.5 is a full English-language station operating all day.

As well as these local stations, the major international radio services can be picked up on short wave. These services operate on different frequencies during the day so you need current information to find them. In the mornings you will find some of these services as follows:

Voice of America	5:00-8:00 A.M.	7.275MHz, 9.770MHz, 15.185MHz
Radio Australia	5:00-8:00 A.M.	15.240MHz
Radio Canada	5:00-5:30 A.M.	11.705MHz
BBC	5:00-7:30 A.M.	6.195MHz, 11.955MHz
KY01 Saipan	6:00-9:00 A.M.	15.405MHz

Thailand was the first country in southeast Asia to have regular TV transmission. When I first visited in the early 1970s, the country had a television blackout between about 6 and 8 P.M. so that people would at least leave the TV set for that period of the evening. Of course, that is long gone. Television is almost entirely in Thai and even original English-language programs are dubbed in Thai. It's weird watching familiar characters with strange voices speaking a language you can't understand.

News broadcasts and the original soundtrack of English programs can be heard on FM radio. Details are in the English-language newspapers. Many of the major hotels have in-house movie programs showing modern English-language movies from the U.S., Australia, Canada, and Britain.

Customs and Courtesies. The Thai people have evolved a culture rich in customs and traditions. These traditions pervade every facet of Thai life and most visitors will come in contact with many of them.

Thailand is justly celebrated for its tolerance and hospitality and the average tourist will have no difficulty in adjusting to the local customs. All the same, as when coming into any unfamiliar society, a visitor may find it helpful to be aware of certain do's and don't's and thus avoid giving accidental offense. Basically, most of these are simply a matter of common sense and good manners—not really all that different from the way one would behave in one's own country—but a few are special enough to be pointed out.

By far the most commonly encountered Thai custom is the *wai*, the traditional gesture of greeting. This is performed by bringing the palms of both hands together, fingers extended, and raising them to the level of the face, while at the same time bowing the head slightly. Unlike the Western handshake, the *wai* is more than simply a gesture of greeting. It is a sign of respect offered to one who is older or of higher social status. It is considered improper to *wai* someone who is younger than you are, or of a lower social position. Rather than struggling to work out the relative social standing of everyone you meet, it is easiest for the first-time visitor, at least in the beginning of his or her stay, simply to return those *wais* which are offered.

The Thai people have a deep, traditional reverence for their royal family, and a visitor should also be careful to show respect for the king, the queen, and the royal children. In a cinema, for example, a portrait of the king is shown during the playing of the national anthem, and the audience is expected to stand. When attending some public events at which a member of the royal family is present, the best guide as to how to behave is probably to watch the crowd and do what it does.

Thai law has a number of special sections concerning religious offenses and these cover not only Buddhism, the religion of the majority of the people, but also any other faiths represented in the kingdom. It is, for instance, unlawful to commit any act, by any means whatever, to an object or a place of religious worship of any community in a manner likely to insult the religion.

Here are a few tips on what to do and what not to do on a visit to a religious place. Dress neatly. Don't go shirtless, or in shorts, hot pants, or other unsuitable attire. If you look at the Thais around you, you'll see the way they would prefer you to be dressed—which, in fact, is probably not very different from the way you'd dress in a similar place back home.

It's all right to wear shoes while walking around the compound of a Buddhist temple, but not inside the chapel, where the principal Buddha image is kept. Don't worry about dirt when you have to take your shoes off. The floors of such places are usually very clean.

In a Muslim mosque, men should wear hats and women should be well covered with slacks or a long skirt, a long-sleeved blouse buttoned to the neck, and a scarf over the hair. All visitors should remove their shoes before entering the mosque and you should not be present if there is a religious gathering.

Buddhist priests are forbidden to touch or to be touched by a woman or to accept anything from the hand of one. If a woman has to give anything to a monk or novice, she first hands it to a man, who then presents it. If a woman particularly wants to present it with her hand, the monk or novice will spread out a piece of saffron robe or handkerchief in front of him and the woman will lay down the material on the robe which is being held at one end by the monk or novice.

All Buddha images, large or small, ruined or not, are regarded as sacred objects. Hence, don't climb up on one to take a photograph or, generally speaking, do anything that might show a lack of respect. In Thailand, Buddhist monks are looked upon as seekers after religious truth and as such are much respected. If introduced, one should always *wai* a monk (even the king does) but one should not expect a *wai* in return.

The don'ts of Thai social behavior are less clearly defined than those concerning the monarchy or religion—especially in a city like Bangkok where Western customs are better known and more widely accepted. However, what is acceptable in Bangkok may be much less so in the countryside, where the old ways are still strong. Here, then, are a few things to keep in mind.

It's considered rude to point your foot at a person, so try to avoid doing so when sitting opposite anyone. The foot is a low-class limb to most Thais, so don't point your foot to show anything to anyone, but use your finger instead.

Thais regard the head as the highest part of the body both literally and figuratively. As a result they don't approve of patting anyone there, even in a friendly gesture. Similarly, if you watch Thais at a social gathering, you'll notice that young people go to considerable lengths to keep their heads lower than those of older ones, to avoid giving the impression of "looking down" on them. This isn't always possible, of course, but it's the effort that counts.

Public displays of affection between men and women are frowned upon. You may see some Westernized young Thai couples holding hands, but that's as far as it goes in polite society.

Losing your temper, especially in public, will more than likely get you nowhere. The Thais think such displays denote poor manners and you are more apt to get what you want by keeping a cool head and concealing your emotions.

Don't be surprised if you are addressed by your first name as, for instance, Mr. Bob or Miss Mary instead of by your surname. This is because Thais refer to one another in this manner, usually with the title "Khun" (Mr., Mrs. or Miss) in front.

Follow the customs of the Thai people as far as possible and you'll make more friends during your stay. And the more friends you make, the more you'll want to go back.

Embassies and Consulates. Bangkok is a true international city, and as the capital of Thailand, it is home to representatives of the world's governments. Here is a list of the embassies and consulates represented in the city.

Apostolic Nunciature—217/1 Sathon Tai Rd. (Tel. 211-8709).
Argentina—20/85 Prommitr Villa (Tel. 259-0401).
Australia—37 Sathon Tai Rd. (Tel. 286-0411).
Austria—14 Soi Nantha (Tel. 286-3019).
Bangladesh—8 Soi Charoenmit (Tel. 391-8069).
Belgium—44 Soi Phraya Phiphat (Tel. 233-0840).
Brazil—8/1 Soi 15 Sukhumvit (Tel. 251-2989).
Bulgaria—11 Soi Ramkhamhaeng 11 (Tel. 314-3056).

Burma—132 Sathon Nua Rd. (Tel. 233-2237).
Canada—11th Floor, Boonmitr Building (Tel. 234-1561).
Chile—15 Soi 61 Sukhumvit (Tel. 391-8443).
China—57 Ratchadaphisek Rd. (Tel. 235-7030).
Czechoslovakia—197/1 Silom Building (Tel. 234-1922).
Denmark—10 Soi Atthakan Prasit (Tel. 286-3932).
Egypt—49 Soi Ruam Rudi (Tel. 253-0161).
Finland—16th Floor, Amarin Plaza (Tel. 256-9306).
France—35 Customs House Ln. (Tel. 234-0950).
Germany—9 Sathon Tai Rd. (Tel. 286-4223).
Greece—1977 New Phetchaburi Rd. (Tel. 314-7333).
Hungary—28 Soi Sukchai Sukhumvit (Tel. 391-2002).
Iceland—59 Soi Nawin (Tel. 249-1300).
India—46 Soi 23 Sukhumvit (Tel. 258-0300).
Indonesia—600-602 Phetchaburi Rd. (Tel. 252-3135).
Iran—602 Sukhumvit Rd. (Tel. 251-0205).
Iraq—47 Pradiphat Rd. (Tel. 278-5335).
Israel—31 Soi Lang Suan (Tel. 252-3131).
Italy—339 Nang Linchi Rd. (Tel. 286-4844).
Japan—1674 New Phetchaburi Rd. (Tel. 252-6151).
Korea (S)—Sathon Thani Building (Tel. 234-0723).
Laos—192 Sathon Tai Rd. (Tel. 286-0018).
Malaysia—35 Sathon Tai Rd. (Tel. 286-1390).
Nepal—189 Sukhumvit 71 (Tel. 390-1877).
Netherlands—106 Witthaya Rd. (Tel. 254-7701).
New Zealand—93 Witthaya Rd. (Tel. 251-8165).
Norway—20th Floor, Chokchai Building (Tel. 258-0513).
Pakistan—31 Soi Nama Nua (Tel. 252-7036).
Peru—Louis' Building, Siphraya (Tel. 233-5910).
Philippines—760 Sukhumvit Rd. (Tel. 259-0139).
Poland—61 Soi Prasanmit (Tel. 258-4112).
Portugal—26 Captain Bush Ln. (Tel. 234-0372).
Romania—39 Soi 10 Sukhumvit (Tel. 252-8515).
Saudi Arabia—10th Floor, Sathon Thani Blvd. (Tel. 235-0875).
Singapore—129 Sathon Tai Rd. (Tel. 286-2111).
Spain—104 Witthaya Rd. (Tel. 252-6112).
Sri Lanka—48/3 Sukhumvit Soi 1 (Tel. 251-2789).
Sweden—11th Floor, Boonmitr Building (Tel. 234-3091).
Switzerland—35 N. Witthaya Rd. (Tel. 253-0156).
Turkey—135/2 Soi Mahadlek 1 (Tel. 251-2987).
United Kingdom—Witthaya Rd. (Tel. 253-0191).
U.S.A.—95 Witthaya Rd. (Tel. 252-5171).

U.S.S.R.—108 Sathon Nua Rd. (Tel. 234-9824).
Vietnam—83/1 Witthaya Rd. (Tel. 251-7201).
Yugoslavia—28 Soi 61 Sukhumvit Rd. (Tel. 391-9090).

Consulates

Bolivia —1362-63 Banthatthong Rd. (Tel. 214-1501).
Chile—Bangkok Bank Building, Silom Rd. (Tel. 233-2177).
Dominican Republic—92/6 Chaeng Watthana Rd. (Tel. 251-0737).
Greece—412/8-9 Siam Square Soi 6, Rama Rd. (Tel. 251-5111).
Iceland—59 Soi Nawin Chuaphloeng Rd. (Tel. 249-1300).
Ireland—205 United Floumill Building, Ratchawong Rd. (Tel. 223-0876).
Korea (N)—81 Soi Ari 7 Phahon Yothin Rd. (Tel. 251-0803).
Mexico—Soi Annopnaruemit 1, Dindaeng Rd. (Tel. 245-7820).
Oman—134/1-2 Silom Rd. (Tel. 235-8868).
Peru—723 Siphaya Rd. (Tel. 233-5910).
Senegal—2/092 Chaeng Watthana Rd. (Tel. 588-1976).
Sri Lanka—1/7-8 Soi 10 Sukhumvit Rd. (Tel. 251-0803).

Travel Tips

Before you go

• Consider all the airline options. The lowest airfare is not always the cheapest in the long run. There are more things to consider than the initial asking price.

• The stop-over options may be an important consideration in your choice of airfare and airline. The cheapest fare probably allows you the smallest choice.

• Travel insurance is almost a "must." Particularly with the cheapest airfares, there are many restrictions on what changes you can make. If you become sick you may be penalized severely if you cannot catch your scheduled flights.

• Arrange unlimited medical insurance because illness or an accident overseas can be ruinously expensive. If you need to claim on insurance, obtain a medical certificate at the time of the treatment. It helps if you have a photocopy of your insurance policy with you.

• If you are travelling with someone, make sure both of you have some traveller's checks and credit cards. Everyone should take a combination of checks, credit cards, and cash.

• Travel light. Your baggage will get heavier each day you are away and it's important to be able to move your own bags even if it's just from a railway station to a taxi or through a large airport.

- Learn at least a few words of Thai before you arrive. Half a dozen key words from chapter three would be enough to get you started.
- Get your timing right. Bad weather can spoil a vacation or make it much more expensive. No one wants to sit around while it rains for five days straight and it's rather a waste if you won't leave the airconditioning because it's too hot outside.
- Don't be late at the airport. Airlines often overbook to compensate for "no-shows." If too many people turn up, it's the last people who are usually in trouble.
- If you are travelling overnight, buy an inflatable pillow. They may not look great but they allow you to doze comfortably in aircraft, trains, and buses because they give good head support.
- Watch out for excess baggage charges. In North America you are allowed two cases of a prescribed maximum size but elsewhere in the world it is 20 kilos in economy class and 30 kilos in business class. The excess baggage charge is dictated by international agreement and can be quite high. Try to carry small heavy items in your hand baggage if you know you are over the weight.

While you are away

- Always confirm onward flights as soon as possible after you arrive at your destination.
- Don't change money at hotels. Banks will almost always offer far better rates.
- Understand what your money is worth. Find some simple way to convert from baht to your own currency. For U.S., Canadian, and Australian dollars, the conversion is simple.
- Report lost credit cards promptly. Your liability is then small.
- Carry your travel documents and medical and toilet items in your hand baggage, just in case the airline, coach company, or hotel misplaces your main bag.
- Never order a second drink in a hotel or bar until you have found out what you are being charged.
- Don't buy breakfast at the hotel if you are on a tight budget. You can usually get something outside for half the price.
- Don't wear or carry anything that looks as if it is worth stealing.
- Always put your valuables in the hotel safety deposit.
- Don't tip unnecessarily. In restaurants if there is a service charge, just pay the last amount. Don't tip taxi drivers, airline porters, or guides.
- When shopping, look around at the alternatives. You will need to bargain but do it with a smile. Never show that you desperately want anything.

- Where possible, eat where the locals eat, drink in local bars, and use public transportation to the maximum. You will save money and will gain a better understanding of the country and people.
- Don't wear new shoes while you are away. Remember comfort is more important than appearance.
- Report anything lost or stolen immediately to the local police and try to get a written acknowledgment of your report.
- Take your time in strange airports, railway stations, or bus terminals. Find out beforehand what transportation alternatives are available to get you to your destination.
- Don't expect hotels to hold rooms indefinitely. If you know you will be checking in late at night, advise the hotel beforehand and consider giving your credit card number when you make the booking.

Visit the Region

Thailand has become the hub of southeast Asia so any visitor wanting to see more of the region will have no difficulty with air transportation from Bangkok. Thai Airways International currently flies to twenty-three destinations in Asia outside Thailand. Visitors should be aware that they will require visas to enter some of these countries and it can be several days before these are issued. You should obtain as many as possible before you leave home, or allow several days in Bangkok before you wish to travel to another country. Laos, Vietnam, and Burma are currently the most difficult.

You could consider including one or more of the following countries in your Thailand vacation.

Malaysia borders Thailand to the south and visitors can freely cross the border for tourist purposes. Malaysia shares with Thailand palm-fringed beaches, coral reefs teeming with fish, and tropical forests. But other aspects of the country are quite different. Kuala Lumpur, the federal capital, is a modern city of tall buildings, gold-domed mosques, and lush gardens. There are well-developed highland resorts, tea plantations, and tropical rain forests. The islands of Penang, Langkawi, and Tioman offer excellent facilities for visitors in idyllic surroundings.

Singapore is connected to Thailand by air, rail, and road. This bustling city-state has many contrasts and surprises. High-density living is the "norm" in much of Singapore yet this is probably one of the cleanest, safest, and most orderly cities in the world. There are dynamic skyscrapers, quaint old Chinese shop-houses, quiet back lanes, massive expressways, and bustling bazaars. This is the world's busiest port, the third largest oil refinery center in the world, and one of the world's key financial centers. The population is predominantly Chinese with Malay and Indian minorities.

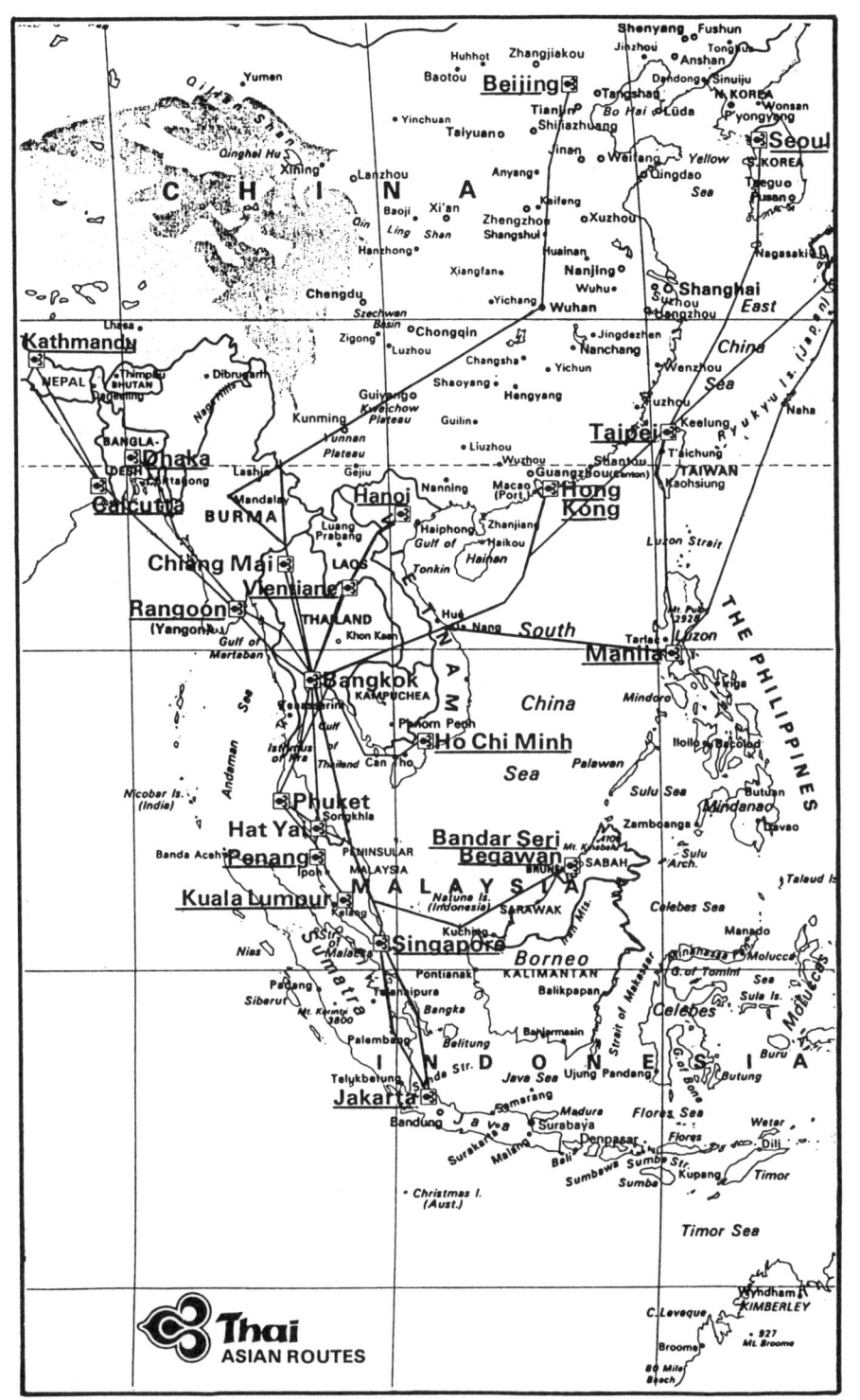

Courtesy Thai Airways International.

Indonesia is a string of 13,000 islands once known to the West as the Fabled Spice Islands. The capital of the republic, Jakarta, is situated on the island of Java, a fertile land of live volcanoes, misty mountains, paddy fields, and countless ancient temples. Major tourist development has occurred on the island of Bali, where a succession of festivals, dances, gentle people, handicrafts, and breathtaking beaches keep visitors happy.

Burma borders Thailand to the west, yet this is one of the least known destinations in Asia. The country's lack of modern material development makes this an "adventure trip," but the warmth of the people is delightful and the sightseeing opportunities are superb. There are temples, pagodas, monasteries, and shrines everywhere, many of them of great antiquity. Rangoon is the sleepy colonial-style capital. Pagan is a center for temples, while Mandalay is an area for traditional arts and crafts.

Vietnam has only recently reopened for tourist travellers and tourism opportunities are still limited. Most visits are restricted to the southern capital, Ho Chi Minh City, formerly known as Saigon. All visitors require visas and these may be refused without any reason being given. Tour arrangements are handled by the state-run Vietnam Tourism. Despite all these difficulties, Vietnam is an unusual and interesting travel destination, reflecting an ancient history and great creative traditions, with a later French colonial period still much in evidence.

Nepal is a country opened to the outside world largely by the efforts of Thai Airways International in the 1970s. The country is famous for the incredible Himalaya Mountains and its ancient forms of art and architecture. Kathmandu, parts of which date from the third century, is the capital city, where a visit is like travelling back in time. Accommodations and other facilities are now of a reasonable standard but some visitors would still consider this an adventurous trip.

The Philippines is an English-speaking nation where visitors can see the strong influences of Malay, Chinese, Spanish, and American periods of history as well as the considerable achievements of the modern independent nation. The archipelago of 7,000 islands has a great diversity of ethnic, cultural, and geographic features. The Filipinos are a warm race that love color, music, dancing, and enjoying themselves. Facilities for visitors are of a very high standard.

Hong Kong is probably the most visually dramatic and exciting port in the world. It is dynamic by day and spectacular by night. Traditional China and colonial Britain blend here to provide a unique travel experience. There is a wide range of sightseeing and endless shopping opportunities. The hotels, restaurants, and transportation facilities are some of the best in Asia.

Taiwan, named Formosa by the Portuguese, has been occupied over the centuries by Chinese, Portuguese, Spanish, Dutch, French, and Japanese. In

1949, two million mainland Chinese refugees arrived, bringing with them their culture, artistic skills, commercial abilities, and antique treasures. The island has some spectacular, rugged scenery and the capital, Taipei, has temples, shrines, parks, and the magnificent National Palace Museum, which contains the world's finest collection of Chinese antiques and art treasures.

Korea is a varied and attractive country with a stormy history but a thriving present. The country offers everything from skiing to subtropical beaches and there is superb mountain scenery and seascapes. Seoul, the capital, is a bustling, clean, modern city with luxurious hotels and other facilities. Transportation around the country is good and visitors are welcome.

Japan has four major and many small islands and a civilization that presents many bewildering contrasts between the traditional and the ultra-modern. Tokyo is one of the most frantic cities in the world yet rural Japan has some of the most delightful, serene landscapes to be found anywhere. A ride on the "bullet train" will show you a wide range of the country's rural landscape.

Demonic carvings on riverboats.

3

The Land and Life of Thailand

Thailand is about the size of France, or about one-twentieth the size of the United States. It extends a relatively long way in a north-south direction and the topography varies widely. This has a significant influence on the climate, and while the whole country is classed as tropical, winter minimum temperatures can vary between 5 and 20 degrees Celsius (40-70 F) in different parts of the country.

The country is divided into four regions. The mountainous north, which shares borders with Laos and Burma; the rolling semi-arid plateau of the northeast that borders Laos and Cambodia; the flat fertile central region, which rises to mountains in the east and west; and the Isthmus of the south, with long stretches of coast facing both the Gulf of Thailand and the Andaman Sea, leading to a land border with Malaysia.

The major river system in the country drains to the Chao Phraya River, which flows through Bangkok to the Gulf of Thailand. This region is extremely rich and provides much of the wealth of the whole country. The other dominant river system is the mighty Mekong, which forms much of the border between Thailand and Laos. Parts of the north and much of the northeast drain to this river. It passes through Cambodia and Vietnam before discharging to the South China Sea.

Throughout its long history, Thailand has been affected by many outside influences but few have been accepted outright and adopted in the way they are seen in other countries. Buddhism, for instance, is entirely imported yet the Thais have adapted it to their own cultural forms. The Thai language and many art forms are hybrids in which an indigenous core has been diversified by outside influences.

Over the centuries, many forces have interacted to form a powerful, complex culture which remains firm but is flexible enough to adapt to world changes and new developments. By understanding these concepts and the way they influence the Thais' perception of their life-style, their country and the world, we can gain an insight into the life of Thailand that is invaluable to the visitor who wishes to understand this "foreign" country.

It is also fascinating to talk to some of the "achievers" in a society and we do this throughout the next two chapters in highlighted profiles. We see that Thai society is as diverse and complex as our own and we learn how the leaders are coping with change and the pressures of modern life. They are bringing improvements that will have great influence on the lives of millions. I salute them.

Religion

More than five hundred years before the birth of Jesus Christ, an Indian prince attained Enlightenment and founded Buddhism. Over the next few centuries the religion spread through much of Asia, molding attitudes, tempering morality, coloring customs, and inspiring some great art, architectures, and sculpture. Buddhism first appeared in Thailand during the third century B.C., when Indian missionaries visited Nakhon Pathom, west of Bangkok, today a provincial capital and site of the world's tallest Buddhist monument. Now more than 90 percent of Thais are Buddhists and the religion influences most aspects of Thai life.

Buddhists believe that a person's life does not begin with birth and end with death, but is a link in a chain of lives, each conditioned by acts committed in previous existences. This concept of Karma, the law of cause and effect, suggests that selfishness and craving result in suffering. Conversely, compassion and love bring a person happiness. The ultimate Buddhist aspiration is to attain perfection through Nirvana, an indescribable state in which a person simply is existing yet is completely at one with his surroundings.

Fundamentally, Buddhism is an empirical way of life rather than a strict religion. It is free of dogma and is a flexible moral, ethical, and philosophical framework within which people find room to fashion their own salvation. It has had a profound role in shaping the Thai character. The concept of earthly impermanence and the idea of uncertainty in an ever-changing existence have done much towards creating that relaxed, carefree character that is one of the most appealing elements in the country. With its emphasis on accepting human faults and shortcomings as inevitable, Buddhism has helped form the Thais' remarkable tolerance and lack of prejudice. This has allowed them to embrace diverse cultural influences regardless of the origin.

The best place for the visitor to gain an understanding of Buddhism's influence is in a country village. This is where the majority of Thailand's 27,000 Buddhist temples are found. The temple is usually located on the village outskirts and comprises a tree-shaded walled compound enclosing a cluster of simple, steeply sloping, multiroofed buildings. The temple's main role is to aid aspirants in their search for Nirvana, but over the years it has also taken on the role of village hotel, employment and information agency, community center, place of safe deposit, and refuge for the mentally disturbed and the aged. In some instances it also acts as school and hospital.

Besides being teachers, many of the orange-robed monks are village councillors, herbal-medicine dispensers, and distributors of Buddhist amulets. The amulets are tiny Buddha images worn around the neck to ensure good fortune, provide protection, and enhance wealth. They are almost universally revered in Thailand and to give an amulet to someone is to be remembered for life, yet Buddha amulets are nowhere mentioned in Buddhist scriptures.

Buddhist monks have always been accorded great respect for renouncing worldly pleasures and seriously undertaking study of the Buddha's teaching to attain "perfect manhood." A monk's life is not unduly severe and daily contact with the general population is commonplace. Except for the three months of the annual Rains Retreat, a monk is free to travel and visitors will see many on the streets, in buses, and in aircraft. This is a legacy from Buddhism's earliest days, when the Buddha and his disciples led itinerant lives.

A monk may leave the monkhood any time he wishes. The Thai ordination is a simple public notice of a man's intention to follow the Buddha's teaching. He is not obliged to remain a monk for life, nor does any stigma attach if he decides to return to his old life. People acquire "merit" by donating food to the monks, by building and renovating temples, by constructing hospitals, and by showing kindness and compassion to all living creatures.

The monks are also an important part of everyday life. They chant auspicious verses blessing the opening of new businesses. They officiate at house warmings. They annoint new ships and aircraft. Brides and grooms make meritorious offerings of food on their wedding days and are blessed and sprinkled with holy water. Most families have at least one member who has studied the Buddha's teachings in a temple. After discharging their family obligations, many men will spend their remaining years as Buddhist monks.

It has long been a Thai custom for Buddhist males over twenty to be temporarily ordained as Buddhist monks, generally during the annual Rains Retreat. Government departments, parts of the armed forces, and larger private companies make temporary ordinations easier by granting their employees three months' leave with full salary. Everyone from a farmer's son to royalty may take this unique chance for self-improvement. Both the present Thai king and his son have been monks for short periods.

Although Buddhism is the primary religion, Thais have always subscribed to the ideal of religious freedom. While the Thai constitutions have stipulated that Thai kings must be Buddhist, monarchs are invariably titled "Protectors of All Religions." The country thus has religious minorities of Muslims, Hindus, Sikhs, and Christians together with Confucianism and ancestor worship.

Muslims comprise Thailand's largest religious minority. Most are concentrated in the southern part of the country adjacent to Malaysia. It is believed that Islam was introduced to the Malay peninsula by Arab traders during the thirteenth century. The king or his representative presides during the annual celebrations commemorating the Prophet Muhammad's birthday, and a respected Muslim religious leader is appointed state counsellor for all Islamic affairs. Government-employed Muslims are allowed leave for important Muslim festivals and are allowed to work half-days on Friday, the Muslim holy day.

Christianity was introduced in the sixteenth and seventeenth centuries by Portuguese and Spanish missionaries. Later Protestants of the Presbyterian, Baptist, and Seventh-Day Adventist churches arrived. Although only a few Thais are Christian, the churches have made major contributions in health and education. Many Thai schools and hospitals are Christian-affiliated. Thailand's first printing press was Christian-introduced, as was Western surgery, the first smallpox vaccinations, and the training of Thai doctors in Western medicine.

Thais of most persuasions are still affected by other older beliefs that existed even before Buddhism. Spirits, astrology, good and bad omens, and other such things all figure prominently in the Thai life-style. Astrologers are consulted to learn the most auspicious time for weddings, important journeys, and business openings. The spirits are believed to exist in many forms and to be huge in number so that they can play a part in every activity of the day.

If you stroll through the business or residential areas of any Thai village or city you will see that there is a miniature house in nearly every compound. It may be a simple wooden structure like a Thai-style house or it may be an elaborate minitemple. These houses are the homes of the compound's resident spirits and you will see that the residents and workers make offerings of food, fresh flowers, and incense sticks to ensure that the spirits

Thai Style

M. L. Tritosyuth Devakul spent much of his school days in the United States. He lived with Dean Sayre of the prestigious Washington Cathedral, attended high school in Washington, then went to Dartmouth College in Massachusetts and finally to Harvard University, where he received a master's degree in architecture.

When he returned to Thailand in the early 1970s after so many years abroad, M. L. Tri felt, in some ways, more foreign than Thai. His first important commission in Bangkok, the design of the Bhirasri Institute of Modern Art, showed influences from his years in the United States.

Subsequent buildings have allowed him to explore cultural roots that may have been unused during his years abroad, but that now exert a powerful influence on his designs. The Australian Embassy in Bangkok stands partly on columns over a small lake, and with its broad expanse of plate glass it has an undeniably modern appearance, yet it is also strikingly reminiscent of traditional Thai architecture. This happy blend also appears in other work—the Indian chancery, some town house and residential projects, and the Thai restaurant for the Oriental Hotel.

M. L. Tri has made a significant contribution to the Thai tourism industry with his developments on Phuket Island. His first major job was the design of several buildings for the Club Mediterranee on Kata Beach. This was followed by the spectacular cascading Phuket Yacht Club on Nai Harm Beach. More recently we have seen the development of Le Meridien Phuket, with its more than four hundred rooms on Relax Bay.

A basic philosophy has been applied to all these developments— there is a need to upgrade the travel infrastructure but at the same time we must preserve the island's main attraction, which is its natural beauty. That principle has also been applied to his own Phuket house, which sprawls over a headland site incorporating a spectacular rock-strewn saltwater swimming pool.

M. L. Tri's activities are not limited to pace-setting buildings. He has served as a senator since 1981 and is on numerous committees covering a wide range of subjects. Clearly here is a Thai who has been spectacularly successful in combining the influences of two cultures to the benefit of his country.

While extremely successful today, M. L. Tri's thoughts are often on tomorrow. He has just launched a massive high-rise residential

> development beside the Chao Phraya River, which he says takes many Thais back to their roots amongst flooded ricefields. Also in his future is more time to pursue his love of sculpture—not the stone-carving kind but the development of space and the individual's relationship to it. Clearly the world will see much more of this man's remarkable talents.

favor them. To the average Thai, there is nothing inconsistent about the intermingling of such beliefs with Buddhism.

The Modern Monarchy

It would be difficult to exaggerate the intensity of respect that the Thai people feel for their king. Within days, every visitor to Thailand will have come into contact with this devotion which extends across all strata of society. The king is both a symbol and a person. With the present king, all Thais have come to respect both sides of a man who has made the Thai monarchy stronger than at any time this century.

While 1932 saw an end to the absolute monarchy that had been practiced for 700 years, the modern monarchy remains the central unifying element in Thailand and it has been in no way diminished by the curtailment of its political power. Visitors should be very aware that no Thai will tolerate any disrespect of the monarchy, even from a foreigner.

In the past, particularly during the Ayutthaya period, Thai monarchs were venerated almost as celestial deities and for centuries the kings were inaccessible to most of their subjects. The present monarch, King Bhumibol Adulyadej, has established a different relationship with his people. He is constantly travelling the country visiting schools, farms, town fairs, graduation ceremonies, and other places where he can talk to, and be seen by, his subjects.

This is reciprocated by an amazing affection for him. Pictures of the king and queen hang in almost every house in the country. Most shops, offices, and factories have framed pictures and quotations from the Royal Family in a prominent position. They are not there because of some dictatorial decree by a fanatical ruler. They are there because of genuine love for the man and the Head of State, Upholder of Religions, and Head of the Armed Forces.

King Bhumibol's apparent natural flair for kingship has been a wonderful thing for Thailand but it occurred almost by chance. When he was born in 1927 in Cambridge, Massachusetts, there was little likelihood that he would ever become king. A succession of events, including the mysterious death of

King Ananda, led to Prince Bhumibol ascending the throne as Rama IX in 1950. The king is an accomplished composer, musician, painter, sailor, mathematician, photographer, sculptor, engineer, inventor, and polyglot. But his greatest love seems to be for the development of Thailand for the benefit of all citizens.

The king has visited every single Thai province—by jeep, train, helicopter, plane, boat, or on foot. During these provincial visits he consults not only officials and monks but seeks firsthand information from farmers, laborers, factory workers, and home help about their common problems, needs, and hopes. On returning to Bangkok, he often initiates steps to ensure that the required assistance is received. Sometimes he uses his own funds to start up the projects, with government agencies later taking over responsibility for the work.

Thailand's northern hilltribes have benefited from a royally inspired self-help program which is assisting them to turn away from the ecologically disastrous slash-and-burn farming of the opium poppy as their sole source of income. Instead they are growing a variety of crops which can be sustained on land close to the village. In the drought-prone northeast, the king instigated a program of artificial rain making and has been instrumental in a scheme to reforest large areas of the country.

The king and queen are also required to take part in innumerable royal ceremonies that crowd the year. There are the various Buddhist holy days, the seasonal robing of the Emerald Buddha in the Grand Palace compound, the opening of the Parliament, the Royal Ploughing Ceremony, and many, many more. The king receives foreign heads of state during state visits and accepts the credentials of each new foreign ambassador to Thailand. Every draft law is submitted to him for his signature before promulgation.

Queen Sirikit's interest in rural people's welfare closely parallels the king's. She has been particularly active in encouraging rural women to employ traditional skills to earn extra income. The king and queen have three children: H.R.H. Prince Vajiralongkorn, H.R.H. Princess Sirindhorn, and H.R.H. Princess Chulabhorn.

There are two major Bangkok building complexes associated with royalty—the Grand Palace, for nearly 150 years the first home of kings, and Chitralada Villa, the estate which King Bhumibol has chosen as his family's residence. The riverine walled Grand Palace was conceived by Rama I as a way of recreating Ayutthaya's splendor. Subsequent kings built Thai- and European-style buildings until the complex assumed its present form. Today it is one of Bangkok's most magnificent attractions. In comparison, Chitralada Villa is small and simple. So too are the other five royal palaces that are maintained around the country in Bang Pa-in, Hua Hin, Chiang Mai, Sakon Nakhon, and Narathirat.

One of King Bhumibol's most spectacular royal possessions is his fleet of ornately carved royal barges, most of which were built by Rama I and resemble barges used by Ayutthayan kings for river transportation. The barges, powered by brilliantly costumed chanting oarsmen from the Thai military, have been used on several ceremonial occasions in recent years. Visitors can see them at other times at anchor in Thonburi.

As can other monarchs, King Bhumibol can bestow awards and honors on ordinary citizens who have served Thailand with distinction or who have rendered great service to the crown. Royal titles are not inherited in perpetuity but lapse gradually over five generations. As British titles descend in rank through prince, earl, knight, etc., Thai titles descend through Chao Fa, Phra Ong Chao, Mom Chao, Mom Rajawongse, and Mom Luang. The children of any one rank inherit the next-lowest rank. After five generations they are plain "mister" or "miss."

Over the forty years since his coronation, King Bhumibol has proved himself a worthy successor to his ancestors. He is now the longest-ruling Thai monarch and must rank among the most successful and most loved of all Thai kings.

The Thai Language

Very few Westerners have a complete understanding of the Thai language, so visitors will not be expected to speak Thai. There are, however, decided advantages in learning even a few Thai words. You will impress the locals with a few words in their own language and you will find that this is a great way to strike up a conversation with just about anyone. Your poor attempt at speaking their language will encourage many Thais to try their limited English on you. Once that happens you will be surprised how much conversation you can have with so few words.

If you are touring outside the recognized tourist areas you will find that few people speak much English, so it can be a great help to have a phrase book or dictionary and a sense of humor. Fortunately the Thais are so friendly and easygoing that they will spend a long time with you trying to understand what you want. They may laugh at your inability to speak correct Thai, but those laughs are more an appreciation of your attempts than a laugh at you. I have found myself in several villages where language had become a stumbling block to my activities. In every case the locals made extraordinary attempts to understand what I was saying and eventually located someone who could speak English or simple Thai to me.

Written Thai employs an alphabet of forty-four consonants and thirty-two vowels that join to form syllabic sounds. The sounds are combined with five different tones to fashion a melodious, complex language. The language is very flexible in everyday usage and you can begin speaking Thai without spending a lot of time learning all kinds of complicated grammar rules. If you know only a limited number of Thai words, you can start speaking complete sentences that will be understood by everyone. The beauty of speaking Thai in everyday life is that a Thai sentence need not be a complete sentence. If the meaning is clear and understandable, then no one cares or even notices what words have been left out.

That is the good bit. The bad bit is that at other levels, it can be very complicated indeed. There are, for instance, seventeen ways of saying "I" and nineteen ways of saying "you." Because the language has no prefixes or suffixes, no genders for nouns, no articles, no plurals or no verb conjugations and because the language structure illustrates rank and intimacy, it can be extremely difficult for a foreigner to understand the precise meaning of some sentences. This is further complicated by the fact that there are in effect four different languages—a royal language, an ecclesiastic language, a polite everyday vernacular, and a pithy expressive slang. A foreigner can find that while he can make himself understood by Thais, he can listen to two Thais talking and not understand a single sentence.

Thai is a monosyllabic tonal language. The meaning of a single syllable may be altered by means of five different tones: mid, high, low, falling, and rising. This makes it rather difficult for English speaking people used to a nontonal language. It means that when speaking Thai, we should remove all emotion and tone modulation from our speech.

The basic word order of a sentence is subject-verb-object, with modifiers following each appropriate word. "Fried rice," for instance, becomes "rice fried." Males usually refer to themselves as "phom," meaning "I" or "me," and females correspondingly use "chan" or "de chan." Suppose you want to say, "I love you." For males it comes out "Phom [I] rak [love] khoon [you]." For females it is "Chan rak khoon."

The last point to remember when speaking Thai is that politeness and gentleness in speech is probably more important than in most other languages. The most important word of all for a male speaker is "Khrap." This is spoken only by a male and can mean "sir, ma'am, yes sir, yes ma'am." The average male in Thailand says this word many times a day. When being ultrapolite, to the boss or an important official, a Thai male will end every sentence with this word. The equivalent word for a female speaker is "Ka." Males never say "Ka" and females never say "Khrap."

Here is a selection of words and phrases that you will find useful in Thailand.

Numbers

zero —soon
one —nung
two —sorng

three	—sarm
four	—sec
five	—ha
six	—hok
seven	—jet
eight	—paet
nine	—gow
ten	—sip
eleven	—sip-et
twelve	—sip-sorng
twenty	—yee-sip
twenty-one	—yee-sip-et
twenty-two	—yee-sip-sorng
thirty	—sarm-sip
forty	—see-sip
one hundred	—nung roy
one hundred nine	—nung roy gow
two hundred	—sorng roy
one thousand	—pan

Days of the Week

Sunday—wun athit
Monday—wun chan
Tuesday—wun angkaan
Wednesday—wun bhut
Thursday—wun paruhat
Friday—wun suk
Saturday—wun sao
today—wun nee
tomorrow—pru nee
yesterday—meua wun

Greetings

hello, goodbye—sawardee khrap/ka
excuse me—cor tort
never mind—my pen ry
How are you?—sabidee ler
Thank you—kop khun
Please come in—choo-en kow
May I come in?—kow di mi

Other Handy Words and Phrases

where—tee ni
when—mua ri
water—narm
spicy hot—phet

no—mi
not—mi di
very good—de mark
what—a-ri
who—kry
cold—yen
hot—rorn
rice—kow
hospital—rong pi ya barn
left—si
right—kwa
straight ahead—trong pi
slowly—cha-cha
stop—yut
drive—khap
be careful—la wung
bus station—satarnee rot meh
railway station—satarnee rot fi
airport—sa narn bin
hotel—rong ram
police station—satarnee tumrooat
embassy—sattarn toot
bath/shower—arp narm

delicious—aroy
hungry—hew kow
thirsty—hew narm
big—yi
small—lek
to like—chorp
how much?—tor-I
Westerner—furung
restaurant—rong aharn
pedicab—samlor
motorized pedicab—tuk-tuk
canal—klong
lane—soi
road—ta non
village—barn
island—ko
district—amphor
downtown—amphor maoung
mountain peak—doi
river—mennarm
Buddhist temple—wat

post office—prisarnee
market—talart

Where is the bathroom?—Hong narm tee ni
I do not understand—Mi kow ji
I would like a ticket—yark di too-a
I would like to go—yark ja pi
Very expensive—pang mark

When you are in Thailand, you will see various attempts to translate Thai into English by Thai speakers. There is no uniformity in this translation at all, so you will find words spelled in quite different ways. This is very confusing but you will fairly quickly understand that "wan ni," "wan nii," "wun nee," and "wan ne," all mean "today." Good luck.

Orchid World

Dr. Rapee Sagarik is simply called "Mr. Orchid." His influence on the Thais' attitude towards these beautiful flowers has been enormous. His lifetime passion began in childhood and he has pursued it relentlessly ever since.

Foreigners have a good knowledge of Thai orchids. Travellers aboard Thai Airways International emerge with the blooms pinned to their lapels; hotels, restaurants, shops, and others use the word in their names; and many a foreign lady has been thrilled by the gift of a genuine cut flower from Thailand or a gold-plated blossom in a piece of jewelry.

Most foreigners would assume that Thais have had a romance with orchids since the days of the early Thai kingdoms. They are wrong. Until the late 1950s, orchids were either a hobby for the elderly or the domain of the wealthy. Then along came Rapee Sagarik and he created a peaceful revolution in the orchid establishment.

Dr. Rapee graduated from Thailand's top agricultural institution, Kasetsart University, and set about changing community attitudes. He gave lectures, appeared on television, and wrote extensively about orchids. He was spectacularly successful. Serious hobbyists appeared, prices plummeted so orchids were accessible to most Thais, and orchidology was introduced to the Kasetsart curriculum.

Now Dr. Rapee turned to scientific research. He began developing hundreds of hybrids which replaced the expensive imports that were coming in at that time. A thriving orchid industry was in the making.

In 1970, low-income farmers came to Dr. Rapee for help in their dispute with cut-flower exporters. The outcome was the Bangkok Flowers Centre Company, a cooperative directed by farmers, managed by business people, and advised by Rapee and others. Since then the cooperative has prospered, growing into one of the largest in the orchid market and becoming a leader in the lucrative export field.

Each day, workers bind the stems of hybrid orchids, ferns, and wet cotton wool to form bouquets which are air freighted to the markets of the world—western Europe, Japan, Australia, Canada, and the United States. Thailand has become the world's largest exporter of orchids due largely to the work of one dedicated man.

> But Dr. Rapee worries that control of the industry might fall to outsiders. Already international companies are entering the industry. He sees this as a reflection of the great change that is underway in Thailand and hopes that it is not too rapid.
>
> Today Dr. Rapee is working hard on preparations for the Fourth Asia Pacific Orchid conference in Chiang Mai in 1992. If his past record is a good guide to the future, it will be a great success.

Thai Food

A few years ago Thai food had a reputation for being so hot that it was unsuitable for foreigners. Then Thai restaurants began appearing around the world and Westerners flocked to them in droves to enjoy slightly Westernized Thai food. If you have enjoyed Thai food in the U.S., Europe, or Australia, you will still be surprised at Thai food in Thailand—it is so much better than you have tasted before. For those who are unfamiliar with the exotic flavors of Thai food, eating in Thailand will be an adventure that shouldn't be missed.

China, India, Malaysia, and Indonesia have all exerted an influence on Thai cuisine over the centuries, contributing certain spices, herbs, and other ingredients. Some were incorporated almost unchanged, while most underwent a gradual change as the Thais shaped them to local tastes. The result today is a unique blend of salt, sweet, sour, and pungent which distinguishes Thai food from all others.

Traditional Thai food as eaten in the rural areas is simple and straightforward. Rice and vegetables plus perhaps some dried fish, soup, and a couple of sauces make an excellent meal for most households. This is occasionally varied by a dish of noodles, a curry, or a papaya salad. It is this food which is readily available in small street stalls and markets throughout the country. Western visitors will generally find it satisfying and nourishing, at a very cheap price.

Restaurants throughout the country have in recent years conjured up other dishes that are far more elaborate and these have been readily incorporated into the urban Thais' cuisine. These are the ones which Westerners are more likely to know and enjoy, but in most cases they are a fairly new occurrence in Thailand.

A Tutor for Thai Tastes

"If I was seeking a single-word summation of Thai food," says one of Thailand's leading culinary teachers, **Charlie Amatyakul**, director of the Thai Cooking School at the Oriental Hotel, "the word would certainly be 'harmony.'"

The Thai Cooking School was set up on the Rim Naam Terrace across the waters of the Chao Phraya River from the Oriental Hotel. The interior of the old, Thai-style colonial house was converted into a classroom, demonstration room, and kitchen and Charlie was the obvious person to be asked to run the school.

Charlie is not your conventional chef. In fact he prefers not to be referred to as a chef at all, nor for that matter as a food expert. "I am not trained as a chef; I just fell into lecturing and then into writing for local publications about food," he says. "But I do love food and I like cooking for pleasure."

Charlie learned his cooking as a child, watching and helping his mother. She taught him the history of the cuisine, what goes or does not go with what, and how things should be cooked. But at first it was purely a hobby. After graduating from Bangkok's Chulalongkorn University with a degree in international studies and political science, he spent two years studying language and literature in France, then two years studying interior design in Vienna. When he returned to Thailand, he entered the hospitality business.

He has been invited to supervise several state banquets for Her Majesty Queen Sirikit and he has accompanied Her Majesty to the United States to look after her entertaining on such official tours. His book, *The Best of Thai Cooking*, is considered to be an A to Z of Thai cuisine. Yet any visitor to Thailand can learn from Charlie the knowledge and use of the essential ingredients that make Thai cuisine so appealing. The classes operate each morning Monday to Friday and foreign visitors are welcome. It's best to contact Charlie direct at the Thai Cooking School, Oriental Hotel, Bangkok, Thailand for details and costs. Your travel agent may be able to do this for you.

"I want to introduce my students to the subtleties of Thai cooking," he says. "I demonstrate to my class recipes that complement each other. They are not my own; I just translated and perfected them. I want to stay as faithful to the traditional recipes as is practical."

Charlie finds the school a challenge, but he revels in it. By nature

> he is gregarious and his wide experience has made him knowledgeable about much of the best in Thai society. Clearly he is an enthusiast about Thai food and you just have to mention the words to spark that wicked smile which is so much an expression of a mischievous character. A week of learning from Charlie would be great fun. No wonder the classes are so popular.

In traditional Thailand, there was rarely any formal protocol at mealtimes and eating was delightful for its simplicity. Tables and chairs were absent and everyone gathered around a mat on the floor. The men sat cross-legged, the women with their legs tucked behind them. Plates, bowls, or pieces of paper were placed at random and the food was put in a central area. This is still the custom in much of rural Thailand and it makes for a lovely informal, intimate meal. Some of my most memorable meals have been had in this way. Unfortunately most visitors do not have the chance to experience this side of Thai life. The nearest you can get to it is in a small rural restaurant where cutlery may be placed in a central container on each table and where dishes will arrive in any order and will be shared by all.

The wide range of tastes associated with Thai food comes from the extraordinary array of herbs, spices, and other ingredients that the average Thai cook would regard as essential. Undoubtedly the most celebrated are the chillies, which come in perhaps a dozen different varieties. The most dangerous for the visitor are the smallest, called "phrik khi nu." These have proved the downfall of many a brave Westerner. The larger chillies are several degrees milder and these are used when a less aggressive flavor is called for.

Chillies, however, constitute only one of the many ingredients which give flavor. Green peppercorns find their way into several dishes as do the leaves of the coriander plant, which are sprinkled lavishly on just about everything from soups to curries. When used properly, none of these ingredients should ever overshadow the delicate citron taste of the lemon grass or the kaffir lime or the elusive flavor of turmeric. Each cook will vary the recipe according to taste, and the blending will differ from one cook to another and from one province to another.

These ingredients come in different forms: roots from ginger, leaves from coriander, stalks from bamboo shoots, seeds from sesame, and so forth. Some are bought from the nearest market but many are picked fresh from the garden by many Thai households and restaurants. Lime is squeezed into countless soups, salads, and curries and is used to adorn many dishes. Equally essential is coconut; the milk is used in both curries and sweets and the grated meat is a frequent addition as well. Tamarind is eaten sugared a candy but it also adds its distinctive flavor to many dishes.

A wide range of dried spices—such as white pepper, the skins of the kaffir lime, cumin seeds, nutmeg, bay leaf, clove, cinnamon, and saffron—is found in many Thai kitchens. The proper use of these ingredients, together with others, is regarded as a culinary art in Thailand.

A Thai meal is not regarded as complete without soup. Soup is eaten by Thais from dawn to dusk from small street soup stalls and during mealtimes. They are eaten throughout the meal, a few spoonfuls at a time. There are three main Thai soups. "Kaeng chut" is a mild Chinese-style broth with meat and vegetables and a gentle taste to complement spicier dishes. "Khao tom" is a clear rice soup claimed to be a cure for fevers, colds, and hangovers which is often flavored with vinegar, chilli, and pieces of meat or poultry. Then there is the famous "tom yung goong," a delicious hot, spicy shrimp soup flavored with lemon grass, lime leaves, shallots, chillies, coriander leaves, lemon juice, and a fish sauce. It is often served in a charcoal-heated bowl so that it continues to simmer during the meal.

Sauces are essential to any Thai meal, often to provide a salty contrast to the blend of sweet and sour that characterizes many dishes. The most popular are "narm pla" (fish sauce), sometimes transformed into "narm pla phrik" by the addition of chopped chillies, and "kapi" (shrimp paste), which is a concoction of dried shrimp and assorted spices. Other sauces that are used are "narm oy" (oyster sauce) and "narm se yu" (soy sauce). Boiled rice is "khao," fried rice is "khao padt," and sticky rice is "khao niaw."

Everyone has their own favorite dishes so it would be stupid of me to suggest what you should eat. The following dishes are some of my favorites and they provide a reasonable variety from which, hopefully, you will also find some favorites.

Rice and Steamed Chicken (Khao Man Kai) is a very simple dish that will offend few people. Chopped, steamed chicken is served over boiled rice with cucumber and tomato as decoration. It is eaten with soy sauce.

Thai Fried Noodles (Kuai Tieo Phat Thai) is a simple delicious noodle dish made from noodles, egg, prawns, and bean sprouts. It is served hot and is garnished with lemon, onion, and coriander leaves.

Crispy Noodles (Me Krop) is a delicious combination of dried vermicelli, prawns, pork, and egg, deep fried and served with grated lemon rind, chopped onion, chopped coriander leaves, and bean sprouts.

Chicken in Coconut Soup (Kai Tom Kha) is a dish quite different from anything in Western cuisine. Chicken, coconut milk, fish sauce, lime juice, and sliced galanga root combine to produce a unique taste.

Fried Beef in Oyster Sauce (Nua Phat Narm Man Hoi) is perhaps more a Chinese dish but it is found on the menu of many Thai restaurants. It is served with chopped, cooked broccoli spears.

Fried Fish in Red Sauce (Pla Chian Narm Daeng) is particularly popular in the south but it is obtainable almost everywhere. The fish is served whole, covered with a sauce made from ginger, chillies, garlic, vinegar, and vegetable oil.

Green Chicken Curry (Kaeng Khreo Wankai) is a combination of chicken, coconut milk, eggplant, chillies, lemon grass, shallots, and curry paste.

Spicy Minced Beef (Larp) is a favorite from the northeast and is made from minced beef, garlic, onion, chilli, lime juice, and fish sauce. It is served cold.

Roast Chicken (Kai Yung) is Thailand's answer to American fried chicken. A mixture of ginger, garlic, coriander root, pepper, and vegetable oil is used to marinate the chicken before it is baked or barbecued.

Papaya Salad (Som Tum) is an ideal complement to Kai Yung or Larp. Green papaya is grated with tomato, carrot, lime rind, dried shrimp, garlic salt, and chilli to make a most unusual dish.

While meat and fish dishes, soups, and salads are always served and eaten together, Thai desserts are always served separately at the end of the meal. Thailand places little emphasis on wheat or corn so until recently there were few cakes, pies, or tarts on menus. This is slowly changing in the tourist areas but most meals will end with fruit rather than puddings or cooked desserts. Mangoes, bananas, papaya, litchis, and pineapples are the most popular fruits and they are often served in combination, sliced on a large plate. There are a few desserts which are not fruits. These tend to be brightly colored and made from gelatin, coconut meat, or rice. A particular distinctive dessert called Gold Threads (Foi Thong) is made from egg yolks, castor sugar, and water.

Eating Thai-style is an experience in sharing, a part of the Thai "sanuk" way of life, the joy of living. This determination to enjoy every facet of life requires the feeling of well-being and the Thais achieve this as they enjoy the food and atmosphere of a Thai meal. It is more difficult for a visitor but I guarantee that if you take the time, you too can experience the same feeling and be touched by the happiness and hospitality of the people around you. It is well worth trying.

To accompany the food, Thais drink one of three things—beer, whiskey, or cola. I find the local Kloster beer to be about right for my taste buds with Singha Gold a close second. The most popular beer on the market is Singha, which is more strongly flavored and probably goes well with many Thai foods. Both Singha and Kloster come in two bottle sizes but many restaurants claim to have only the full-size bottle. The beer has a higher alcohol content than in many countries so beware. Small bottles cost B30-45 and large bottles B60-80 in most restaurants.

I am not usually into local spirits but I must confess to enjoying the Thai

Mekong whiskey. It is far from Scotch in taste but when mixed with cola or lime and soda it makes a very pleasant drink. Customers normally buy Mekong by the bottle or half-bottle and the waitress will bring the bottle to the table with a bucket of ice and mixers. She will never let the glass fall below half-full without filling it again, and before you know it the bottle will be gone. At about B80 for the whiskey and perhaps B20-25 for cola it can be cheaper than drinking beer.

While imported Scotch whiskey has a great status attached to it, Thais rarely drink other imported spirits. That is mainly because of the cost. One gin and tonic in a restaurant is likely to cost you more than a whole bottle of Mekong. Many Thai women and a growing number of men are avoiding alcohol so there is probably more cola sold in Thai restaurants than in most countries on earth.

Just a word about ice and water. Tap water is not recommended for drinking anywhere in Thailand so a thriving bottled water industry has emerged. There are a few "national" water companies and many small local concerns. I have no idea what the controls or hygiene standards of these companies are, but the Thais seem to put their trust with anything that comes in a bottle and I must admit that I have never been ill from Thai bottled water anywhere in the country. Ice is almost impossible to avoid and it appears that in most cases it is made from bottled water. When you order a drink in most places outside the tourist areas, it will automatically come with ice—even the beer. If you want it cold, you will accept the ice and hope for the best.

Rural Life

A short-term visitor to Thailand who spends a few days in Bangkok then a few more at one of the beach or northern resorts could well leave the country without any real appreciation of what life in Thailand for the ordinary Thai is all about. These areas have developed a veneer which is difficult for the foreigner to penetrate. Yet it is likely that the actual life-style of the hotel receptionist or the immaculately dressed shop assistant, outside their place of employment, is little different from that of their parents or cousins back upcountry.

The best way to understand the fabric of Thai society is to look at family and village life in the rural areas. Visitors who are prepared to get away from the "package tour" regime will be well rewarded. Every family has within it a system of relationships and attitudes governing personal contacts which is repeated on all levels of society and which makes the Thai nation one huge extended family. Thais learn a code of behavior in the home that they find perfectly viable when they go to school and then later when dealing with the workplace and the government. It really is a wonderful system.

A rural girl.

Angel of the Slum Children

One million people live in the slums of Bangkok, 60,000 of them in the Klong Toey district. The slums are squalid but in Bangkok they serve a useful purpose, providing homes cheap enough for very poor people to afford.

Prateep Ungsongtham was brought up in Klong Toey slum but now this remarkable woman devotes her energy to making life better for the thousands of children who know no other life.

"We are trying to improve the conditions of Klong Toey, not get rid of it," she says. "Beside, only when Thailand's poor disappear will there be no more Klong Toey. If you are poor in this country it means you have no education, no job security, and no chance of earning high wages. I grew up in this slum and understand the problems of these people. I learned from an early age that the only way to improve the condition of life is through education."

Prateep spent only four years at primary school before she started working, yet even at twelve she had a fierce determination to achieve a better life. By working in factories and on the docks, Prateep saved enough money to pay for a secondary education at night school. Then she was awarded a place at a teaching college. It was during this time that she opened her first school in the space beneath her house in the slum. Just eight small pupils turned up on that first day, but when others saw what was happening the numbers soon grew. While the idea was to give the children a formal education, Prateep found that much of her time was spent helping the children and their families cope with slum life, rather than in normal teaching.

Then the young girl, still not twenty, was asked to fight the Port Authority and the government against an eviction order that would see the entire area closed. She did the impossible and won the battle, and it helped bring Prateep the Magsaysay and Rockefeller awards that led her to establish the Duang Prateep Foundation. A career of public service on behalf of the urban poor had begun.

When a part of Klong Toey had to be moved, the original school was rebuilt by the slum people at their own expense. The new building was first a single-story structure then later other buildings were added. In 1974, the government acknowledged the school's right to exist and the local authority assumed responsibility for it. Prateep became the head teacher of Klong Toey's first official slum school. Today the Foundation has several schools and kindergartens attended by more than four thousand children and there is happiness and hope for many.

Of course the problems are far from over but the Foundation has achieved much for the slum dwellers. Significantly it has the trust of the people and the government. A recent achievement has been the success of a community initiative called the Freedom From Drug Abuse Campaign. This aims to make all of Klong Toey a drug-free zone by dividing it into six project areas, each with rehabilitation centers and a job-training scheme. The Foundation says that fighting against drugs is not an impossible task, but it recognizes that it is difficult. It believes the key to success is people involvement, not only participation but *doing* and taking *responsibility*. That seems a very practical approach. Prateep says the three-year campaign has, with the help of local police, greatly reduced drug-dealing in the slum.

The work of the Foundation is now widespread. It includes a lunch program for kindergartens run by local mothers who buy, prepare, cook, and serve the food. Then there is the educational sponsorship scheme which currently helps 2,500 young people take their place in the state primary and secondary education system. The New Life project is another enormously successful program that takes slum children to a farm in southern Thailand. Here they learn farming and ancillary skills and learn to live together in a spirit of cooperation. The children take the produce they have grown to the local market and for the first time in their lives discover that they too have a part to play in life, and that they can play it successfully. The young people return to the slums to the same challenges as before but now they are ready to face them with new courage and new hope.

A visit to the slum is a daunting experience. Much of it has rotting wooden boards, hovering over a stinking swamp, as walkways. Mangey dogs roam wild while people scavenge through piles of garbage for anything of value. In the wet season, the garbage- and sewage-filled swamp water rises almost to the floorboards of the shanties that are home to thousands. Yet even in this squalor there can be smiling and laughter. Much of this is brought about by the presence and love of Prateep Ungsongtham.

The achievements of this remarkable lady and the Foundation she established are outstanding. This is community work of the best possible type. I am truly impressed by the attitudes and determina-

> tion of the staff and would love for you to see for yourself what is being achieved. Prateep says she is always happy to welcome visitors to the Foundation and particularly those who wish to see the programs in action and see where their donations are used. Certainly I was made most welcome. I would love to think that readers would be able to contribute to Prateep's work in a large or small way.
>
> Thailand can provide you with the holiday of a lifetime. A small donation to the Foundation can provide a lifetime for many Thai children. That's something they deserve.
>
> The Angel of the Slum Children has started a miracle. She has given a generation new hope. Despite the poverty, the sickness, the drugs, and the despair they respond with a simple message: "We love you."

A typical Thai family will almost always extend beyond the nucleus of parents and their children to include grandparents, cousins, an uncle or aunt or even the children of upcountry relatives, all living amicably together in the same house. A family often lives in a wooden house with a large single room serving as bedroom, living room, kitchen, or dining room as the situation demands. This communal life-style, in which everyone lives together in an open space with little or no privacy, obviously requires tact, compromise, courtesy, and tolerance if social harmony is to be preserved. It has a major influence on Thai attitudes.

Respect for elders is taught from a very early age, and is universal in Thailand. This is formalized in a complex system of words and titles used to distinguish between older and younger brothers and sisters and aunts and uncles. The young Thai learns to defer to the superior age and position of the village headman or the workplace boss and this attitude guarantees a strong degree of cultural conservatism.

One of the prime responsibilities placed on children is that of taking care of parents in their old age. There is no feeling of being inconvenienced by caring for aged parents, and their accumulated wisdom gives them an elevated place in the household. Thailand's aged actively help in bringing their grandchildren and great-grandchildren into adulthood.

The next larger unit of social organization is the village. In most of the country this is a simple collection of wooden houses on stilts and a Buddhist temple or wat. In the south there is likely to be a mosque. The setting may vary—a beach front, a dusty track, a palm-fringed canal bank, or a treed area surrounded by green ricefields—but in essence most Thai villages are similar. Each is a self-contained social unit which after many centuries still survives in its basic form.

Villages are self-governed. An elected headman frequently consults with an informal, though influential, council of elders and monks, often headed by the village abbot and schoolteacher. The wat acts as the major unifying element, particularly during festivals and merit-making ceremonies when the temple becomes the social center giving villagers their sense of community. Each day, the fields surrounding the village are tended, with all able-bodied villagers pitching in during busy periods such as harvests. The village is a peaceful place, its slow pace reflecting the serene, unassuming natures of the villagers themselves.

For reasons of protection and efficient administration, village houses are commonly arranged in groups. Most houses are elevated on stilts to avoid flooding and unwelcome animal intruders and to improve air circulation. The open area beneath the house is used for storing implements and is often the sleeping quarters for the household's animals. During the day it is the coolest part of the house and is used for social contact and handicraft making and as a children's play area.

The village school, communal spirit house, and wat are located on the village outskirts, often close together. They are sometimes separated from the houses by an open field that serves as the village common where cattle graze and children play games and fly kites. Village wells are often in this area and a village store may be at one side.

Thais are highly individualistic people, yet they believe that inner satisfaction is dependent upon an emotionally and physically stable environment. Social harmony is thus best preserved by avoiding any unnecessary friction or turbulence in their contacts with others. This leads to an extreme reluctance to impose on anyone or disturb his personal equilibrium by direct criticism, challenge, or confrontation. It leads to the occasional frustration for visitors because when a problem arises, the Thai may have a natural tendency to go away rather than try to find a solution.

Outward expressions of anger are also discouraged. During normal social activities, strong public displays of dismay, despair, displeasure, disapproval, or enthusiasm are frowned upon. As a visitor you will find that faster progress is usually made when you keep your temper and a smile on your face than when you start to shout and cause a confrontation. When you have just missed your bus or discover the hotel has no available rooms, you will find this very difficult but you could do well to adopt the Thai "Mi pen ri" (never mind, it doesn't matter). Try to accept that you should gracefully submit to external forces beyond one's control.

All Thais gauge the enjoyment of any activity by "kwarm sanuk," the pleasure to be had in doing that particular activity. It is a concept which Westerners would like to adopt but feel unable to do so because of modern life pressures. The Thais have successfully maintained this concept in the

A spirit house.

modern world and extend it to school and work activities. Repetitive work, standard routines, and any activity which involves drudgery is definitely "mi sanuk" or no fun and should be avoided. Going to temple festivals, meeting old friends, finding a new work routine, meeting new people, and preparing merit-making ceremonies are all "sanuk."

Another "sanuk" activity enjoyed by all Thais is the concept of "pi teo," or to go around. It means leaving the house for relaxation, curiously wandering around markets, visiting neighboring villages, walking in the evening air, going to out-of-the-way restaurants, or ambling through festivals or down busy streets. It almost always involves informal socializing and can lead to a wide circle of casual acquaintances that can even include visitors to the country.

All rural life revolves around the seasons, and with rice being by far the most important of all crops, its seasons affect the entire community. Rice is the principal food for humans and animals throughout the country and it provides major government revenue from exports. In a widespread complex pattern of communal cooperation, farmers prepare their fields, repair bunds, plough, and transplant rice seedlings into each family's prepared field. At this time every active family member works in the field. If all goes according to plan, monsoon rains arrive to inundate the farmland and the farmers can literally watch the rice grow.

During the rainy season much of rural life revolves around Rains Retreat observances, which involve study and meditation. When these end, monks throughout the country receive new robes in an annual ceremony called "Tod Kathin," which allows groups of people to combine holidays with merit-making and thus provide an intricate pattern of countrywide support for temples. Work in the fields is now concerned with keeping birds away from the ripening rice crop and with catching fish, which are a vital part of the staple rural Thai diet.

In early November, the most spectacular of Thai festivals, "Loy Krathong," takes place. By moonlight, people light candles and incense, make a wish, and launch their banana leaf "krathongs" on canals, streams, rivers, lakes, and ponds. Water spirits are thus honored and it is commonly believed that the "krathongs" carry away the past year's sins.

By early December rice in many parts of the country is ready for harvesting. Harvesting schedules are determined by common consent within each village. Starting early each morning, cooperative work groups harvest each farmer's crop. The host family provides lunch and dinner. Cut rice is spread in the field to dry and then taken to the family compound where it is threshed.

The hot season after the rice harvest is marked by the important "Songkran" festival. Shortly after this time, showers signal the approaching rain and villagers once more prepare for rice planting.

Lady Chairman

Mrs. Chanut Piyaoui is a petite, soft-spoken lady who is a formidable businesswoman of rare determination and ability. Today she heads Thailand's largest domestic hotel chain as chairman and managing director of the Dusit Thani Hotel Group.

Born in Bangkok, she finished her secondary schooling, then enrolled in Thammasat University. At the end of her first year of studies, the family moved to the country to avoid the risk of bombing during World War II. When the war was over she decided not to resume her university studies but instead went to the United States.

Twice she attempted to enter a university in the U.S. but was rejected because her English was not good enough. This period, however, determined her future career because the experience of seeing many different hotels across the country convinced her that she would enter the hotel business in Thailand.

She talked with many friends in Thailand and they all advised her against the hotel industry. Despite this she persisted, borrowed the money, and built the Princess Hotel in New Road. The hotel had a swimming pool and an airconditioned lobby and it was used by airline staff staying over in Bangkok.

Mrs. Chanut met all guests, was prepared to work as room maid if need be, and through hard work made the Princess a great success. But she wanted more. Her aim was a 500-room true international-standard hotel. In Bangkok in the sixties, it was almost unthinkable. But that didn't stop her.

By 1970, the twenty-two-story Dusit Thani hotel was a fact. Mrs. Chanut had raised the money and put her stamp on the design and construction. Against all advice she insisted on a Thai name for the hotel. Then after three years of Westin management she took over management herself so she could handle the finances.

The results have been spectacular. Not only has the Dusit Thani remained a leading Bangkok hotel, it has become the flagship of a group that now has hotels in Chiang Mai, Pattaya, and Phuket, with others planned for Chiang Rai, Cha-am, Rayong, and a further major hotel for Bangkok. A recent development has been the establishment of a new Princess Hotel which will be the start of a proposed chain of smaller hotels.

Mrs. Chanut proceeds slowly but each move has been carefully researched. It has not been easy but with hard work, a love for the

> industry, great determination, and an unfailing belief in her own ability, she has been outstandingly successful. At the same time she has managed to remain a charming person to meet and a staunch believer in the ability of the Thai people and the young generation to enter business.
>
> This gracious and tranquil lady has recently been honored with the royal title Khunying, for her contribution to Thailand's economy. It is a fitting tribute to an outstanding personality.

Despite the arrival of sealed roads, electricity, radio, and television, village life remains relatively undisturbed. It is a simple yet satisfying life-style that most rural Thais would not wish to change. Contentment to most is a well-fed family, productive land, peace, no debts, and a little "sanuk." It has much that can be recommended.

The Economy

Your visit to Thailand will be much more fulfilling if you know a little about the country's economy. A visitor arriving in Bangkok expecting a third-world country will be in for a very great shock, for modern Thailand is as much attuned to the microchip as it is to its traditional Buddhist culture. On the other hand, those arriving with the expectation of a Western industrial nation will perhaps be amazed at the poverty and "backwardness" in some parts of the country.

The truth is that Thailand is in a transitional state. For centuries it was a slightly feudal agrarian nation with a determination to remain "free" from foreign control. Now it has one of the developing world's strongest economies based largely on overseas trade, embracing industries employing the latest and most sophisticated technology.

The importance of agriculture, though, cannot be over-emphasized. Blessed with large expanses of fertile land and ideal growing conditions, Thailand not only enjoys agricultural self-sufficiency but along with nations such as the U.S., Canada, and Australia it is one of only a few net exporters of food in the world. In recent years agribusinesses with emphasis on value-added food exports have developed in the heart of the countryside. Besides increasing the value of the area's produce, the new industries have the added benefit of employing laborers who might otherwise have gone to Bangkok to find jobs.

With the government providing support and exerting relatively limited control over private industry, a free enterprise system has emerged, allowing rapid development. The introduction of improved technology and marketing

Planting the ricefields.

expertise has made Thailand a world leader in the sales of staple commodities. It has also transformed the country into a fast-rising manufacturer of sophisticated products built to international standards.

Rice forms the core of the Thai economy. It was the country's largest single foreign exchange earner for well over a century. Now it has been joined by tapioca, sugar, maize, rubber, tobacco, beans, and other crops. A myriad of delicious tropical and temperate fruits thrive in Thailand's humid climate. They include mangoes, durians, watermelons, papayas, rambutans, oranges, bananas, strawberries, and pineapples. Much fruit is exported and canned fruit is contributing to export earnings. Flowers are also an important export crop. Thailand is the world's largest supplier of orchids and export of other fresh flowers is rapidly growing.

Beef production until recently was a farming sideline in some areas. But growing demand brought about by the increase in population, urbanization, and a rising standard of living has led to scientific stockbreeding and farming. Thailand was always a forested country but heavy timber cutting and encroaching farmland has made huge inroads into the softwood and hardwood forests. The government has banned the export of logs and most sawn timber but has encouraged the local processing of timber into furniture, wood carvings, household utensils, and parquet, most of which is exported.

Export and production of fish and shellfish has also grown. These have always been important ingredients in the Thai diet but now frozen fish, shrimp, squid, and other items are sent around the world. Mining production is also important. Tin has been an important revenue earner for centuries and Thailand's colored gems are considered some of the world's best. Other minerals are being mined for local use, thus reducing the country's imports. Gas and oil have been discovered in the Gulf of Thailand and long pipelines now crawl ashore feeding processing plants southeast of Bangkok.

On the manufacturing front, Thailand now exports goods ranging from cement to watches, including television sets, chemical products, transportation equipment, clothes, material, publishing, and so on. Thailand's prospects for further industrial exports appear bright. It is now a manufacturing base for many Japanese and international companies. With its low-cost skilled labor and a relatively well-functioning economic system, future expansion is sure.

Manufactured goods have become an increasingly important source of foreign exchange earnings and a rapidly growing percentage of the population is engaged in the manufacturing and industrial sectors. The government has focused on the development of light industries such as textiles and electronics and this has achieved spectacular results.

Finally there is tourism. Five million tourists visited Thailand last year—a 25 percent growth rate each year for the past four years. Tourism is the country's top foreign exchange earner and a major catalyst for the booming construction, transportation, and service industries. There is little doubt that the tourism industry has been a great success story for Thailand. It has provided jobs for a sizeable proportion of the population in some areas and the industry reaches into almost all sectors of the Thai economy.

Financial institutions, particularly the commercial banks, have played a very important role in mobilizing savings for domestic investment. There are over two thousand bank branches throughout the country which support a major banking system. It is part of a sophisticated private industry sector that could become a model for many adjacent countries.

Thailand has shown a great ability to expand its economy and improve the welfare of its citizens. Some basic economic problems such as income disparity, the need to conserve natural resources, and the need for improved administration efficiency require attention and improvement. But judging by recent past performances, the problems will be tackled and solved.

Leisure Time

An unfailing penchant for "kwan sanuk" combines with a natural gregariousness here, making both spontaneous and formal leisure activities vital parts of the Thais' social fabric. Thais everywhere share a common interest in gambling, "pi teo," and sports. The national lottery excites imaginations and card games are almost a national pastime.

"Pi teo" by foot, boat, bus, or motorbike is a favorite way to relax and the Thais are their country's most avid explorers. In Bangkok, food, "sanuk," the art of bargaining, and "pi teo" are all inherent in visits to the famous Weekend Market. In the rural village a visit to a neighboring village festival serves the same purpose.

The growing Westernizing of Bangkok has meant that leisure activities in the capital appear somewhat different from those in the rural areas, but it is really a matter of degree. The international recording stars and comedians that sophisticated Bangkokians see in the plush supper clubs are serving a purpose similar to that of the folk drama troupe in the provinces. But even in Bangkok there are local temple fairs featuring food and entertainment stalls and the ever-popular satirical comic opera performances featuring outrageous puns and double-entendres, sly ribaldry, and popular folk songs.

Sporting events, museums, a planetarium, art galleries, cinemas, and amusement parks draw large crowds in Bangkok. Yet many people still prefer to join the crowds of strollers, loungers, food and drink vendors, ballplayers, and joggers in Lumpini Park, just like they would if they were in a rural village or country town.

The Thais are some of the world's most passionate sports enthusiasts.

Sports are a social as well as recreational pleasure for a very large segment of the population, ranging from a group of children kicking a ball around a temple playground to tens of thousands of fans under National Stadium floodlights boisterously encouraging a local team against foreign competition.

Of organized sports, soccer is probably most popular with boxing a close second. Cycling, shooting, athletics, swimming, squash, basketball, badminton, gymnastics, horse racing, hockey, table tennis, yachting, golf, tennis, weight lifting, and rally driving all have their adherents. Inherent in sports is physical fitness so early each morning or late afternoon, joggers and walkers of all sizes, shapes, ages, and nationalities pound the streets. Similarly from dawn each morning, Bangkok's Lumpini Park is packed with Chinese practicing their Tai Chi, a balletlike slow-motion set of calisthenics performed by young and old alike.

One of the most interesting sports for a visitor to watch is Thai kite-fighting. In Bangkok you can see it at Sanam Luang near the Grand Palace during March and April but it is also practiced at many other places throughout the kingdom. The spectacular aerial acrobatic displays can be enjoyed from a rented chair with ice-cold beer in hand while you nibble on local specialties like peppery grilled squid and fiery salads. Nothing could be more memorable.

Thailand has one of the world's most thriving movie industries. The local films are unashamedly made for entertainment purposes and consequently they enjoy large audiences who demand exaggerated "soap operas" or escapist entertainment. Popular Thai actors and actresses are in great demand and many feature in ten or more low-budget movies each year. Thai moviegoers adore stars who consistently play sympathetic roles, and speak of them in a way usually reserved for close friends. The films in which they star usually include everything thrown in together: pathos, romance, hatred, love, loss, gain, joy, despair, violence, gentility, comedy, and tragedy, all woven around a major plot and several subplots. Unfortunately for the visitor, no English versions of these films are made.

Foreign films are shown throughout the country but except occasionally in Bangkok they are always shown with a dubbed Thai dialogue. In some cases you can hear the English version through headsets or by sitting in a special sound room, but this will generally have little appeal to short-term visitors.

Art forms have always been popular in Thai culture and they remain so today. Literature is the strongest Thai art form, probably because it has proven to be the most adaptable. Early Thai literature was primarily concerned with Buddhism and until 1850 all literature was in verse form. The epic *Ramakian*, a unique Thai version of the Hindu *Ramayana*, is the major Thai literary work. Today a growing readership eager for quality poems, prose, and fiction supports well-known Thai writers such as Seri Snowapong, Kamsingh Srinawk, and Suwance Sukhontha.

In the purely classical form, Thai drama and dance are indivisible. The "khon" masked drama is derived from Indian temple rituals and dancing and draws its story lines from the *Ramakian*. "Lakon" dance drama is less formal and most actors do not wear masks. These two forms depict what is loosely called "classical dance." Other drama forms include "Li-la" folk dramas, shadow plays, and puppet shows. In recent times Western ballet and modern dance have appeared on stage while the rock culture go-go dancing has found an instant market in the bars and lounges throughout the country.

Traditional Thai painting has suffered this century because of the influence of the West. Classical Thai painting was confined to temple and palace interiors and book illustrations. Murals decorated chapel interiors with excerpts from the Buddha's life; scenes of Buddhist tales; and tiers of gods, goddesses, spirits, holy men, and angels. Sometimes there were scenes of contemporary Thai life with lovers embracing, drunkards asleep under trees, and dogs stealing food from palace kitchens. Modern Thai artists are still struggling to find a suitable Thai contemporary form of expression. While in this transitional period, they are showing a powerful Western influence, providing interesting opportunities for Western visitors to purchase originals that would not be out of place on a New York, Toronto, or Melbourne wall.

Thai sculptors traditionally concentrated on religious statuary, particularly Buddha images. Several million Buddha images have been created ranging in size from Sukhothai's gigantic seated Buddha to tiny fingernail-size necklace Buddhas worn as amulets. Other religious statuary includes demonic and mythological figures—some humans, some animals, some hybrids—which grace all major Thai temples. Today there are many places in Thailand where sculptors can be found working in stone or wood. Many of the subjects now are birds, animals, or women—a reflection of what is likely to appeal to the visitor or the Western-educated Thai.

Thailand enjoys a particularly rich heritage of folk arts, handed down over the generations since the early days of the kingdom. Some, like the shimmering silks and the superb wood carvings, have become major export items and are internationally renowned. Others have been rarely seen outside rural villages. In Thailand, as in many other countries, the introduction of cheap, mass-produced goods from abroad inevitably had an adverse effect on the production of such crafts and more particularly on their sale in Bangkok. Changing fashion and style of living saw Bangkokians turn away from local products.

A Thai classical dance.

While this was happening in Bangkok, in a few provincial areas such as Chiang Mai in the north and Nakhon Si Thammarat in the south, the old traditional arts not only survived but continued to show a remarkable vigor. Fashionable ladies in the capital might have given up their richly embroidered silk costumes for Parisian dresses and city households might take to the latest imported gadgets, but in the country homespun cloth continued to be woven by time-honored processes, rice and other produce was still carried in baskets that have changed little over the centuries, and even children's toys remained much the same.

Now in the last fifteen years there has been a major revival of interest in Thai folk arts. One reason has been a growing awareness of the cultural importance of these traditional crafts and their intrinsic beauty in a world of plastic and other artificial materials. Not only anthropologists and other scholars but also collectors, dress designers, interior decorators, and ordinary Thais have come to appreciate them. This has resulted in countless shops in Bangkok that now specialize in such arts, and these crafts can be found in many modern homes.

4

Who Are the Thais?

Historians find it hard to agree on the exact beginning of the Thai civilization. Certainly it was in existence in the thirteenth century when a group of princes came together with common purposes to defeat the Khmer Empire in what is now northern Thailand. Perhaps it existed six centuries earlier when a distinctive kingdom was established in southern China in Yunan. But was it really started by the sophisticated civilization that existed in northeast Thailand 4,000 years before that?

Ban Chiang is a tiny village in one of the least-developed parts of Thailand. The village was unknown to the outside world until, by chance, a remarkable discovery was made about in the 1970s. Heavy rain had washed away some topsoil to reveal fragments of a strange pottery, and an American student, Stephen Young, literally stumbled on to it. That find and the later scientific studies have proved to be so startling that they challenge long-established theories of man's first steps towards civilization.

Systematic excavations of burial mounds in Ban Chiang have unearthed a treasure of artifacts which include bronze and iron tools, jewelry, hand-painted pots adorned with intricate fingerprint patterns, ceramic figurines, and stone and glass beads. If the dating of these objects is correct, this civilization was the first in the world to produce bronze and bimetallic tools and utensils. It certainly was a well-developed civilization in many respects. People dressed well and printed their own silk textiles. They lived in sturdy houses and used domesticated cattle to cultivate the rice paddies.

While the Ban Chiang people's metallurgy was extremely sophisticated, their general farming methods were not. They often employed a slash-and-burn agricultural system which eventually led to deforestation and soil exhaustion, forcing them to move about. Eventually they moved off the northeast plateau down into the rich Chao Phraya Valley to the west. This basin covers most of modern central and northern Thailand and is fertile, well watered, and well protected from excessive outside influence. This natural, self-contained geopolitical unit was destined to play a central role in Thailand's development.

Historically and agriculturally, this valley was as important to the Thais as the Nile was to the Egyptians or the Mississippi was to the early Americans. Later it would become the Thai heartland, contain future Thai capitals, and provide transportation routes to keep the nation together.

Early Settlers

The influx of immigrants into this area took many centuries. When the Ban Chiang people arrived, they encountered a Neolithic valley proto-Malay tribe that later moved south under pressure from migrations from the north. These people settled in the heavily jungled Kanchanaburi area, 100 kilometers west of present-day Bangkok. They appear to have entered the Bronze Age in about 2000 B.C. and were advanced in the arts.

Next came the bearers of the Lungshan culture, who arrived in 1800-1600 B.C. from China. They brought with them sophisticated methods of rice cultivation. At one time they occupied most of southern Thailand and as far north as Lopburi, about 150 kilometers north of present-day Bangkok. These groups were able to more or less coexist because they all sought a degree of autonomy and shared a common desire for a better life.

Two of the most important immigrant groups were Khmers and Mons, who arrived around the first century B.C. The Khmers came over the high Burmese mountains, settling east of the Chao Phraya Valley in eastern Thailand and deep into present-day Cambodia. Twelve centuries later their civilization culminated in the magnificent Angkor period with the construction of the fabled temple complex of Angkor Wat in Cambodia and numerous other temple-cities in the region. The Mons settled the western half of the valley and founded the Dvaravati kingdom, which became a major producer of rice and an important religious center. The Mon seat of power was Lopburi.

Still more migration waves occurred. In the sixth and seventh centuries A.D., Tibeto-Burmese people moved into the northern part of the area. Today they form part of the itinerant hilltribes of northern Thailand. Then in the eleventh and twelfth centuries, the people who would eventually form the present Thai nation began arriving. They came from Yunan in China, where for 600 years they had developed their own distinctive culture. Under pressure from China's Mongolian conquerors, these people moved steadily south and settled in what is now northern Thailand.

By the thirteenth century, the Thais had successfully established themselves among the Khmers and Mons and had a major presence in the north. The Thais brought with them an advanced rice technology and they set about turning marshland into fertile ricefields. These people were not a completely homogeneous group. In fact, they formed several small independent Thai states. But they provided the setting for the first truly independent Thai kingdom which eventually led to modern Thailand.

Sukhothai: "The Dawn of Happiness"

The early-thirteenth-century northern Thai kingdoms were actually city states with very limited resources. They were usually located in fertile surroundings and were self-sustaining in terms of fuel, food, and building materials but they were separated by dense jungle and were individually powerless to stop overall Khmer control. Each state was obliged to pay tribute to Angkor. But although Khmer power was paramount, it was, because of its distance from the Thai kingdoms, far from absolute.

In 1238, two Thai chieftains, Khun Bang Klang Tao and Khun Pa Muang, combined forces and defeated the local Khmer commander. They then formed the first truly independent Thai kingdom in Sukhothai. In the next sixty years the influence of Sukhothai expanded at a great rate until it extended over much of present-day Burma, Thailand, Malaysia, and Singapore. Bang Klang Tao became the first king and ruled as King Sri Intratit.

Sukhothai reached its zenith during the reign of Ramkamhaeng the Great (reigned 1275-1317), the third Sukhothai king, often known today as "The Father of Thailand." Ramkamhaeng was an accomplished warrior with a fearsome reputation. He ensured Sukhothai's continued security and stability by concluding pacts with the powerful neighboring kingdoms of Chiang Rai, Chiang Mai, and P'ayao. In a series of diplomatic coups, he established trade treaties with India and Burma, made close contact with Ceylon, and promoted friendly relations with the Chinese emperor.

In 1283, Ramkamhaeng created the Thai alphabet and thus formed the tool for uniting scattered tribes into a nation with an identity of its own. The capital flourished as a trading center. Chinese artisans were brought to teach Thais how to make the Sawankaloke celadon pottery. Rice, fruits, and timber were exported to China, Burma, and Persia. The king ruled his ethnically diverse subjects—Mons, Laotians, Malays, Burmese, Khmers, Chinese, and

Sukhothai.

Thais—wisely and well. There is little doubt that life in Sukhothai at this time was good for almost everyone.

On Ramkamhaeng's death, Sukhothai started to decline. His son Lo Thai ruled for thirty years but lost the outlying feudal states as fast as his father had gained them. He was more interested in religion than power politics and spent much of his time developing relationships with Ceylon, the center of orthodox Buddhism. When his son, Lu Thai, became king in 1347, he continued the emphasis on religion. This directly led to the meteoric rise of Ayutthaya, one of Sukhothai's former states. King Lu Thai was forced to acknowledge Ayutthaya's sovereignty. Deprived of his independence, the king eventually joined the monkhood. His family continued to rule for three more generations as hereditary governors, but when the center of administration was transferred to Phitsanulok in 1378, Sukhothai became a deserted city.

The Rise of Ayutthaya

Ayutthaya was a river-island city-state founded in 1350 by King U-thoney (later crowned King Ramathibodi). From the very beginning, the king launched Ayutthaya on a rigorous diplomatic and military campaign to make it the dominant force throughout the Chao Phraya basin. His success is seen by the fact that Ayutthaya was the Thai capital for 417 years until its fall in 1767. In all, thirty-three kings ruled Ayutthaya during its glorious four centuries.

Throughout the Ayutthaya period, power was centered in the royal palace. Wars were fought for territorial reasons rather than religious reasons or to repulse invading neighbors. Victory meant greater wealth from treasure and from captive prisoners and it meant greater prestige, deterring would-be invaders.

Many of the captives brought skills as painters, writers, dancers, sculptors, architects, musicians, and so forth. The Thais selectively adopted those techniques or fashions that seemed useful and modified them into clear Thai forms of expression. Laotian, Malayan, Cambodian, Burmese, and Vietnamese people were gently absorbed into the Thai community as were subsequent arrivals of Persian, Chinese, Japanese, and Indian immigrants.

Wealth became synonymous with land ownership and the kings levied taxes on all produce. They also taxed external trade so that a widespread levy system financed the royal court, wars, and public works. Taxes were paid in food, cash, precious metals, or labor. Through such central control, trade flourished. Potters, swordmakers, goldsmiths, and jewelers emerged to serve the new economy. Architects, sculptors, and painters serenely fashioned the beautiful temples and palaces that were so much a part of Ayutthaya.

Condom Man Sets Sights on Rural Poor

When **Mechai Vivavaidya** started handing out condoms to masses of people, the skeptics laughed and some people were outraged. Yet since the establishment of his nonprofit, nongovernment family planning program in 1974, the results have been spectacular.

Population growth has dropped from 3.2 percent to 1.4 percent a year—that's the most dramatic decline of fertility achieved anywhere in the world—and it is estimated that 70 percent of couples now use contraception. The Population and Community Development Association (PDA), which was originally founded by Khun Mechai in 1974 as the Community Based Family Planning Service, has played a major role in this success.

The success of PDA's community-based approach to family planning has encouraged the Association to adopt a similar strategy for other development needs in Thailand. Now Dr. Mechai has come up with a bold attempt to bridge the ever-widening gap between the rich and poor. To do this he has initiated a plan called "T-bird," which calls for the active participation of large businesses in rural development.

"I believe the government can provide basic infrastructure for rural areas but what the poor villages need to develop their economies is the kind of business initiative that private sector companies alone can provide," he says.

Under T-bird, a company fosters a village in much the same way as parents can "foster" a child by providing the necessary skills and support. The scheme is already working. Swedish Motors identified a need for decorative trees, encouraged a village to grow them, brought in experts to teach the villagers, and identified a company that would buy the trees. Now the business is showing a profit and some of the villagers are experimenting with other marketable crops.

Dr. Mechai is a man of enormous energy, flair, and skill. I have little doubt that the T-bird program will achieve a success similar to his earlier endeavors. As secretary-general of PDA he has a mammoth task. But he still finds time for his role of senator in the National Parliament; as visiting scholar at Harvard University; as a member of the Club of Rome, the Population Council of New York, the Global Commission on AIDS, the NGO World Bank Committee; and several other posts.

AIDS is another major issue occupying Dr. Mechai's time. PDA

> has mounted a nationwide campaign to educate the public on AIDS. He believes that if ordinary Thais remain unaware of the dangers of AIDS, it will soon be too late to stop the disease from spreading into general Thai society. In typical Mechai style, audio tapes, videos, books, and pamphlets are being distributed free to schools, offices, and public places. He even has been able to enlist the help of door-to-door salesmen.
>
> Thailand and the whole world are continuing to benefit from the drive, determination, and vitality of the "Condom Man."

The Khmer threat gradually lessened. Ramathibodi invaded Angkor in 1369 and his son attacked it again in 1393. Finally in 1432, the Khmers abandoned Angkor because of its increasing vulnerability to Thai attack and moved their capital eastward to a Mekong riverbank site known as Phnom Penh.

Recurring cycles of war, consolidation, and peace marked the reigns of Ramathibodi's successors. In 1512, the first Europeans arrived in Ayutthaya. These were Portuguese who, having captured Melacca and subsequently discovering that Ayutthaya claimed control over the region, decided that the smart way to avoid future conflict was to establish relations with the Ayutthayan king, Ramathibodi II.

The next fifty years were declining years for Ayutthaya. A war was fought with Burma in 1538 which the Thais won with help from 120 Portuguese mercenaries. In return, the Portuguese were given land in Ayutthaya for their own church and houses. Successive wars with Burma followed in 1549, 1563, and 1569. This last war was just too much for a weakened Ayutthaya and it fell to the Burmese. The city was thoroughly sacked and much of the city's population was forceably moved to Burma.

The Rise Again

If the Burmese thought Ayutthaya was finished they were very wrong. In 1584, the greatest of all Thai warrior kings, Naresuan the Great, emerged to expel the Burmese and restore Thai independence. During the following nine years, the Burmese made several attempts to recapture Thai territory but each time they were expelled. Finally a 1599 Thai campaign fragmented the Burmese empire and for the next 160 years, Ayutthaya would be safe.

Peace brought a great increase in foreign traders and missionaries that made Ayutthaya, by the 1650s, a truly cosmopolitan city. The Chinese, Japanese, French, Dutch, Spanish, English, and Portuguese all had their own enclaves and Ayutthaya's population and wealth exceeded that of

London. Some Western visitors compared Ayutthaya to Venice and called it the "most beautiful city in the East." It was at this time that the country became known to the West as Siam. Europeans were primarily attracted to Ayutthaya because of the China trade but the Siamese home market was also important. There was great wealth in Thai society and hence great demand for luxury items such as Oriental porcelain and silk.

Naresuan's brother, Ekatotsarot, eventually became king and he sent emissaries to Holland—the first recorded appearance of Thais in Europe. In subsequent years the English and Japanese arrived and then in the reign of King Narai (reigned 1656-88) the French became favorites. This coincided with the amazing rise of a colorful Greek adventurer, Constantine Phaulkon. A talented linguist, Phaulkon had originally been employed as an interpreter by the Thai Treasury. Phaulkon did his job brilliantly, closing gaping loopholes in customs and duties collection and winning himself rapid promotion as a Thai nobleman. He had access to the king, whose confidence he slowly and surely cultivated.

Phaulkon, a Roman Catholic convert, willingly helped the French in establishing a close relationship with Ayutthaya. There was an exchange of ambassadors and the French expected to be able to convert the whole of Siam to Christianity. After French troops arrived, King Narai became suspicious of French motives, while the Thai nobility increasingly resented Phaulkon's powerful influence over the king. Then it was rumored that Narai intended to appoint his adopted son, Prince Piya, a Roman Catholic convert, as his successor and the situation became tense.

Consequently in 1688, when the king fell seriously ill in his Lopburi Palace, an anti-French movement took immediate action. Phaulkon was arrested for treason and executed. Prince Piya was assassinated. The French were expelled and within a month King Narai was dead. The new rulers, now deeply suspicious of Europeans, all but closed their country to foreign trade for 200 years.

After King Narai, the country was led by a series of ineffectual rulers. The only bright period was during the reign of King Boromokot (1733-58), when literature and the arts flourished as never before. This is often known as Ayutthaya's Golden Age.

It was not to last for long. In 1766, the Burmese attacked Ayutthaya and after a fifteen-month siege, irreparably destroyed the city. The Burmese looted and set fire to everything, effectively obliterating four centuries of Thai civilization. Temples and palaces were stripped of priceless treasures and most written records were burned. A hundred thousand survivors of the holocaust were marched off to Burma as prisoners, and a once-resplendent city of one million was left with about ten thousand inhabitants.

During the last months of the siege a young general named Phya Taksin gathered a small band of followers together, broke through the Burmese encirclement, and escaped to Chantaburi in eastern Thailand. There he assembled an army and navy and seven months after the fall of Ayutthaya, he and his forces sailed back to the capital and expelled the Burmese. However, Ayutthaya was finished and Taksin decided to move the capital to a site nearer the sea which would be easier to defend and better for trade. He chose the west bank of the Chao Phraya river at Thonburi, now part of metropolitan Bangkok. In 1769, he was crowned king.

Bangkok, the New Capital

The rule of Taksin was full of difficulties. Ayutthaya's destruction was a catastrophic loss to the Thais and the kingdom rapidly fragmented. Taksin set about reuniting the provinces. He fought battles with the Burmese and finally liberated Chiang Mai and the rest of northern Thailand. He continued his campaigns and eventually brought most of present-day Cambodia and Laos under Thai control. It was from the Laotian campaign that Thailand obtained the famed Emerald Buddha, regarded by Thais as the most sacred of all Buddha images.

Ten years' continued military campaigning took its toll on Taksin and his behavior became increasingly erratic. In 1782, a successful coup was mounted and Taksin was forced to abdicate. The vacant throne was offered to Taksin's leading general, Phya Chakri, and he assumed the throne as Rama I on April 6, 1782, a day still commemorated each year. This was the start of the present Chakri dynasty. The present king is Rama IX. One of the first acts of Rama I was to transfer his administrative headquarters across the river to Bangkok. There he set about building a new palace in the grand manner of Ayutthaya. The complex incorporated the residences of the king and royal family, the government and judicial offices, and the Royal Chapel.

Modern Thailand owes much to Rama I. He and his two successors devoted themselves to Thailand's overall reconstruction and they prepared the ground for the country's eventual modernization. They revived the arts and culture of Ayutthaya, built many fine temples and buildings, and slowly re-established relations with the West. Then followed a great period in Thai history.

Rama IV (reigned 1851-68), or King Mongkut, was forty-eight years old when he was crowned. He had spent the previous twenty-seven years as a reform-minded Buddhist monk and exceptional scholar. He was taught Latin and English and this enabled him to study Western history, geography, mathematics, modern science, and astronomy. Mongkut travelled extensively as a monk and had much contact with common people. He realized that traditional Thai values would not save his country from Western encroachment so he entered into trade deals with England, France, the United States, and other Western nations.

The king wanted his children to gain the same benefits from the English language as he had. For this purpose he engaged a governess called Anna as an English teacher. She resided in Siam from 1862 to 1867 and her autobiography was partly depicted in the famous Western musical comedy *The King and I*. It should be said that the whole affair erroneously maligns Mongkut as a frivolous autocrat. In truth he was a great understanding king whose reign successfully transformed Thailand from the old to the new.

Despite his many official activities, King Mongkut found time to follow his love of astronomy. In 1868, European and Asian skeptics joined him in marshy countryside south of Bangkok when he predicted a total eclipse of the sun. He was proved to be right but only enjoyed brief satisfaction, as he contracted malaria during the trip and died two months later.

On ascending the throne, his son Chulalongkorn strengthened Thailand's independence and smoothly advanced modernization by introducing reforms whenever he saw fit. In his eventful forty-two years as king (reigned 1868-1910) he abolished slavery, constructed Thailand's first railways, built schools, sent hundreds of young Thai men to Europe, and revitalized government bodies. He also reformed provincial administration, thus extending government control to the remote parts of the kingdom. He improved health and communications by establishing hospitals and introducing postal and telegraph services.

But all was not easy. Chulalongkorn was forced to cede large areas of undefendable Thai territory in the south to the British and in the north and northeast to the French. By gradually acceding to those territorial demands, Chulalongkorn preserved Thai independence in the vital Chao Phraya basin so that Thailand remains the only southeast Asian country never to be colonized by a European power. By the time of his death in 1910 his reforms had borne fruit—the country's economy was flourishing and the Thai peasantry was very well off in comparison with neighboring countries. He had successfully completed the transformation of Thailand and today he is the most honored of Thai kings. The anniversary of his death, October 23, is a national holiday.

Chulalongkorn's Oxford-educated son, Vajiravudh (Rama VI), continued his father's and grandfather's reforms. He established Chulalongkorn University, supported the Red Cross, founded the Thai Boy Scouts, and ordered his subjects to adopt surnames. This last law caused much initial bewilderment, particularly in rural areas, so the king personally coined many of the Thai family names in existence today.

In 1925 Vajiravudh was succeeded by his half-brother, Prajadhipok, who was unprepared for the task. His reign was beset by financial crises caused mainly by Vajiravudh's sweeping reforms, which had left Thailand vulnerable to the world depression of the late 1920s. Prajadhipok was unable to

Thai American

Gerald Pierce has been in Thailand for over ten years. Like many Westerners, he planned to stay for only two or three years but time has turned him into a permanent resident.

The big Louisiana native has an extensive background in fashion design and for the past ten years he has been the Director of Product Design for famous Jim Thompson Thai Silk. He is a good example of how a Westerner can adapt to a Thai life-style but still be tied to his own culture.

Gerald Pierce admits that Thais still think he leads a Western rather than Thai life-style. "Because I'm a Western-reared and -educated person, I don't have any Thai culture," he says. "I very much like Thai handicrafts, art, and life-style but the way I deal with these is certainly Western."

The growth in the Thai silk industry over the last several decades has been staggering, but Gerald Pierce claims no credit for that. Perhaps he is being too modest because undoubtedly he has done much to keep Jim Thompson Silk as the pace setter for the industry. His ability to create new fabric designs and products using some of the world's best artists and designers has enabled the industry to progress and win many followers worldwide.

Thai silk is a craft that goes far back in Thai history but one man is credited with transforming it into a thriving industry. That man is Jim Thompson, a former American army officer who settled in Thailand in 1945. He introduced color-fast chemical dyes and looms capable of producing longer and wider cloths. He popularized the fabric to the point that it was causing a sensation in the world of high fashion and interior decoration. Jim Thompson mysteriously disappeared in 1967 while vacationing in Malaysia, but both the company he founded and the Thai silk industry in general have continued to flourish.

Today the company is truly international. Jim Thompson Thai Silk is managed by an American but most of the other executives are Thai. It has a cooperative agreement with a group from China and receives design input from artists worldwide. It has moved away from its original cottage industry base but it now directly employs thousands of people at its weaving facilities, showrooms, and head office. Of all silk exported, Jim Thompson Thai Silk accounts for more than a third.

> Despite being a permanent Thai resident, Gerald Pierce has not forgotten his native Louisiana. "There are a surprising number of similarities between Thailand and Louisiana," he says. "There is the same friendly attitude of the people, the climate and, in parts, even the landscape. Yes, even though I am thousands of miles from my original home, I still feel part of it. There are places over on the Thonburi side of the river where you can go and not see any Thais or Thai architecture. I'm sure that I could make anyone from Louisiana think they were home."
> Just maybe that is one of the factors that makes him stay.

hold off the crises; unemployment rose and salary reductions were implemented just at a time when hopes for a better future were high. The economic malaise exacerbated the frustrations of returning Thai students who had embraced democratic ideals during their European school days. In June 1932, nearly seven hundred years of absolute monarchy ended with a bloodless coup organized by middle-level civilian and military officers.

New Directions

King Prajadhipok continued his reign as a constitutional monarch but in 1935 he resigned. The government then elected Prajadhipok's nephew, the ten-year-old Prince Ananda Mahidol, to be king. A Council of Regents was appointed to rule until he became of age.

After 1932, the power once exclusively the king's was shared among the government and civil service administrators, the armed forces, and a growing merchant class. Immediately after the Revolution there was a period of experimentation with various forms of Western parliamentary democracy. But they seemed too vague after centuries of totally centralized control by absolute monarchs. The result was a series of autocractic regimes which changed the "permanent" constitution several times. Two major figures dominated Thai politics through the 1930s and 1940s. One was a brilliant lawyer, Pridi Phanomyong. The other was a soldier, Lt. Luang Pibulsongkhram.

Pibul became prime minister in 1938 and in 1941 was forced into collaboration with the occupying Japanese. Pridi meanwhile was sympathetic to the Allies and worked with Thailand's underground resistance movement. At the end of the war, Pridi became prime minister and King Ananda Mahidol (Rama VII), who had been studying for many years in Switzerland, returned to Thailand. The public enthusiastically welcomed the king, but their contentment was shattered only one year later when he was found shot dead in his bedroom. Pridi was forced into exile and Pibul again assumed power. This time his period of leadership would be a long one and Thailand grew as a nation. In 1946 it had joined the United Nations and in 1950 it committed a military force to the United Nations contingent in Korea.

Pibul was deposed and exiled in 1957 by one of his generals, Sarit Thanarat, who immediately initiated sweeping bureaucratic reforms to promote economic development. Sarit became the most popular Thai leader of the postwar period. His dynamism gave Thailand the stability, security, and sense of direction it had lacked for the previous thirty years. Sarit met the needs of Thailand's rapidly increasing population by stressing economic development as the government's first priority. Many bodies were established to plan and administer national development and to encourage foreign investors to take an active part in the country's growth. By the time of his death in 1962, Sarit had provided the nation with a sound infrastructure on which to build.

The Vietnam War years were traumatic for Thailand. Western opinion saw Thailand as a "domino" likely to fall if communism was allowed to triumph in Indochina. So Thailand allowed the United States to build several massive air bases on Thai soil in return for monetary aid to be directed towards highway development.

The king proclaimed a new constitution in 1968, but two years later the war and a local terrorist insurgency resulted in the proclamation of martial law. In October 1973, there was a student uprising which resulted in about 70 dead and 700 injured. It was enough to topple the military government.

The next three years saw pressure groups, strikes, demonstrations, and brief coalition governments. The fall of Vietnam, Laos, and Cambodia and the withdrawal of U.S. troops and equipment from Thailand compounded these problems. In 1976 another violent confrontation between the police and students led the army to seize control from the elected government.

The 1980s saw the political situation consolidate and Thailand is no longer considered a country in political or economic chaos. The situation is actually the opposite. Politics is openly practiced, censorship is relaxed, and the country is booming. The king has provided an enormous stability and continuity which was lacking in the early political days. As a constitutional monarch, he maintains neutrality at times of crises and all coup-makers have declared their loyalty to him.

Prem Tinsulanonda assumed the position of prime minister in 1980 and served until 1988. His administration is credited with the stabilization of the country, the dismantling of the Communist party and its military activity, and Thailand's gradual democratization. In the 1988 elections, Prem was succeeded by Chatichai Choonhavan, who has since set about creating a cabinet of former business executives rather than military officers.

Thailand was a frontline nation for the West during the 1960s and 1970s. Today it proudly remains a "free land," better able to take an active part in world affairs than ever before.

BANGKOK 1.

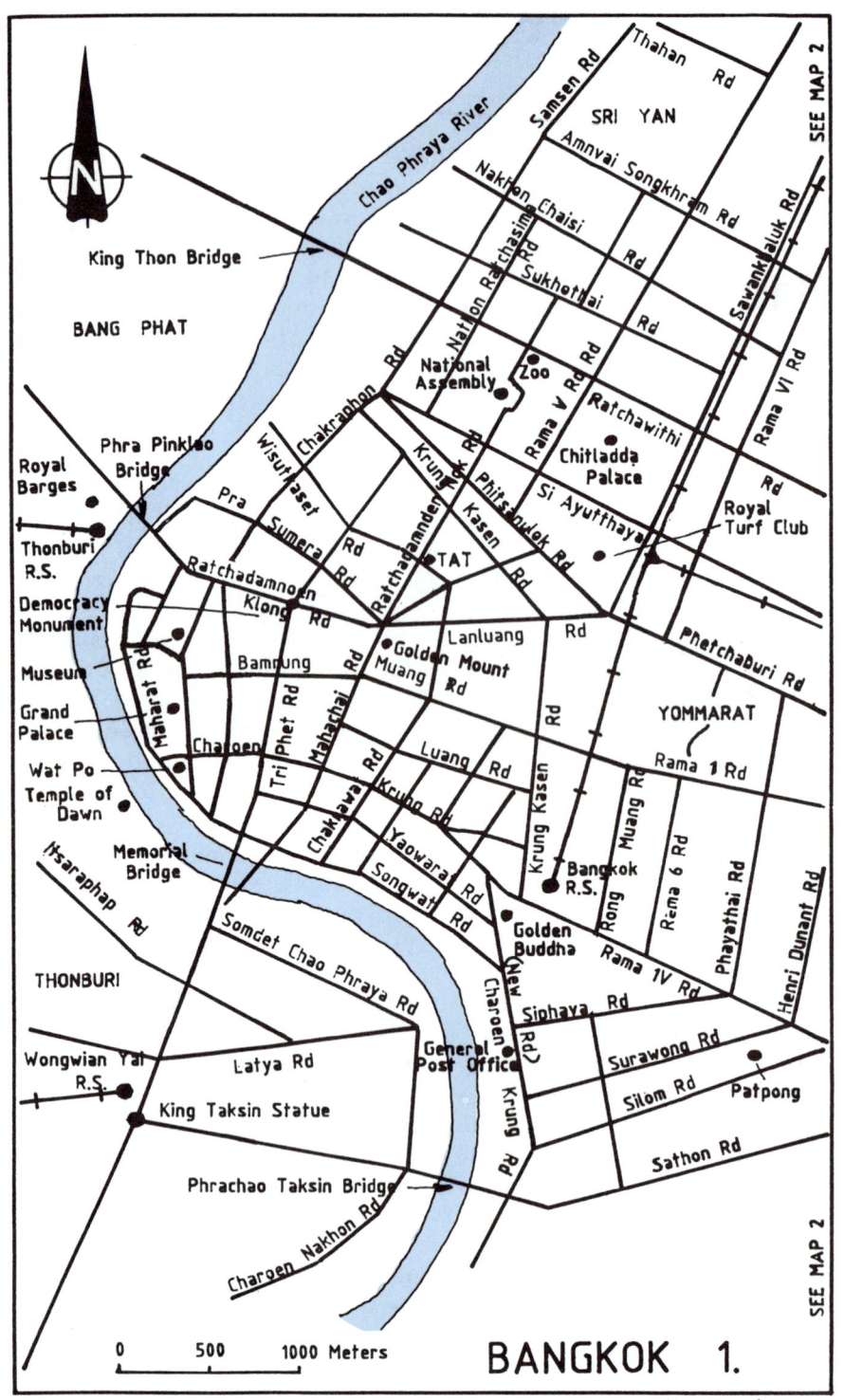

5

Bangkok

1. The General Picture

Bangkok is certainly not one of the world's most beautiful cities but it must qualify as one of the world's most exciting.

A city that is flat, low-lying, polluted, and crowded is unlikely to win any beauty contests. But if you add some of the world's most enterprising and attractive people, a flamboyant architectural style, a booming economy, and a natural love of life, you will end up with variety, excitement and, believe it or not, style. That is Bangkok today.

Bangkok, known to the Thais as "Krungthep" (City of Angels), was established in 1782 by King Rama I as the capital of Siam. Since then it has developed into a cosmopolitan city of about six million people with an intriguing mixture of East and West, the traditional and the modern.

Driving from the airport for the first time, visitors could be forgiven for thinking they were entering a large, slightly worn Western city. Stay a few days, however, and wander down some back streets and you will discover that beneath the veneer, traditional ways are very much part of Bangkok life. This is certainly not the West. It is very much southeast Asia.

Bangkok dominates Thailand in many ways. In a country of 55 million people, this is the only large city. In almost every facet of life, Bangkok is the leader and at times it seems that the citizens of the capital care little about the rest of the country. But even that image gets shattered when, at the time of major festivals, almost half of the population heads upcountry and returns to the villages and towns that were home until very recently.

Major visitor attractions are luxury hotels, glittering Buddhist temples, palaces, floating markets, canal scenes, legendary nightlife, and some of the best shopping available anywhere. If you forget the heat, the rain, the smog, the unbelievable traffic, and the dirt, this is a truly great city. At the very least, it is a wonderful place to have a good time and sample some of the attractions of an amazing country.

2. Getting There

Bangkok International Airport (called Don Muang by the Thais) is new, modern, and vast. It is competing for the position of major southeast Asian hub and it has been very successful in attracting much new traffic. It is ideally situated for airlines to provide a nonstop service to Europe, Australia, or Japan and it has captured much of this market.

Passing through Bangkok Airport is simple. Aircraft nose into landing bridges and passengers enter one of several corridors which lead to a central spine. Arrivals and departures are on different levels so traffic generally is one way. Moving walkways help to speed movement throughout the terminal.

The **immigration area** has upwards of fifty slots, so at most times processing of incoming passengers is fast. Escalators take you down one flight to the baggage claim carousels and large monitors inform you where baggage from specific flights can be found.

Customs work on the honesty system, with most passengers passing through the "nothing to declare" gates without interruption. From here you go into the arrivals hall. There are banks for money exchange, taxi and limousine counters, a hotel counter, and a branch of the Tourism Authority of Thailand.

The airport is a good place to change some money. Several banks provide competition but bank rates vary little within the country and unlike some places, rates are not higher at the airport than elsewhere. If you have not prebooked your accommodation, I strongly urge you to use the hotel service at the airport before you head into the city. At times Bangkok is almost booked solid so it is much easier to have someone telephone around for you than to travel around yourself.

Travel from the airport to the city (18 kilometers) can be by public taxi, airport taxi, limousine, coach, or public bus. For first-time passengers, particularly if there are two or more of you travelling together, I recommend the **airport taxi** service. You buy a ticket for B300 at the taxi desk and you are then shown to a special car which is clean, new, and airconditioned. The driver will speak some English and he will take you to your hotel or other

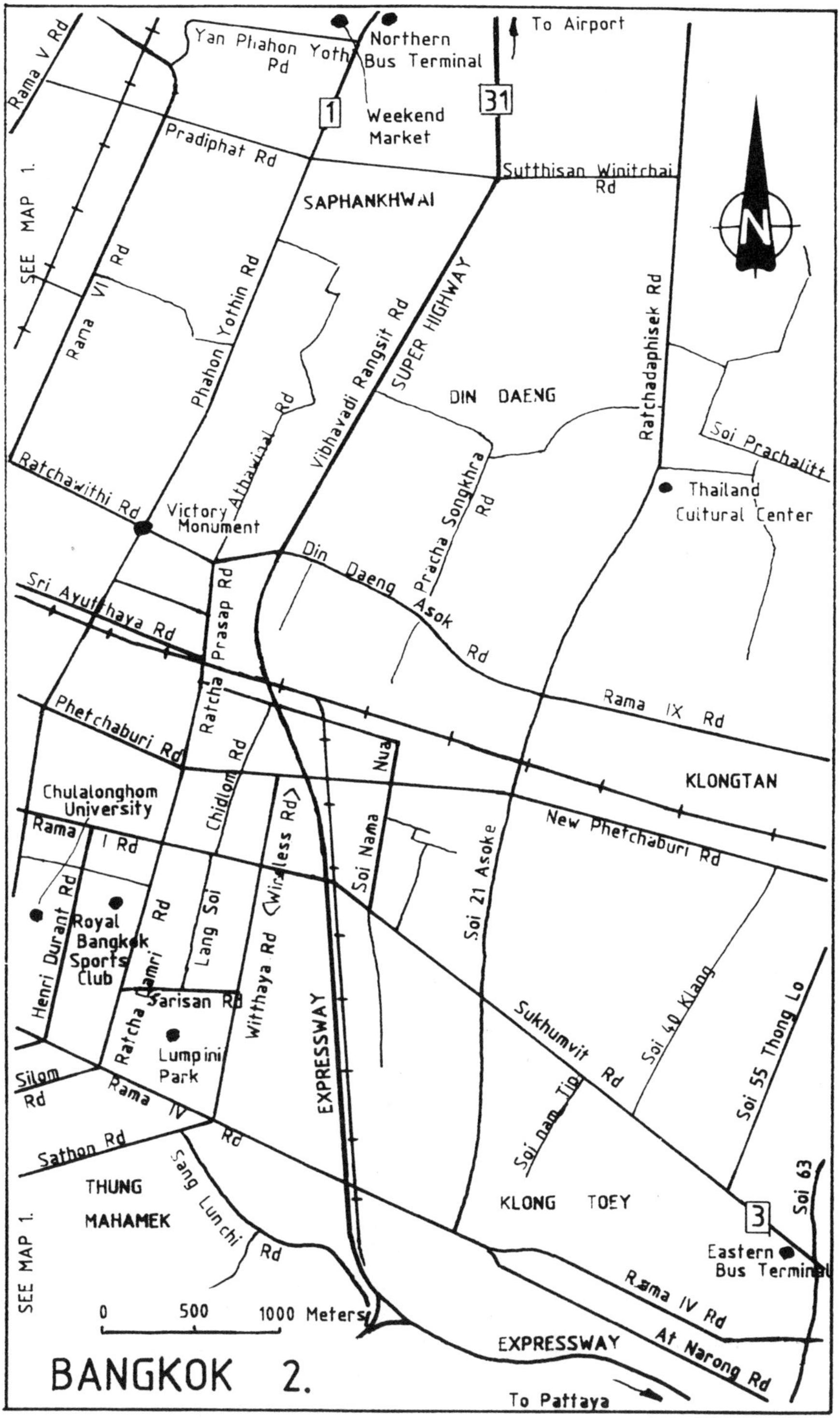

L.R. Copyright

destination. When you reach there, give him the ticket and sign the log. He will not expect a tip. The service is excellent.

If you know your way around, a public taxi will cost about B180 for the same trip and a public bus only a few baht, but US $12 for the airport taxi does not seem exhorbitant for a journey that could take anything up to one hour. Airconditioned bus numbers 3, 4, 10, and 107 and ordinary bus numbers 29 and 59 all pass close to the airport terminal so they can be used by the adventurous. Turn right as you exit the terminal, walk about 100 meters to the main highway, and you will see the bus stop clearly marked.

There is a separate arrivals/departure terminal for internal flights about 800 meters from the international terminal. It is too far to walk in the heat with baggage. Fortunately Thai Airways International provides a complimentary shuttle bus which operates about every 30 minutes between terminals. My experience indicates that it rarely operates to the posted schedule, so don't wander away or you could well miss the next service.

The other possible way to arrive in Bangkok is by rail. The Singapore-Malaysia-Bangkok Express is popular with young people and it lets you see much of the country on the way. You can board the train in Singapore, Kuala Lumpur, Georgetown (near Penang in Malaysia), or at several places in southern Thailand. It takes about two days from Singapore to Bangkok with at least one change of train. You arrive in Bangkok at the main rail station adjacent to Chinatown.

Local Transportation

Bangkok has no subway, almost no suburban rail system, little river transportation and, as yet, no above-ground light-rail system. That leaves the roads as the only means of transportation. No one walks for any long distance, so you have three choices: buses, motorized samlors (called tuk-tuks), and taxis (both public and hotel-owned). Getting around Bangkok is difficult at first for the newcomer. But once you understand the system, it is not too hard to get to your destination without it costing a fortune.

Bangkok has some of the worst traffic and pollution problems in the world so it's good to keep this in mind when you try to go somewhere. During the morning and late afternoon peak periods, it is often faster to walk. On occasion, buses which sometimes have their own lanes will be faster than taxis.

You can view all this as a frustrating waste of time or you can consider it part of the Bangkok "experience." Whichever way you look at it, there is nothing you can do about it. When you are stopped in a long line of noisy trucks, buses, tuk-tuks, and other vehicles, look around and take the chance to see the stonework of the old buildings, the amazing "spaghetti" electric wiring along the streets, the cool private courtyards of many buildings, and the cosmopolitan life that is all around you.

Hotel taxis are the easiest and most expensive form of transportation. There is a desk by the front door of all the major hotels. You tell the porter (in English) where you wish to go and he tells you how much it will be. You pay him, get a ticket, and are taken smoothly and efficiently to your destination. You cannot hail a hotel taxi on the street so if you wish to travel back to the hotel later, you will need to ask him to wait for you. Naturally this costs money.

Public taxis should be about half the cost of hotel taxis but often, for the international visitor, they are not. The problem is that taxis don't operate on a meter system so you have to negotiate a fare before you move off. This involves bargaining hard with the driver to reduce his initial offer by 20-30 percent. That can be difficult if you speak no Thai and he speaks little English.

Most public taxis are airconditioned and reasonably clean. I have never had an argument about a fare once it has been negotiated and there is no incentive to go the long way around, so I consider Bangkok taxi drivers to be basically honest. If you have learned a few words of Thai, most drivers will show some interest in conversation. These days more and more speak some English. You will find that most drivers come from the provinces but despite this, they seem to know Bangkok well.

Fares to most places within central Bangkok will be B40-B80. If you consider that the fare should be less than B40 you should probably use a tuk-tuk.

Tuk-tuks, those noisy, smelly, jaunty little three-wheel motorized contraptions, are useful for short-distance travel and are a "must" experience for most visitors. As with taxis, you have to negotiate the fare. For short distances, up to say two kilometers, you should be able to convince a driver to accept B20. Three to four kilometers should cost B30-40. That's about the limit of their usefulness.

Most tuk-tuk rides are hair-raising. The drivers are obsessed with speed and see each new fare as a personal challenge to beat some mythical "best time." Because of this and their reckless approach to traffic rules, tuk-tuks are often involved in minor (sometimes major) accidents. The other problem is that the open tuk-tuk exposes you to all the pollution pouring from surrounding vehicles.

Despite all this, tuk-tuks are useful. They are easy to find, they operate twenty-four hours a day, and in heavy traffic they can be faster than taxis. Late at night, when traffic is light, they can even be fun.

Buses are by far the cheapest way to travel around Bangkok, but they are often very crowded and you need to know where you are going. While some buses have destination boards, these are not in English so you will have to travel around by knowing route numbers. The best way to start is to purchase the yellow and blue City Bus Map (costing B35) from a hotel or bookshop. This shows bus routes and numbers.

Buses, both private and public, operate set routes—often the same set routes. This leads to some initial confusion but it really makes little difference to the passengers. Buses can be classified into four groups and each has a flat fare for journeys up to about 10 kilometers. You generally pay a conductor on board and receive a ticket and any necessary change. Most conductors do not speak English so just indicate the number of people for whom you are paying.

The blue-white buses have a fare of B2, the red-cream buses cost B3, and the smaller green minibuses cost B2. After 10 P.M. the fare rises to B3.50. The curtained buses with automatic doors are the airconditioned ones. Five baht will get you to most places in the central area on these, while some longer trips may be B10 or B15. These stop running at 11 most nights.

Boat transportation is very limited even though Bangkok was once known as "Venice of the East." Many of the original canals have been filled in and today boat transportation is restricted to the Chao Phraya River and some canals in the Thonburi (western) side of the city. Some of the major hotels with river frontage—the Oriental, Shangri-La, Royal River, Menam, and Royal Orchid Sheraton—have their own boats which provide a service along part of the river.

A more extensive service is provided by the riverboat express which operates from the Menam Hotel (in south Bangkok), through central Bangkok. It stops at places such as Chinatown, River City, and the Grand Palace then goes as far north as Nonthaburi. The whole journey will take about 90 minutes (one way) and will cost about B15.

4. The Hotel Scene

Bangkok has some of the best hotels in the world. By world standards they are still reasonably priced although rates have risen significantly since the mid-eighties.

Before deciding on a hotel you need to consider a few fundamentals about the city. Bangkok lies on the flat floodplain of the Chao Phraya River. There is a large area of the city on the west bank of the river but this can be almost ignored by the visitor.

Visitor interest is concentrated in several areas on the eastern side of the river. Bangkok has no well-defined downtown area so hotels, shopping facilities, and nightlife are scattered. We can, however, generalize as follows:

The historic area is close to the river in the westernmost area of eastern

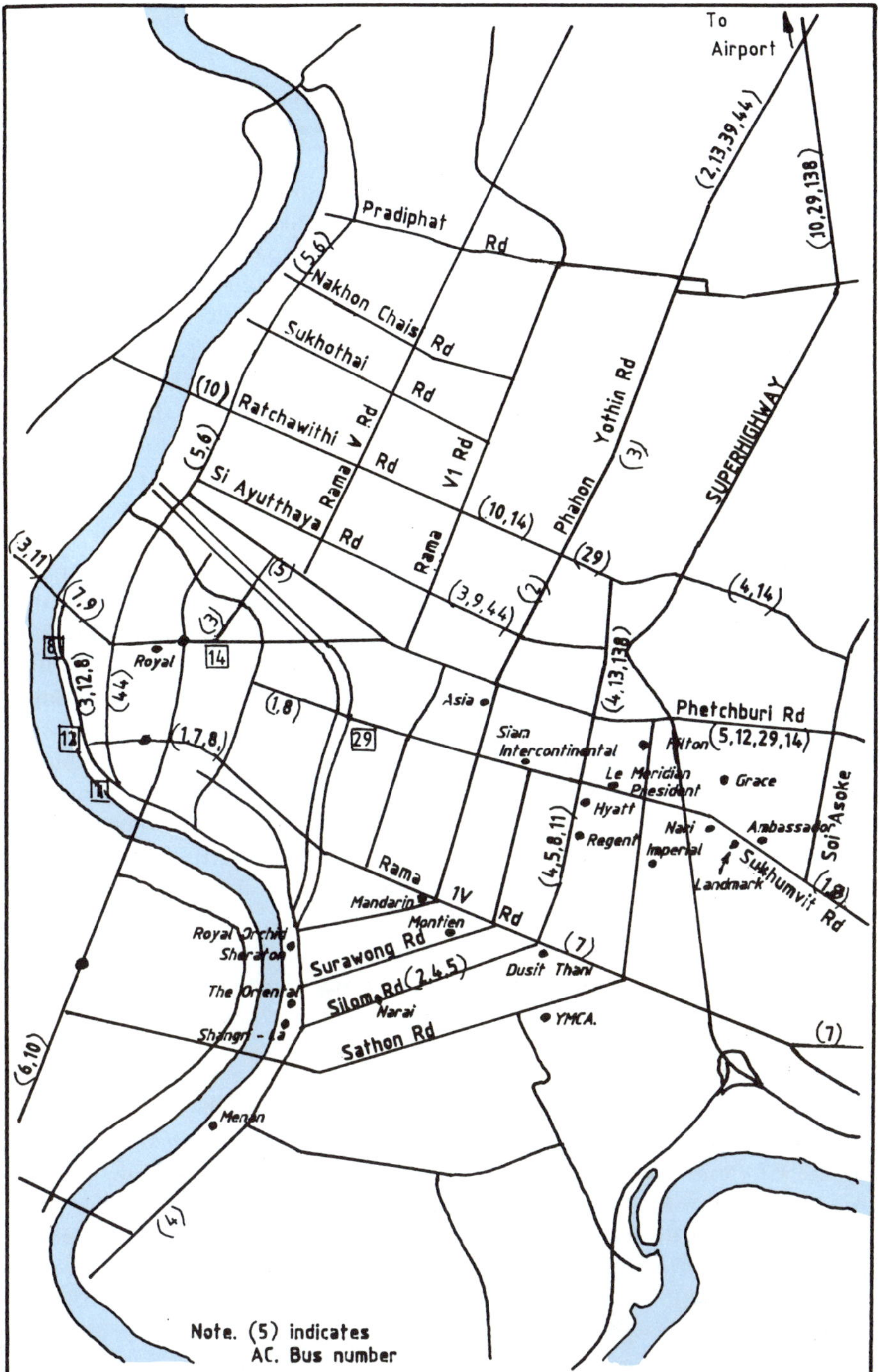

Note. (5) indicates AC. Bus number

5 terminus of route.

HOTELS and AC.BUS ROUTES.

L.R. Copyright

Bangkok. Of major interest here is the Grand Palace, the National Museum, and Wat Po. Most people consider this to be the most attractive area of the city.

The government area is northeast of here. The southern end is marked by the Democracy Monument, and Ratchadamnoen Nok Road is its spine. Here you will find offices for major government departments, the Tourism Authority of Thailand information center, Wat Sakhet and the Golden Mount, the National Assembly, Wat Benchamabopit, the Dusit Zoo, and the royal residence at Chitladda Palace.

Chinatown is an area, south of the government area, which stretches along Yaowarat Road and Charoen Krung Road. This is still a major shopping area for antiques, gold, Chinese medicines, and so on. The area also has some of the city's major banks and companies. The eastern edge is at Bangkok's main rail station while the southern end runs into the major hotel area by the river.

Shopping areas can be found almost everywhere. But the area close to the intersection of Rama I Road and Phayathai Road has developed into a major point with Siam Center and the Mah Boon Krong emporium. The area around the Rama I Road and Ratcha Damri Road intersection has shopping facilities to the north, south, and east, and Silom Road remains a major attraction.

I have long agonized over which area of Bangkok is best for tourist accommodation and have reluctantly come to the conclusion that no one area meets all needs. Fortunately, as the facilities of the city develop, the choice of location becomes less important. Shopping, nightlife, restaurants, and even sightseeing attractions are spreading to all areas.

Bangkok has more than twenty top quality hotels, a wide range of mid-market hotels, and a huge number of small hotels, guesthouses, and budget accommodations. The following is a personal selection which is by no means complete, but I have been satisfied with my stay in these establishments.

You will find that all hotels in the Expensive and Medium-Price categories have airconditioned rooms with attached bathrooms, a selection of bars and restaurants, direct dial local (and often international) telephone facilities, safe-deposit boxes or room safes, room service, and shopping areas. Hotels in the Cheaper category will have many of these facilities while Budget Accommodations will have much more limited offerings.

A word of warning about hotel telephone charges. It seems to be a fact of life that in general, the more expensive the hotel, the more they charge for telephone calls. Local calls will not be too expensive but be very careful with international calls, even collect calls.

The magnificence of a temple door.

EXPENSIVE HOTELS

The Oriental Hotel (Tel. 236-0400), 400 rooms, has long been a Bangkok institution. For many years, the Oriental was the only quality hotel in Thailand and almost every famous person who has stayed in Bangkok in the last 115 years has visited here. The hotel has a river frontage and presently consists of the original wing built in 1876, a tower block added in 1958, and a large river wing opened in 1976. The old wing contains several exotic suites that are simply magnificent. My favorite is the Somerset Maugham suite in the Authors' Wing, which honors the writer who stayed at the hotel in 1923.

The road approach to the hotel is through narrow, crowded streets and when you get to the entrance, this is also somewhat disappointing. The moment you enter the huge lobby doors, however, it is a different world. The lobby is cool and grand. Large decorative sculptures hang from the ceiling, comfortable lounges invite you to sit and watch the passing parade, and huge windows look out over the pool and through to the river. The check-in desk is to your extreme right and the elevator just to its left. Within minutes you will discover the service that has kept this hotel on top in Bangkok for so long. Facilities include six restaurants, four bars, two swimming pools, a shopping arcade, tennis and squash courts, a disco, and chauffeur-driven Cadillacs.

You won't get a room at the Oriental under B5000 these days and suites climb to a high of about B50000. For many people the experience is worth the price. (Reservations through Mandarin International Hotels or write to the hotel at 48 Oriental Ave., Bangkok 10500; Fax: 662-236-1939.) You may get to share the pool or restaurant with a VIP or even royalty.

The **Shangri-La Hotel** (Tel. 236-7777), 700 rooms, shares a close-by river frontage with the Oriental. The modern high-rise hotel has been well designed to take advantage of river views and its management has set out to try and capture the "best hotel" title. This is a fine hotel. The rooms are large and well-appointed and the facilities throughout the hotel are superb. My only reservation is the hotel's size. It is difficult to maintain a personal touch particularly if you are also accepting group tours. Despite my feelings I see that the hotel has recently won some "best" awards so it is obviously doing the right thing in the eyes of many people.

The entrance is impressive, and as you drive up the steeply inclined driveway your expectations rise. When you enter the lobby you are not disappointed. The check-in desk is in a separate area to your immediate left, but your eyes will be drawn to the right to the huge lounge-bar area with its spectacular light fittings and huge windows. During your stay you will discover that this is a great place to spend a few relaxing hours. Hotel facilities include four restaurants, two bars, a disco, shopping arcade, swimming pool, tennis and squash courts, and health club.

The Somerset Maugham suite at the Oriental Hotel.

Shangri-La Hotel.

Shangri-La room prices have climbed to over B5000 with suites going as high as B50000. For this you receive almost everything that a room can promise. (Reservations through the Shangri-La Group or write to the hotel at 89 Soi Wat Suan Plu, New Rd., Bangkok 10500; Fax: 662-236-8579.)

The Royal Orchid Sheraton (Tel. 234-5599), 780 rooms, is the third major hotel in this area. In Sheraton tradition, the operation is smooth and efficient. The adjacent River City Shopping Center provides a real bonus. The 28-story hotel has seven restaurants, three bars, two swimming pools, tennis court, sauna, billiards, and jogging track. This is a lively hotel much liked by several group-tour operators.

Sheraton room rates start at about B3500 and rise to B30000. Most have lovely river views. (Reservations through the Sheraton Organization or direct with the hotel at 2 Captain Bush Ln., Siphaya Rd., Bangkok 10500; Fax: 662-236-8320.)

The Regent of Bangkok (Tel. 251-6127), 420 rooms, is probably my personal favorite. The hotel is elegant rather than flamboyant. It makes excellent use of landscaped atrium gardens to create a quiet atmosphere in contrast to the frantic activity outside. The entrance from the street is appropriately impressive. You alight in an area that seems remote from the frenzied traffic that has been all around until now, and as you walk towards the main doors, past the fountains and pools, it all seems quite unreal. The lobby sets the tone of the hotel. It is vast, but it is not impersonal. It is a great place to sit, have a quiet drink, and watch the world pass by. The check-in counter is across the lobby and slightly to your right. The elevators are to the left. The other delight is the Garden Terrace, reminiscent of the open-air restaurants much loved by the French. I know of no better place in Bangkok to enjoy breakfast.

The Regent has good shopping facilities close by, and a horse racing track and 18-hole golf course across the road. The rooms are large and delightfully furnished. All have a separate dressing area and a fully equipped bathroom with hair drier, scales, and so forth. Best of all, however, is the feeling of caring that you receive from the staff. It reminds you of home. There are three restaurants, a coffee shop, bars, shopping arcade, pool, health club, two squash courts, and an impressive fleet of limos.

A large Regent room will cost you B4000 and up. If you need a suite you can pay up to B60000. (Reservations through the Regent Group or direct with the hotel at 155 Ratcha Damri Rd., Bangkok 10500; Fax: 662-253-9195.) Room service is great but try breakfast in The Garden Terrace one morning.

The **Dusit Thani Hotel** (Tel. 233-1130), 525 rooms, is part of a Thai-owned and -managed company. The high-rise building is in spacious grounds opposite central Bangkok's major park and close to Robinson's department store and other shopping facilities. Among other facilities, the hotel houses one of the capital's most popular discos. The lobby is both

The lobby of the Regent of Bangkok.

elegant and subdued. The check-in desk is situated straight ahead when you pass through the entrance doors and the elevators are a short walk to the rear. There is a nice atmosphere of quiet elegance helped by the woodgrain paneling and solid furnishings. This is a hotel that takes time to enjoy. Once you know your way around you will find that there are some delightful hideaways that are perfect for relaxing and getting away from it all. For your wellbeing the hotel houses six restaurants, three bars, a pool, squash court, tennis court, and health club.

The Dusit Thani has rooms from B4000 and suites from about B8000. (Reservations with the hotel at 946 Rama IV Rd., Bangkok 10500; Fax: 662-236-6400.) Once you have been here for a few days, it will be very hard to leave.

The **Montien Hotel** (Tel. 234-8060), 600 rooms, was one of the first hotels to open in the 1970-80 hotel building boom. It is not trying to compete with the best of the newer properties but is consolidating its reputation as an up-market, friendly hotel in an excellent location. For those into nightlife, the hotel is directly opposite the famous Patpong area, and the surrounding shopping facilities are extensive. Within the hotel there are three restaurants, three bars, a pool, and a shopping arcade.

Room rates start at a very reasonable B3000 and rise to about B7000. They represent a good value. (Reservations with the hotel at Surawong Rd., Bangkok 10500; Fax: 662-236-5219.)

The **Ambassador Hotel** (Tel. 254-0444), 1,050 rooms, is by far Bangkok's largest hotel. The complex actually consists of several different buildings with a wide price range. The Ambassador is in the center of the Sukhumvit Road hotel and restaurant area, some distance from the hotels previously mentioned. In fact this area has developed into the major mid-market hotel area of the city and it is also home to most of the city's best restaurants. The size of the Ambassador is somewhat overwhelming. There are over twenty restaurants and bars within the complex including the famous Food Center. There are four arcades with over 100 shops and there are the most extensive convention facilities in the city.

Because the hotel has been added to at different times, the various buildings do not fit together as well as they might. The entrance, for instance, can be reached through a carpark from Sukhumvit Road or off a narrow *soi* (lane). If you are staying in the Tower Block there is quite a long walk from the check-in desk, and you will need a map to find some of the restaurants. This can be a problem for short-stayers but it will not worry those with more time.

Room rates here start at about B2000 but the best accommodation (Tower Block) is from about B3500. (Reservations with the hotel at 171 Sukhumvit Rd., Bangkok 10100; Fax: 662-253-4123.)

The **Airport Hotel** (Tel. 566-1020), 300 rooms, is a modern hotel connected to the international terminal building by elevated walkway. Many flights arrive and depart either very late or very early, so many travellers choose this hotel for their first or last night in the city. Facilities at the hotel are good but you are a long way from the attractions of downtown. The hotel goes some way towards overcoming this problem by providing a shuttle-bus service during the day and at night until midnight. The rooms are good and the hotel is trying to provide more entertainment with a fitness club, a disco, and a live band in the lounge at night. There are three restaurants, bars, a pool, and a shopping arcade. One excellent facility is the in-room TV flight arrival and departure information.

The hotel has a high occupancy rate most of the time and this is reflected in the room rate of about B4000. (Reservations with the hotel at 33 Choet Wudhakat Rd., Bangkok 10210; Fax: 662-566-1941.)

Other top hotels in the city include the following. The **Hilton International** (Tel. 253-0123), 390 rooms but undergoing further development, is a very popular business hotel in the diplomatic section of town. Room rates are from B4000. (Reservations through the Hilton International reservations system or direct with the hotel at 2 Wireless Rd., Bangkok 10500; Fax: 662-253-6509.) The **Siam Intercontinental** (Tel. 253-0355), 400 rooms, is set in 26 acres of parkland near Siam Square. Room rates are from B3800. (Reservations through the Intercontinental reservations system or direct with the hotel at 967 Rama I Rd., Bangkok 10500; Fax: 662-253-2275.)

The **Le Meridien President** (Tel. 253-0444), 400 rooms, is part of the well-known and respected French-managed chain and has room rates from B3800. (Reservations through the Le Meridien reservations system or direct with the hotel at 137/26 Gaysorn Rd., Bangkok 10500; Fax: 662-253-7656.) The **Imperial** (Tel. 254-0023), 400 rooms with rates from B3500 is in a fine garden setting. (Reservations with the hotel at Wireless Rd., Bangkok 10500; Fax: 662-253-3190.) The **Regal Landmark** (Tel. 254-0404) has 415 rooms with rates from B4000. (Reservations with the hotel at 158 Sukhumvit Rd., Bangkok 10110; Fax: 662-253-4259.) I have never stayed at any of these properties so I am unable to comment further.

Two soon-to-open hotels which will undoubtedly make an impact in the next few years are the **Holiday Inn** on Silom Road and the **Hyatt Regency** on Ratcha Damri Road. Both are huge and each occupies a commanding location.

MEDIUM-PRICE HOTELS

Just below these top hotels in price is a collection of other properties which either because of location, facilities, or service do not quite qualify for top billing. In some cases these are older properties, in other cases they are deliberately aiming at the mid-market tourist.

The **Royal River** (Tel. 433-0300), 400 rooms, is the only major hotel on the west bank of the river. This area is a long way from Sukhumvit Road or the nightlife areas but it is reasonably handy to the older part of the city. The hotel itself is new and extremely popular with groups from Australia and Europe so it is often fully booked. There are three restaurants, three bars, a night club, shopping arcade, health club, pool, and riverboat shuttle service. Room rates start at B3000 but you may be able to secure a "special deal" during the low season. (Reservations with the hotel at 670 Charansanitwong Rd., Bangkok 10700; Fax: 662-433-5880.)

The **Indra Regent** (Tel. 252-1111), 440 rooms, is at the top of this price category and has facilities to match. The hotel has a huge shopping complex and the area surrounding the hotel is a maze of markets and alleyways that have thousands of small shops and manufacturing businesses. For someone completely new to Asia this can all be a bit daunting, but when you get used to it, this is a good bargain shopping area. Within the hotel there are five restaurants, three bars, a pool, and a night club. Room rates are from B3000 with the best rooms now nudging B4000 and suites B6500. (Reservations with the hotel at Rajprarob Road, Bangkok 10400; Fax: 662-253-3849.)

The **Mandarin Hotel** (Tel. 233-4980), 350 rooms, is on Rama IV Road not far from the Montien. This is another hotel that caters extensively to groups. There is a certain flamboyance about the interior but it is also clearly well used and slightly dated. The location is not bad and the price is attractive to many. There are two restaurants, a night club, a shopping arcade, and a swimming pool. Room rates start at about B2200 but your travel agent may be able to do better because this hotel is in many packages at discounted rates. (Reservations with the hotel at 662 Rama IV Rd., Bangkok 10120; Fax: 662-234-1399.)

The **Asia Hotel** (Tel. 215-0808), 640 rooms, is large and it is only a short walk to a major shopping area. The hotel has a full range of facilities and is becoming well known as a very good mid-market property. There are several restaurants, bars, a disco, two swimming pools, a health club, and a shopping arcade. The rooms are large and comfortable and have been recently refurbished. Rates are B2800 with suites up to B25000. (Reservations with the hotel at 296 Phayathai Rd., Bangkok 10400; Fax: 662-215-4360.)

The **Narai Hotel** (Tel. 233-3350), 500 rooms, is a good option for those looking for mid-market facilities in the Silom Road area. The hotel is close to the shopping and restaurant attractions of the Central Department Store and Silom Village. There are three restaurants, three bars, a swimming pool, and five shops within the hotel. Room rates begin at B2500. (Reservations with the hotel at 222 Silom Rd., Bangkok 10500; Fax: 662-236-7161.)

The **Rama Gardens** (Tel. 579-5400), 380 rooms, is out towards the airport.

Because it is somewhat isolated, the hotel has good facilities and space. It operates a shuttle-bus service to the city. Room rates are around B3000. (Reservations by writing to 9/9 Vibhavadi Rangsit Rd., Bangkok 10900; Fax: 662-561-1025.)

CHEAPER HOTELS

The next group of hotels fall into the B600 to B1200 category. There are numerous small properties in this category in the Sois off Sukhumvit Road but others are scattered throughout the city. Most offer reasonable facilities, are generally clean, and are an excellent value.

Some that are recommended are:

The **Y.M.C.A.** (Tel. 287-2727), 190 rooms, on Sathon Tai Road near several embassies.

The **Grace Hotel** (Tel. 253-0651), 550 rooms. Many Arab guests, popular hangout for the night crowd, a bit run-down, good location, good rooms on the upper floors.

The **Royal Hotel** (Tel. 222-9111), 300 rooms, one of the few large hotels near the historic and government area of the city.

The **Nana Hotel** (Tel. 252-0121), 500 rooms. Many Arab guests, opposite new nightlife area, off Sukhumvit Road.

The **Tower Inn** (Tel. 233-9060), 120 rooms, on Silom Road.

The **Quality Inn** (Tel. 253-7705), 28 rooms, clean, small, convenient, on Sukhumvit Road.

It is still possible to find a cheaper room and have private bathroom facilities. The establishments may lack a restaurant and other facilities but you will find substitutes in the streets close by. The following are in the B300 to B600 category:

The **Niagara Hotel** (Tel. 233-5783), 100 rooms, some with airconditioning, off Silom Road.

Madral Lodge (Tel. 235-6761), similar area, smaller property.

SRI Guest House (Tel. 381-1309), small hotel in quiet area, off Sukhumvit Road.

Amar Inn (Tel. 235-7182) near the Shangri-La Hotel and the **Riverview Guest House** (Tel. 234-5429) near the Sheraton Hotel are two popular small places near the river.

BUDGET ACCOMMODATIONS

Below B300, the choice is huge. So many small guesthouses have sprung up in recent years that it is impossible to keep up with them. Best areas for these are around the Democracy Monument, on the fringes of Chinatown, or in the Sukhumvit Road "tourist area." The rooms will not be airconditioned but some have attached bathrooms. Here are a few suggestions:

Ruamchitt Mansion (Tel. 251-6441) is off Sukhumvit Road. Good range of room prices.

PS Guest House (Tel. 282-3932) is a new property near Democracy Monument.

Prasuri Guest House (Tel. 280-1428), in similar area.

Marco Polo Guest House (Tel. 282-9227), near Tourism Authority of Thailand.

The New Empire Hotel (Tel. 234-6990) is at 572 Yaowarat Rd. in Chinatown. The hotel has a swimming pool and is popular with southern Thais.

5. Dining and Restaurants

Thai food has become popular worldwide so it is no surprise to discover that Bangkok is a gourmet's delight. Restaurants range from street stalls where individual dishes cost as little as B10 to exotic restaurants which have decor, service, and food to rival the world's best.

Bangkok has a huge tourist trade and a large foreign community, so it not only has great Thai restaurants but others for Western and Asian food as well.

Some visitors find the street stalls and small cafes so cheap and satisfactory that they rarely venture into the better restaurants. That is a pity. Equally foolish are those visitors who eat all their meals in the hotels. The best arrangement is to try as many different restaurants and food styles as possible. My recommendation would include a Thai food center, a top-class hotel restaurant, a riverside (or riverboat) meal, a top-class Thai restaurant, a Western restaurant with music, and perhaps a meal with a Thai classical dance performance.

All this is possible without it costing a fortune. Here are a few more details.

THAI FOOD CENTERS

These have become very popular and now appear in most department stores and at other places around the city. They are an excellent place to first sample Thai cuisine. The food is inexpensive and good tasting without being too exotic, and the surroundings are generally clean. Dishes cost from about B15 to B40 and there are photographs of some of the dishes together with labels in English and Thai.

The usual system is that you buy tickets (usually in B5 or B10 denominations) which you get at a central point and use to pay at the stall where you buy a particular dish. You wander from stall to stall buying what you want before going to a table with all your purchases. Any unused tickets may be returned for a refund when you have finished. The system works very well once you know what to do. A meal like this will only cost B100-B150 for two, including soft drinks and a Thai dessert.

I have tried most of the department store food centers and find them all satisfactory. My favorite is probably Robinson's on Silom Road, on the top floor. There is also a restaurant here (one or two floors down) which is a good value.

Another popular location is the food center on Sukhumvit Road under the elevated superhighway. In my mind, however, none can match the Ambassador City Food Center at the Ambassador Hotel on Sukhumvit Road near Soi II. It takes a conscious effort on my part to eat elsewhere when I am in Bangkok. The variety is excellent and the food good and inexpensive. Apart from Thai food you can buy Japanese, Chinese, Korean, and other dishes and they have great ice cream and Thai and Western desserts. You can eat outside or in airconditioning. It opens from about 10:30 A.M. until late at night.

TOP-CLASS HOTEL RESTAURANTS

Most of the major hotels have at least one superb restaurant where the food, atmosphere, and service are beyond reproach. I don't guarantee that the following are the best hotel restaurants in Bangkok but I do know that I have found them excellent and I am sure you will not be disappointed with any of them. Most of these restaurants have made lasting memories for me.

Le Vendome French Restaurant in the Ambassador Hotel opens for lunch and dinner with a full a la carte menu. This is only one of about 20 food outlets at this huge hotel but it never fails to please. Similar cuisine is available at **The Normandie** in the Oriental Hotel. This very sophisticated restaurant requires men to be dressed in suits. There is a special set menu for lunch costing B400-B500. Dinner can be a la carte or again there is the option of a set menu for B1700.

The Dusit Bussaracum at the Dusit Thani Hotel features Thai cuisine in the ancient "royal" style. For classical Thai food it is hard to beat and it opens for both lunch and dinner. Dinner for two will cost in the order of B2000. If Italian food is your choice, I recommend **Giorgio's** at the Royal Orchid Sheraton. This authentic Italian restaurant has a buffet luncheon and a la carte dinner with Italian music. Entree prices range from a reasonable B200 upwards.

The Salathip Thai Restaurant at the Shangri-La Hotel is almost in a class by itself. Magnificent classical Thai architecture, a lush riverside setting, and excellent food and service guarantee a great dinner. You have a choice of dining indoors or under the stars while you listen to Thai classical music. Unfortunately, the restaurant only opens for dinner.

If intimate surroundings are what you want, try **Avenue One** at the Siam Intercontinental. The French menu is excellent and entree prices range from B250 to much higher. It is only open for dinner. Not so **Le Cristal** in the Regent of Bangkok. You can sample the French cuisine at lunch and dinner while you admire the imposing Thai murals or the nice outdoor garden. While elegant casual apparel is suitable attire, this really is a top-class restaurant.

When I think of seafood, I recall a memorable meal at **Lord Jim's** in the Oriental Hotel. This fine restaurant in nautical surroundings offers a buffet lunch and full a la carte dinner. You will not get much change from B2500 for two but you will long remember the meal for its excellence.

RIVERSIDE AND RIVERBOAT RESTAURANTS

The Chao Phraya River provides the setting for some of Bangkok's nicest restaurants. Apart from the facilities at the riverside hotels—Oriental, Shangri-La, Sheraton, Menam, Royal River—the following are worth visiting.

The **Savoey Seafood Restaurant** (Tel. 234-9365) is in the River City shopping complex near the Royal Orchid Sheraton hotel. You have a choice of dining outdoors overlooking the river or in the airconditioned lounge. Outdoors on a calm evening is a magical setting I strongly recommend even though prices are on the high side.

Some five kilometers upriver from here the **Baan Khun Luang** (Tel. 241-0521) is also strongly recommended. The restaurant is just north of the Krungthon Bridge opposite the Royal River hotel and you will best reach it by taxi. There is a very good value lunch buffet at B100 but dinner will cost you several times this amount.

The **Dusit Rimtarn Restaurant** (Tel. 437-9671) sits in the Supakarn Entertainment Complex on Charoen Nakhon Road on the Thonburi bank of the river. Many locals consider this to be one of the best seafood restaurants in Bangkok so who am I to disagree. If you wish to go the whole way and actually dine on the river, the **Floating Restaurant** (Tel. 437-9603) is also found at this location.

TOP-CLASS THAI RESTAURANTS

You have never tasted Thai food anywhere outside Thailand that is anything like the food in Bangkok's top Thai restaurants. It took me several visits before I found my way to many of these tucked-away places but now, on each visit, I take time out to have at least one meal in one of the following.

Lemon Grass (Tel. 258-8637), in Soi 24 off Sukhumvit Road, is my favorite Thai restaurant. The food is magnificent and the setting in an old Thai house amid statues and antiques is difficult to better. The restaurant has been very successful and it worries me a little that some of the staff have become offhanded. Also more and more foreigners have discovered this gem so now you find more Western than Thai faces on some occasions. Nevertheless, I still keep going back. Entree prices start at about B100 and two can have a great meal for less than B1000.

Bussaracum (Tel. 235-8915) in Soi Pipat off Convent Road near Silom Road is worth the search. Some of my Thai friends argue that this is the best Thai restaurant in central Bangkok. The "royal" Thai cuisine served here is excellent but individual dishes do not appeal to me as much as my favorites from Lemon Grass. Nevertheless I thoroughly enjoy each visit and acknowledge that the freshness and quality of the food cannot be faulted. Lunch can be quiet, but dinner with its accompanying live classical music can be very busy. A meal for two will cost B750-B1000. In the same general area, **Thanying Restaurant** (Tel. 236-4361) also offers "royal" Thai cuisine. This restaurant in Soi Pramuan off Silom Road has never been a disappointment to anyone that I know so that indicates to me that quality is consistent.

Laikhram (Tel. 392-5864) in Soi 49/4 off Sukhumvit Road is something quite different. It is difficult to find and I strongly recommend taking a taxi or tuk-tuk but it is well worth the effort. The food here is authentic modern Thai and the atmosphere is homey. Locals from the surrounding expensive residential area use this as their community restaurant so prices are not overly high. It opens for lunch seven days a week and dinner every evening except Sunday. Two can eat for about B400 but watch for the strange system which makes you pay for "extras" including the hand towels, cold water, and butter.

WESTERN RESTAURANTS

Bangkok is one of the few places in Thailand where you can find good Western food outside the international hotels. When you need a change from rice and noodles, you will enjoy the food and atmosphere at any of the following.

Prime Beef (Tel. 253-2443) is off Soi 13, Sukhumvit Road behind the Ambassador Hotel. The restaurant is house-style within a lovely lawned garden decorated with tropical flares. Beef in all its forms is the specialty and the quality is high. Dinner for two will cost about B1500. It is not open for lunch.

Bobby's Arms (Tel. 233-6828) is in Patpong carpark. This most unlikely location for a great pub and restaurant does not appear to be a disadvantage because most evenings you need to book to ensure getting a table. There's entertainment on Friday and Saturday nights and on Sunday evening there is a swinging jazz session. Draft beer, fish and chips, and a selection of pies add variety to a menu which includes roast beef, steak, and other Western favorites. You can drop in for a drink and snack (about B100) or a full meal (B150-300).

Two other places worth trying are **Neil's Tavern** (Tel. 254-5875) and **Two Vikings** (Tel. 258-8843). Neil's Tavern off Vithayu Road near the U.S. Embassy offers a relaxed atmosphere with good steaks and seafood at attractive prices. Two Vikings on Soi 35, Sukhumvit Road is intimate and elegant with fine wines, first-class service, and acclaimed European cuisine. The restaurant is open for lunch and dinner. Dinner for two will cost about B1500.

THAI-DANCE RESTAURANTS

These are great time-savers for people on a super-fast tour. You eat and see Thai classical dancing at the same time. Of course, that is not the idea of these restaurants and it would be unfair to say that food and dance quality both suffer because of the compromise.

In fact, an evening at one of these establishments can be extremely enjoyable. They vary from the Ruen Thip, which is crowded and casual, to the more formal Dusit Bussaracum and Sala Thai. Here are some recommendations.

Ruen Thip (Tel. 234-4761), in the Silom Village Trade Center, is a reasonably priced, a la carte, indoor-outdoor restaurant. Very popular. Dancing is not the main feature.

Dusit Bussaracum (Tel. 251-1111) in the Indra Regent Hotel is open from 7:30, with a show at 8:30. Set price is B300 per person. Good presentation.

Tump Nak Thai (Tel. 277-8833) at 131 Ratchadaphisek Rd. is the world's largest restaurant. Food is delivered by waitresses on roller skates. Quality is surprisingly good. Atmosphere is nice because the restaurant is Thai-style buildings over water. Dancing is not the main feature of the evening.

Piman Thai Theatre Restaurant (Tel. 258-7866), Soi 49 off Sukhumvit, also features Thai food and dancing.

OTHER SUGGESTIONS

Be brave and sample some food from one of the street food stalls. You may not know what it is but you will enjoy the taste.

For those who would die without fast food you can find McDonald's, Kentucky Fried Chicken, Pizza Hut, ACW Family restaurants, Dairy Queen, Dunkin' Donuts, and others in Bangkok. There are also a growing number of small Thai restaurants which will provide continental breakfasts, sandwiches, spaghetti, etc., for the homesick.

Good northeastern Thai food is found at restaurants around the

Ratchadamnoen boxing stadium, near the TAT office. I found a similar restaurant in Pradiphat Road opposite the Mido Hotel.

Here are a few more general suggestions:

D'Jit Pochana (Tel. 279-5000) on Phaholyothin north of Victory Monument has a reputation for excellent Thai food. Prices are quite reasonable. There is also a branch at Sukhumvit Soi 20. Both have great lunch buffets.

Roberto 18 (Tel. 258-1327), Soi 18 off Sukhumvit. A branch of the longtime popular Trattorio Da Roberto in Patpong. Good Italian food, wine cellar, and Piano Bar. Prices range from B50 for soup through B80 for pizza or B150 for steak.

Moghul Room (Tel. 253-4465), Soi 11 off Sukhumvit. Probably Bangkok's best Indian restaurant. Good decor and atmosphere. Also serves Muslim cuisine. Dinner for two will cost B500-B800.

Silver Palace (Tel. 235-5118), Soi Pipat off Silom Road, is good for fine Chinese food. Serves a dim sum lunch and a full a la carte dinner.

The Whole Earth Restaurant (Tel. 252-5574), Soi Langsuan off Ploenchit Road (near British Embassy). Well-regarded vegetarian food. Also some Thai dishes. Lunch and dinner. Two can eat well for under B500.

Cabbages and Condoms (Tel. 251-0402), Soi 12 off Sukhumvit. This restaurant is run by the Thai Population and Community Development Association and certainly has novelty value. The food is good too. Lunch will cost about B300 for two.

6. Sightseeing

For a city that I have previously described as flat, crowded, noisy, and polluted, Bangkok has an amazing amount of charm. Everywhere you go you will see something of interest. It is that kind of city. Narrow leafy canals run between concrete high-rise buildings. Palaces rub shoulders with cinemas and row houses. Swallows happily roost in some of the noisiest streets in the world. On the river, tugboats pulling long strings of barges loaded almost to the gunwales compete with ferries and sampans scurrying back and forth between riverbanks.

Bangkok also has some world-class sightseeing attractions and these help make it a true international metropolis. Many of these are connected with the monarchy and the Buddist religion, two of the major forces in Thai life even today. From a distance, the city skyline is a silhouette of stupas and temples all thrusting skywards.

There are an estimated 400 wats (temples) in Bangkok so it is not difficult to find one close to where you are. All are worth a visit. Shoes should be removed before entering the sanctuary or chapel (bot) in any temple.

The Grand Palace and Wat Phra Keo (Tel. 222-8181) is something that must be on every visitor's itinerary. This complex rivals the very best European palaces and cathedrals in interest and attraction. From certain angles this represents all that is best about Thailand and Thai culture. It is a sight guaranteed to impress the most blase traveller.

The huge white walled complex is in the center of "historic Bangkok" near the river. The Palace was originally built in 1782 by the first king who ruled from Bangkok. Since then almost every other king has added to it so that today the complex is an amazing mixture of architectural styles that somehow work together to create a very impressive feature. The Grand Palace is no longer used as a royal residence but it is used for state functions, the presentation of ambassadorial credentials, and some other ceremonies. The royal family now reside at Chitladda Palace some three kilometers to the northeast.

The best part of the original palace building is known as the Dusit Group. The main structure is a splendid example of classic Thai architecture with its four-tiered roof and nine-tiered spire. Near the main building is a beautiful pavilion where the king alighted before entering the main audience hall. Please take a close look—it really is exquisite. Visitors are allowed to see the reception rooms of what was the royal residence. These were constructed by King Rama V and they are an impressive mix of classic Thai and Victorian Western style. A major highlight is the magnificent Chakri Throne room, where the king receives ambassadors.

Wat Phra Keo, more commonly known as the Temple of the Emerald Buddha, adjoins the Grand Palace and serves as the royal temple. It is difficult for Westerners to understand fully the significance of this rather small statue, kept in a glass case ten meters above the kneeling worshipers, but you can sense the power and the role that this has played through centuries of Thai history. Three times a year, at the beginning of the cool, hot and rainy seasons, the king changes the Emerald Buddha's robes in a simple ceremony of great meaning to the Thais.

The sanctuary is surrounded by a spectacular collection of structures—pavilions, chedi, prangs, statues, and so forth—encrusted with bits of porcelain or glass or covered by brilliant gold leaf. There are huge murals which depict the colorful story of the Hindu epic poem, the *Ramayana*. See the mother-of-pearl inlaid doors of the Royal Chapel. They are stunning.

The main entrance to the palace grounds is from Tha Phra Cham Road opposite the end of Sanam Luang. Airconditioned buses 3, 8, 12, and 44 all go reasonably close to this point. There is an admission charge of B100 to the complex and visitors are required to wear modest dress. The best time to visit is the morning (it opens at 8:30), when crowds are less. This gives you the chance to see the impossibly colorful and dramatic complex in its full glory. You will come away exalted.

Wat Po, located just south of the Grand Palace, is the oldest and largest temple in Bangkok and is often called Thailand's first university. The huge site is divided into two by narrow Jetupon Road and it is from here that access to the complex is gained.

The temple complex is so large, yet so crammed with buildings and other structures, that it is initially somewhat overpowering. To help you overcome this problem there is a guide service available at the main gate. This can help you get the most from a visit. The main attraction for most visitors will be the gigantic 46-meter-long Reclining Buddha, entirely covered in gold leaf. The huge feet are marvelously inlaid with mother-of-pearl with the 108 signs of the Buddha.

Among the many other features, it is fascinating to see the traditional medical practitioners who still dispense treatment daily at the wat. Also, the massage school (teaching the ancient form of Thai traditional massage) is open to the public so that you can experience the pleasure of this art form.

Remember that the early kings regarded the temple as a primary source of public education, so objects were placed in the compound to instruct people. There are statues or paintings showing methods of massage, details of military defense, literature, archaeology, and so forth. Geological education was helped by the displays of stone specimens from different parts of Thailand. Many of the rubbings on sale in Bangkok come from the beautiful Ayutthaya reliefs within Wat Po. It is also a favorite place for Thais to buy an amulet offering protection and help to the wearer. There is no admission charge to the wat but you pay B10 to see the Reclining Buddha.

Wat Arun (the Temple of Dawn) is another classic Bangkok landmark that is one of my favorites. The temple is at its best when silhouetted against the sky in the early morning.

The temple has a riverbank site in Thonburi, across from Wat Po. It takes its name from the Indian god Aruna. The main feature of the temple is the 80-meter-high prang, built in the first half of the nineteenth century. Very steep and narrow steps lead to a balcony high on the central tower. From here there is an impressive view of the Grand Palace and other central Bangkok landmarks.

The towers of Wat Arun are built of brick covered with stucco. This is further decorated with thousands of pieces of multicolored Chinese pottery which shine and sparkle when caught in the sun's low rays. It is believed that the wat which was previously on this site was the last home of the Emerald Buddha before Rama I took it across the river to its present location. Admission to the wat grounds is B5. There is a ferry from near the Grand Palace which will take you across the river to a landing adjacent to the temple.

The **National Museum** (Tel. 224-1333) is close to the Grand Palace and

Wat Arun (the Temple of Dawn).

is said to be the largest museum in southeast Asia. Like some of the major European museums, the main complex was originally a palace, built in 1782. It is an excellent place to learn about some aspects of Thai life.

The first building to the left of the entrance contains the prehistoric art collection (many pieces come from Ban Chiang in northeast Thailand). Behind this another building has an excellent collection of furniture used by early royalty. The main palace building has ceramics, weapons, and various other objects, while the new buildings on either side contain the Buddhist art collection and contemporary works.

Guided tours of the museum in English are provided by the Museum Volunteers' Group. The tours last about 1 1/2 hours and leave at 9:30 A.M. The museum is currently open from Wednesday to Sunday, 9 to 4. The admission fee is B30.

In this same area there are other places of interest. **Wat Mahathat** was built during the reign of Rama I and is now an important Buddhist teaching institution. Inside the atmosphere is quiet. This is rarely visited by the hordes of foreign tourists who pass by outside. If you go there, you will come away with a better appreciation of the Thai need for tranquility and the Thai personality that it nourishes.

Close by is Thammasat University which, although only founded in the 1930s, has become one of Thailand's leading educational institutions. The buildings are nothing special but you will almost certainly find a student happy to talk to a visiting foreigner.

Opposite all these buildings is an open area known as **Sanam Luang.** Traditionally this royal field has been used for royal ceremonies, then for some years it held the famous Weekend Market. Today it is used on weekends for such diverse purposes as free concerts, political rallies, bicycle riding, and kite flying. It is a good area for people-watching and you can pick up some cheap Thai food from the food stalls.

Wat Sakhet and the Golden Mount are something seen by most visitors but they are rarely visited. The main attraction is to climb the 320-step circular stairways to reach the gilded Chedi. From the top you have a fine view, but the climb is fairly exhausting, especially on a hot day. Each November the wat grounds contain food stalls and various displays and travelling shows as part of a religious festival, and there is a candlelight procession to the top of the mount which is very impressive. Admission to the wat is free except for the final climb to the summit, which will cost B5.

Tree-lined Ratchadamnoen Nok Road leads north from here, past various government offices to the **National Assembly building.** The square in front of the building contains an equestrian statue of King Chulalongkorn, who was instrumental in developing this part of Bangkok. The imposing building of white marble with a huge cupola in classic European style is delightful, but it is not generally open to the public.

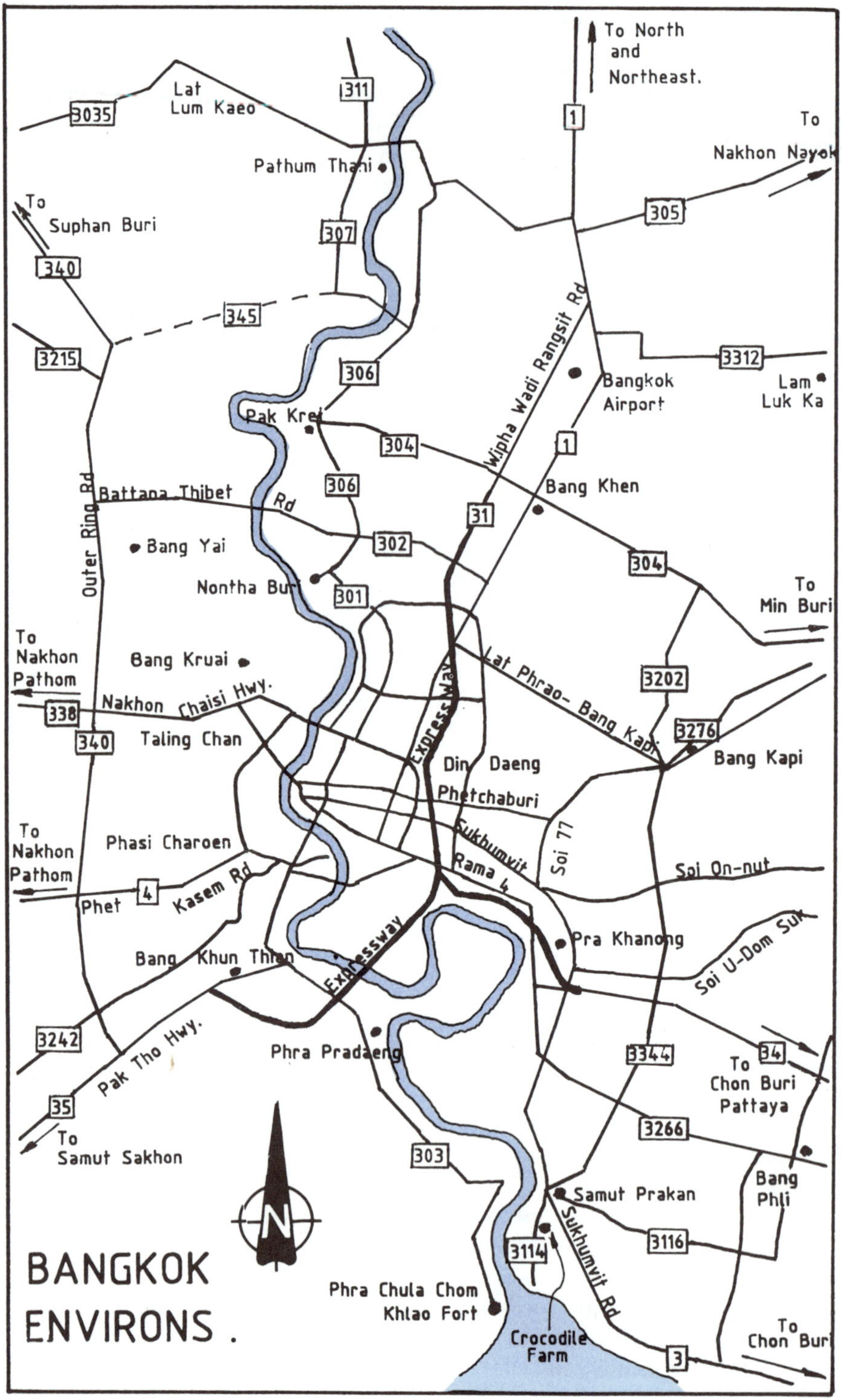

BANGKOK ENVIRONS.

To the left, **Amporn Gardens** are refreshing with fountains, trees, and gardens. **Dusit Zoo** (Tel. 281-0000) is situated on the right and is worth a visit, particularly if you are travelling with children. There are gibbons swinging in trees, giant carp to feed in ponds, aviaries full of colorful birds, and little paddle-boats to rent on the lake. The zoo opens every day and admission is B20.

Nearby you will find **Vimanmek Mansion** (Tel. 281-1518), billed as the largest golden-teakwood building in the world. The Mansion was built by King Chulalongkorn in 1901 as a royal residence. After being deserted for decades, HM Queen Sirikit had it renovated a few years ago and it is now open daily from 9 to 3. It contains priceless royal treasures and memorabilia but it's the building itself and its lovely setting that appeals so much to me. Admission is B50.

The last place of interest here is **Wat Benchamabopit** (the Marble Temple), also built by King Chulalongkorn. It is the newest of the royal temples in Bangkok and one of the most unusual. This is a major departure from traditional Thai architecture with light marble, an enclosed courtyard, and yellow Chinese roof tiles. The courtyard has a strangely European feel. A large collection of bronze Buddha images lines the walls. The main chapel is open daily with an admission fee of B10.

Jim Thompson's House is something quite different. This was the residence of Jim Thompson, an American who settled in Thailand after World War II and turned his energy to reinvigorating the Thai silk industry. His efforts were highly successful and in the process he made considerable profit. But he disappeared in the Cameron Highlands in Malaysia under quite strange circumstances in 1967 and has never been seen since.

The house, or actually seven fine old wooden buildings assembled together, is at the end of a narrow dirty soi off Rama I Road, in a small tranquil garden which is a world apart from Bangkok's traffic and noise. The house is a great example of real tropical luxury. I would love to recreate such an atmosphere for myself. The B100 entrance fee seems steep but I have decided that it is well worthwhile. The house contains a splendid Asian art collection together with personal belongings from Thailand, Burma, Cambodia, and China. The guided tour tells you about these objects and shows how Thompson was able to improve the traditional Thai architecture in several ways. There is no entrance fee to the garden. The house is open daily except Sunday from 9 to 5.

The **Royal Barges** are worth a visit. They are situated in Thonburi on a creek close to the Chao Phraya River and are housed in a huge boathouse. These fantastically ornamental boats are used in ceremonial processions on the river. The longest is about 50 meters (160 feet) and all have carved prows and lush red, gold, and black decorations. The boathouse is open daily from 8:30 to 4:30 and admission is B10.

Wat Benchamabopit.

The **Weekend Market** is Bangkok's "flea market." It is held at Chatuchak Park on Phahonyothin Road, north of the central city area. The crowded market is a bargain-hunter's delight. Even if you are not buying, it makes an interesting few hours because of its huge size and the variety of goods. Every Saturday and Sunday crowds buy and sell plants, fruit, cloths, pets, handicrafts, antiques, and junk. See faith healers, musicians, herbalists—they are all part of the scene. You can reach it by airconditioned bus Nos. 2, 3, 9, 10, 12, and 13. There is no admission fee.

The **Snake Farm** is near the corner of Rama IV Road and Henri Dunant Road near the Patpong nightclub area. Each morning at 11 there is a public snake-handling display and extraction of venom. This is very popular with camera-popping visitors. For the brave, there is a large python which will be draped around your shoulders while cameras record the event for posterity. The farm is open daily from 8:30 to 4 and admission is B80.

The **Samut Praken Crocodile Farm** (Tel. 387-0020) is claimed to be the largest in the world. No one will argue; there are crocodiles everywhere. The farm was begun as an attempt to save the species from extinction in Thailand. It now has over 30,000 crocodiles and is a major supplier of skins, meat, and other products. Crocodile wrestling shows are staged at various times each day and a relatively new zoo adds further appeal. The farm is about 30 kilometers south of central Bangkok at 777 Taiban Rd., Samut Praken. Admission is B80.

The **Rose Garden** is one of Bangkok's most popular tour destinations, about 30 kilometers west of the city. Of course there are roses, but this is not the major attraction. There are delightful gardens, fountains, ponds, boats to ride, a hotel, restaurants, and several Thai-style bungalows to rent. While this is nice, it's the daily cultural show that brings tourists by the thousands. The show includes Thai folk dances, sword fights, Thai boxing, classical dance, a mock wedding ceremony, and more. Afterwards there is an elephant performance. As these things go, this is rather good. Admission to the garden area is B10; then you pay another B150 for the show.

The **Ancient City** (Tel. 226-1226) is strangely named. This "world's largest outdoor museum" consists of small-scale replicas of many of Thailand's most famous buildings, monuments, and temples. The museum covers some 80 hectares (200 acres) in a shape roughly similar to Thailand. It is open every day from 8:30 to 6:00 and it is located about 30 kilometers along Sukhumvit Road to the southeast of the city. Admission is B270.

GO NORTH

The obvious destination for any trip north from Bangkok is the old capital of Ayutthaya. This can be seen on a day trip from Bangkok (see Section 7).

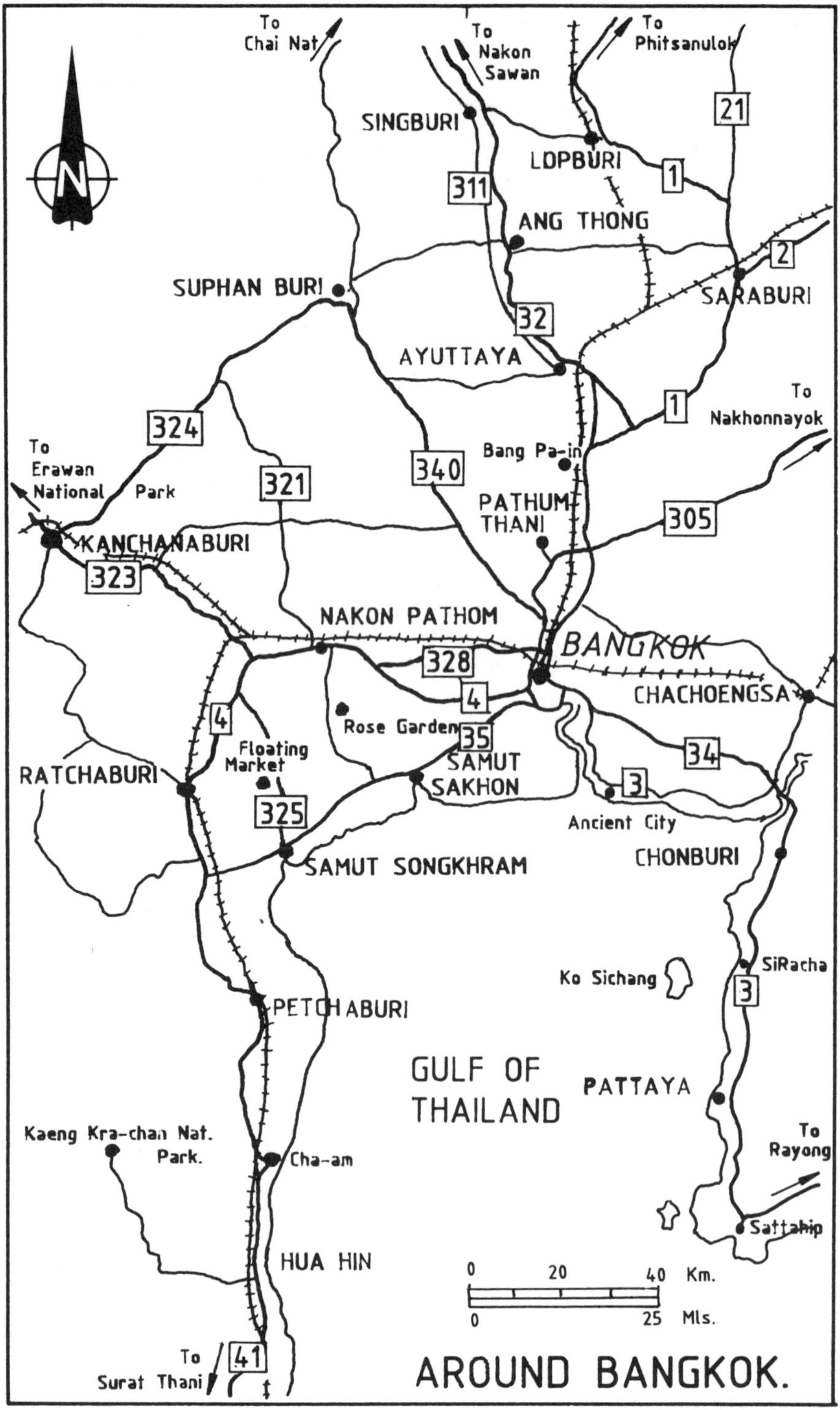

To Chai Nat
To Nakon Sawan
To Phitsanulok
21
SINGBURI
LOPBURI
1
311
ANG THONG
2
SUPHAN BURI
SARABURI
32
AYUTTAYA
To Nakhonnayok
1
324
To Erawan National Park
321
340
Bang Pa-in
PATHUM THANI
305
KANCHANABURI
323
NAKON PATHOM
BANGKOK
328
4
CHACHOENGSA
4
Rose Garden
35
Floating Market
SAMUT SAKHON
34
RATCHABURI
3
325
Ancient City
SAMUT SONGKHRAM
CHONBURI
SiRacha
Ko Sichang
3
PETCHABURI
GULF OF THAILAND
PATTAYA
To Rayong
Kaeng Kra-chan Nat. Park.
Cha-am
Sattahip
HUA HIN
0 20 40 Km.
0 25 Mls.
To Surat Thani
41
AROUND BANGKOK.

But it will justify a longer stay if you have the time and are particularly interested in history or Thai culture.

If you are prepared to tackle Thailand's roads, there are several excellent two- and three-day trips from the capital which I highly recommend. The road surfaces and alignment are usually good but the traffic is less disciplined than in many Western countries. Remember, traffic keeps to the left in Thailand.

Finding your way north out of Bangkok is not difficult. Follow the signs to Don Muang (Bangkok) Airport and then keep going. You will be on Route 31, then Route 1. The road is a four-lane divided highway for the 65 kilometers to the Ayutthaya turnoff. If you have a few days for your trip, ignore Ayutthaya at the moment and continue along the divided road for another 50 kilometers until you come to the town of **Saraburi.** Route 1 continues north while Route 2, to northeast Thailand, turns off to the right.

There is nothing of particular interest in this town for the visitor although there are a couple of reasonable hotels and restaurants. The town has several religious festivals during the year (see Section 8). Continue along Route 1 and some 15 kilometers further on, a turnoff to your left takes you to **Phra Phuttabaht.** This beautiful shrine houses a revered Buddha footprint encased in gold. It is a most holy place.

Your immediate destination now is **Lopburi,** a town some 150km north of Bangkok. The town has been occupied since at least the sixth century, when it was called "Lavo." Few traces of that culture remain today, however, except in the artifacts in the Lopburi National Museum. Much remains though from the next two periods—the Khmers from the tenth to the thirteenth centuries and the Sukhothai/Ayutthaya Thais from the thirteenth century to the early eighteenth century. King Narai of Ayutthaya fortified Lopburi in the mid-seventeenth century and used it as a summer capital. Several interesting buildings remain from that period.

Lopburi today is really two towns. The old town within the fortified walls is still alive and thriving but a new town has been built some 4 kilometers to the east. Between the two are army barracks, government buildings, and a steady stream of traffic. Old Lopburi has enough interest for you to overnight here. Although the accommodation is not fancy, I strongly recommend staying in the old town. I chose the **Asia Hotel** (Tel. 411-892), which is clean and has both airconditioned and non-airconditioned rooms. It is opposite King Narai's palace on Sorasak Road.

The Palace and Museum is the best place to start a Lopburi visit. The palace was built (1665-77) with the help of French architects and it is an interesting blend of Khmer and European styles. The main entrance is opposite the Asia Hotel, in Sorasak Road. It leads into well-kept gardens and eventually to the main buildings and museum. This whole complex is well

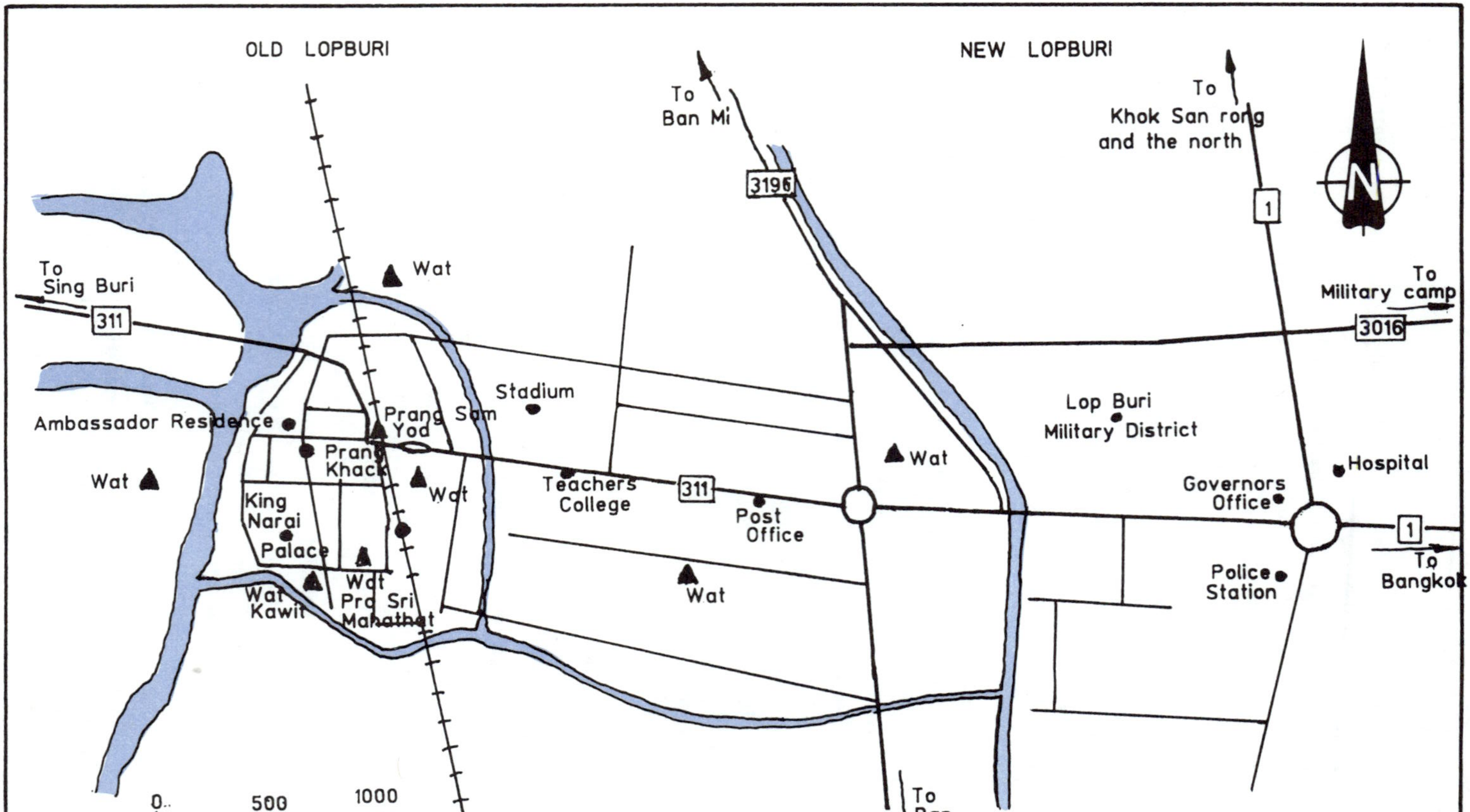
OLD LOPBURI
NEW LOPBURI
To Ban Mi
3196
To Khok San rong and the north
1
N
To Sing Buri
311
Wat
To Military camp
3016
Stadium
Lop Buri Military District
Ambassador Residence
Prang Sam Yod
Prang Khack
Wat
Wat
Wat
King Narai Palace
Teachers College
311
Post Office
Hospital
Governors Office
1
To Bangkok
Police Station
Wat Kawit
Wat Pra Sri Mahathat
Wat
0
500
1000
meters
To Ban Pa Wai

LOP BURI.

worth seeing. Parts of it have been nicely restored; others are in ruins. The museum is interesting and most descriptions are in English.

Other places worth visiting include **Wat Phra Sri Ratana Mahathat,** a large twelfth-century Khmer wat opposite the railway station. Much of this has been fairly recently restored and the grounds are well kept. There are numerous structures over a large area.

Chao Phya Vijayen was a Thai-European palace built as a residence for foreign ambassadors. Unfortunately the building is in a state of disrepair and is not open to the public. **Prang Khack** is just a shadow of its former self but what remains has been restored and it now sits in the middle of a busy street. Take a quick look.

Prang Sam Yod is an impressive building on a somewhat restricted site beside both the main northern railroad line and the main highway through the old town. The shrine is in classic Khmer-Lopburi style and was originally built as a Hindu temple. The temple has three prangs and is well known by Thais as it has been featured on bank notes, in advertisements, and in tourist publicity.

If you are spending the night in Lopburi, wander down by the railway station at dusk and buy some food from the numerous vendors who set up stalls in this area. There is a night market close by. Four telephone numbers worth having are the Railway Station, Tel. 411-022; the Bus Station, Tel. 411-701; the Anantarnathidon Hospital, Tel. 411-623; and the Police, Tel. 411-013.

From Lopburi we want to head back to Ayutthaya. If you do not have your own vehicle you can do this by bus or train. The trip takes about 1 1/2 hours. The best way by car is to take the road towards Singburi, then when you reach route 32, turn left towards Bangkok.

Ayutthaya is Thailand's major historical site and certainly the one which is most visited. Nevertheless, I have never quite come to grips with the city and usually come away slightly disappointed. I guess I am probably expecting too much from a place that was totally devastated after being overrun. What remains today are just a few basic structures from what was probably the world's greatest city in its heyday. It was the Thai capital for over 400 years until it was destroyed by the Burmese in 1767.

The historic large central city area, which was protected by water on all sides, is today part modern town, part ruin, and part unused wasteland. Most visitors arrive in Ayutthaya on group tours, so insufficient thought has been given to signposting and general visitor information for those travelling independently. As an unescorted visitor you can wander around for quite some time without knowing which are the major sites and how to get to them.

When you eventually find **Wat Phra Si Sanphet** (see our Ayutthaya map), you will know that you are in the center of things. This was the largest temple

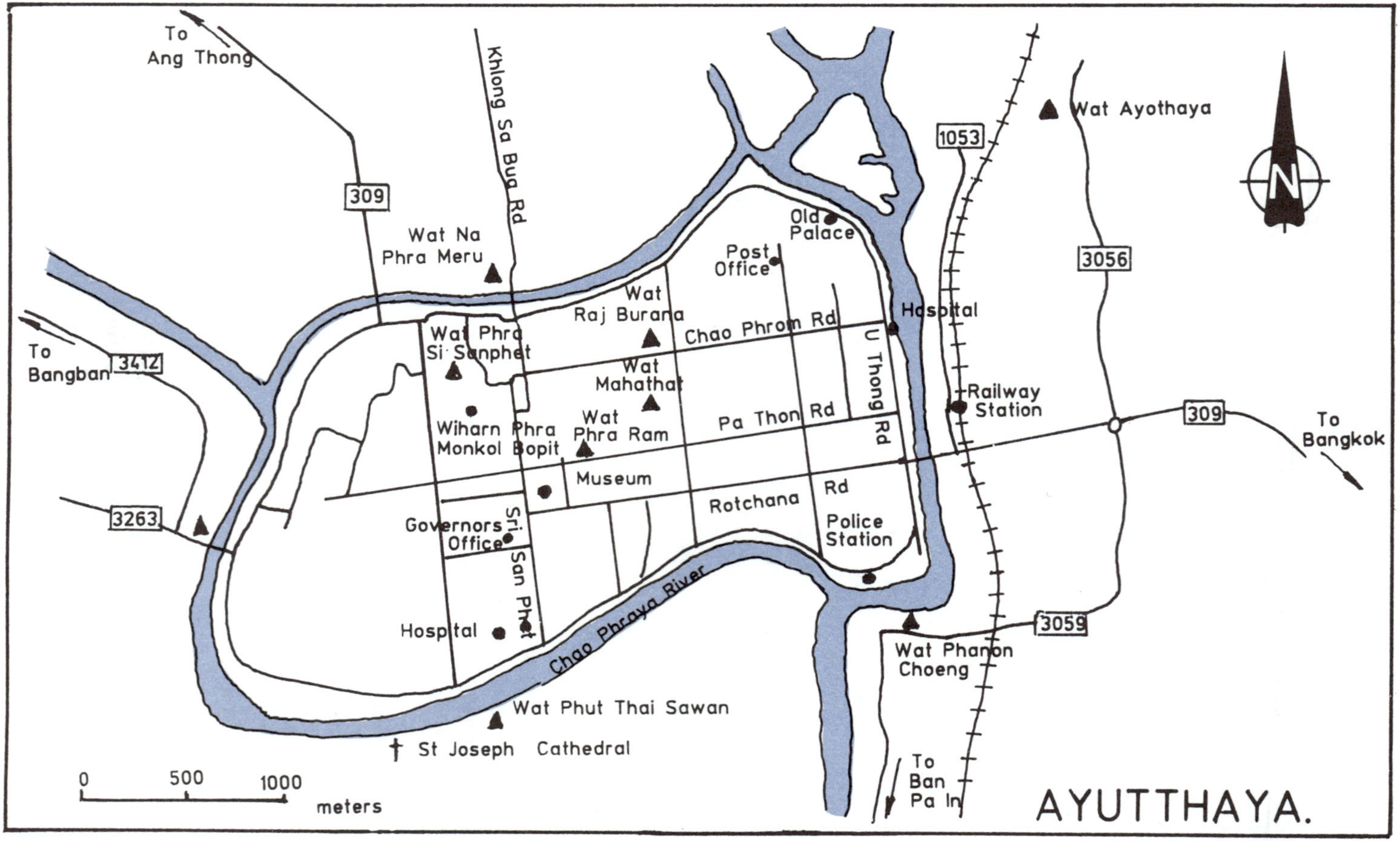
AYUTTHAYA.
N
To Ang Thong
309
Khlong Sa Bug Rd
Wat Na Phra Meru
To Bangban
3412
3263
Wat Phra Si Sanphet
Wiharn Phra Monkol Bopit
Wat Raj Burana
Wat Mahathat
Wat Phra Ram
Museum
Chao Phrom Rd
Pa Thon Rd
Rotchana Rd
U Thong Rd
Post Office
Old Palace
Hospital
Police Station
Governors Office
Sri San Phet
Hospital
Chao Phraya River
Wat Phut Thai Sawan
St Joseph Cathedral
0
500
1000
meters
1053
Wat Ayothaya
3056
Railway Station
309
To Bangkok
3059
Wat Phanon Choeng
To Ban Pa In

in Ayutthaya and it served as the Royal Temple for many years. The huge gold-covered Buddha which gave the wat its name was destroyed by the Burmese and today nothing remains. However, the three central chedis of the wat have been restored and are today photographed from all angles by visitors who see them as representing the peak in Thai art form. This is a "must" for visitors. Admission is B10. Close by is the **Wiharn Phra Monkol Bopit,** which was built in the 1960s to house an ancient Buddha statue that had just been restored. The building is interesting but does not seem large enough for the crowds that flock to this point on weekends and holidays.

Other ruins and restorations are scattered around for quite some distance. What will appeal to you will depend on what you are looking for in Ayutthaya. I believe that **Wat Phra Ram, Wat Raj Burana,** and **Wat Mahathat** are all worth visiting. These old temples all date from the fourteenth century and are in various states of repair. They are all built around a lake which provides good reflections and, at certain times of the year, brilliant color.

Other places of interest within the main town area are **Chandrakasem Palace,** which was destroyed by the Burmese but rebuilt by King Mongkut and today houses a small museum (admission is B10); **Wat Suwan Dararam,** which was built towards the end of the Ayutthaya period and is still used today as a temple; and the **Chao Sam and Phya National Museum,** which has some good original pieces from the old city and considerable information on what Ayutthaya was like in its heyday. The museum provides enough to show you that what you see of the city today is purely a stripped shell. The original brilliant gold exteriors to the buildings must have been magnificent—something like Bangkok's Grand Palace but on a far grander scale. The museum is open Wednesday to Sunday and admission is B10.

Outside the "island" of the ancient city it is worth seeing **Wat Na Phra Meru,** which escaped destruction from the Burmese; **Wat Phanon Choeng,** which was a favorite of the Chinese community; and **St. Joseph's Catholic Cathedral,** which is a reminder of the large European community that once lived here.

Ayutthaya covers a large area and you need transportation to travel between points of interest. You can hire a samlor to take you around, but it's also interesting to do a tour of the rivers by long-tail boat. No local hotels are great but the **Thai Thai** (Tel. 251-505) has some good rooms for about B300 and the **U-Thong Inn** (Tel. 242-618) has 100 nicely furnished rooms, a restaurant and bar, and prices from B500 a night. The following telephone numbers may be useful: Police, Tel. 241-663; Phra Nakhom Si Ayutthaya Hospital, Tel. 241-027; the Railway Station, Tel. 241-521; and the Bus Station, Tel. 241-273.

Twenty kilometers south of Ayutthaya is **Bang Pa-In Palace,** former country residence of Thai kings and princes. This is a curious collection of

PHETCHABURI.

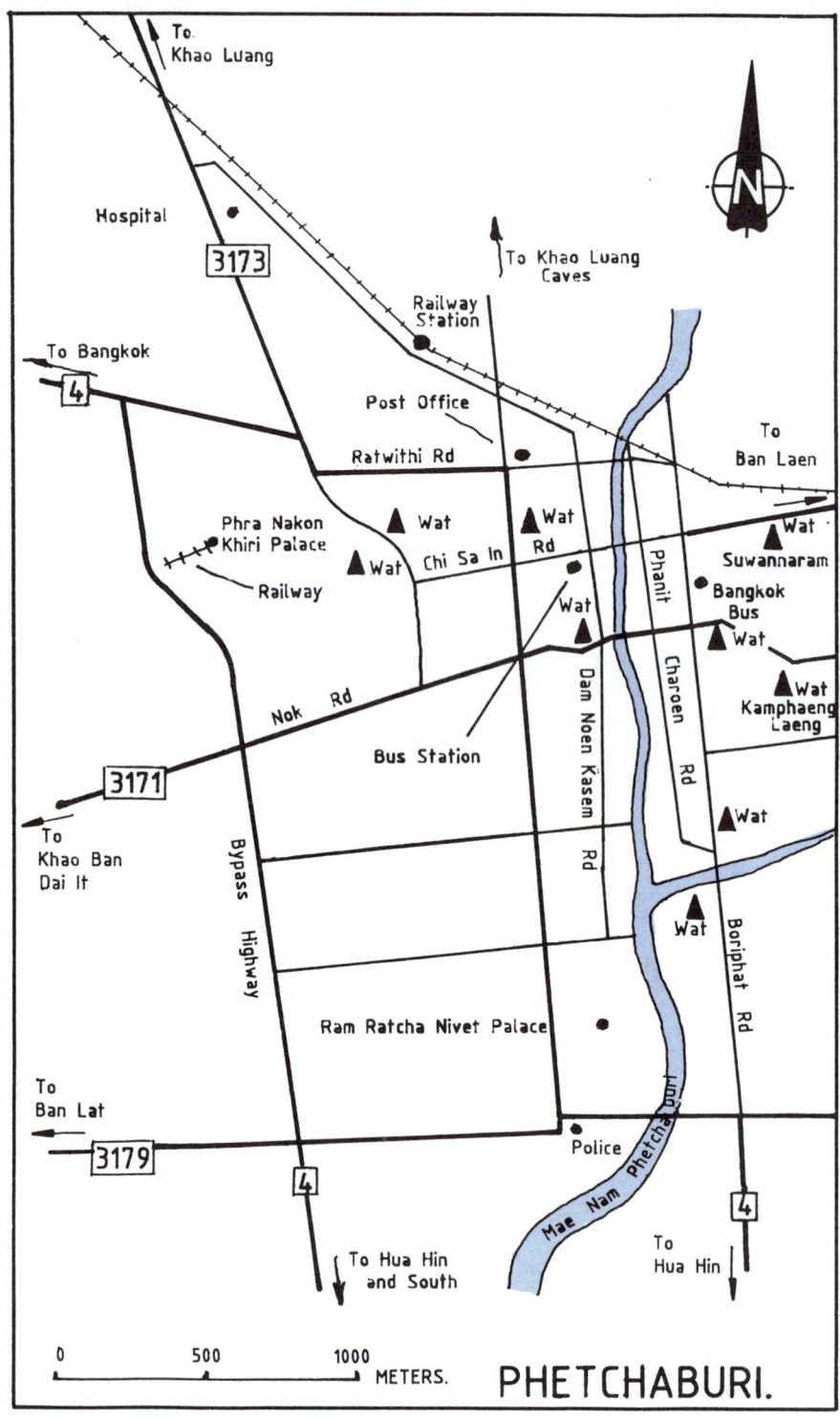

buildings in a strange mixture of Oriental and Western architectural styles. The palace grounds and a few buildings are open to the public (B10 admission fee) and it is well worthwhile walking around. There is a pretty Thai-style pavilion in the center of a lake, a Chinese-style palace, European statues, and a strange observation building that looks vaguely like a lighthouse.

From here it is a comfortable 60-kilometer drive back to Bangkok. Or if you are lucky, you can enjoy three hours on the river as you travel back by the *Oriental Queen* (see Section 7 for details on this tour boat).

GO SOUTH

If you travel about 200 kilometers (only about a three-hour trip) southwest then south from Bangkok, you will reach Hua Hin, Thailand's royal beach resort and a real delight. There is much to see on the way.

You can reach Hua Hin by train or by coach (and maybe by hydrofoil) but it is a good trip by car or even motorcycle. Cross the Chao Phraya River by the Taksin or Rama IX bridges and head for Route 35. This initially runs through the new industrial and residential outer urban areas, then there are some vegetable gardens and ricefields. The first 20 kilometers of this road is not a particularly pleasant drive. Heavy vehicles slow your progress and the road is dusty in the dry season and liable to flooding in the wet. It is these outer semi-urban areas which seem to be suffering most in Bangkok's hectic development.

After about 40 kilometers, a road to the left takes you to the port of **Samut Sakhon**. This busy fishing port is built where the Tachin River flows into the Gulf of Thailand. It's fun to walk along the waterfront and maybe stop for a seafood lunch in one of the excellent restaurants. If you are there in the early morning or late afternoon, visit the fish market and see the fish, prawns, squid, and crabs out on display.

It is possible to reach Samut Sakhon (also called Mahachai) by rail and this is by far a more pleasant or perhaps more intriguing trip. The railway is a relic but it is kept alive by the rural people it serves. The train leaves Bangkok from a small rail station in Thonburi called Wongwien Yai. Convincing a taxi driver that you actually want to go there will be your biggest problem. Once aboard the train for the 50-minute ride, there is little to do but plenty to see. Inside the carriage your fellow passengers will be mainly rural people returning home after selling produce in Bangkok. There will be no other foreigners.

The train crosses swampland of vivid green, punctuated here and there by slumbering stations. Within minutes most of your fellow passengers will be sound asleep, coaxed no doubt by the heat, the gentle rocking, and the clickety-clack. You should stay awake and watch the uniformed conductor, the railside flagmen, and the stationmasters going about the business of getting you safely to your destination. Outside, workers in conical hats are stooping low to plant rice in the flooded fields exactly as they have for centuries. You could be way back in time, yet you will be the only person on the train to recognize that or perhaps even to see it. On reaching Samut Sakhon, walk down to the river, find a table overlooking the harbor, order a serving of Tom Yum Goong, and sit back knowing that you have just experienced a part of Thailand unknown to all but a handful of the five million visitors who go to Thailand each year. But I have digressed.

Back on the main road, it's another 35 kilometers to **Samut Songkhram,** then a further 20 kilometers to the main southern road, Route 4. Travel is now more pleasant. The scenery is interesting, there are fewer heavy vehicles, and sections of the road are a divided highway.

The 35 kilometers to **Phetchaburi** pass quickly. This provincial capital has several worthwhile sights. At the top of the list for me is the Palace and Wat on a hilltop on the left of the main by-pass road around the town. **Phra Nakon Khiri Palace** was built last century by King Mongkut and is now used as a museum. You reach the hilltop by a cable railway that has been recently installed so that you can avoid the strenuous walk. The railway costs B5 each way and admission to the Palace is B20. From the top the view is quite spectacular, particularly in the late afternoon. Visit the museum, then walk around the well-formed pathways to see some of the other structures on the hill. All in all this is a very pleasant place and one I recommend to anyone.

After visiting the palace, it is worth seeing the town with its many old temples. Don't miss **Wat Suwannaram,** with its Ayutthayan-style wooden teaching hall dating from the early 1700s and its lovely chapel murals. Also worth seeing is **Wat Kamphaeng Laeng,** an old Khmer site with four prangs and part of the original wall still standing.

The **Khao Luang Caves** are just outside town on the north side. Midday shafts of sunlight illuminate stalactites and Buddha images. It is a nice place. Telephone numbers worth having are Police, Tel. 425-500; Phetchaburi Hospital, Tel. 425-700; the Railway Station, Tel. 425-211; and the Bus Station, Tel. 425-256.

The country south of Phetchaburi is interesting. There are caves, verdant limestone outcrops, hilltop temples, fertile farmland, and gentle bays. Some 15 kilometers south, a road to the right goes inland for about 20 kilometers to Kaeng Kra-chan Dam and the **Kaeng Kra-chan National Park,** Thailand's largest. The Irrigation Department provides accommodation here overlooking the reservoir in bungalows which rent from B350 to B800.

The next point of interest is the seaside town of **Cha-am.** Actually the town is on the railway and highway which are about 2 kilometers inland, but it's the beach that has the appeal. The popular beach is long, straight, and shaded with casuarina trees. By some standards the sand is not particularly good, but the Thais who frequent this place don't spend too much time on the sand or in the water.

The narrow beachside road fronts cabins, hotels, shops, restaurants, and bars. Weekdays are relatively quiet but the weekends can be quite hectic with a large influx of Thai students. Vendors sell food from small stalls under the trees on the beach and there are several good seafood restaurants along the beach road.

Cha-am is developing rapidly. There are already several large beachfront hotels and huge billboards advertise condominiums which are about to be started. The largest hotel is **The Regent Cha-am** (Tel. 471-483), 550 rooms. It has huge grounds, which appear difficult to keep in order, and most facilities of a first-class hotel including a vast swimming pool, three restaurants, a night club, tennis and squash courts, and a fitness center. A room here will cost B1800 up. (Reservations with the hotel at 849/21 Cha-am Beach, Phetchaburi 76120; Fax: 6632-471-492.) Other properties are the **Beach Garden Cha-am** (Tel. 471-350), 250 rooms, and the **Cha-am Methawalai Hotel** (Tel. 471-145), 120 rooms. There are many small bungalows.

Hua Hin is 30 kilometers to the south. In the 1920s, when the railway reached Hua Hin, the town became an exotic new resort for the socialites of Bangkok and their foreigner friends. It was not long before there was a first-class hotel (the Railway), a golf course, and a royal residence.

For some time Hua Hin was *the* beach resort of Asia. Then just as quickly as it had come, fashion abandoned Hua Hin. For twenty years it languished and it was only in the 1980s that Thais rediscovered the pleasures of this resort. Now they are not so sure that they want to tell the world. Perhaps it is because they have seen what happened to Pattaya and what is happening to Phuket. Some people don't want to see Hua Hin go down the same track.

Fortunately, common sense may save Hua Hin. If the renovation of the old Railway Hotel into the beautiful **Hotel Sofitel Central** (Tel. 512-021) is an example of Hua Hin thinking, then all is well. The hotel is a delight. In some ways it is the nicest hotel in Thailand. The renovations have retained all the style of the past but have added the conveniences and facilities of today. A huge new wing has been added in traditional style to give a total of 200 rooms. The garden has been improved with the addition of a nice beachfront swimming pool and a magnificent Thai restaurant. Inside, Satchmo appetizers and drinks are available to the accompaniment of some of the best jazz music in Asia. Take my tip—try a "Summertime" while listening to some of the hottest music around. Room rates start at B2000. (Reservations with the hotel at 1 Damneankasin Rd., Hua Hin 77110; Fax: 6632-511-014.)

Other top-class resorts at Hua Hin are the **Royal Gardens Resort** (Tel. 511-881), 220 rooms, on the beachfront just south of the main town with four restaurants, a disco, and a well-protected pool; and the **Royal Garden Village**

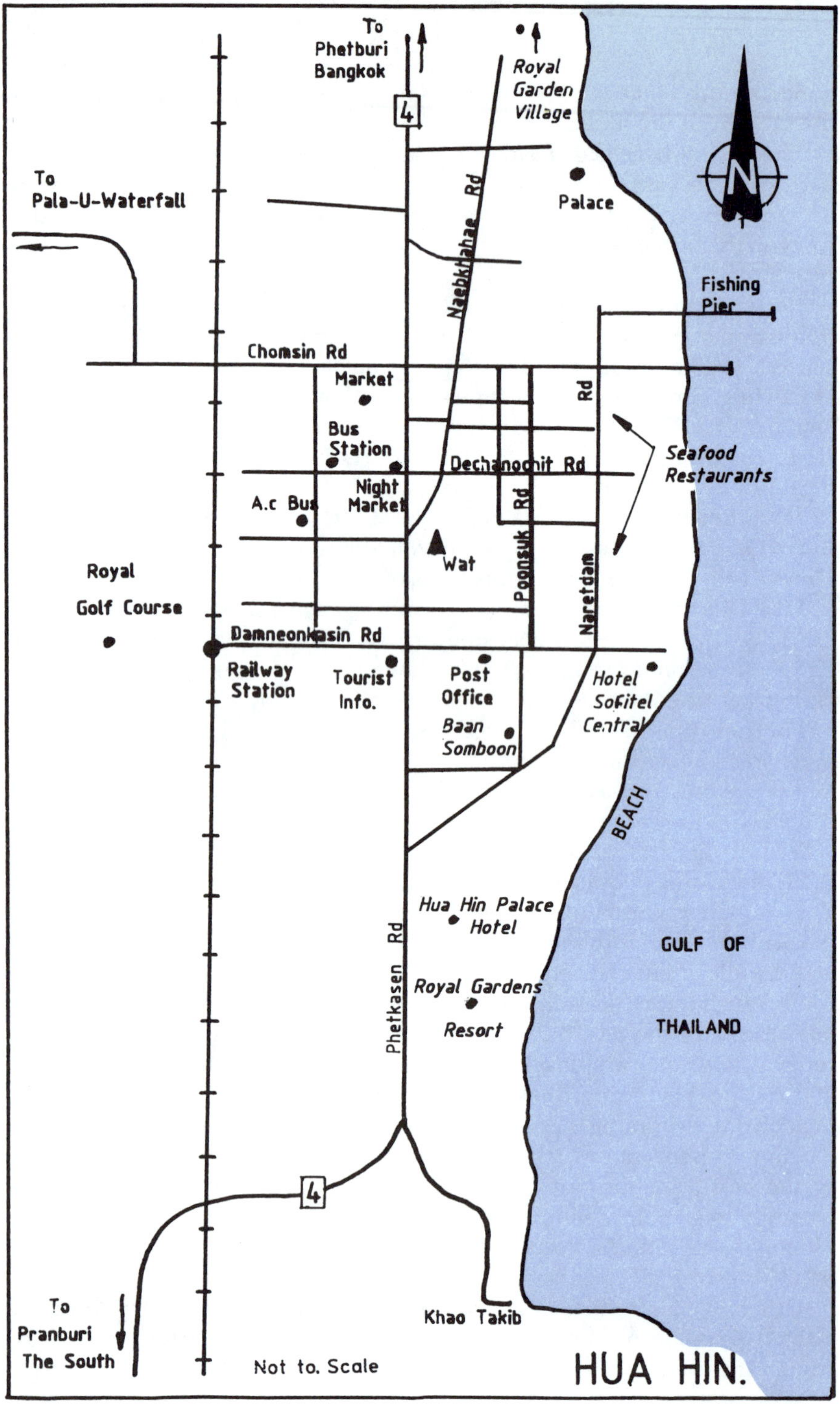
To
Phetburi
Bangkok
4
Royal
Garden
Village
N
To
Pala-U-Waterfall
Palace
Naebkhahae Rd
Fishing
Pier
Chomsin Rd
Market
Bus
Station
Rd
Seafood
Restaurants
Dechanochit Rd
Night
Market
A.c Bus
Rd
Wat
Poonsuk
Naretdam
Royal
Golf Course
Damneonkasin Rd
Railway
Station
Tourist
Info.
Post
Office
Baan
Somboon
Hotel
Sofitel
Central
BEACH
Hua Hin Palace
Hotel
Phetkasen Rd
Royal Gardens
Resort
GULF OF
THAILAND
4
Khao Takib
To
Pranburi
The South
Not to. Scale
HUA HIN.

(Tel. 512-412), 165 rooms, a newish low-rise resort with a huge pool, several restaurants, and a superb sports center, a few kilometers away to the north. Both these properties cost about B2000 a night. (Reservations with the hotels as follows. Resort—107/1 Phetkasen Rd., Hua Hin 77110; Fax: 6632-512-422. Village—45 Phetkasen Rd., Hua Hin 77110; Fax: 6632-512-417.) Down-market from these but still providing good accommodation are the **Hua Hin Palace Hotel** (Tel. 511-151), the small **Baan Somboon Resort** (Tel. 511-538), or the budget-style **Jed Pee Nong Hotel** (Tel. 512-381), almost next to the Post Office where rooms with fan are B300, B400 for airconditioning.

Eating is one of the delights in Hua Hin. Almost all the restaurants along the shore are good and the seafood is wonderfully fresh. Wander along the road from the Sofitel Hotel towards the pier and choose one that suits your mood. Some are simple, low-budget affairs, others are in garden settings, while some provide airconditioning. Eat seafood and eat it cooked Thai-style. You will long remember the experience.

Hua Hin beach is not great but it is particularly pleasant in the late afternoon, when you cast long shadows across the sand into the water. Swimming is okay, but relaxing in a deck chair under an umbrella with a book in hand is hard to beat. Wandering ladies will offer you something to eat, a drink, a massage, or a ride on one of the little ponies. If you have the time, accept everything on offer.

A popular day trip from Hua Hin takes you to **Pala-U-Waterfall.** This is about 100 kilometers away within the Kaeng Kra-chan National Park. The falls themselves are not great unless you trek for quite some distance to the higher levels. On the way, though, you pass through some pretty country. There are some caves, and you can even visit a Karen peoples village. It's a problem using public transportation to get to this area, so you will have to drive yourself or take one of the organized day trips.

The main attraction south of Hua Hin is **Khao Sam Roi Yod National Park.** The 60-kilometer trip is worth the effort because the park contains some really exciting scenery. The park consists of spectacular limestone hills that rise dramatically from the sea and coastal marsh. The hills are dotted with trees while the valleys are densely forested. Wildlife is an outstanding feature of the park—goat antelope, crab-eating macaques, shorebirds, barking deer, and porcupines. So too are the caves, with **Phraya Nakhon Cave** the most popular.

The recently opened **Club Aldiana Siam,** midway between the Park and Hua Hin, has low-rise accommodations set amid coconut trees fronting a nice beach. It is being marketed heavily to Germans as a Club-Med type of complex, but at most times you will be welcomed if you just turn up at the gate.

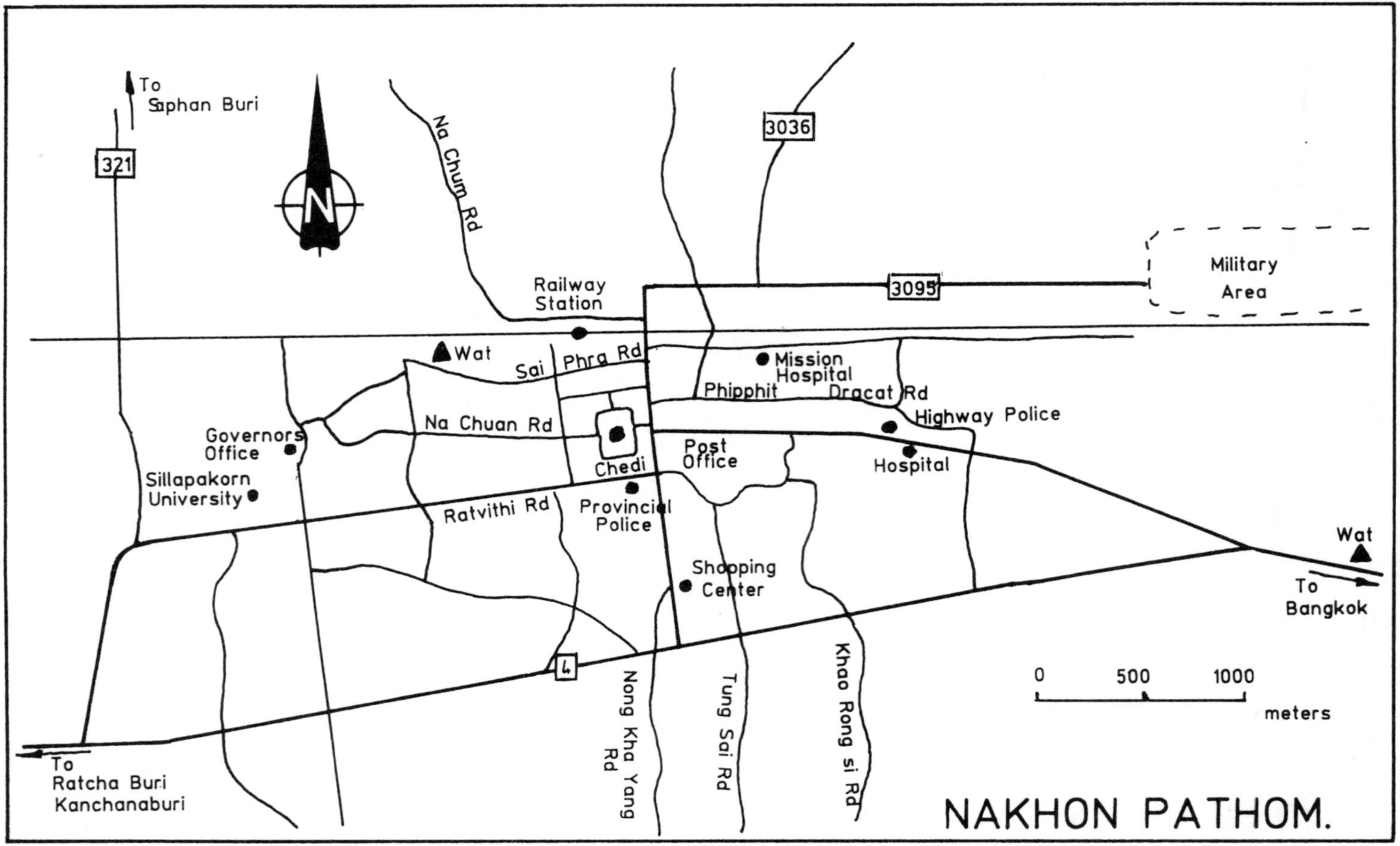
To
Saphan Buri
321
Na Chum Rd
3036
Military
Area
3095
Railway
Station
Wat
Sai Phra Rd
Mission
Hospital
Phipphit Dracat Rd
Highway Police
Na Chuan Rd
Governors
Office
Sillapakorn
University
Chedi
Post
Office
Hospital
Ratvithi Rd
Provincial
Police
Shopping
Center
Wat
To
Bangkok
4
Nong Kha Yang
Rd
Tung Sai Rd
Khao Rong si Rd
0
500
1000
meters
To
Ratcha Buri
Kanchanaburi
NAKHON PATHOM.

The trip back to Bangkok can be made in 3 1/2 hours from here following Route 4 through Hua Hin and Phetchaburi. This time, continue along Route 4 after the junction with Route 35, through **Ratchaburi** until you eventually reach Route 323. If you turn right at this point (still on Route 4) you will return to Bangkok. If you turn left, Route 323 takes you to Kanchanaburi and the River Kwai.

GO WEST

In a direct line, the Burmese border is only 120 kilometers west of Bangkok. However, there is no road connection and no crossing points. There is, however, very interesting country west of the capital and a few tourist sights that should not be missed.

The two major centers are Nakhon Pathom (about 60km) and Kanchanaburi (about 130km). Regular coaches and trains operate to both. If you are travelling by rental car or motorcycle you leave Bangkok on either Route 4 or 338. These two roads join about halfway to **Nakhon Pathom.** This was the center of a kingdom that flourished from about the sixth to the eleventh centuries A.D., but it is believed the town was occupied from at least the third century B.C. Nakhon Pathom is thus regarded as the oldest city in Thailand.

The major attraction today is the famous **Phra Pathom Chedi,** the tallest Buddhist monument in the world. The 127-meters-high "handbell" towers over the town and is most impressive. The present structure has been built over at least three other structures which span fifteen centuries. It is set in a park on a huge circular terrace, and even though Route 4 does not pass directly by, you cannot miss it. Small bell towers encircle a round pavilion which, in turn, encircles the chedi. Four chapels are built into the pavilion at the four points of the compass.

Each November, the chedi is the site of a three-day fair. Part market, part amusement park, the fair has stalls, temporary restaurants, sideshows, fortune tellers, freak shows, folk dancers, exhibitions, and so on which provide opportunity for merit-making and fun for everyone. If you plan to stay here you should consider staying at the **Rose Garden Resort** (Tel. 311-171). It is some 20 kilometers out of town but provides by far the best accommodation in the area. Room rates start at B1000. (Reservations with the hotel at 21 Mu 2, Sam Phran, Nakhon Pathom 73110; Fax: 662-253-2625.) In town, rooms are available at the **Mit Phaisan Hotel** (Tel. 242-422) from B100 a night. Useful telephone numbers in town are Police, Tel. 242-794; Hospital, Tel. 251-551; Railway Station, Tel. 242-305; and Bus Station, Tel. 242-214.

The fast divided road continues west and after about 10 kilometers, Route 4 bears left while Route 323 continues west to **Kanchanaburi.** This town was

Bridge on the River Kwai.

established by Rama I as a first line of defense against a possible Burmese invasion, but it was the Japanese 150 years later who brought fame to the town. During World War II, the Japanese used Allied prisoners of war and local labor to build the infamous Death Railway. It is estimated that 16,000 prisoners of war and 100,000 local laborers lost their lives through beatings, starvation, disease, and exhaustion when constructing the railroad. It will forever be a shame on the Japanese nation.

The story was told in the book by Pierre Boulle, *The Bridge Over the River Kwai*, and later made into a movie. The bridge is still there and so are the graves of the soldiers. It is hard not to be moved by a visit. Shortly before the end of the war British bombers managed to destroy three spans of the bridge. No attempt was made to match the original spans when the bridge was rebuilt but today the railway is operating once again.

The bridge is about 5 kilometers west of the town center and can be reached by songthaew. It will cost about B5 to get there. At the bridge there are several steam engines and other miscellanea, a number of fair restaurants, souvenir shops, and a reasonable viewpoint. A footbridge between the rails has been provided so that you can walk across the railway bridge. At times it is crowded. This is particularly so during the River Kwai Bridge Week (see Section 8), when there is a nightly light and sound show at the bridge. At this time it is very difficult to find accommodation. At other times it is not too bad because most foreigners visit Kanchanaburi on a day trip from Bangkok.

The Tourism Authority of Thailand has a branch office on the main street of Kanchanaburi (Tel. 511-200), with a small selection of literature and a fair map. Don't try to find out about accommodation though, because the personnel believe all foreigners want airconditioned accommodation in the center of town. In fact this is just what I did not want. Nevertheless, I ended up in the expensive **River Kwai Hotel** (Tel. 511-269) because the TAT man convinced me there was nothing else worth considering. One night was enough. High price, average rooms, poor service, and an offhanded attitude saw me happy to leave the next morning.

I then found the delightful river-fronting **Prasopsuk Garden Resort** (Tel. 513-215) and could have happily stayed there for a week. At B400 it was a good value. The resort has lovely gardens and a delightful floating bar and restaurant where you sit Thai-style on the floor. I'll be back for more. (Reservations with the resort at 6/1 Gaeng Seant Village, Patthana Street, Kanchanaburi 71000.) I have not seen the **Kasem Island Resort** (Tel. 511-603) on an island just south of town but it has a good reputation and prices from B600.

In town, the **Kanchanaburi War Cemetery** contains the remains of almost 7,000 prisoners and the **Chong-kai War Cemetery** across the river contains another 1,750. Both of these cemeteries are run by the Commonwealth War

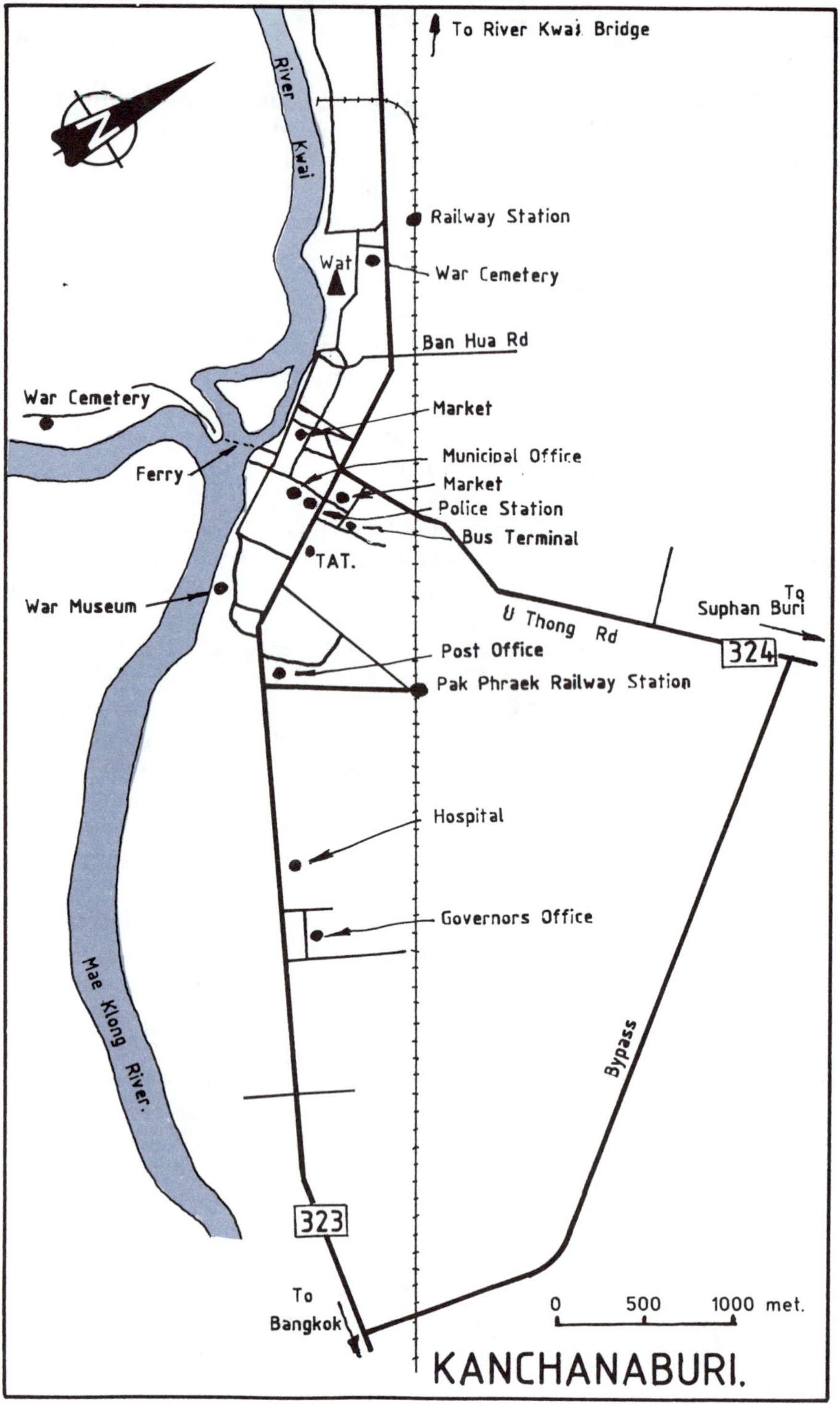

L.R. Copyright.

Graves Commission. They are well kept, there are permanent attendants, and they rarely fail to move the many visitors who stop to look.

It's strange how places affect different people. I had been told that Kanchanaburi had a delightful atmosphere and friendly people. On three visits I have yet to come to this conclusion myself. I'm always happier when I am away from the town.

My favorite trip is to **Erawan Falls,** about 70km northwest of Kanchanaburi. The falls are situated within a national park and they consist of a series of rapids and falls which provide great opportunities for picnics, relaxing, and swimming. To reach the higher falls you need a pair of sneakers and good stamina but even if you only visit the first two or three, you will soon realize this is a delightful spot. Buses operate from Kanchanaburi and there are restaurants at the car park nearest the falls. After visiting Erawan Falls, if you have your own transportation, you should go a few kilometers farther along the main road to the top of **Sri Nakharin Dam** for a great view of the valley and a modern hydro-electric facility. The road continues to **Si Sawat** and around the lakeside there are several raft resorts offering meals and accommodation.

There are several other touring options. Route 323 crosses the River Kwai a few kilometers upstream from the rail bridge. This road goes for 60 kilometers to **Namtok,** which is now the end of the railway, then another 90 kilometers to **Thongphraphum,** and eventually a further 80 kilometers to **Sangkhlaburi.** There are various caves, waterfalls, and raft resorts along this stretch of road and river. Some of the resorts are fairly basic while others are modern with good facilities. Perhaps the best is the **River Kwai Village Hotel** (Tel. 251-7532), 60 rooms. This is a hotel rather than a raft, but it is surrounded by forests and waterfalls. The hotel organizes trips to local points of interest.

A recent development has been the opening up of the Hell Fire project which commemorates the prisoners of war who died while constructing some of the most difficult sections of the Death Railway. Visitors can walk along a trail which follows the old railway through Konyu cutting. The site is about 80 kilometers from Kanchanaburi on Route 323.

A further alternative is to travel north from Kanchanaburi to **Ban Nong Pru** (95 kilometers) and then visit the **Than Tarn-lod National Park.** The park has beautiful caves and good waterfalls.

Back in town a visit should be made to the **Jeath Museum.** As you enter a notice tells you that "Death" sounded too horrific so it was decided the museum would be named using the initials of the nations largely involved with the railway—Japan, England, Australia, Thailand, and Holland. There is a replica bamboo hut similar to those that were used for housing the Death Railway workers, which contains photographs and paintings from the period. There are some weapons and other war memorabilia.

Damnern Saduak floating market.

Special trains run from Bangkok on Saturdays, Sundays, and holidays. These leave Bangkok at 6:15 A.M., stop at Nakhon Pathom for 40 minutes, stop at the River Kwai Bridge for 30 minutes, then proceed along the Death Railway to Namtok. A three-hour stop here enables you to have lunch and visit local sights. Then, on the return journey, a 45-minute stop is made in Kanchanaburi to visit the War Cemetery. The train arrives back in Bangkok at 7:30 P.M. If you enjoy trains and your time is short, this is an ideal way to "go west" in one day.

Useful telephone numbers in Kanchanaburi are: Police, Tel. 511-562; Hospital, Tel. 511-233; Railway Station, Tel. 511-285; Bus Station, Tel. 511-182.

7. Guided Tours

Many different companies operate half-day and one-day tours in Bangkok. If you are on a group tour, your tour company will have made arrangements with a particular operator. If you book through your hotel, they will have an arrangement with some operator. In neither case do you have much say in it. For some people this is of no concern but for those watching the budget, generally the companies that are not in league with the major hotels will be cheaper than those that are. At the same time there is no guarantee that they will be as good. As with most things, it's best to make a few local inquiries. Most companies make hotel pickups and almost all travel agencies offer tours. You could check prices and availability with **Major Home Travel Agency** (Tel. 250-1685) or **Touch of Travel Agency** (Tel. 279-8869) as well as the agency in your hotel.

The half-day **Grand Palace Tour** is by far the most popular tour. This operates daily both morning and afternoon. It visits the palace grounds and the Temple of the Emerald Buddha. Afterwards you are likely to visit a shop with "wholesale" prices where a free drink encourages passengers to look and perhaps buy. At B300-B350, this tour is highly priced by Bangkok standards. But nevertheless, if you are doing your sightseeing by tour, this is a "must."

The half-day **Temples Tour** is interesting. This will visit three or four city temples other than the Temple of the Emerald Buddha. In the process it will take you through several different areas of the city. Unfortunately, because it is on the other side of the river, the Temple of Dawn is never included. The operator will select from Wat Po, Wat Sakhet, Wat Benchamabopit, Wat Raajanadda, and Wat Traimit (with its 5-ton solid gold Buddha). Cost is about B250.

The **Floating Market Tour**, departing at 7 A.M. and returning by 11 A.M., is probably only for those who cannot afford a full day to travel to the much better floating market at Damnern Saduak. The half-day tour explores some of the canals off the Chao Phraya River in Thonburi. I believe it is a tour filled with interesting sights but don't expect too much frenzied market activity. A stop is made at the Temple of Dawn on the way back. Cost is B250.

The full-day **Damnern Saduak and Rose Garden Tour** is one I strongly recommend to first-time visitors to Thailand. This tour gives a varied look into many aspects of Thai life. It visits an upcountry floating market about 100 kilometers from Bangkok which is less affected by modern influences than those near the city. It shows you the huge chedi at Nakorn Pathom (the country's largest), gives you lunch on a floating restaurant, and visits the Rose Garden to see the Thai Village show. In the process it takes you through a variety of industrial, residential, and rural countryside and you see how modern Bangkok is encroaching on once remote fields and villages. The tour will cost B600-700. There is a half-day afternoon **Rose Garden Tour** which costs B300-350.

Another tour that I recommend is the **Rice Barge Cruise.** This departs mid-afternoon and returns in the early evening. You have a thrilling ride in a long-tail boat along rural canals before stopping to visit several farmers' homes. You then board a converted rice barge and travel slowly along a broad canal, watching life on the banks and in small communities. The countryside takes on a different appearance as the sun sinks low in the sky.

There is an evening **Thai Dinner and Classical Dance Tour.** This visits a restaurant which serves a typical Thai dinner, then afterwards you watch performances of Thai classical dances (see Section 5). Costs vary depending on which restaurant is visited but typical prices are B350-400.

One of my favorite tours is the whole-day **Ayutthaya Tour** by coach and boat. Ayutthaya (see Section 6) is a former capital of Thailand where only magnificent ruins remain. The tour can be done boat first or coach first. I strongly recommend coach first. You travel 90 kilometers north to Ayutthaya (1 1/2 hours), then spend some time visiting the major ruins. About midday you travel a short distance back towards Bangkok, then divert into the old Royal Summer Palace at Bang Pa-In. There is time for a quick look around this fascinating complex before you are taken to the airconditioned river cruisers *Oriental Queen* and *Orchid Queen* for lunch and a leisurely three hours back to Bangkok. The B750-800 cost is worth paying. This tour departs from and returns to the Oriental Hotel. A very similar tour commenced in 1990 from the Shangri-La Hotel using the newly constructed luxury *Ayutthaya Princess*. The fully airconditioned cruiser can accommodate 200 passengers and departs daily.

For those with a little more time, **Asia Voyages** (Tel. 235-4100) has a 1 1/2-day tour to Ayutthaya aboard a converted rice barge named the *Mekhala*. The luxury vessel, which has six airconditioned cabins with attached bathrooms, departs Bangkok at 3 P.M. and overnights at riverside Wat Kai

Tia. The next morning *Mekhala* reaches Bang Pa-In and passengers visit Ayutthaya by long-tail boat and return to Bangkok by minibus. Cost is about B3000 per person.

Some companies offer a **Pattaya Day Tour**. Pattaya is a bustling seaside resort about two hours from Bangkok. When you reach there, you are taken by boat to Coral Island for lunch and coral viewing. There is time for a swim or maybe parasailing or water skiing before you return to Bangkok.

Longer tours are on offer. You can visit Kanchanaburi and the Bridge over the River Kwai (two days) or Chiang Mai (three or more days). Tour companies also have air/land tours to Phuket, Chiang Mai, Ko Samui, and other destinations.

8. Culture

Cultural activities in Thailand are rarely far removed from Buddhism or royalty. It is difficult for Westerners to understand just how powerful a role these two symbols play in Thai life. Suffice it to say that in almost two decades I have never heard one Thai seriously criticize either.

The best way for a foreign visitor to see genuine Thai culture is to participate in one of the country's festivals, which are held with such grace and elegance. Whether it's a parade of floral floats or beauty queens, a ploughing of the soil to mark the start of the rice-planting season, or a thundering of elephants across a field, it's all done with great panache.

This single event brings people, place, and history together in a colorful occasion that can be a highlight of any visit. The following events can be enjoyed by anyone visiting Bangkok at the appropriate time of the year.

New Year's Day is a public holiday in Thailand. This provides a good excuse for parades, religious ceremonies, and private get-togethers. These are not huge events but if you are in the city, it is worth asking the locals for advice on a good vantage point. You may even find yourself invited to a private party. Take along a bottle of local "whiskey" and you will be very popular.

The **Phra Nakon Khiri Fair** is held in the old city of Phetchaburi, about two hours' drive southwest of Bangkok. The city is overlooked by Phra Nakon Khiri (City on the Mount), a hill on which there are a number of religious shrines and temples and a fine nineteenth-century palace. An historical light and sound presentation, street stalls, dancing, firecrackers, and parades are all part of this popular fair held for six days early February.

Makha Puja is a national holiday and important Buddhist holy day. This celebrates the occasion when 1,250 of Buddha's disciples gathered without pre-arrangement to hear him preach. Merit-making, such as offering food to monks and freeing captive birds, is interspersed with sermons throughout the day. After sunset, monks lead candlelight parades which circle Buddhist chapels throughout the country. Each participant silently carries flowers, glowing incense, and candles in homage to the Buddha. The festival is held in late February on the full-moon night of the lunar month.

The **Phra Buddha Bat Fair** is held in mid-March near Saraburi, about 1 1/2 hours northeast of Bangkok. The Shrine of the Buddha's Footprint—Phra Phuttabaht—is one of the most sacred places in Thailand. The large "footprint" has been encased in gold and is on view in the main building of the seventeenth-century shrine. Large numbers of Buddhist pilgrims come to the shrine during the seven-day event which also features folk music performances, dance dramas, and a lively bazaar selling some excellent handicrafts.

Chakri Day, April 6, is a national holiday celebrating the establishment of Bangkok as the Thai capital. This occurred in 1782, when King Rama I, the first king of the current Chakri dynasty, moved from Thonburi to Bangkok. This day honors the king with parades and floral tributes.

The **Songkran Festival** (April 13-15) is something most Thais look forward to for weeks. This is a three-day national holiday to coincide with the old Thai New Year. Celebrations occur nationwide but are taken to their peak in Chiang Mai in northern Thailand. This is a time for wearing casual wash and wear clothes, because if you venture out on the streets you are guaranteed to get wet. An old tradition of sprinkling water on Buddha images and on the hands of elders has, over the years, turned into the tossing of bowlfuls of water on everyone. Visitors won't escape dry, but it's considered an honor to be soaked. Fortunately this is the peak of the hot, dry season.

In Bangkok, the festivities begin with the parading of the Phra Buddha Sihing on the parade ground outside the Grand Palace. Then it rapidly turns into a "wet" event. In Phra Pradaeng district of Samut Prakan province on the southern outskirts of Bangkok, a large community of Mon people, some of Thailand's earliest settlers, celebrate with a thorough cleaning of the house, religious observances, and colorful parades.

The **Sweet Grape Fair** is held in the area around the famous floating market at Damnern Saduak (see Section 7), some 100 kilometers southwest of Bangkok. This is a typical rural fair featuring displays, a beauty competition, parades, and folk art. It is held in late April.

The **Royal Ploughing Ceremony** is held on a moveable date in the early part of May. This ancient Brahman ritual celebrates the official commencement of the rice-planting season and is held at Sanam Luang outside the Grand Palace. It is said that this ceremony can be traced back more than 3,000 years to the time of Buddha. It was once regarded as a signal that it was the auspicious date to start ploughing for the new rice crop. Even today it is seen as a reliable indicator of what sort of year it will be for crops and rainfall. Colorful costumes are worn by the participants, and there is drumming, chanting, and conch-shell blowing. Then rice seed is scattered so that people can collect a few grains to plant with their own crops to ensure a good yield, or tuck into their pockets to attract money.

Visakhaa Bucha is a national holiday held on the full-moon day in May. This is the holiest of all Buddhist days, marking the birth, enlightenment, and death of the Buddha. Temples throughout the country are crowded with people who listen to sermons by several monks. In the evening there is a solemn candlelight procession around the main monastery buildings. Merit making happens in a similar way to Makha Puja.

The **Thailand International Swan-Boat Races** is an event which was first staged in 1988 but it is set to become an increasingly important sporting event for the capital. It is held on the Chao Phraya River near the Rama IX Bridge. Competitors from several countries take part in the races and there is a procession of decorated boats, displays, handicrafts sales, and cultural shows. The races are held in the last week of June.

Tak Bat Dok Mai is a merit-making festival held in mid-July at Saraburi. This coincides with the start of the annual three-month Rains Retreat when Buddhist monks must remain in their monasteries. Young men are ordained for this period of study and meditation.

HM the Queen's Birthday Celebration (August 12) is a spectacular occasion. Throughout Thailand, public buildings are decorated to honor Queen Sirikit on her birthday. The most spectacular are in Bangkok, where government offices and streets are garlanded with colored lights like you have never seen before. Handicrafts are on sale in bazaar stalls set up for the occasion.

Ok Phansa is the end of the Buddhist lent and is a joyous occasion celebrated the day after the full-moon night in October. It also introduces the Kathin period when, throughout Thailand, the people present monks with new robes and other items deemed necessary for the monkhood's upkeep during the next year. Processions of gift-bearing people can be seen dancing their way to monasteries for the presentations.

Chulalongkorn Day (October 23) is a public holiday to commemorate popular King Chulalongkorn, Rama V. He is remembered in Bangkok on the anniversary of his death in 1910 with parades and the placing of flowers and incense at the foot of the equestrian statue at the end of Ratchadamnoen Nok Road.

Loi Krathong is perhaps Thailand's loveliest festival. It is held on the full-moon night of November and it sets rivers, canals, and ponds throughout the country alive with banana-leaf boats glittering with tiny flames from candles and incense. It is most spectacular. There are several large celebrations in Bangkok and the same thing happens throughout the country. A particularly impressive ceremony is held at Sukhothai, the old capital 350 kilometers north of Bangkok. Many temples also are the scenes of special festivities at this time and the Golden Mount Temple in Bangkok (see Section 6) and Phra Pathom Chedi in Nakhon Pathom (see Section 6) put on fairs and night bazaars.

The **Thailand Long Boat Racing Championships** are held during November at Bang Sai, about 80 kilometers north of Bangkok. Located on the Chao Phraya River not far from the ancient capital of Ayutthaya, the Bang Sai Arts and Crafts Center was set up by Her Majesty the Queen as a training center for artisans. On this day it is also the picturesque setting for festive boat races in which both local and foreign crews compete for trophies.

The **Royal Orchid Regatta** is an annual charity event in mid-November sponsored by the Royal Orchid Sheraton Hotel and other organizations. It brings together rowing teams from various parts of Thailand to compete in long boats on the Chao Phraya River. There are also demonstrations of precision parachute jumping by the Royal Thai Air Force.

River Kwai Bridge Week is held in late November-early December at Kanchanaburi, about two hours west of Bangkok. The bridge on the River Kwai is the setting for this series of events that include a light and sound presentation, archaeological and historical exhibitions, and rides on vintage trains.

Trooping of the Colors (December 3) is presided over by Their Majesties the King and Queen and is held in the Royal Plaza near the equestrian statue of King Chulalongkorn. Dressed in colorful uniforms, amid much pomp and ceremony, members of the elite Royal Guards swear allegiance to the king in a stirring ceremony.

HM the King's Birthday Celebration (December 5) is a great day to be in Bangkok. This is a national holiday and is the last major event for the year. The deep reverence felt by all Thais for their king is given public expression on this day. Government buildings, businesses, and homes all over the country are elaborately decorated with spectacular illuminations. Nighttime Bangkok, particularly around the Ratchadamnoen Nok Road-Grand Palace area, is a fairyland of colored lights unrivaled, in my experience, by anything else in the world.

If you cannot be in Bangkok during one of these festival times, all is not lost. A visit to the National Museum (see Section 6) will give you an insight into some aspects of Thai culture. Right next door is the **National Theater,** which has regular displays of traditional dramatic arts on weekends. Historic-mythical dramas are staged with instrumental and voice accompaniment in the main auditorium. Call 224-1342 to check performance details. There are popular performances most Saturday and Sunday afternoons which are social occasions for the Thais.

The **Siam Society** (Tel. 258-3491) on Sukhumvit Soi 21 (Soi Asoke) is a group under royal patronage, founded in 1904 to promote studies in the history, botany, zoology, anthropology, and linguistics of Thailand. The premises are open daily except Sunday and Monday and there are exhibitions of folk art and a reference library. One of the main attractions is a northern house dating from 1860 that was dismantled, brought to Bangkok, and reassembled in a garden compound.

The **Erawan Shrine** at the intersection of Rama I with Ratcha Damri Road is currently on the edge of a construction site for the new Hyatt Hotel and opposite the just completed World Trade Center. This is an important site for Thais where requests are made and devotional offerings promised. There is a small group of classical Thai dancers in traditional dress.

9. Sports

Thailand is a sports-minded country and most of the best facilities (except for water sports) are in or near Bangkok. You will find facilities for your favorite sport—tennis, golf, horse racing, fishing, shooting, soccer, bowling, and so forth. But you will also come across other sports which you may not know.

Thai boxing is undoubtedly the most spectacular of the local sports. This originated in the Ayutthaya period when it was transformed from a self-defense art into a spectator sport. Foreigners are bewildered by the strange rules and the apparent mayhem in the ring as boxers are permitted to use feet, knees, and elbows along with kicking and pushing. Before the fight starts the boxers go through an odd, slow-motion dance designed to show off their talents in stylized form. Each boxer has a different series of movements which is devoted to his guru as well as to the spirit of Thai boxing. This is done to the rhythm of a ringside musical orchestra of Thai oboe, cymbals, and drums. The musicians continue to play throughout the match and the volume and tempo of the music rises and falls depending on the action. The bout lasts for five three-minute rounds or until one boxer is injured.

There are two major boxing stadiums in Bangkok. The **Ratchadamnoen Stadium** is next to the TAT office and boxing takes place here on Mondays, Wednesdays, Thursdays, and Sundays starting at 6 P.M. The **Lumpini Stadium** on Rama IV Road opposite Lumpini Park operates Tuesdays, Fridays, and Saturdays. Visitors may be surprised to find that ringside seats cost B500 and up while the cheapest seats in the house will be about B150. Activity in the seating area is often as frenzied as in the ring with referee's decisions often strongly debated. There is also heavy gambling activity.

Horse racing also has a big following for the gambling element. There are two courses—the Royal Turf Club on Sri Ayudhya Road and the Royal Bangkok Sports Club on Henri Dunant Road. Races are held on Saturday and Sunday and both are easy to reach by public transportation.

Golf has become very popular among rich Thais and Thailand offers some of the best and challenging courses in Asia. Many of the clubs are

Thai boxing.

private but foreign visitors are welcome, particularly during the week when courses are far less crowded. Low labor costs in Thailand mean that clubs here can afford large ground staffs to maintain the fairways and greens in top condition. Most courses have clubhouses with restaurants, pro shops, and other sporting facilities. All the major courses have clubs, shoes, umbrellas, and other accessories for rent. Caddies, often beautiful but knowledgeable young girls, are almost universally used—golf carts are not. On many courses, ice-cold towels are provided every half-hour and strategically placed refreshment stalls allow you to quaff a cold beer to kill that thirst.

In the Bangkok area the best courses are probably **Navatanee** (Tel. 374-6127), the venue for the 23rd World Cup Tournament in 1975; **Krungthep Kritha** (Tel. 374-0491), also known as Huamak Golf Course and very popular with players with higher handicaps; and **Unico** (Tel. 377-9038), which has recently been upgraded. The **Railway Training Center** course (Tel. 271-0130), which was relandscaped for the 1987 Thai Open, is flat but has well-placed lakes and bunkers, and the **Rose Garden Course** (Tel. 374-6127) is arguably Thailand's most attractive course. Several new courses opened during the 1980s and, when fully mature, many of these will be magnificent facilities.

Bangkok has several driving ranges where players can exercise their swings. The best known are the **Huamak Range** on Ramkamhaeng Road and the **Soi 18 Range** at the end of Sukhumvit Soi 18. Of the hotels, the Oriental's Sports Center in Thonburi has a range and resident pro, while the Siam Intercontinental hotel has a floodlit 30-meter driving range and putting green.

Tennis facilities at the major hotels are good. Courts can be found at the Ambassador, Hilton, Central Plaza, Imperial, Indra Regent, Siam Intercontinental, and Menam hotels. Most of the golf and sports clubs also have facilities.

Health club facilities are even more prevalent so there is no excuse for visitors to go home flabby. The following major hotels have worthwhile facilities: the Airport, Asia, Hilton, Central Plaza, Rama Gardens, Royal Orchid Sheraton, Shangri-La, Menam, and Regent.

Kites are a sport most visitors will know little about but kite watching can be very enjoyable and relaxing. February to April is the kite-flying season and during this time visitors can see hundreds of them flying over Sanam Luang. Aerial battles occur between large "male" kites and smaller, faster "female" kites. These often involve teams of players, both young and old, trying to capture the opposing kite and drag it over into their territory.

Takraw is a simple demonstration of skill rather than a competitive sport but it is a joy to watch. A small ball of woven rattan is kicked back and forth or around in a circle. Players can use their bodies and feet but not their hands to keep it airborne.

10. Shopping

Bangkok is a treasure trove for shoppers. Thanks to a wide range of attractive locally produced goods available at reasonable prices, Thailand has become the best shopping destination for clothes, silk, silverware, leather goods, and certain handicrafts in all of Asia. It offers the convenience of browsing in modern, airconditioned malls as well as the thrill of discovering bargains in back-alley markets and out-of-the-way places known mainly by locals.

Bargaining is an art well established in Thailand. It is applicable in most shops and stalls except the fixed-price department stores. Generally shop owners will initially quote a price 20-30 percent above the one for which they will ultimately settle. Most Thai shopkeepers tend to be fairly honest, so if you enjoy the bargaining game while being polite and firm, you will get your purchase at about the right price.

Ask for receipts so that you can verify prices at customs when you arrive back home. When buying gems and antiques, ask for a certification of authenticity. If you can, buy from stores which display prominent Tourist Authority of Thailand signs on their doors.

Here are some of the better shopping buys in Bangkok:

Ready-to-wear clothes. This is a boom industry in Thailand which produces articles for export and local sale. The industry initially concentrated on T-shirts and jeans but recently there has emerged a full range of men's and women's clothing to meet international tastes. Boutiques sell genuine label products while cheaper versions are offered by vendors in most markets.

Custom tailoring. Frequent visitors to Bangkok arrive with only one change of clothes and an empty suitcase knowing that they can have clothes custom tailored at prices far less than most ready-made items back home. There are thousands of outlets which can produce almost anything you want in a matter of days. Twenty-four-hour tailoring is available but you are much better off allowing time for fittings so you can make alterations. Both locally made and imported materials are available.

Gems and jewelry. Exceptional bargains can be found in local rubies, sapphires, zircons, garnets, and turquoise. Bangkok has established a worldwide reputation for quality and artistic beauty so jewelry exports are now big business. Most shops have a wide selection of original items and can make others to specific designs supplied by the customer.

Gold and silver. Gold prices are fixed so the ultimate cost depends on the gold weight and the cost of the workmanship. Gold chains, earrings, bracelets, and pendants, all delicately handcrafted, are excellent buys. Most goldsmiths are still concentrated in Chinatown. Silver is also a good buy. Bangkok is good for fashion accessories while northern Thailand is better for bowls and tableware. Inexpensive silver is in abundance but the silver content can vary so you need to be careful when comparing prices.

Thai silk. This is justifiably famous throughout the world and few visitors leave without buying some of this handwoven fabric. Silk is available by the meter or made into clothing, place mats, neckties, scarves, and so on or to cover such souvenirs as notebooks, jewelry boxes, and cushions.

Thai cotton. This is also gaining a good reputation around the world because of its subtle texture and durability. It comes in a wide range of colors and prints and often comes adorned with delicate embroidery.

Bronze ware. High-quality bronze ware has long been a favorite for visiting shoppers. The craft is used to make bowls, cutlery, and striking figures ideal for home decorations.

Antiques and art objects. Most genuine antiques can only be taken out of the country with permission of the Fine Arts Department (see Section 10 of next chapter on Chiang Mai). Only buy in a shop that can provide the necessary documentation on pieces it offers. The best buys are probably wood carvings from the north, Chinese and Thai porcelains, and Burmese tapestries. Many shops offer paintings by Thai artists. These can be excellent buys and local framing is inexpensive and of high quality.

Leather goods. This craft has grown enormously in recent years and now jackets, footwear, belts, handbags, and various accessories are available in modern designs at very competitive prices. Leather clothing and shoes can be custom made in a number of places.

Because Bangkok shopping is spread out over many areas rather than concentrated at one central location, visitors may be restricted to the area close to their hotel or to one particular part of the city. Actually this is no problem because each area has a full range of facilities. The following areas are the most likely ones where visitors will be shopping. The specific shops mentioned are by no means the only recommended outlets and visitors should visit several shops before making a purchase.

The **Rama I Road/Phayathai Road** intersection is a major shopping area with a large department store, teeming emporiums with hundreds of shops, and one of Bangkok's largest food-shop complexes.

Major centers here include the Mah Boon Krong Center, which has the Tokyu department store and hundreds of shops and fast food outlets. This is a particular favorite of younger Thais. Then there is Siam Center, a well-known, multistoried, airconditioned shopping center with boutiques, souvenir shops, banks, and restaurants. Siam Square is a shopping area with a large number of ready-to-wear, textile, book, and sports shops plus clinics, restaurants, and several cinemas.

The following outlets have proved reliable:

Treasure Siam Co.—Rm. 306, Siam Center (silverware), 251-3597
Khanitha Ltd.—Siam Center (Thai silk), 251-2933

Krirk Optical—Mah Boon Krong Center
Nike (Thailand)—Siam Square (sports products), 252-4523
Bangkok Books—Siam Square, Soi 4, 251-6348
Maharajas Tailors—Siam Square, Soi 5, 251-6539
D. K. Books—Siam Square, 251-6335

Chinatown is the area centered on Yaowarat Road. This is undoubtedly the best area to buy gold and jewelry. The workmanship is excellent and the designs are creative. For those who are adventurous and love bargaining, there is a "thrift market" close by which has a huge range of goods. Here are a few suggestions:

Yoo Long Kim Kee—484 New Rd., 222-1427
Tang Toh Kang Co.—345 Venichi Rd., 224-2422
Seng Heng Tee—410 Yaowarat Rd., 224-2036
Liang Seng Heng—303 Yaowarat Rd., 224-8139

Silom-Surawong area is the most important business district in Bangkok. It is also a significant shopping area, particularly for jewelry, antiques, ceramics, leather products, and art objects. The area includes Robinsons Department Store in Silom Center, the Charn Issara Tower shopping complex, Jim Thompson silk, the Patpong night market, Silom Village, and the Central Department Store on Silom Road.

It is well worth checking out the two department stores. They often have specials on offer which are cheaper than you will find in the market street stalls. At the other end of the scale they have excellent ready-made clothing, shoes, and so forth.

The Patpong night market has developed into one of the best in Bangkok. This is a great place to buy cheap watches, cassettes, videos, T-shirts, jeans, and a variety of other goods. Prices are cheap; quality is fair.

I recommend the following:

Century Gems—328 Silom Rd., 233-6484
Chartered Gems—292 Silom Rd., 234-4376
Central Dept. Store—306 Silom Rd., 233-6930
Jim Thompson Silk—9 Surawong Rd., 234-4900
Robinsons Dept. Store—Silom Rd., 235-6708
Associated Lapidaries—Patpong 2 Rd. (gemstones), 233-9691
Nike—Silom Rd. (sportswear), 233-1544
Anita Thai Silk—294 Silom Rd., 234-2481
Design Thai—304 Silom Rd., 235-1553

The **Ratcha Damri/Phloenchit Road** intersection is currently undergoing major redevelopment but this is already a great shopping area. To the east is the Amarin Plaza shopping center and the huge Central Department Store. To the south is Galleries Lafayette and the Peninsula Arcade and to the north is Ratcha Damri Arcade and the Daimaru Department Store.

Just to the north of here is the amazing Pratunam market, which is reminiscent of a Middle Eastern bazaar with its covered alleys jam-packed with tiny shops overflowing with goods. This is a great area for ready-made clothing and leather goods.

Try these stores for starters:

Indra Siam Gems—Indra Center, Ratcha Prasap Rd., 251-1111
Peninsular Gems—Peninsula Plaza, Ratcha Damri Rd., 251-8211
Bangkok Dolls—85 Ratcha Prasap Rd., 245-3008
Central Dept. Store—1027 Phloenchit Rd., 245-3243
House of Handicrafts—36 Amarin Plaza, 256-9732
La Grace Ltd.—502 Amarin Plaza (silk), 251-0711

Sukhumvit Road has numerous hotels, apartments, guesthouses, and restaurants so it's no surprise to find that this is a good shopping area catering to the visitor. This area has perhaps the greatest concentration of tailors in the city but almost everything else can also be found here. Here are some suggestions:

Pop's Fashion—Sukhumvit, Soi 11 (tailor), 253-4798
President Tailors—Sukhumvit, Soi 11, 255-4237
Euro Fashion—Sukhumvit, Soi 4, 251-8563
Siam Antique—Sukhumvit, Soi 11, 253-5296
International Jewelry—Sukhumvit, Soi 1, 251-1584
T. Shinawatra—Sukhumvit, Soi 23 (silk), 258-0295
High Art—875 Sukhumvit Rd., 258-7787
Asia Books—221 Sukhumvit Rd., 252-7277

Chao Phraya River Area encompasses the large, modern River City shopping complex, the New Road area, and the shopping areas around the Oriental and Shangri-La hotels. River City is one of the best places in the city to buy antiques and decorative articles, while other shops in the area have a wide range of other goods.

These outlets are worth trying:

Honey Fashion—1132 New Rd. (tailor), 233-8625
You Lim Gems—1180 New Rd., 234-0422
Exceptional Gems—261 River City, 235-2970
Lin Oriental Gems—Soi Oriental, Charoen Krung Rd., 233-0904
Bogies Thai Silk—Soi Oriental, Charoen Krung Rd., 234-0419

Banglampoo is one of the city's largest retail centers for top-quality ready-made garments. There are several department stores and countless small outlets selling leather goods and other products.

Victory Monument is an area frequented by few visitors but there are good shopping facilities much used by Thais.

The **TAT Duty Free Shop** was opened at 888 Ploenchit Rd., central Bangkok, in 1990. The shop carries a wide range of international brand names and various local Thai products and handicrafts. All products sold are accompanied by the shop's guarantee of authenticity.

11. Entertainment and Nightlife

By now you will know that Bangkok has plenty to occupy most people during the sunlight hours. To make certain you have plenty to do, here are three more suggestions.

Siam Park is a gigantic fun park in the Bangkapi area some 20 kilometers northeast of the central city. The main attractions are an immense artificial lake with man-made waves, a series of water slides and swimming channels, and some exciting rides including a looping roller coaster. The area is a bit run-down but it's a good place for the young-at-heart. Admission is B100.

Magic Land (or "Dan Neramit" in Thai) is a large fun park on Paholyothin Road about 20 kilometers north of the central city. There are amusement rides for the kids, some more hair-raising rides for the adventurous, and a number of fast-food outlets.

The Planetarium, on Sukhumvit Road next to the Eastern Bus Terminal, and the nearby Science Museum provide a few hours' fun for those so inclined. Unfortunately there is little description in English and the commentary is in Thai.

As the sun sets, the bright flashing neon signs appear on hundreds of night spots around the city. It is difficult to write about Bangkok nightlife because its reputation precedes me. Unfortunately what is "known" about the nightlife is a series of half-truths, caused by sensational writing and a total lack of understanding of the Thai spirit of "sanuk" or fun.

Night spots are scattered throughout the city and many are patronized solely by Thais. Western tourists tend to stick to certain areas where English is spoken and where they are made especially welcome. For first-time visitors there is plenty in these areas to keep you satisfied for weeks. Nighttime activities can be more or less classified into discos, cocktail lounges, beer bars, live band pubs and clubs, go-go bars, massage parlors, and coffee shops.

Discos may be the same in most parts of the world but some in Bangkok are different. The **Nasa Spacedrome** (Tel. 314-3368) on Ramkamhaeng Road, some 15 kilometers east of the central city, is claimed to be the world's largest discotheque. You haven't seen anything quite like it. Because of its

Dickens Pub.

more central location, **The Palace** (Tel. 270-0302) on the airport road claims to be the most popular discotheque in the city. **The Paradise** (Tel. 433-4965) on Arunamarin is another with an amazing light and sound system. Of the hotel discos, I believe that **Bubbles** (Tel. 233-1130) at the Dusit Thani, **Diana's** (Tel. 236-0400) at the Oriental, **Talk of the Town** (Tel. 236-7777) at the Shangri-La, and **Flamingo** (Tel. 251-0404) at the Ambassador are the best. Most discos operate a cover charge that generally includes the first two drinks and admission.

Cocktail lounges are a popular feature of Bangkok's nightlife. Unfortunately it is not immediately clear what you are getting when you see the words "cocktail lounge." Some of these spots have soft music, gentle lighting, and your favorite cocktail; others are expensive, sophisticated places with dancing and hostesses. The ones in the major hotels are drinking places with music, while some others are gay bars, go-go bars, and bars with shows. My recommendation would be to use the ones in the hotels and give the others a miss.

Beer bars—those open-air establishments much favored at the beach resorts—are not all that popular in the capital. They do exist, however, and there is a cluster of twenty or so behind the Night Bazaar opposite Sukhumvit Soi 1. There are more sophisticated German beer gardens on Sois 3, 7, 15, and 23 and the Singha Bier Haus on Soi Asoke, off Sukhumvit, is popular.

Live band pubs and clubs offer some of the best value in Bangkok. Some are in hotels, others are outside. Many have excellent music, a good atmosphere, and reasonable prices. The following are my recommendations.

Dickens Pub (Tel. 255-0444), Ambassador Hotel, Sukhumvit, is a great place for a quiet drink while listening to some of Bangkok's best groups and solo artists. Music starts in the early evening and goes late with each group playing for one hour. Most of the songs are in English.

The Basement (Tel. 233-1130), Dusit Thani Hotel, Rama IV, is a recent addition to the scene but it already succeeds with flair and atmosphere. **Blue Moon** (Tel. 253-7603), upstairs near the President Hotel on Phloenchit Road, has great rhythm and blues, rock, or jazz every night of the week from 8 P.M. **Milestone** (Tel. 253-7607) is almost directly opposite Blue Moon. This features some of the up and coming rock bands in the city. Opens 7 P.M. The **Glass** (Tel. 254-3566) is a great jazz and rock hangout in Soi 11 off Sukhumvit. Very popular with the Thai in-crowd.

Go-go bars are what gives Bangkok its great nightlife reputation. Those that cater to visitors are clustered in **Patpong roads 1 and 2** between Silom and Surawong roads, **Soi Cowboy** between Sukhumvit Soi 21 and 23, and **Nana Plaza** on Sukhumvit Soi 4. Together there are probably close to one hundred bars, each with ten to fifty go-go dancers and hostesses. It is quite an industry.

The go-go bars vary in atmosphere from raunchy to reasonably refined. At Patpong, stick to the street level bars if you are travelling with your mother-in-law. The atmosphere in most of the bars is noisy, happy, and friendly. If you are a single male you will be joined by one of the hostesses who will talk to you and try to get you to buy her a drink. When business is slow, you may find yourself with several ladies. In most bars, if you indicate you want to be alone, you will not be hassled. Show some interest in a companion and you will be well looked after.

These bars change ownership and atmosphere regularly so it's impossible to give recommendations. The best way is to walk in, see the atmosphere, then walk out before ordering if you don't like what you see. This is quite acceptable behavior and will cause no problem.

Some of the upstairs bars have "special shows" which are occasionally raided by police. You take your chances with these.

Massage parlors have a dubious reputation in the West and you will find some similar facilities in Bangkok. In addition though, you will find ancient massage parlors which will give you a healing art massage in the tradition that is centuries old, and other modern massage parlors where a young masseuse will bathe and rub your body in the gentlest of ways. Many massage parlors cater to ladies as well as men and some even provide private rooms for couples. Rates vary from B150 to B300 per hour depending on the establishment. A body massage—which implies the masseuse uses her whole body rather than just her hands—will cost you something like B500-B800 for two hours.

In most massage parlors the masseuses sit together in a room behind glass, waiting to be selected by a customer. The whole process is degrading to some Westerners but it is not regarded that way by most Thais. It appears to be a system adopted even in small Thai towns where international tourism is totally unknown. The big parlors are **Atami** and **Mona Lisa** on New Phetchaburi Road, **Darling** and **James Bond** on Sukhumvit, and **La Cherie** on Surawong.

Coffee shops are not places where you drink coffee. They are establishments used by Thais to get drunk in the company of attentive hostesses. You can recognize them by their dark paint, colored flashing lights, and doorman out front. They are somewhat pointless to visitors as most people inside will not be able to speak English.

12. The Bangkok Address List

Airport—International Airport, Vibhavadi Rangsit Rd. (Tel. 531-0022).
Ambulance—Sri Ayutthaya Rd. (Tel. 246-0199).
American University Alumni Association—Tel. 252-4021.

British Council—Tel. 252-6136.
British Dispensary—109 Sukhumvit Rd. (Tel. 252-9179).
Bus Terminals—Northern & Northeastern lines, Phahonyothin Rd., Tel. 271-2379 or airconditioned Tel. 271-0101; Southern Line, Pinklao Nakhon Chaisi Rd., Tel. 434-5557 or airconditioned Tel. 435-1199; Eastern Line, Sukhumvit Rd., Tel. 391-2504 or airconditioned Tel. 391-3301.
Churches—Calvary Baptist Church (interdenominational), Tel. 251-8278; Christ Church (Anglican-Episcopalian), Tel. 234-3634; Holy Redeemer Catholic Church, Tel. 253-0305; International Church, Sukhumvit Rd., Tel. 253-2205.
Embassies—Australian, 37 S. Sathon Rd., Tel. 287-2680; British, 1031 Phloenchit Rd., Tel. 253-0191; Canadian, 138 Silom Rd., Tel. 234-1561; Malaysian, 35 Sathon Thai Rd., Tel. 286-1390; New Zealand, 93 Wireless Rd., Tel. 251-8165; Singapore, 129 Sathon Thai Rd., Tel. 286-2111; United States, 95 Wireless Rd., Tel. 252-5040.
Hospital—Chulalongkorn Hospital, Rama IV Rd. (Tel. 252-8181).
Immigration Office—Soi Suan Plu, Santhontai Rd. (Tel. 286-4231).
Lost Credit Cards—American Express, Tel. 253-8377; Diners Club, Tel. 233-5644; Mastercard/Visa, Tel. 252-2212.
Medical Center—Sukhumvit Medical Center, Soi 31 Sukhumvit Rd. (Tel. 258-0255).
Newspapers—*Bangkok Post*, Tel. 233-8030; *The Nation*, Tel. 392-0050.
Police—Tourist Police, Worachak Rd. (Tel. 221-6206).
Post Office—Central Post Office, New Rd. (Tel. 233-1050).
Railway Station—Rama IV Rd. (Tel. 223-7010).
Tourism Authority of Thailand—4 Ratchadamnoen Nok Rd. (Tel. 280-1305).

6

Chiang Mai and the North

1. The General Picture

Northern Thailand is a world apart from the Bangkok region. Stunning mountain scenery, exotic hilltribes, colorful festivals, ancient cities, and invigorating cool-season weather are just some of the attractions which make this region a "must" for every visitor's itinerary.

Bordered by Burma and Laos and characterized by forested mountains and fertile river valleys, the region encompasses part of the infamous Golden Triangle and was the cradle of Thai civilization.

Northern Thailand is dominated by Chiang Mai, Thailand's second largest city. Anyone expecting a smaller replica of Bangkok, however, will be very disappointed—the city is only one-tenth the size of the Thai capital and is quite unlike it in most respects. In the hot season thousands of orchids burst spectacularly into bloom, showering the city with shades of mauve and brilliant yellow. At other times of the year, the city is awash with the color and shape of every kind of fruit and flower imaginable.

Whereas Bangkok is 200 years old, Chiang Mai was founded in the thirteenth century and is one of the oldest continuously inhabited cities in Thailand. It was once the capital of Lanna, an independent Thai kingdom, and it has preserved many of its ancient temples, arts, and culture to give it unique charms. To see the city and surroundings from a high-flying aircraft or from atop a mountain peak is memorable. The sun reflects off hundreds

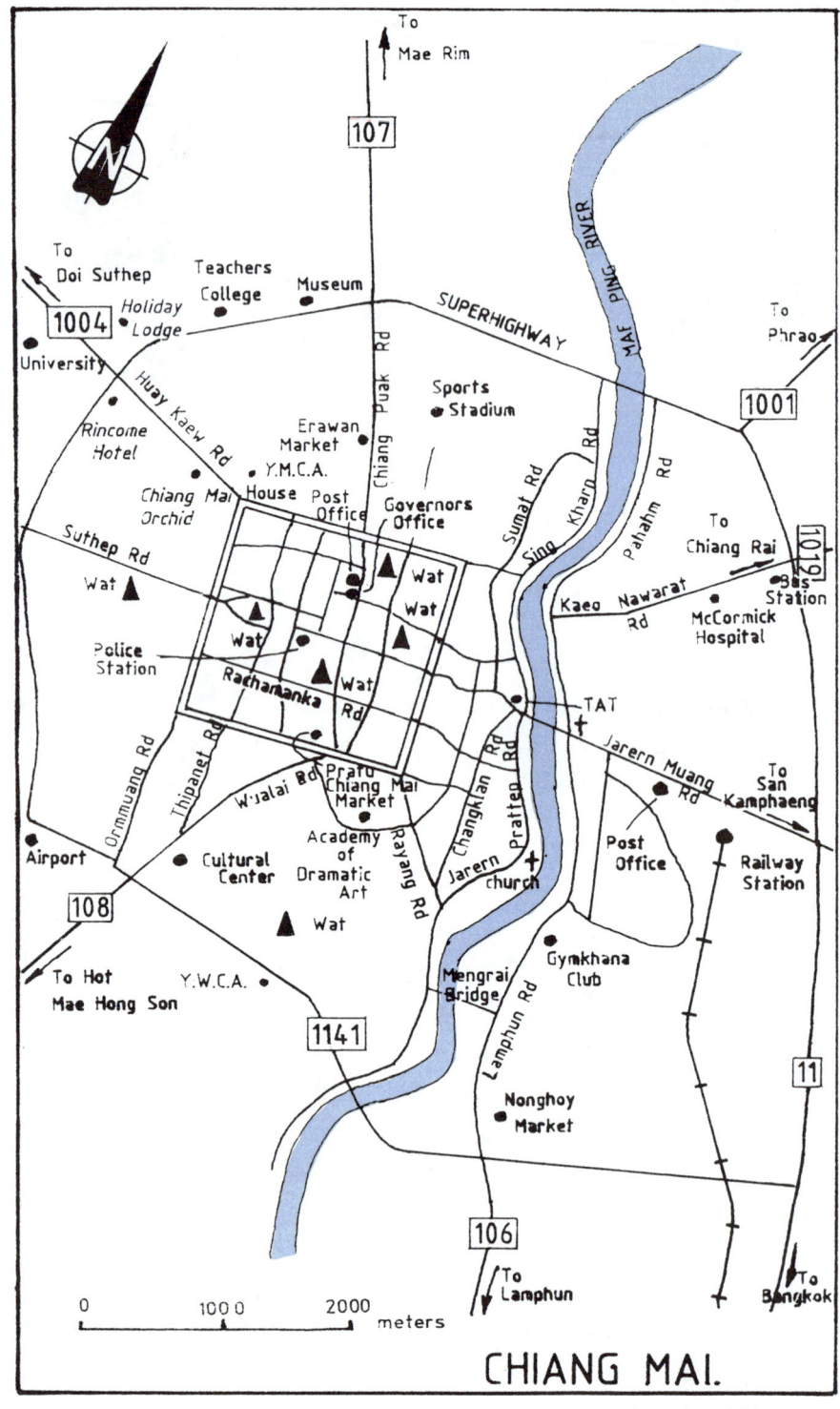

CHIANG MAI.

of steel-grey flooded ricefields with their small green islands crowded with wooden houses on stilts, and the gold and orange temple rooftops that appear as colorful freckles on the valley floor.

Chiang Mai is further characterized by being a major center for cottage industries. Numerous handicrafts are traditional to the region and craftsmen continue to produce silverware, lacquerware, shimmering silk and cotton, hand-painted umbrellas ablaze with color, pottery, and more. This somehow helps to produce a people who have a gentle, rather languid charm. Thai men have long admired the astonishingly beautiful girls with their pale, flawless skin, their bright eyes, and their silken voices.

Then there are the hilltribes. There are seven major tribes, each with its own distinct culture, religion, language, and dress style. These people maintain independent life-styles from each other and from mainstream Thais. They are a fascinating addition to the natural beauty of the region. You see them best when you trek this land of lost valleys, mysterious caves, and misty mountains. Distances have little meaning on these steep mountain slopes but each new ridgeline brings vistas to take your breath away.

2. Getting There

Thai Airways International has the occasional international flight into **Chiang Mai Airport,** however, most visitors will travel from Bangkok. Chiang Mai Airport is modern with good facilities and it is only about 4 kilometers from the city center.

There are currently seven jet flights a day in each direction between Bangkok and Chiang Mai. During the peak holiday season there are additional flights. A recent initiative has seen Chiang Mai linked with both Pattaya and Phuket with direct jet services. Chiang Mai is also the hub for a series of short regional flights which connect with Chiang Rai, Mae Hong Son, Nan, Mae Sot, Tak, and Khon Kaen. The Bangkok-Chiang Mai flight takes one hour. In Bangkok call 280-0070 for bookings and in Chiang Mai call 211-044.

Chiang Mai is the terminus for the northern **rail** line and overnight train travel from Bangkok is still popular. There are three levels of service: special express (12 hours), express (13 hours), and rapid (15 hours). The express is the only train to offer first-class airconditioned sleepers. It also has airconditioned and fan-only second-class sleepers. Most trains have a restaurant car. In Bangkok call 223-3762 for bookings and in Chiang Mai call State Railways of Thailand at 242-094. The station is about 2 kilometers from the city center.

Both airconditioned and non-airconditioned **buses** connect Bangkok with Chiang Mai. All public buses leave from Bangkok's northern bus terminal. Buses take from 8 1/2 to 12 hours for the trip depending on the route and type of service. Buses are cheaper than sleepers on the train but may not be as relaxing. In Chiang Mai all long-distance buses arrive and depart from the Arcade Bus Station on Kaeo Nawarat Road (Tel. 242-644).

There are also a variety of **private tour companies** which operate airconditioned buses to Chiang Mai from Bangkok. They leave from various places in Bangkok and usually offer a hotel pickup. The cost of these is more than on the public bus service and round-trip tickets are always cheaper than two one-way tickets. Bookings can be made at Bangkok hotels or travel agencies.

3. Local Transportation

Chiang Mai is not a large city and public transportation is good, but it pays to learn a few tricks to save time and money.

Don't wait on a street corner for a **taxi.** You could be there forever because Chiang Mai must be one of the few cities around that doesn't have conventional taxis. The nearest thing you get is a **"see-lor"** (literally, "four-wheel"), which is a communal taxi. These red pickup trucks with a canopy on the back collect as many passengers as they can, then drop each passenger off when their destination is reached.

To travel by see-lor, tell the driver where you wish to go. If he nods his head, board through the back and pay 5 baht per person when you get out. If he shakes his head, it means he is not going in your direction. If he asks, "How much will you pay me?" it means that he wasn't planning to go your way but could be persuaded to go if you offer him enough money.

Down-market from the see-lors are the **motorized samlors** (three wheels). While these have been popular in Bangkok and some other cities for quite awhile, they are a relatively new addition to the Chiang Mai scene. Many of the motorized-samlor drivers have come from Bangkok and they tend to be quite aggressive. Tourists are often charged far higher prices than locals so fix a price before you travel. Most fares should be in the 15-30 baht range. Be wary of those motorized samlors that park in front of the first-class hotels, if you are on a tight budget.

The most relaxed way to travel short distances within the city is by **bicycle samlor.** While these are a relic of the past, they are still very popular with the locals and are easy to find. In many cases you will ride with the samlor owner so you get more personal attention. With the motorized samlors and see-lors, the driver is almost always an employee of a large or family company.

It may seem strange but many drivers do not speak English, cannot read a map, and few know the names of streets in Chiang Mai. Local people often state their destination by naming a well-known nearby landmark. You can do the same by carrying a map which has hotels, wats, and other major features clearly shown. Just point to the landmark and at least you will end up close to where you plan to go.

For those visitors who want complete independence and for those travelling away from the city, a **rental car or motorcycle** can be a good investment. In most cases you will need either an international driver's license or a Thai license but some companies now accept foreign driver's licenses for short-term rentals.

Many travel agents handle car rental, or you can deal directly with the rental companies. These are some of the more reasonable companies:

AOD Car Rent—49 Changklan Rd., 249-197
A.T.M.—139 Changklan Rd., 251-213
Avis—14/14 Huay Kaew Rd., 221-316
Erawan—211/14-15 Changklan Rd., 236-548
Hertz—12/3 Loi Kroa Rd., 235-496
Inthanon—100/19 Huay Kaew Rd., 212-373
Suda Car Rent—18 Huay Kaew Rd., 210-030
Thanom Patanakhet—105/5 Phrapokklao Rd., 222-607

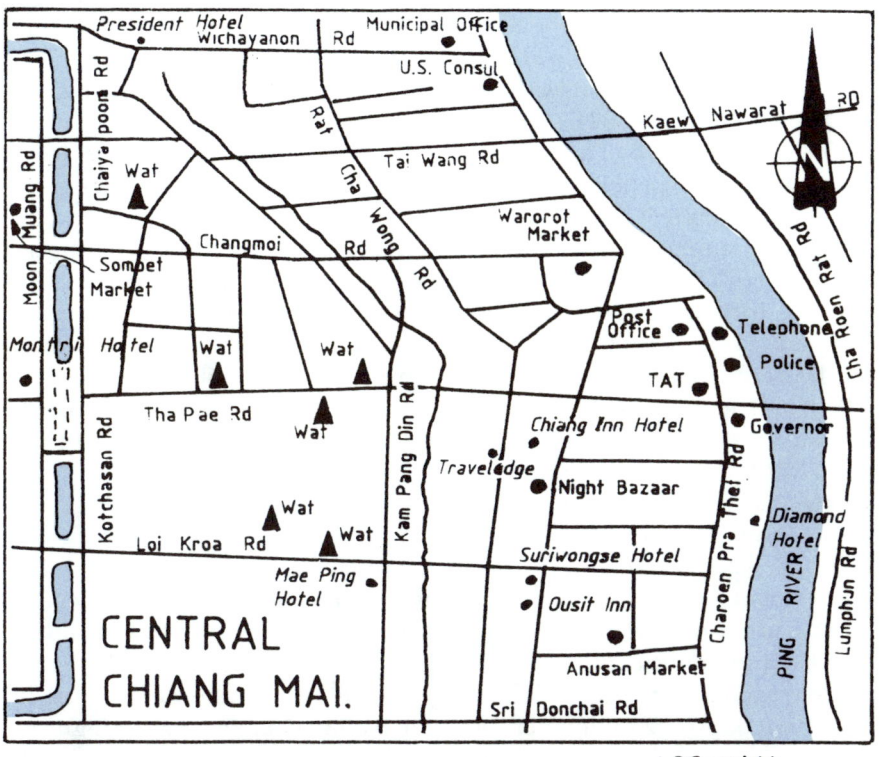

4. The Hotel Scene

Chiang Mai accommodation costs range from many thousand baht a night to a low of about B40. Because the city is much smaller than Bangkok, it is much easier to compare different offerings. You will certainly find that friendliness and service have little connection with price.

EXPENSIVE HOTELS

There are about ten major four- or five-star hotels in Chiang Mai. These are clustered in the area of the night bazaar or scattered throughout the other areas of the city. No one hotel dominates the city and which one you choose will depend on personal preferences.

After staying in most, my preference is for the **Novotel Suriwongse** (Tel. 236-733), 168 rooms, or the **Rincome Hotel** (Tel. 221-044), 158 rooms. The Novotel Suriwongse has a great central-city location just 100 meters from the night bazaar. At night this area really buzzes and the hotel gets into the same mood with lively bars and restaurants catering to guests and locals alike. The lobby is not spectacular but it is large, and there is a constant stream of people passing through. Rooms are adequate rather than lavish and the views are nothing to write home about. But the hotel has a pool and the usual features and a comfortable feel which I enjoy. The Suriwongse has rooms from B1400. (Reservations with the hotel at 110 Chang Klan Rd., Chiang Mai 50000; Fax: 6653-251-024.)

The Rincome Hotel appeals to me for entirely different reasons. It is a great place to relax because it is out of the hustle and bustle and has lovely grounds. If you feel like an afternoon in the sun you can relax around the biggest swimming pool in the city. If you feel like a game of tennis you can do that too. The large split-level lobby-lounge area is conducive to sipping a quiet drink by yourself or forming a party with friends. This is a sister property to the Airport Hotel in Bangkok and the Coral Beach at Phuket. Both the Rincome and the Novotel have good bars and restaurants and efficient, friendly service. Rincome rooms start at B1500 and rise to B5000. (Reservations with the hotel at 301 Huay Kaew Rd., Chiang Mai 50000; Fax: 6653-221-915.)

Here are some other night-bazaar area hotels worth considering. The **Dusit Inn** (Tel. 236-835), 198 rooms, at 112 Chang Klan Rd., Fax: (6653) 251-037, has two restaurants, two bars, a disco, and a swimming pool. It is right next door to the Suriwongse and is part of the Thai-owned Dusit chain. Rooms are from B1800. The **Chiang Inn Hotel** (Tel. 235-655), 170 rooms, 100 Chang Klan Rd., Fax: (6654) 234-299, with a restaurant, coffee shop, disco, swimming pool, and shopping arcade, is literally surrounded by nighttime activities. Rooms here are from B1400. Then there is the high-rise but slightly stark **Mae Ping Hotel** (Tel. 251-060), 374 rooms, from B1600, at 153 Sridonchai Rd., Fax: (6653) 251-069. All have good rooms and a choice of bars and restaurants. My experience with each of them is restricted to one visit but I have no complaints about the facilities or service.

If you arrive with a car or rent one locally, it could make sense to try one of the new hotels a few kilometers from the central-city area. On my most recent trip I checked out of the B2000-plus **Chiang Mai Orchid Hotel** (Tel. 221-625, with 250 rooms, restaurant, bar, disco, and pool) after two nights and found better and more friendly service at the **Chiang Mai Holiday Lodge** (Tel. 210-901), 66 rooms, at 16/16 Huay Kaew Rd., Fax: (6653) 210-905, for B500 a night. In fact I found the Holiday Lodge, which is basically a three-floor motel with very small rooms but with a good restaurant and pool, a real delight and I look forward to a return visit. It is a mid-market property with the attitude of a friendly luxury hotel.

MEDIUM-PRICE HOTELS

There is a wide range of tourist- and business-class hotels in the B400-800 category. Prominent among these are the **Chiangmai Travel Lodge** (Tel. 251-572), 40 rooms, near the night bazaar; the **Montri Hotel** (Tel. 211-070), 77 rooms, on the edge of the old city; the **Diamond Hotel** (Tel. 233-947), 145 rooms, near the river; and the **Y.M.C.A. International House** (Tel. 221-819), 57 rooms. Which would suit you best will depend on your own particular needs. The Travel Lodge or the Diamond would be best if shopping and nightlife are your thing. The Montri is better situated if you wish to explore the old city on foot. The Y.M.C.A. is the most modern of them all but is a little farther from downtown. If you have the time to come to grips with the transportation system, it doesn't really matter too much where you stay because it is quite easy to get to the place you are interested in.

BUDGET ACCOMMODATIONS

Down-market from here there are a vast number of small guesthouses which cater to foreigners. Prices range from B50 to about B300. Some have airconditioned rooms. Most have basic restaurants. For the young at heart these are a great meeting point, information center, and accommodation all rolled into one. It is impossible to make specific recommendations which I can absolutely guarantee because this market changes quite rapidly, but the following have either been inspected or come with a long-held reputation.

Candy House—1 Soi 4 Charoen Pra Thet Rd., 236-457
Chiang Mai Youth Hostel—31 Phrapokklao Rd., Soi 3, 212-863
Lek House—22 Chaiyapoom Rd.

Pornphan Court—20 Soi 8 Phrapokklao Rd., 211-423
Portobello House—191/1 Wungsingkhum Rd., 232-997
Top North—15 Moon Muang Rd., Soi 2, 213-900

5. Dining and Restaurants

Chiang Mai has an excellent range of restaurants but the northern region has not developed its own distinct menu to any great extent. Certainly there are a few local dishes which are a variation of Bangkok-style Thai food, and you can best sample these at a Khantoke (dinner show), but there is not the distinction that you find in the south or the northeast.

It is no surprise to find that the major hotels all have excellent restaurants. My choice from a good selection would be one of the following. **Fuang Fah** at the Novotel Suriwongse Hotel is a popular meeting place serving Thai and Western food in a casual atmosphere. Lovely Thai singers add a touch of glamor. The service is good and the staff friendly.

The **Jasmine** at the Dusit Inn is one of the best Chinese restaurants in town. It opens for lunch and dinner and serves dim sum and an excellent extensive menu. This is a very popular place for local Chinese to party, so that is probably the best recommendation you can get. **La Grillage** at the Chiang Inn Hotel serves a buffet lunch, then offers gourmet evening dining for those with a love for fine French food, light music, and good wine. Good Western food is hard to come by in many places in Thailand but in Chiang Mai this restaurant meets all requirements.

Le Pavillon at the Chiang Mai Orchid Hotel offers dinner with classical-guitar entertainment. This restaurant is renowned for chateaubriand. A complete contrast is provided at the **Rajawadee**, a waterfront restaurant at the smart Rim Ping Garden Hotel (Tel. 236-208), where the specialty is grilled pork knuckle with sauerkraut. It also offers a variety of Thai, Chinese, and Western favorites. Then there is the **Tong Kwow,** the lovely French restaurant at the Rincome Hotel which opens for lunch and dinner and provides live piano music as an accompaniment.

It is my belief, however, that you must eat outside the hotels to experience the true local flavor. In Chiang Mai, the opportunities are endless. I am sure that you will not be disappointed with any of the following, provided you understand the level and atmosphere aimed at by each restaurant.

For excellent Thai food in fairly basic surroundings you can do no better than **Aroon (Rai)** restaurant (Tel. 236-947) on Kotchasan Road overlooking the moat of the old city. The restaurant has been run since 1957 by Piejit and the food has remained basically the same—cheap, good, and straightforward. It's a popular place with locals and dishes start at B25. The success of this restaurant has drawn other establishments to this area and many are similar in style and price.

The **Baan Suan** (Tel. 242-116) on the Chiang Mai-San Kamphaeng Road, a few kilometers from town, is almost at the other end of the scale. Here tables are set out amid lawns and huge trees and the atmosphere is relaxed. This restaurant tends to cater to Western groups so the food is not necessarily great but the setting, particularly at night, is quite enchanting. If you are into romantic settings, this place is for you.

A further contrast is provided by **The Hill** (Tel. 222-614) on Bamsungburi Road near Buak Haat Park. Here you can combine good local food, an exotic atmosphere in a great setting, and live country music. The clientele here is mostly Thai, young, and progressive. It was one of the places I enjoyed most on my most recent stay in the north. I strongly recommend it to all young-at-heart travellers.

There is quite a large Western population in Chiang Mai and a major Western tourist market as well, so there are some excellent "European" restaurants. My favorite is probably **The Pub** (Tel. 211-550) on the Huay Koew Road, run by a Swiss engineer and his charming Thai wife. This was featured in *Newsweek* magazine in 1986 as one of the "world's best bars," which underplays the excellent menu and high standard of food. The restaurant is in a garden some way back from the road and is a bit hard to find but it is worth the effort. Another one not to miss is **The Chalet** (Tel. 236-810) at 71 Charoen Pra Thet Road, where French cuisine is served in a beautiful old northern teak mansion.

For something more casual, try the **German Beer Garden** (Tel. 236-179) at 48 Charoen Pra Thet Road, close to the night bazaar; **La Villa Pizzeria** (Tel. 215-403) on Ratchadamnern Road for pizza baked in a wood-fired oven by an Italian chef; **Dave's Cantina** (Tel. 223-021), Rajwithi Road, for Mexican food; or an old favorite, the **Riverside Restaurant** (Tel. 243-239) on Cha Roen Rat Road for a cozy setting with river views, good Thai and Western food, and live folk and country music.

Vegetarian, Thai, and Pakistani food is available at **The Whole Earth Restaurant** (Tel. 232-463) on Sri Donchai Road. This has the same owner as the Bangkok restaurant of the same name. It is in a nice setting, is always popular, and serves great fruit, yogurt, and honey smoothies which you should try.

Khantoke dinners are almost exclusively for foreign tourists but they provide a safe and simple way to experience some local food and culture. You sit on the floor (with pillows for support) and eat from a low, round, teak table. After dinner you will be offered a cigar made of ground tamarind bark, tobacco, and banana leaf. Try it, then watch the northern traditional dancers performing some of their amazing repertoire. You will long remember the beautiful girls, dressed in brilliant brocaded Thai silk costumes that shimmer and flash alluringly in the restaurant lights.

The best places to have a khantoke dinner are **The Old Chiangmai**

Cultural Center (Tel. 235-097) on Wualai Road near the airport or the **Diamond Hotel** (Tel. 234-155) near the night bazaar. Both dinners are priced at about B200. It is a fun-filled few hours that most people thoroughly enjoy.

6. Sightseeing

Chiang Mai is an old city with a proud history. It was founded by King Mengrai, who united several tribes, called the new kingdom Lanna Thai, and built a new capital between Doi Suthep Mountain and the Mae Ping River.

The new city was completed, then surrounded by a wall and a moat in 1296. It was the capital of Lanna Thai for a long time until it finally came under the control of Ayutthaya and then Burma. In 1774 King Taksin of Thailand recovered it from the Burmese and since then Chiang Mai has been a province of Thailand. This history is important for today's visitor, because it reveals that Chiang Mai has a long and significant past. It places great importance on Chiang Mai's wats and I believe these should be the starting point for any sightseeing.

There are many wats within the old city walls and at least three of these should be visited. Start at the city's oldest temple, **Wat Chiang Man**, on Ratchaphakhinai Road near the northeast corner of the old city. King Mengrai is believed to have lived here for some time. Unfortunately these days the doors of the main buildings are often locked, but the tiny crystal Buddha and the Sila Buddha are on display on Sundays. Both figures are believed to be at least one thousand years old.

Wat Chedi Luang, on Pra Poklan Road, is probably the most impressive temple for me. This has a huge chedi and there was formerly a massive pagoda. The big earthquake of 1545 caused considerable damage and the 90-meter-high chedi is just a remnant of its former glory. There is presently an appeal in progress to return it to its original height. Even in its ruined state it is extremely impressive. It is said that the Emerald Buddha, now in Bangkok, was housed here for eighty years.

Wat Phra Singh, on Sarnlarn Road in the west part of the old city, was started in 1345 when King Pha Yu constructed the large chedi to house the ashes of his father. Within the grounds there is much of interest. See the scripture repository which held delicate pages of scripture or folklore. It's the unusual-looking building on a high stucco-covered stone base. Look at the chapel walls to see murals illustrating Lanna customs and dress, and visit the lovely Lai Kam chapel, which houses the revered Phra Singh Buddha image.

Many visitors would be content with these three wats, but for enthusiasts, there are many more. A complete contrast is provided by **Wat Jed Jod** on the superhighway near the Chiang Mai Museum. Built in 1455, its name means "seven spires," which describes the chedi's construction. It was copied from the Mahabodi Temple in India, where Buddha achieved enlightenment. **Wat Koo Tao** near the sports stadium has a delightful, almost whimsical chedi constructed of five spheres all intricately decorated with pieces of colored porcelain. **Wat OO-Mong** was built in the fourteenth century in a forest close to the old city. A highly respected monk had to practice Lord Buddha's teachings in a peaceful environment, so King Mengrai built him this wat. Today it contains some interesting modern art by various monks who have resided there in recent years.

While wats give us a glimpse of yesterday, Thailand's markets are very much of today. Chiang Mai is an excellent city in which to explore markets. A few hours spent browsing through the stalls will provide visitors with an opportunity to experience a facet of daily Thai life completely different from anything in the West. There is a chance to sample local food and exotic fruits, to experience the aromas of oriental spices (and waste disposal systems), and admire the beauty of freshly cut flowers and freshly picked fruit and vegetables.

Warowot Market on Changklan Road, Chiang Mai's central and largest market, is frantic from 6 to 9 A.M. but is busy and colorful at any time of the day. Almost everything is available in the market or surrounding shops. The second floor has stalls selling clothing, shoes, and hilltribe articles at very reasonable prices but you must bargain hard. The escalator, incidentally, seems more often out of order than operable.

The Pratu Chiang Mai Market at the Chiang Mai Gate is convenient for visitors staying south of the old city. It is a busy neighborhood market with good prepared food both inside the market and in street stalls. At night the parking lot transforms into a large open-air restaurant.

The Sompet Market on Moon Muang Road serves the same purpose for visitors staying north of the old city. It has excellent fresh produce and fruits and very colorful flower stalls. Best times are early morning or early evening.

The Anusan Market off Changklan Road south of the night bazaar is not really a market, but an entire area of open-air restaurants and food stalls. It is an excellent place for very reasonably priced food and is very popular with locals and visitors "in the know."

Another major attraction for everyone is the **night bazaar** along Changklan Road. This market has an incredible variety of northern Thai goods, general rubbish, cheap clothing, and souvenirs at very low prices—if you bargain well. There are so many stalls selling the same type of goods that competition keeps prices low, so haggle seriously with vendors or you will get caught. Even if you are not in the mood to buy, it's a most interesting scene. Some say it's unfortunate that the whole area is becoming more organized and in some ways I must agree. Much of the old excitement and glamor is fading, but with crowd numbers increasing all the time, that was inevitable.

The Chiang Mai National Museum is on the superhighway north of the old city about 4 kilometers from downtown. There are a good selection of Buddha images in several styles, pottery, household items, and various other historic exhibits. Note that the museum is closed Mondays and Tuesdays and between noon and 1. Admission is B10.

Chiang Mai is surrounded by sightseeing attractions and for those with limited time there is a major problem in deciding which to visit. At the top of my list would be a trip out road No. 1004 to Doi Suthep. Five kilometers from town, **Chiang Mai University** is the first point of interest. The university is set in spacious grounds and you are welcome to drive around to see the various faculty buildings. Its Tribal Research Institute gathers information and studies Thailand's tribal people.

Next door, the **Chiang Mai Arboretum** has attractive landscaped gardens and a fitness park, while the adjacent **Chiang Mai Zoo** started out as a private collection but now belongs to the city. It is open 8-5 daily, for a B10 admission. You can catch a songthaew from here to Doi Suthep for B30. The road now immediately begins to climb past a statue of the monk Khruba Srivichai who, in 1934, initiated a plan to construct a hillside road to the monastery on Suthep Mountain.

Sixteen kilometers from town, **Wat Phrathat Doi Suthep** is a real attraction. From the parking area you reach the temple via a cable railway or up a serpent-flanked stairway of 300 steps. Be smart—go up by railway and walk down. The temple was built in 1383 and is a most holy place for Buddhists. Visitors are welcome to enter the pagoda and see the magnificent statues and paintings. It is an active wat so you will see several monks ministering to visitors. When the weather is clear there is also a great view of Chiang Mai city far below. Don't forget the camera.

The road continues some 7 kilometers farther on to **Bhubing Palace,** the royal winter palace, built in 1962. The air is wonderfully clear and the atmosphere is relaxed and easy. The palace grounds are open to the public on Fridays, Saturdays, Sundays, and holidays when the royal family is not in residence. The gardens are quite lovely but the buildings are unspectacular.

Ten more kilometers from here, the road leads to a **Meo hilltribe village.** For those who are visiting more remote villages, this is not particularly recommended because it is very "touristy." But for those with limited time it is an attraction. The village has an Opium Museum, which is not worth visiting, and a Hill-tribes Museum which falls into the same category. There are, however, spectacular views of rugged, forested mountains and adults and children in traditional dress selling souvenirs or going about their other business. Despite the commercial sophistication, in many ways the hilltribes still live traditional lives.

It is possible from here to travel on to **Samoeng**, then return to Chiang Mai via route 1096. This takes you through lovely country after you descend the steep road from the mountain. There are many resorts, which offer lunch, and other attractions that can easily fill in a half- or whole day.

The **Chiang Mai Resort** (Tel. 236-548) and the more expensive **Kangsadan Resort** (Tel. 212-209) are both good places for a meal, short break, or overnight stay. They have lush gardens and great scenery and provide the time and atmosphere to sit and contemplate the generosity of nature to this area. At **Ban Hmong Mae Sa Mai** you can learn about the culture and life-style of the Hmong hilltribe people. The village has basic lodging, a campfire, and food for those wanting to stay overnight.

The **Erawan Resort** (Tel. 232-450) provides impressive houses of different styles, nice gardens and lawns, and displays of dances and handicrafts at "Little Chiang Mai" at 2 each day. Three kilometers farther, the **Mae Sa Valley Resort** (Tel. 234-358) has cottages scattered through an attractive garden with gurgling streams, while 2 kilometers more brings you to the **Mae-sa Elephant Camp**. This area is only 25 kilometers from Chiang Mai but it really is another world. The elephant display is roughly from 9 until 11 A.M. and the well-trained elephants captivate most visitors. Short elephant rides and a 2 1/2-hour elephant trek are available.

The **Rose Garden** provides a very attractive setting for roses and other flowers, while **Mae Sa House** is a showplace for private collections of Thai antiques. Close by, the **Mae Sa Falls** in a natural setting with its gigantic trees will impress most visitors. **Orchid Farm** is the center of all northern orchid growing and three nearby orchid farms provide an opportunity for visitors to admire the Queen of the Forest and other blooms. From here it is a 12-kilometer drive back to Chiang Mai.

The other attractions in Chiang Mai are to the east. Take Route 1006 (the Chiang Mai-Kamphaeng Road) past the railway station and across the superhighway (Route 11). For the next 12 kilometers there are many handicraft factories producing and selling silverware, lacquerware, wood carvings, silk, cotton, and pottery. Each small community tends to concentrate on one craft and it is fascinating to watch and talk to the people doing their delicate workmanship. These days it is more difficult to do that because there is a tendency to lump what were individual village works into big sales cooperatives with a relative hard sell.

Two villages are of particular interest. **Bo Sang** (9 kilometers out) is known as the umbrella-making village and is usually ablaze with thousands of hand-painted items drying in the sun. Artisans make umbrellas, temple bells, and paper using an ancient process. Visitors are welcome to visit the factories and you will find the making of hand-painted umbrellas particularly fascinating. Four kilometers farther on, **San Kamphaeng** is a major center for silk and cotton weaving. The shops and factories are a mass of color and noisy

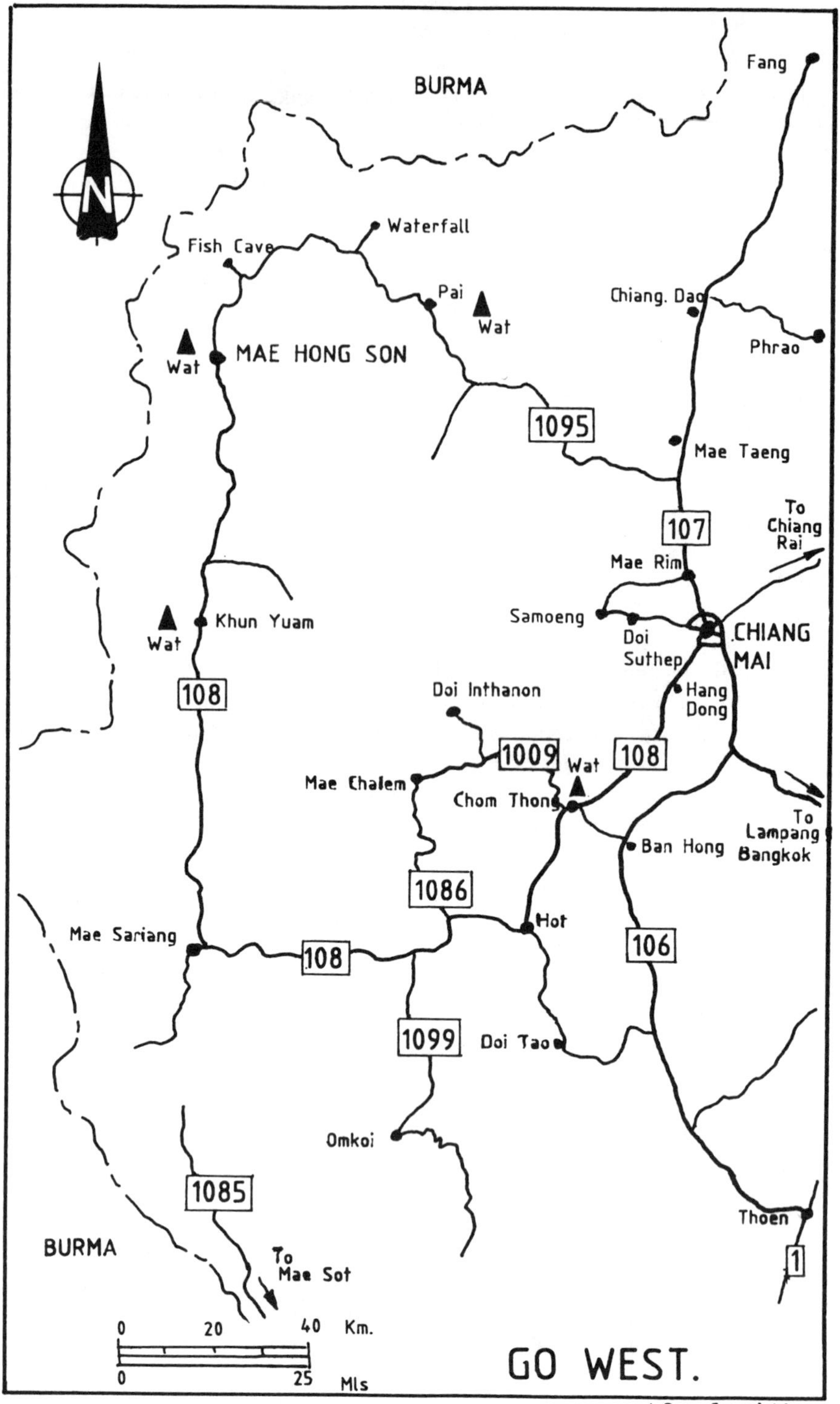

L.R. Copyright

handlooms rattle in the background. Young girls frequently do the weaving, producing cloth that cries out to be taken home. Using these looms a good operator can produce about 6 meters of finished cloth in a day. Several factories describe the silk-producing process from mulberry leaves to designer dresses. If this is your first time to see silk being made, you will find it fascinating.

Continue through San Kamphaeng and turn left onto the Mae on Teak Plantation Road. This runs for 12 kilometers through verdant ricefields that stretch off into infinity and through small settlements, until a road to the left indicates the route to the hot springs. It is 12 kilometers farther along here to an area where thermal mineral waters provide an interesting spectacle of hot pools, water spouts, and steam blows. There are three distinct privately run springs, each charging a nominal admission fee. Most visitors will select only one to visit, and on the advice of the Chiang Mai office of the Tourism Authority of Thailand, I went to **San Kamphaeng Hot Springs.** After lunching on the property and looking around at the various attractions, I was a little disappointed. It was only then that I discovered the adjacent **Roong Aroon Hot Spring,** which in my opinion is far superior (admission is B30 to each). Amazingly, TAT did not mention it, nor the very smart and modern **Roong Aroon Hot Springs Resort** (Tel. 251-191), 36 rooms, where I will stay on my next visit to this region.

The bungalows at the resort are fully airconditioned, have hot mineral water piped to each bathroom, and have a communal living area with a log fire for winter evenings. The resort and the hot springs have amazing natural rock sculptures set in lovely lawns. It was an unexpected and delightful discovery. Rooms are about B900 and slightly more on weekends.

GO WEST

Some of the best scenery in Thailand lies west of Chiang Mai but it is rarely seen by Thais or visitors. Your ultimate destination will be **Mae Hong Son,** a small town of about 8,000 people, in a misty valley close to the border of Burma.

If your only interest is in Mae Hong Son, the best way to get there is by a Thai flight from Chiang Mai. The 35-minute journey takes you over forested hillsides and steep mountain streams before landing right in the center of town.

The alternative is to take a bus or a rental car or motorcycle from Chiang Mai, either via **Pai** or via **Mae Sariang.** Even with recent road improvements, either trip will take 6 hours by car or about 8 hours by bus. For those interested in mountain scenery, isolated villages, farming communities, and delightful forest, the rewards are there for the effort. The northern road via

Pai is by far the most gruelling as this is a true mountain road. The southern route is better described as a road through mountainous country.

If you are planning on doing a circular trip from Chiang Mai, take Route 107 north through **Mae Rim** for about 30 kilometers, then turn left onto Route 1095. The first few kilometers are somewhat uneventful. Then you realize that you are fast running out of valley and the first of a series of long, steep climbs and descents, through deep green ranges, commences.

This is real hair-raising stuff. The views from the peaks are spectacular and the impenetrable jungle in the valleys takes on a vivid green which nearly envelopes you. You pass few other vehicles, except the ever-present motorcycles that mysteriously appear out of nowhere then disappear to places unknown. The road is narrow in places but the bitumen surface is good. After 3 hours Pai appears in a valley far below. It's another 20 minutes, however, before you enter the sleepy, dusty, two-street town and take a welcome break.

Pai is not yet into mainstream tourism but it has discovered the backpacker. English-language handwritten signs along the main street direct visitors to a variety of guesthouses, resorts, and other establishments including one with the delightful name of **Pai in the Sky.** Typical of the accommodation is the **Pai Resort,** close to the Pai River about 600 meters from town, where a room for two in a bamboo bungalow costs the princely sum of B70 for the night. Slightly more up-market is the **Wiang Pai Hotel** in the main street, which will cost you just over B100 for two.

With the backpackers has come the desire to trek, so signs also advertise various one-, two-, and three-day treks and raft trips. The only problem I had was in locating a trek that was actually going in the next few days. It seemed to be a case of "you provide the necessary six people and we will provide a guide." No doubt six people are easy to come by in the tourist season. I did not actually make it into the hills but certainly the surrounding country should provide all the necessary ingredients for fascinating trekking.

Pai restaurants are nothing to rave about but try one anyway. There is little alternative in the next 3 hours to Mae Hong Son.

The Thai Roads Department continues to upgrade the 110 kilometers of the Pai to Mae Hong Son road, but there is still about one-third of this section which is unpaved and very rough. A small section is almost impassable to conventional vehicles after rain because of its very slippery surface. Accept this and appreciate that for Thailand this is a very isolated area and this is very rugged terrain. For a country accustomed to building roads across flat plains, road construction in these difficult mountains must be very daunting. For the visitor this drive can provide a real sense of pioneering and achievement.

Various side roads lead to the right to waterfalls, caves, and villages. If you have stopped overnight in Pai it is easy to spend a day exploring these tracks and seeing a side of Thailand that will not exist in this form in ten years' time. For those with less time, allocate 20 minutes for a stop at Fish Cave, just 100 meters off the main road some 15 kilometers before Mae Hong Son.

I last visited here after floods had washed away the footbridge which gives access to the park area around the cave. In place of the bridge, two park workers were operating a small bamboo raft which they pushed across the fast-flowing stream. When I asked the cost I received the answer, "Something or nothing." At more "sophisticated" locations, the park would have been closed or a set charge made for the boat service. It was nice to be part of a vanishing innocence. In fact the park is not great and the only attraction of the cave is the fish which crowd the water where a spring emerges, but I recommend a visit. The area is controlled by the National Parks Department and there are picnic tables, an old wooden waterwheel, and various bamboo devices constructed by park personnel.

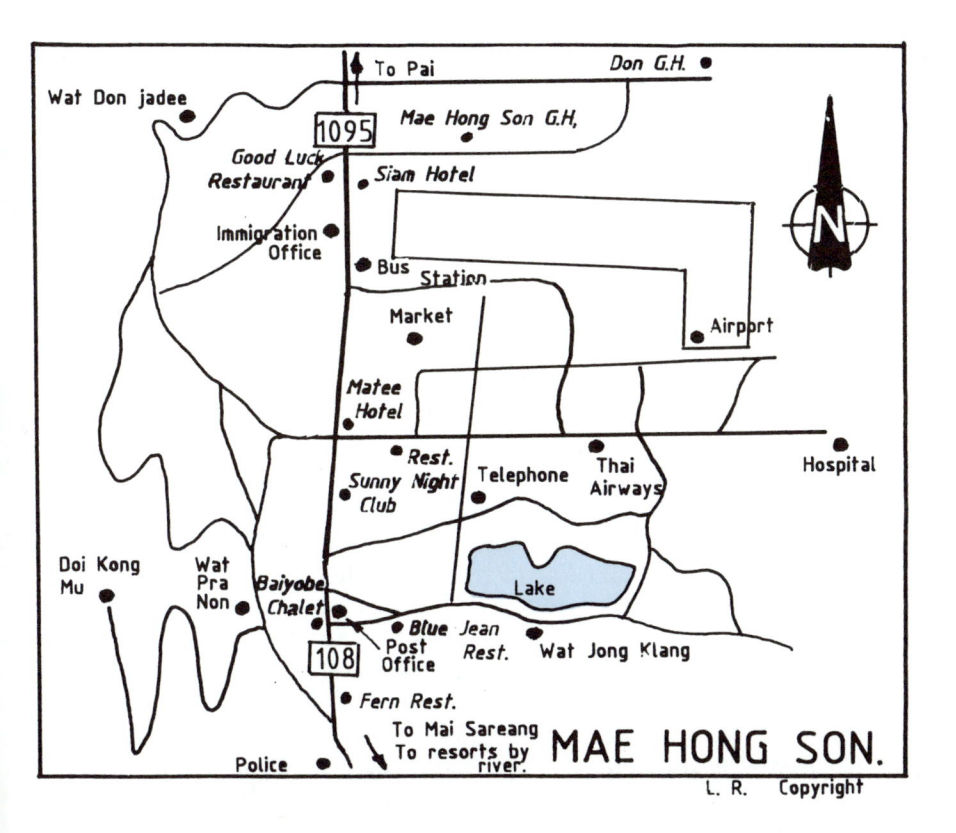

Mae Hong Son is a delight. Perhaps it is the effort to get there that heightens the feeling but I find it a place to enjoy for its own sake. There are a nice small central lake, two reasonably interesting Burmese-style wats, rafting trips, and visits to hilltribe villages, but none of these are world-class attractions in their own right. It's their combination plus the easy atmosphere of the region and the lovely setting that should be savored.

The most expensive accommodation is at the **Mae Hongson Resort** (Tel. 611-504), 30 rooms, 6 kilometers out of town on the banks of the Pai River. My preference, though, is for the **Rim Nam Klang Doi Resort** (Tel. 611-086), 20 rooms, which is considerably cheaper and 1 kilometer closer to town but shares a river location. Popular actor Mel Gibson recently spent several weeks here on a filming assignment and had a special bungalow built for his stay. That now sets a new standard for Mae Hong Son.

There are several hotels and numerous guesthouses in town. On the main street the **Siam Hotel** (Tel. 611-148), 14 rooms, the **Mae Tee Hotel** (Tel. 611-141), 40 rooms, the **Baiyobe Chalet** (Tel. 611-486), and the **Fern House** (Tel. 611-374) all provide acceptable accommodation in the low to medium range. An airconditioned room will cost from B300 and non-airconditioned rooms can be had from about B150. Several other guesthouses are scattered around town and a bed in a shared room will cost no more than B60.

Mae Hong Son is rapidly changing so this is a town to see now rather than ten years in the future. The change is reflected in the town's first traffic lights, several modern-style restaurants, and a growing (but still small) nightlife. The best of the restaurants are **Fern Restaurant** on the main road south of the post office, **Blue Jean Restaurant** on the road beside the post office, and **The Mork Fa Restaurant** near the center of town. If you can't live without nightlife, the **Sunny Coffee Shop** and the **Tawin Coffee Shop** are what you will get. Don't expect coffee!

Visit the **lake** in the late afternoon for tranquility and some delightful reflections. Drive the newly constructed bitumen road to the hilltop Burmese-style **Wat Phra That Doi Kong Mu** for a great view of the town. Call in at **Nick Trekking** or **Don Tour & Tribal Trekking** (both on the main street) for advice on trips to hilltribe villages, border settlements, trekking, rafting, or motorcycle rental. One trip that is being pushed hard is to the Burma border to see the "long-necked" Pa Dawn people. It depends on your point of view what value you see in this trip. I could cheerfully spend a few days around town without going on any trips and I worry about the ethics of keeping humans in social captivity so they can be displayed to visitors.

When you finally decide to leave Mae Hong Son, the southern road, Route 108, provides an interesting journey back to Chiang Mai. The road is bitumen the whole way; however, the alignment for the first 50 kilometers south of Mae Hong Son is extremely poor so travel is slow. The 160 kilometers to **Mae Sariang** will take you about 3 hours. A side trip to a hilltop Meo village, 10 kilometers off the main road to the left at a point 30 kilometers from Mae Hong Son, will add at least another 90 minutes to the trip.

This uncomplicated village is another of those unexpected delights that you happen upon in areas where the tourism industry is not totally organized. It's the kind of experience that trekkers love and it is extremely rare to be able to find it by road.

The last hour of the drive into Mae Sariang is picturesque and the road alignment is good. Mae Sariang has a couple of semi-interesting Burmese-style temples but many people bypass the town as they head back to Chiang Mai. I had hoped to continue driving south, parallel to the Burmese border to Mae Sot, but discovered that one section of this road was impassable to conventional vehicles. It is about 5 hours by motorcycle.

There is one hotel in town called **The Mitaree** (near the bus station) and a new guesthouse, about a kilometer away, with the same name. I would choose the guesthouse. There are several restaurants in the main street. The **Intra Chinese Restaurant** has a good local reputation and served up a good meal for me. The **Reurn Prae** is nice for Muslim food.

Route 108 now heads due east through lovely mountain country. It weaves and winds through pine plantations, cultivated fields, and natural jungle. Many of the villages here belong to the Karen people and they hug the hillsides in locations no vehicles can reach. They now grow strawberries and apples, coffee and tea, garlic and chillies, cabbages and flowers to fill the markets of Bangkok, rather than their more traditional opium crop. There are some wonderful mountain views and, way below, rivers that are carving deep valleys through the ridges.

About 18 kilometers before the town of **Hot,** the road joins a river as it traverses a minicanyon. **Ob Luang Gorge** is a deep cut in the rock which the swollen river races through. There is a good viewpoint just meters off the road. Hot itself has no particular attraction. This is a relatively new town built when the old site was submerged by the huge Bhumibol Dam. I don't think it will win any town planning awards.

For those heading south to Bangkok, there is an excellent road which connects Hot to Route 106 via Doi Tao. Taking Route 106 south, you eventually reach Route 1. If you are heading back to Chiang Mai, however, Route 108 now turns north to **Chom Thong** and the entrance to the **Doi Inthanon National Park.** Chom Thong is noted for its **Wat Phra That Si Chom Thong,** which has a Burmese-style chedi and one of the most beautiful temple buildings in northern Thailand. It is well worth the time for a close inspection of the excellent wood carving and other features.

Doi Inthanon is Thailand's highest mountain (about 2,500 meters) and there are several waterfalls within the park. Mae Klang Falls is the largest, easiest to reach, and most impressive but, particularly on weekends, this area

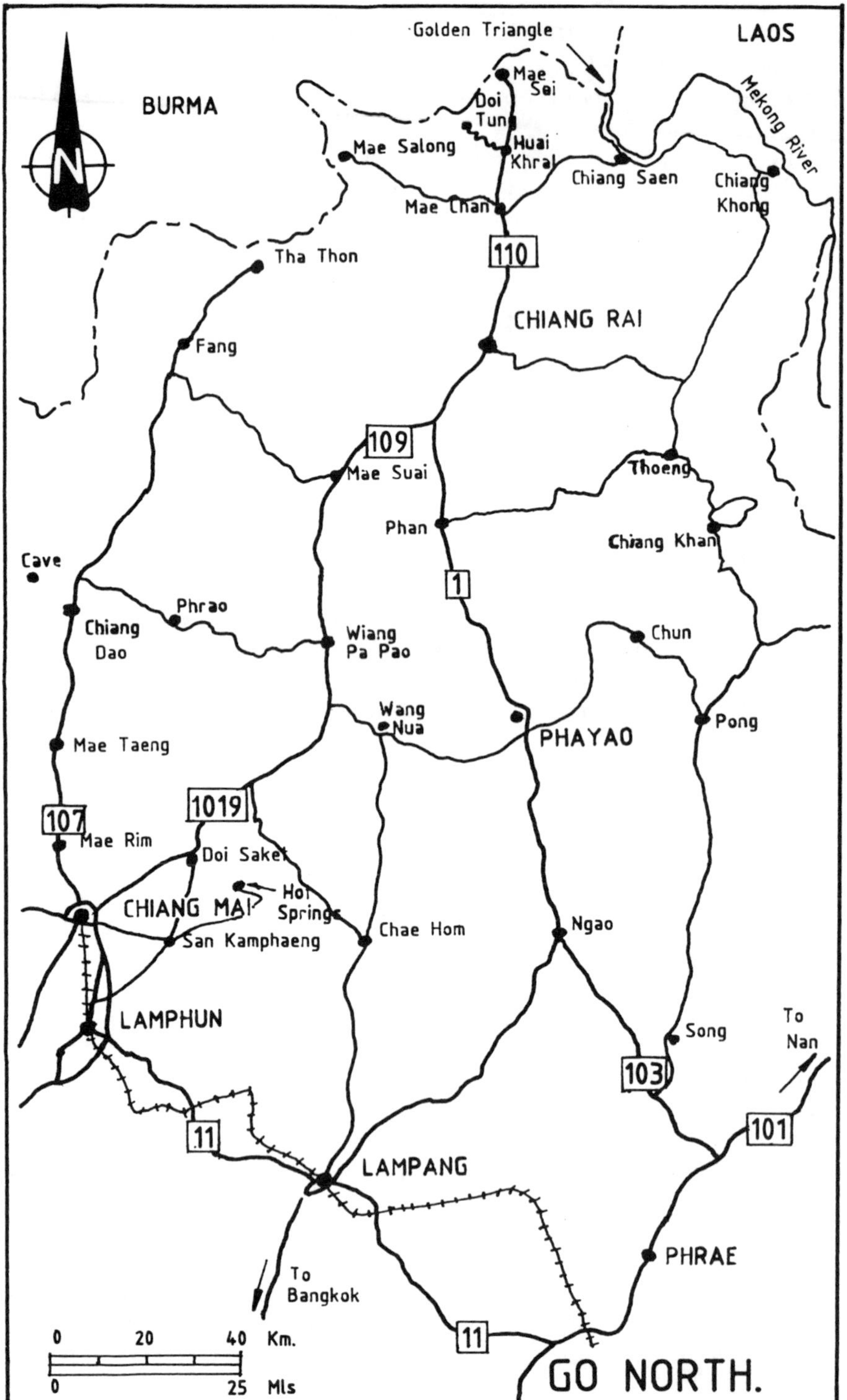
Golden Triangle
LAOS
BURMA
N
Mae Sei
Doi Tung
Huai Khral
Mekong River
Mae Salong
Chiang Saen
Chiang Khong
Mae Chan
110
Tha Thon
CHIANG RAI
Fang
109
Mae Suai
Thoeng
Phan
Chiang Khan
Cave
1
Phrao
Chiang Dao
Wiang Pa Pao
Chun
Wang Nua
PHAYAO
Pong
Mae Taeng
1019
107
Mae Rim
Doi Saket
Hot Springs
CHIANG MAI
San Kamphaeng
Chae Hom
Ngao
LAMPHUN
Song
To Nan
103
11
101
LAMPANG
PHRAE
To Bangkok
0 20 40 Km.
0 25 Mls
11
GO NORTH.

can be very crowded. A road leads to the top of the mountain and there is a minibus that takes passengers for the 2-hour journey.

GO NORTH

To the north of Chiang Mai, the main interest is in the border towns of Fang and Tha Thon, the city of Chiang Rai, and the area known as the Golden Triangle.

Thai Airways International has three flights from Chiang Mai to Chiang Rai each day (fare about B650 round trip) and there are buses of various types leaving at least every half-hour (fare: B50-B100). The flight takes 40 minutes in a 30-seat aircraft while the bus takes about 3 1/2 hours along the most direct route (Route 1019).

For a good circular trip from Chiang Mai, take the northern route from the city (Route 107) through Mae Rim, past the left turnoff to Pai and Mae Hong Son, and on towards Mae Taeng. The road slowly leaves flat farmlands and travels through scenic hill country towards **Chiang Dao.** The main interest here is 6 kilometers off to the left—the **Chiang Dao Cave.** The cave system is quite extensive and only a small section is lit but, as well as the natural attractions, you see the inevitable Buddha statues, the souvenir sellers, and various chedi. The entrance fee is B10.

It is about 80 kilometers from here to **Fang** and the trip is full of interest. This region offers the mysteries of the unexplored. Fang itself was founded in the thirteenth century but it has never made the big time. This area was once a trading point for opium produced nearby. No doubt there is still some trade but the Thai government has been fairly successful in introducing other agricultural crops into the region. The area around Fang has many hilltribe villages and it has become popular for trekking. Reasonable accommodation in town is available at the **Chok Thani Hotel.**

It is only 20 kilometers to **Tha Thon** on the Burmese border and the starting point for popular rafting or boating trips to Chiang Rai. The boat trips are well organized, leave at regular intervals, and cost about B200. All this means that the area is no longer isolated or primitive. In fact, riverside villages along the way seem quite sophisticated. Nevertheless the trip is well worth doing and the 4 hours or so that it takes rapidly pass. It is almost faster to go from Tha Thon to Chiang Rai by water than it is by road. For the road trip you retrace your steps to Fang, then take Route 109 to join eventually the main Chiang Mai-Chiang Rai road at Mae Suai.

Chiang Rai is the capital of the northernmost province of Thailand. It was founded in 1262 by King Mengrai, who later established Chiang Mai. Despite its strategic importance due to its position near the borders of Laos and Burma, it has not grown into a major center—that is, until now. Chiang Rai is at last being discovered by world tourism.

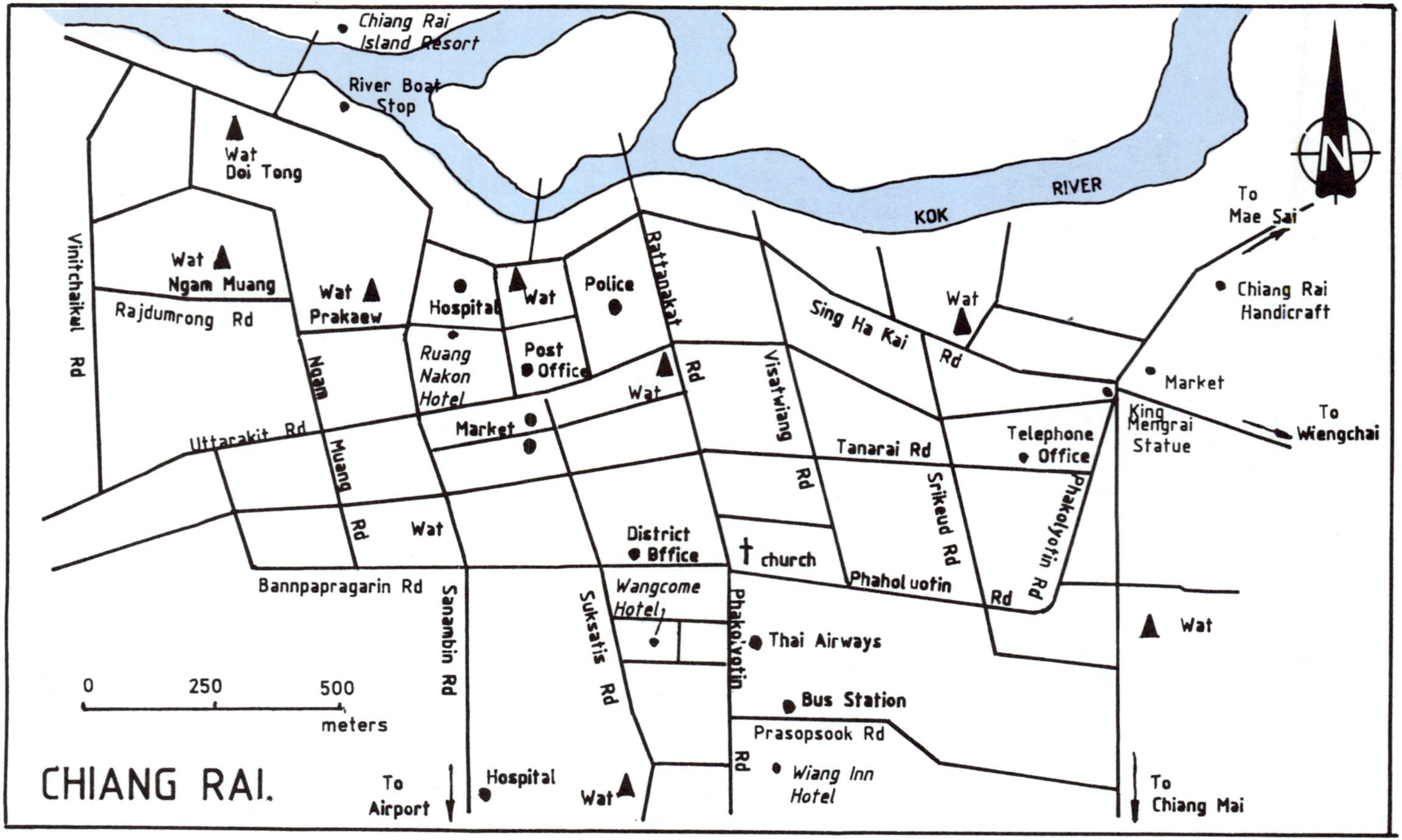
CHIANG RAI.
0
250
500
meters
Chiang Rai Island Resort
River Boat Stop
Wat Doi Tong
Wat Ngam Muang
Wat Prakaew
Rajdumrong Rd
Vinitchaikul Rd
Ngam Muang Rd
Uttarakit Rd
Hospital
Wat
Police
Post Office
Ruang Nakon Hotel
Market
Rattanakat Rd
Wat
Bannpapragarin Rd
Sanambin Rd
District Office
Wangcome Hotel
Suksatis Rd
Phakolyotin Rd
church
Visatwiang Rd
Sing Ha Kai Rd
Wat
Tanarai Rd
Srikeud Rd
Phaholuotin Rd
Phakolyotin Rd
Telephone Office
King Mengrai Statue
Market
Chiang Rai Handicraft
To Mae Sai
To Wiengchai
KOK RIVER
N
Wat
Thai Airways
Bus Station
Prasopsook Rd
Wiang Inn Hotel
Hospital
Wat
To Airport
To Chiang Mai

Frankly there is little in Chiang Rai of great interest. But it is a good base for exploring the surrounding region and the combination of good hotels, pleasant restaurants, reasonable shopping, lack of congestion, and fresh climate has much to recommend it. The best hotel in town is the **Wangcome** (Tel. 711-800), 220 rooms, at 869/90 Pemawiphak Rd., Fax: (6653) 713-844, with a restaurant, bars, and swimming pool. It is a first-class property in a good central location with excellent shopping facilities nearby. Room rates start at B1000. Another major hotel, the **Wiang Inn** (Tel. 711-533) with similar facilities (and a massage parlor), is nearby at 893 Phaholyothin Rd. (Fax: 6653-711-877). As an alternative you could decide on the **Chiang Rai Island Resort** (Tel. 711-865), 25 rooms, which has bungalows on an island in the middle of the Kok River. A new top-of-the-market resort, the **Dusit Island Resort** (Tel. 711-865), 256 rooms, should be open by the time you read this.

There is a large range of guesthouses which offer Western-style rooms for about B300, or Thai-style rooms for B50 and upwards. Some of the better ones are **Boonbundan Guest House** (Tel. 712-914), **Bank and Boom's Guest House** (Tel. 714-854), the **Golden Triangle Guest House** (Tel. 711-339), and the **White House Guest House** (Tel. 713-427).

The larger hotels have good restaurants and you can find some other interesting places around town. The **Hawnariga Restaurant** (Tel. 711-062) can be recommended for good Thai food. The **Chiang Rai Sports Club and Restaurant** (Tel. 713-353) has atmosphere by the river. The **Bierstube Restaurant** (Tel. 714-195) has German and Thai food plus draft beer on tap. The amazingly named **Gub-Duck Garden Restaurant** (Tel. 711-042) is a fun place with Thai and Western food and live music from 9 P.M.

Chiang Rai is not big on nightlife but you do have a selection of the Wangcome Hotel's **Music Room Night Club,** the Ram Hotel's **Cheers Pub** (Tel. 711-344), **Country Road** for international country music and atmosphere, the Wiang Inn Massage Parlor or its disco, or a few smaller cafes or coffee shops.

All of Chiang Rai's sightseeing attractions can be covered in half a day. Start with the **municipal market,** which is clean, covered, and interesting. Then walk west to **Wat Phra Keo,** which at one time was home to the Emerald Buddha now in Bangkok. Walk downstream along the riverbank from here and you will come to the new Tourism Authority of Thailand office near the bridge to the island. If you keep walking in the same direction along Sing Ha Kai Road, you will eventually come to the highway and the **statue of King Mengrai.**

A walk back to your hotel will take you past several hilltribe, jewelry, antique, and art shops. Probably the best of these are **Ego** (Tel. 712-090) opposite the Wangcome Hotel, **Chiang Saen** (Tel. 713-535) on Premwipak Road, **Lanna Souvenir** (Tel. 714-681) on Phakolyotin Road, and **Berries House** (Tel. 712-245) on Pemauipath Road.

Cars, jeeps, and motorcycles are available for rent in Chiang Rai. Try **A.R. Car Rent** (Tel. 713-946), **Fah Luang** (Tel. 712-130) or **Pin Kaew Guest House** (Tel. 715-193) for jeeps, and **Pintamorn** (Tel. 714-161) for motorcycles. Tours from Chiang Mai can be organized through **The Golden Triangle** (Tel. 711-334), **Far East North Tour** (Tel. 713-615), or **Issra Tour** (Tel. 713-166).

Route 110 continues north from Chiang Rai through Mae Chan to the Burmese border at Mae Sai. **Mae Chan** is a small town 28 kilometers from Chiang Rai. The **Mae Salong Guest House** (Tel. 712-962) and the **Laon Tong Lodge** have reasonable rooms. A road to the left leads 12 kilometers to a large **Hill-tribe Center** where the Thai government is weaning the locals off opium poppy growing.

Another 25 kilometers farther on this road is **Mae Salong**, a settlement populated by the families of Nationalist Chinese army members who fled communism in China in 1949. On the way you pass several hilltribe villages where souvenirs are available. Mae Salong has the "highest Chinese restaurant in Thailand" and there's accommodation at the **Mae Salong Resort** (Tel. 714-047) and some guesthouses.

Mae Chan is also where a road to the east (Route 1016) leads to the delightful riverside village of **Chiang Saen**. Experts believe the town was founded in the thirteenth century and was the home of the future King Mengrai. It was heavily fortified at some time and you can see ancient earthen ramparts today. These did not stop the Burmese from overrunning the city-state in 1558, and it was not retaken (and destroyed) by the Thais until the late eighteenth century. The town remained deserted until King Rama IV, in 1861, ordered it repopulated.

The attraction of Chiang Saen is its ancient monuments and its position on the bank of the great Mekong River. The small settlement itself is peaceful and the pace of life is slow. There are ruins of temples, stupas, and Buddhas from the original kingdom now covered with creepers and flowers. There is also a branch of the National Museums of Thailand to visit. It opens daily and admission is B10.

Chiang Saen is not the place to stay unless you have plenty of time but a stop at the **Sala Thai Restaurant,** right on the riverbank overlooking Laos, is strongly recommended. On a day without tour buses, sitting with a beer in hand, gazing across at total inactivity, it is certainly hard to beat. For those with time, **Lanna House** by the river has reasonable accommodation, while the **Poonsuk Hotel** is fairly basic but sometimes has interesting guests. **Chiang Saen Lake** some 4 kilometers south of town has been developed for tourists. There is swimming, boating, and fishing and a good restaurant which specializes in freshwater seafood.

There is an excellent river trip available from Chiang Saen to **Chiang Khong** almost directly to the east. It takes about 3 hours in a long-tail boat and is quite spectacular for about half the way. After passing the mouth of the Kok River, the Mekong curves between beautiful mountains. For 20 kilometers it splashes down rapids beneath steep, jungled mountainsides until you reach Chiang Khong. You can travel to Chiang Khong by road but it is quite rough and not as exciting as the river trip.

In the Chiang Khong area there are a number of Hmong and Yao hilltribe villages which, because they are off the tourist track, provide a reasonably accurate picture of traditional hill life. For those who wish to stay overnight, the **Mae Kong River Resort** will look after you. One of the best buys here is beautiful Lao textile or silver jewelry which has been semilegally "smuggled" across the border.

For those wishing to visit the **Golden Triangle,** it is necessary to return upriver to Chiang Saen, then go on by river or road to the confluence of the Mekong and the Sop Ruak rivers. The Golden Triangle conjures up mystery, legends, intrigue, and danger. In reality this spot where Burma, Laos, and Thailand meet has none of these elements—only lots of tourists. There are restaurants, souvenir stalls, shanty accommodations, and now reasonably sophisticated resorts. They exist simply because the tourism industry demanded a specific location to take countless visitors who wanted to "see" the Golden Triangle.

Probably the best viewing is from a pavilion which is part of the **Wat Phra Thai Pukhao** monastery. Late in the afternoon, when most of the tourists have left and the sun is low in the sky, the river and ranges are beautiful. For those who stay the night, **The Golden Triangle Resort Hotel** (Tel. 714-710) provides the best accommodation. Room rates are being advertised at B1800 but you can get a large discount at some times of the year.

The town of **Mae Sai** is the end of the road. This is the northernmost point in Thailand. There is a bridge which leads to Burma and while Thais may cross, other nationalities may not. You do not really need to cross because Mai Sai has the feel of a Burmese town. Visitors can buy Burmese lacquerware, jade, gems, puppets, and other items at many shops along the wide, dusty main street.

Tourism has left its mark on hilltribe children, who demand payment before you can take their photograph in the street. Other traders tend to be fairly aggressive as they know the average tourist is likely to stay for less than an hour. One attraction here, to many, is the local strawberries, available December through March. They are cheap and delicious. For a good view of the town and into Burma, you can walk up the 200-odd steps from the center of town to a chedi of **Wat Phra That Doi Wao.** It is worth the effort. There are many guesthouses in Mae Sai, two fairly new and clean hotels— the **Sin Watana** (Tel. 731-950), 30 rooms, is the larger, and the **Mae Sai Resort** (Tel. 731-140).

Route 110 heads back south to Chiang Rai but after 19 kilometers, in the

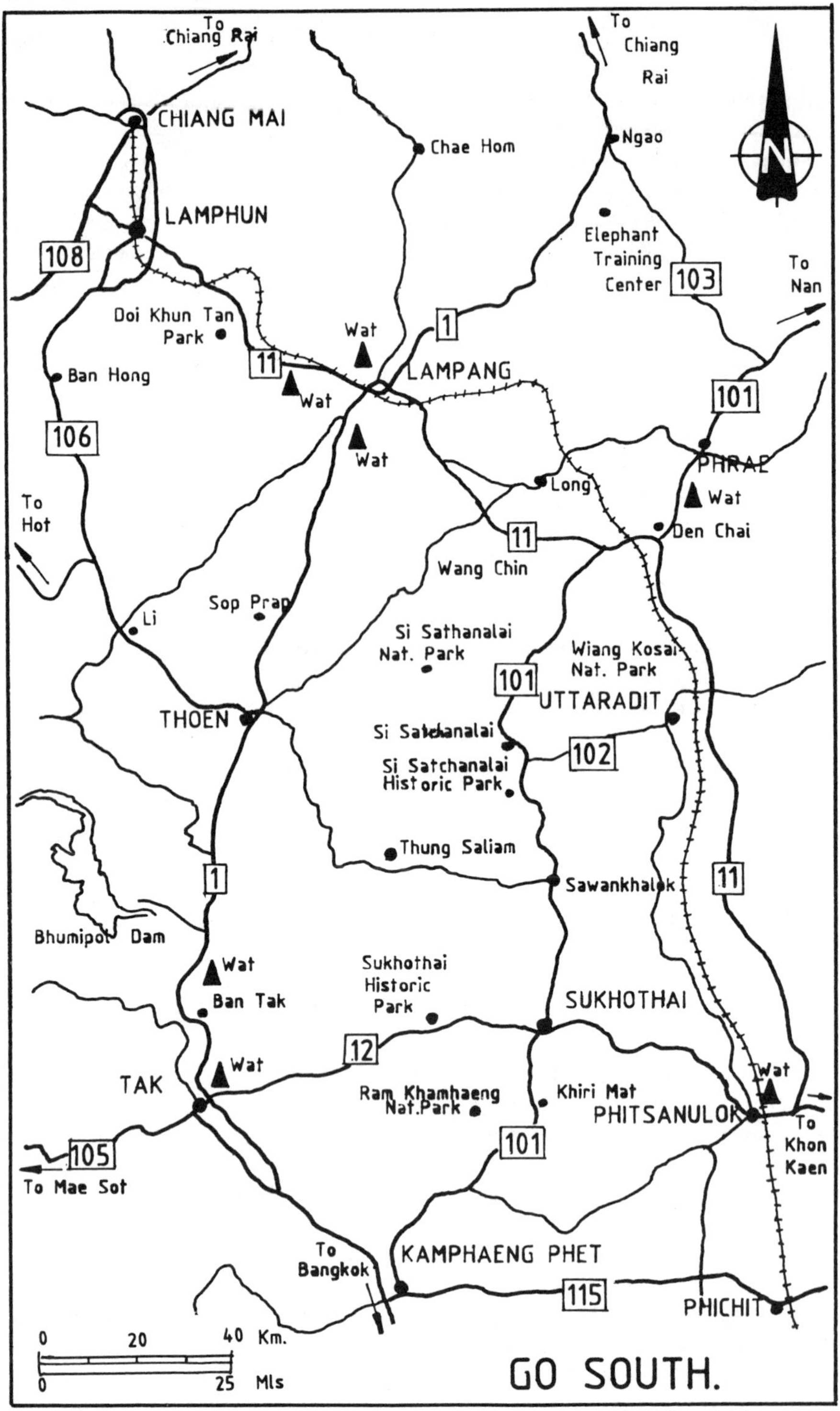

To Chiang Rai
CHIANG MAI
To Chiang Rai
Chae Hom
Ngao
LAMPHUN
Elephant Training Center
103
To Nan
108
Doi Khun Tan Park
1
Wat
11
LAMPANG
Ban Hong
Wat
101
106
Wat
PHRAE
Long
Wat
To Hot
11
Den Chai
Wang Chin
Sop Prap
Li
Si Sathanalai Nat. Park
Wiang Kosai Nat. Park
101
UTTARADIT
THOEN
Si Satchanalai
102
Si Satchanalai Historic Park
Thung Saliam
1
Sawankhalok
11
Bhumipol Dam
Wat
Sukhothai Historic Park
SUKHOTHAI
Ban Tak
12
Wat
TAK
Wat
Ram Khamhaeng Nat.Park
Khiri Mat
PHITSANULOK
To Khon Kaen
105
To Mae Sot
101
To Bangkok
KAMPHAENG PHET
115
PHICHIT
0 20 40 Km.
0 25 Mls
GO SOUTH.

village of **Huai Khrai,** a road leads to the right to **Doi Tung.** This mountain (2,000m), with its temple and royal residence for the Princess Mother, is a very revered place for Thais and devout Buddhists from Burma and Laos. The shrine is reached by a tortuous mountain road which climbs through hilltribe villages and pine trees to the spectacular location. The surface is good, but care needs to be taken on some sections because it is steep and narrow.

The original temple is supposed to have been built in the eighth century and it is believed that the left collarbone of Lord Buddha is "enshrined in the twin pagodas." The complex was extensively rebuilt, however, in 1973 and the present buildings are not terribly special. The location and the views make it impressive. Accommodation at the **Akha Guest House** in one of the hillside villages is basic but you are close to reality.

Back in Chiang Rai you have two alternative roads back to Chiang Mai. Route 1019 will take you about 3 1/2 hours, but the older Route 1 has some interest and should be considered. Some 90 kilometers south of Chiang Rai is the town of **Phayao,** situated by a shallow lake at the foot of a high peak. The town appears uninteresting but it was built in the eleventh century on the site of a deserted city which may be very old indeed.

The next center is Ngao, where Route 103 leads east for 160 kilometers to the isolated town of Nan. Some 20 kilometers later, a road to the right leads to Pha Thai cave, which gives you a climb up nearly 300 steps to the huge arched grotto entrance. There is a great stalagmite rising from the surrounding limestone and green snakes, which apparently are protected.

The road twists and turns over and around hills and ranges between here and Lampang. On the way you pass an elephant training school, millions of teak trees, and hundreds of spirit houses which appear at all the sharpest bends and highest crests in the road. The drive is slow but it is certainly interesting.

GO SOUTH

It is about 700 kilometers south to Bangkok and the fastest route takes about 9 hours. There is really too much of interest on the way to do this quickly, and there is a real problem knowing which way to travel so you can see most of the sights. The answer is to do a circular tour from Chiang Mai south covering the centers of Lampang, Sukhothai, Phitsanulok, Tak, and the Bhumipol Dam and then travel to Bangkok separately.

Route 11 heads south from Chiang Mai then veers east for 100 kilometers to **Lampang.** The city has been occupied since about the seventh century but it is only about a quarter the size of Chiang Mai and far less developed. Lampang is famous throughout Thailand for its horse-drawn carriages. In reality they are fast disappearing, except for tourist transportation.

The lazy Wang River winds through town and it reflects the local mood. For a few decades early in this century, Lampang was the terminus of the railroad from the south. Passengers heading north would disembark, rest for a day or a night, then continue to Chiang Mai by horse or elephant. Then the railroad was extended and no one stopped in Lampang. When the modern highway was built it bypassed the town.

Teak built Lampang; it was the wealth of the town. Now it is mainly gone. Lampang is not dying, it is just resting in the sun. That's not a bad attitude for a visitor to adopt. There are two typical temples in town which are well endowed and cared for. **Wat Phra Keo Don Tao** housed the much-travelled Emerald Buddha for thirty-two years and it is a nice fusion of local and Burmese architecture. **Wat Phra Saeng,** across the river, has seven chapels and a nice chedi. For an overnight stay, try the **Siam Hotel** (Tel. 217-474) with room rates from B200 or the more up-market **Tip Chang Hotel** (Tel. 218-450), 120 rooms from B350. Both are within the main town area.

Route 11 continues southeast and if your destination is Phitsanulok you can follow this the whole way. We, however, will turn right onto Route 101 about 60 kilometers past Lampang because we are heading for **Si Satchanalai.** From the north you enter the small town and wonder why anyone has ever suggested you come here. There are Japanese pickup trucks, noisy motorcycles, cola and Mekong whiskey just like every other town in Thailand.

You have to travel another 13 kilometers, leave the highway, cross the Yom River, and travel back upriver to find what makes this region so magical. Old Si Satchanalai was built in the early thirteenth century and survived until the mid-1700s. It was often mentioned as the twin city of Sukhothai, the first Thai capital. Today only weathered ruins remain but the historical park under the control of the Fine Arts Department of the Thai government is a great place to visit.

While Ayutthaya and Sukhothai receive great publicity, Si Satchanalai does not. Yet in some ways it is equally impressive because of its lovely location, its size, and its relative lack of people. The whole area consists of about 300 hectares with some 140 ancient remains. Many of the best ruins are within the town walls but others are along the river and in surrounding fields. The town had moats, ramparts, and a laterite wall which included bastions and gateways. Some good examples remain.

The walls enclose part of a mountain range and naturally some of the finest chedis and other structures were built at impressive heights. Particularly impressive are **Wat Phra Si Rattanamahathat Chaliang,** with its fine riverfront location; **Wat Chao Chan,** near the bridge; **Wat Chang Lom,** which is probably the "Elephantt-girdled Shire" described in King Ramkamhaeng's stone inscription and built in the 1280s; **Wat Chedi Chet Thaew,** which contains seven rows of stupas; and the hilltop **Wat Khao Suwan Khiri.**

These old ruins in their lovely setting, when seen near sunset or sunrise, are indeed a glimpse into "Old Siam." Fortunately there is no accommodation at the old town so commercialism has largely been kept at bay. On Route 101 about 3 kilometers from the walls, there are two small unsophisticated "guesthouses." For better accommodation you need to go about 50 kilometers south to Sukhothai. If you happen to be at Si Satchanalai near lunchtime, the Kang Sak Restaurant has a lovely setting overlooking the river about 1 kilometer from the historical park.

Sukhothai can be called Thailand's first capital. It flourished from the mid-thirteenth century until the end of the fourteenth century. In many ways the culture of the Thai people originated in Sukhothai. It was the center for technology and knowledge, and it was the birthplace of the Thai alphabet.

Old Sukhothai is situated about 12 kilometers west of the modern city, on Route 12. It is a fascinating spread of ruins which takes time to explore. You see ruins as you approach the old town but the most impressive area is within the old city walls. A good starting point is the **Ramkamhaeng National Museum,** where you can see a miniature model of the old city and its environs. See also a good collection of Sukhothai artifacts and a replica of the famous Ramkamhaeng rock inscription. The museum opens daily and admission is B20.

Extensive restoration and clean-up work has been carried out in the old city in recent years by the Fine Arts Department and UNESCO. The city is considered of world significance and is now being presented as such. The historical park has been divided into several sections and there is a B20 admission charge to each. The most impressive site is **Wat Mahathat.** This is surrounded by brick walls and a moat and has about 200 chedis, numerous Buddha figures, huge towers and buttresses, and some fine stucco friezes. It is believed the temple was started in the mid-thirteenth century but it was extensively remodelled during the fourteenth century when Buddhism of the Sri Lankan school found favor at Sukhothai.

Nearby is **Wat Sri Sawai,** distinguished by its three Khmer-style laterite prangs and surrounding laterite walls. The temple was probably started in the late twelfth century but not finished until the fifteenth century. It was originally a Hindu temple built by the Khmers. **Wat Trapang Ngoen** is just west of Wat Mahathat on a small island in the middle of Silver Lake. There is a fine chedi which can be picturesquely framed by the hills in the background and reflected in the foreground water to make a great photograph.

Another of the impressive temples is **Wat Sra Sri.** This is a beautifully sited and attractive monument with a Sri Lankan-style chedi in good condition and other pieces, including a stucco Buddha image. The sites mentioned so

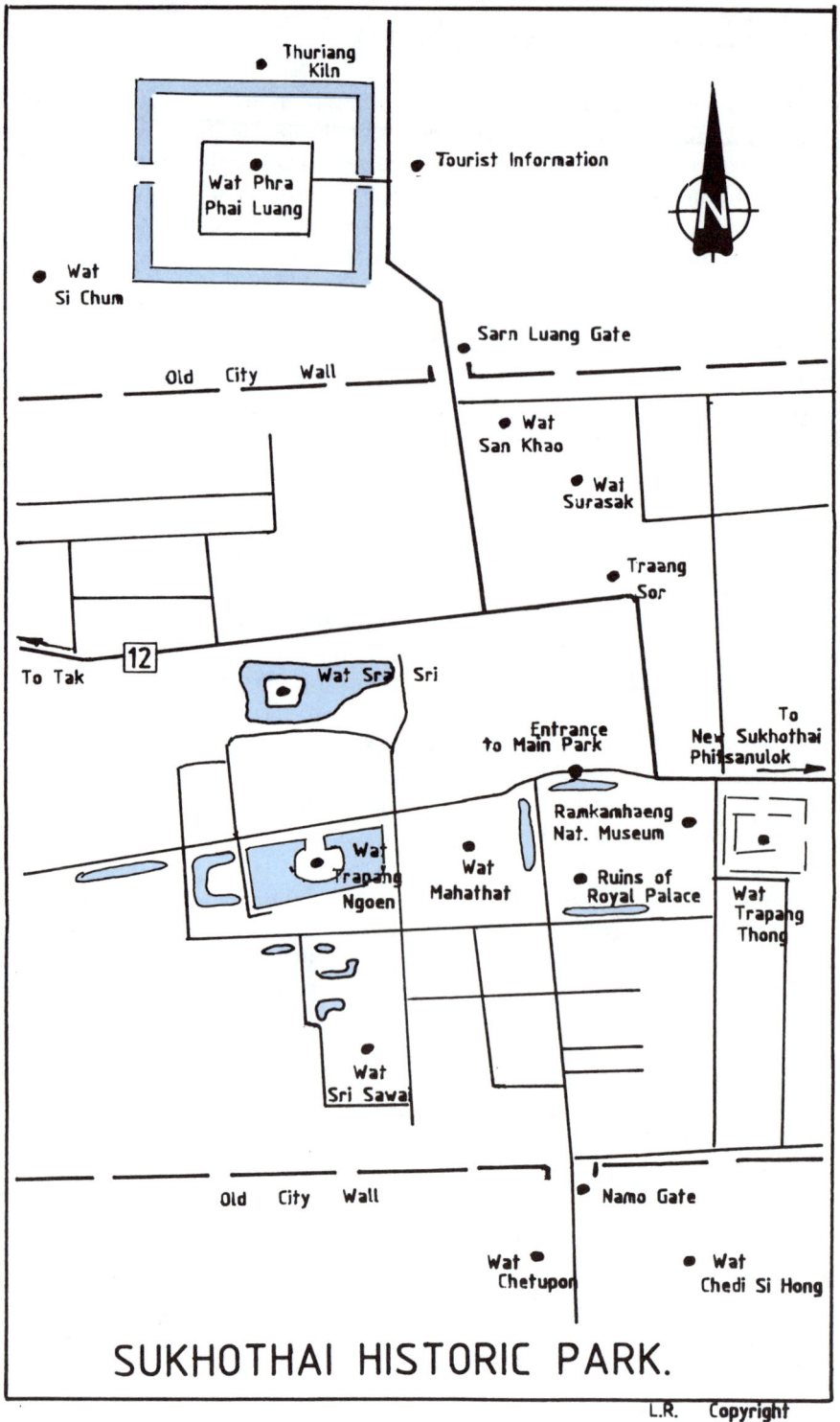

SUKHOTHAI HISTORIC PARK.

far are all within walking distance of each other although it is probably better to have a bicycle or your own vehicle. An interesting alternative is the tram touring service which will transport you between sites and provide a commentary on the way for a cost of B20 per person. The tram leaves from the car park adjacent to the main road in the center of old Sukhothai.

Outside this immediate area **Wat Phra Phai Luang** provides the most extensive remains. This also dates from the Khmer occupation. **Wat Si Chum** has one of Thailand's largest seated Buddhas, while **Wat Saphan Hin** has a slate footpath leading up the hill to the 12.5-meter-high standing Buddha.

There are two small but interesting national parks in the region which are worth a visit. The **Si Satchanalai National Park** in Ban Kaeng has cliffs, grass fields, caves, many small wild animals, and two nice waterfalls located not far from the park headquarters. The **Ram Khamhaeng National Park** is south of Sukhothai at Khiri Mat. The tallest peak in the park is 1,200 meters high and access is via a 4-kilometer-long road. It is a popular spot for camping and sightseeing.

If you wish to overnight in Sukhothai you need to travel 12 kilometers to the new town to find reasonable accommodation. The best hotel in town is the **Ratchathani** (Tel. 611-031), 80 rooms, on the main road before you come to the river. Room rates are from B450. The **River View Hotel** (Tel. 611-656) offers a cheaper alternative with standard rooms at B140 and airconditioned ones from B200. The new **Pailyn Hotel** on the main road between old and new Sukhothai should be open by the time you read this, bringing first-class accommodation reasonably close to the old city. Three useful telephone numbers are: Police, Tel. 611-199; Hospital, Tel. 611-782; and Bus Station, Tel. 611-788.

An alternative chosen by many people is to drive the 50 kilometers to **Phitsanulok.** This is the largest city in central Thailand and it has been well known to Thais for 500 years. What you see today is essentially a modern city rebuilt after an enormous fire in 1960 which destroyed most of the old town. Fortunately the fire spared **Wat Mahathat** and today this is the principal tourist attraction. The wat contains the Jinaraj Buddha, one of Thailand's most revered images. The temple gives you a good idea of older northern-style religious architecture with its low side walls and concentration on the beautiful bronze image. You should also wander around the rest of the complex and in particular see the restored areas, which look quite dramatic.

Phitsanulok has a branch of the Tourism Authority of Thailand so you should visit them for information before going sightseeing. I found this office one of the more helpful TAT outlets. They produce a leaflet on the city which lists information on the attractions together with hotels and restaurants. They also have a Walking Tour Guide. The central area is small enough to walk around and this certainly adds to its charm. Call the TAT office at 252-742.

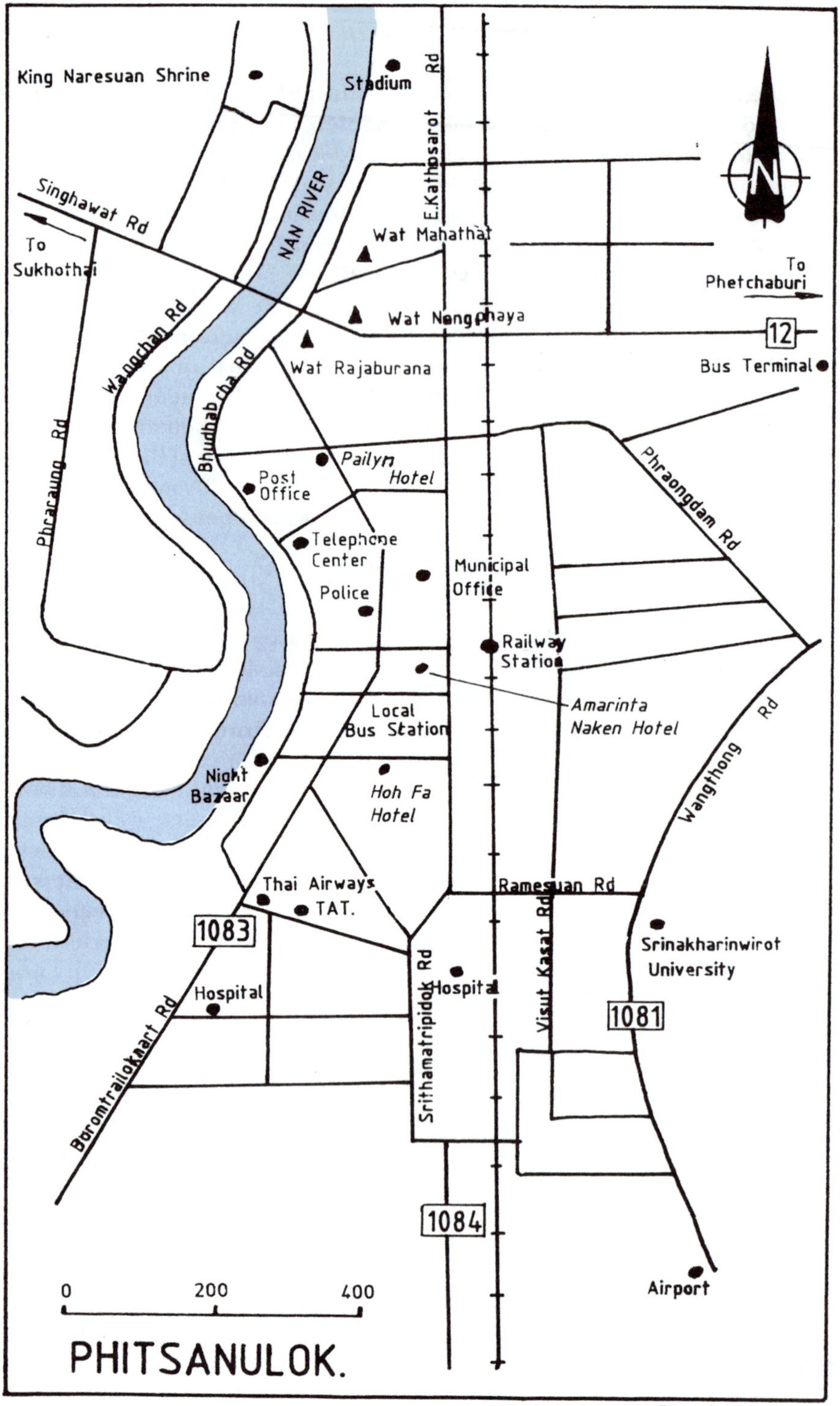

L.R. Copyright

The other attraction, to many visitors, is the good hotel accommodation. I stayed recently at the **Pailyn Hotel** (Tel. 252-411), 240 rooms, and found it excellent. The twelve-floor building would not be out of place in central Bangkok and the service was friendly and efficient. Facilities include a fine restaurant, a 19-hour coffeehouse with a live band at lunch and dinner, a disco, massage, sauna, nightclub, and lobby bar. For B600 it is an excellent value and is justifiably popular. (Reservations with the hotel at 38 Boromtrailoknart Rd., Phitsanulok 65000; Fax: 6655-258-983.)

Another hotel with adequate facilities is the **Amarinta Naken** (Tel. 258-588), 132 rooms. The rooms are small but you can get an airconditioned room without refrigerator for about B300 and still have good car-parking facilities, a cocktail lounge, a 24-hour coffee shop, and some of the best Chinese food in town. Cheaper is the **Hoh Fa** (Tel. 258-484), 69 rooms, which has rooms from B90.

The town has one further attraction. Take a walk along the riverbank in the evening and you will see bizarre towers outside several of the open-air restaurants. Watch closely and you will see a waiter climb a tower and casually catch a plate of cooked vegetables which has been flung into the air by a cook some 20 meters away. This amazing act happens everytime a customer orders "Morning Glory" or "Flying Vegetables" and of course every first-time customer is certain to do so. The restaurants incidentally serve good food at quite reasonable prices. Just head towards the riverbank. Useful telephone numbers are: Police, Tel. 258-777; Kai Sarndajphra Naresvan Matharat Hospital, Tel. 251-128; Railway Station, Tel. 258-005; and Bus Station, Tel. 258-113.

East of Phitsanulok, along Route 12, there are many attractions. **Sakunothayan Forest Park** is at kilometer 33, **Kaeng Song Waterfall** is at kilometer 44, and **Poi Waterfall,** the area's largest, is at kilometer 61. The lovely **Thung Sa Laeng Luang National Park** with its lush green forests, high mountains, and scenic winding roads is at kilometer 80. Travel farther east and you enter I-san—the large northeast section of Thailand.

From Phitsanulok it is a comfortable one-day drive back to Chiang Mai. To complete our circle, however, we will travel southwest to **Kamphaeng Phet,** where there are many ruins both within and outside the old city wall. If this was your first encounter with the Sukhothai dynasty you would be fascinated, but it is not so impressive after you have seen Sukhothai itself. From here Highway 1, then Route 104, takes you north to **Tak.**

This provincial capital is not particularly interesting but **Wat Phrae** and **Wat Sibunruang** will be mandatory stops for temple freaks. An excellent side trip along Route 105 takes you to **Mae Sot** near the Burmese border. On the way you pass **Lansang National Park, Pa Peung Waterfall,** and **Do Musu,** where numerous hilltribe settlements cling to steep slopes. Mae Sot town is

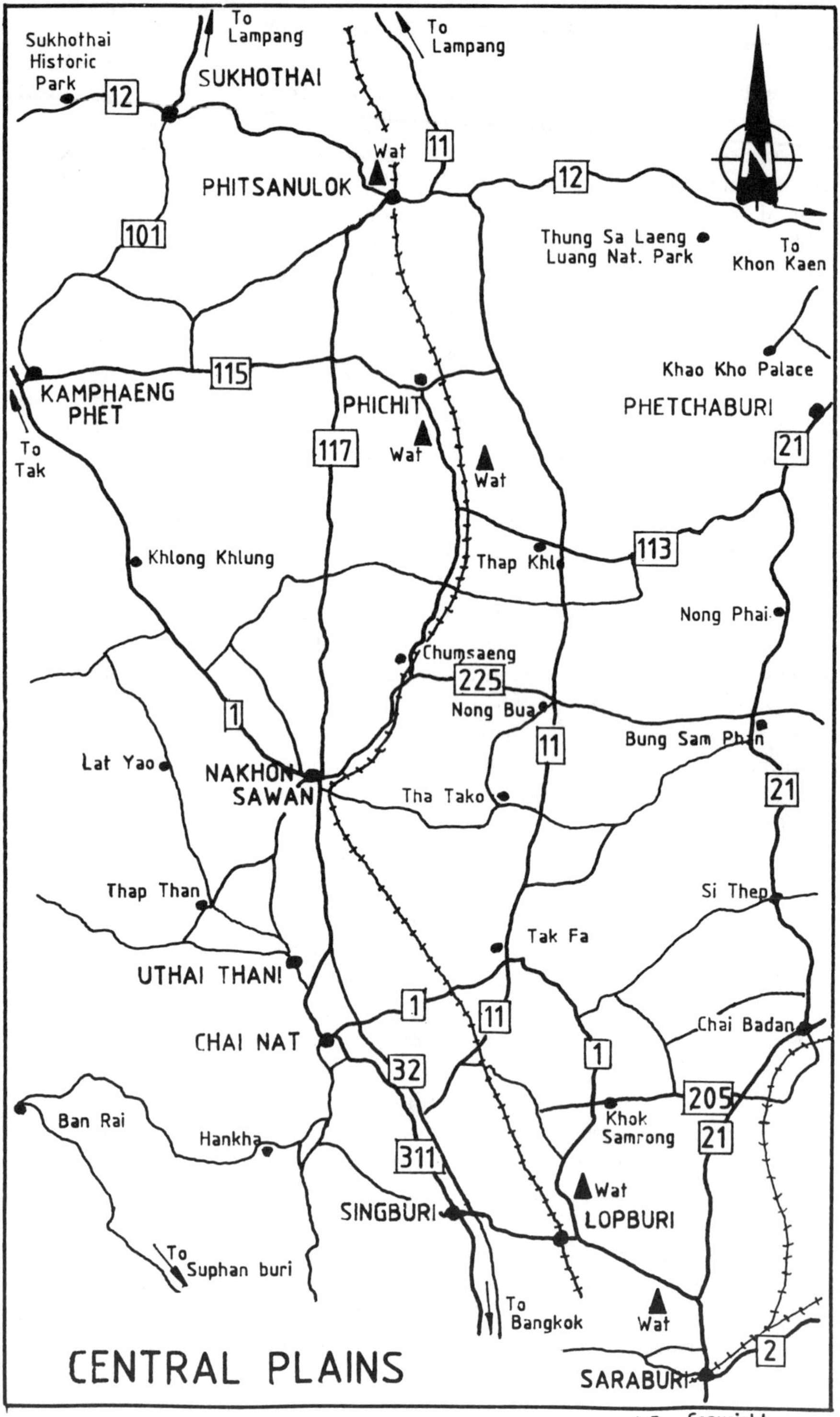

L.R. Copyright

small but it is growing and it has thrust itself into tourism. Walking the streets you see a mixture of dress and ancestry which is quite unique.

If you have the time, it is a good idea to stay in Mae Sot, travel out to the border, and explore some of the local villages. There is some trekking available but you can get a minibus to places such as Mae Kit or Mae Ramet and explore these areas yourself. Some care is required close to the border because there is an illegal trade in narcotics, teak, gems, and guns. Obviously under no circumstances should you get involved in this. Reasonable accommodation is available at the **First Hotel** (Tel. 531-233) in the center of town, with room rates from B160 with fan and B300 with bath and airconditioning, or at the **Mae Sot Hills Hotel** (Tel. 532-600) on the highway from Tak. This 120-room hotel has tennis courts, a swimming pool, a disco, and room rates from B500. Check out the good market for Burmese, Indian, and other unusual items.

The road which heads north from Mae Sot is still not connected to the main northern road network, so you need to retrace your tracks to Tak then head north on Route 1. About 25 kilometers on, there is a well-signposted road to the left leading to **Bhumipol Dam,** Thailand's largest. The electric authority maintains guesthouses and hotel accommodations facing landscaped gardens. There is tennis, golf, and boat trips on the reservoir.

Thoen is 60 kilometers farther along Route 1, then you twist and wind through teak-covered mountains towards Lampang (Route 1) or Lamphun (Route 106). If you decide on Route 1, take the time to visit **Wat Lampang Luang,** an elegant old temple some 20 kilometers south of Lampang. The temple compound is all that is left of an ancient city that was built more than one thousand years ago. The wat was extensively rebuilt in the sixteenth century but even today it is fascinating to most visitors.

Lamphun is only 26 kilometers from Chiang Mai so your journey is almost complete, but the town is worthy of a stop. It is said to have been occupied from at least the ninth century and was for a long time a small principality independent of both the Khmers and the northern Thais. Lamphun today is famous for its two old wats and its beautiful women. The main highway bypasses the town so it has been able to preserve some peaceful atmosphere, appropriate to its age.

Wat Phrathat Haripoonchai stands on the site of an ancient palace. The temple faces the river but most people now enter from the road. The large compound has a school, numerous other buildings, a 50-meter-high gold-topped chedi, a library, and a small museum. **Wat Kukut** is said to be even older with its chedi thought to have been built by Chama Devi, the fabled princess of Lopburi. It has obviously been restored at various times because today it is a mixture of styles. Each of the four sides of the chedi has fifteen Buddha images.

Elephant training camp.

The pleasant treelined road to Chiang Mai returns you to your starting point.

7. Guided Tours

There are two quite distinct forms of touring available in Chiang Mai—coach and trekking. Most of the sightseeing attractions close to Chiang Mai mentioned in Section 6 can be reached on half- or one-day coach tours offered by several companies. Your hotel desk will be able to book these tours (but be aware that they probably only deal with one company and thus can offer limited variety), or you can contact the more reliable operators yourself. These are some of the more reliable operators:

Amata Tour—6 Loi Kroa Rd., 233-406
Discovery Tours—92 Sri Donchai Rd., 252-050
JSJ Tour—Chiang Mai Orchid Hotel, 222-099
Malee Tour—56/3 Chaiyapoom Rd., 251-294
Northern Express Tour—6 Tai Wang Rd., 232-597
Siam Exceller Tour—42/5 Tai Wang Rd., 236-152
Singha Travel—277 Tha Pae Rd., 233-198
Top North Tours—Chiang Mai Plaza Hotel, 252-050

There are four popular half-day tours which can be recommended, but the enjoyment you get from each will depend on your interests. Everyone should enjoy the *tour to Doi Suthep Temple, the Palace, and the Meo hilltribe village*. This is available both in the morning and afternoon. It offers good variety and is not tiring. Likewise, most people will enjoy the morning *tour to the elephant training camp, a waterfall, and an orchid farm*. Watching the huge animals go through their paces is quite fascinating. Then there is the chance to go for a short ride. The half-day *city and temples tour* is a good introduction to Chiang Mai and will quickly help you get your bearings as well as show you five of the best temples. I have reservations about the *home industries tour* because it quickly turns into a shopping expedition, yet for those who want handicraft souvenirs, it is probably ideal. Most operators also offer an evening *khantoke dinner and hilltribe show tour*. It is an experience I can recommend.

The best of the day tours is to Doi Inthanon National Park, which surrounds the highest peak in Thailand (see Section 6). You see Karen and Meo villages, waterfalls, and the Chomthong Temple. The other tours make a full day by visiting the elephant training school then a selection of other attractions such as hilltribe villages, the orchid farms, the hot springs, and then they include lunch. Some give you a chance to ride an elephant or take a short raft trip.

There are two excellent two-day/one-night trips from Chiang Mai. One heads north and visits Chiang Rai, the Golden Triangle, and hilltribe villages (see Section 6), while the other goes west to Mae Hong Son and the Burma border through spectacular hill country.

TREKS

For many years Chiang Mai has been the departure point for treks into the mountainous areas of northern Thailand. Apart from the scenery, the attractions are visits to hilltribe villages and the opportunity to take boat rides, rafting trips, and elephant rides in delightful rural settings. In recent years the trekking industry has greatly expanded and now thousands of foreign travellers take these treks every year.

Most come away with a sense of adventure and achievement but unfortunately some are disillusioned. There are many trekking companies in business in Chiang Mai and there is a considerable difference between the best and the worst. Even within one company there are likely to be treks of varying quality. Two basic things make for a good trek—a good leader-organizer and a good group of trekkers—but there are other considerations as well. Here is a list of guidelines to help ensure that you get what you expect.

1. Use the following list as a guide to the better trekking companies. I acknowledge it is not exhaustive and it can never consider local happenings that just occur from time to time. Using these names, see if you can talk to someone who has recently returned from a trek with the company you choose.

Bamboo Tour—91 Charoen Pra Thet Rd., 236-501
Chiang Mai Fantastic Tour—270 Tha Pae Rd., 236-501
Chiang Mai Holiday Tour—201 Tha Pae Rd., 233-058
Folkways Tribal Trekking—29 Chang Mai Khao Rd., 251-839
Northern Thailand Trekking—59 Moon Muang Rd., 214-572
Summit Tour & Trekking—28 Tha Pae Rd., 233-351
Youth's Tour—31 Phrapokklao Rd., 236-399

2. Each company has its own itinerary and destinations, although some will offer to take you to other areas which you may particularly want to visit. Areas covered by trekking groups include Chiang Dao, Wiang Pa Pao, Phrae, Ngao, Mae Chan, Fang, Chiang Rai, and Mae Hong Son.

3. Don't be afraid to ask questions, and make sure you persevere until you believe the answer. Ask how many people will be on the trek (four to eight seems the ideal size), can the company guarantee no other tourists will stay overnight at the same village, can the guide speak the language of the villages to be visited, and so on.

4. All trekking companies and guides are supposed to be licensed by the government, so ask to see the company registration which gives the name of the owner and company's registered office address. Make sure that the company reports its itinerary and destination to the tourist police in Chiang Mai before you leave. You may also inquire of the tourist police about reports of any problems with the company you have chosen.

5. You must have a thorough understanding of the services the trekking company will provide. Find out how long a three-day trek actually lasts. It may be from mid-afternoon the first day to mid-morning the third day. Get the name of the villages that will be visited and ask what meals are provided. Does the company provide transportation from Chiang Mai before and after the trek or is it just by public bus?

6. If the trekking company or guesthouse offers to keep your valuables, traveller's checks, passport, and so on while you are travelling, prepare a complete listing of the valuables and ask for a receipt covering your list.

7. Don't choose a trek by price alone. The highest-priced tour may not be the best tour but the lowest-priced tour is almost guaranteed not to be.

8. Probably the best time to trek is from November to February. The weather is cooler then (the nights may even be cold) and there should be little or no rain.

9. As more and more trekkers take to the hills and the security situation improves, more people are trekking without a guide. I do not believe that you get as much from an unguided trek and you run the risk of missing much of interest, but it appears that this trend is inevitable. The key to any success at all is careful planning, so visit the Tribal Research Institute at Chiang Mai University and collect as much information as possible on the various tribes, their beliefs, and their customs. There are various maps around that help pinpoint hilltribe villages, so talk to the people at DK Books or the Suriwongse Book Center in Chiang Mai for help.

The term "hilltribe" is used to identify the ethnic minority people who live in the mountainous border regions of north and west Thailand. The term does not, however, embrace a specific race of people. Each of the major "tribes" has its own language, customs, mode of dress, origin, and religion.

There are approximately half a million tribal people living in Thailand, although the number varies because many of them are wanderers who cross the Thai-Burma-Laos borders without regard to nationhood. The Tribal Research Institute recognizes ten different hilltribes but there could be more groups. They appear to have originated in the Tibetan plateau (Akha, Karen, Lahu, Lisu, Meo, and Yao) or more locally in the Golden Triangle countries (H'tin, Lua, Khamu, and Mlabri). Many tribes have traditionally been involved in opium growing and some lead a shifting cultivation lifestyle which causes destruction of the forests and hillsides. The Thai government is undertaking considerable work with the hilltribe people to encourage

A Yao child in northern Thailand.

them to adopt more acceptable practices, with tourism being one of the new income sources for the people.

The *Akha* exist in Laos and Burma and it is believed they arrived in Thailand about one hundred years ago. They are generally among the poorest of the minorities and are shifting cultivators. The women wear headdresses of beads, feathers, and silver ornaments. Villages are located above 1,000 meters, often on steep slopes.

The *Karen* come mainly from Burma and are the largest hilltribe group in Thailand. They live mainly in low altitudes, trace kinship through the mother, and can be Buddhist, Christian, or ancestor worshippers. They wear thickly woven V-neck tunics with unmarried women in white. The group can be further subdivided into four parts.

The *Lahu* come from Tibet and live only above 1,000 meters. The group adopts a shifting cultivation pattern and has traditionally grown opium. They are monogamous and although they worship their ancestors, they believe in a single god. The women wear black and red jackets with narrow skirts and they produce woven shoulder bags which are popular buys for visitors.

The *Lisu* come from Tibet and live at or above 1,000 meters. Their shifting cultivation and opium growing is similar to the Lahu but they have a reputation for being individualists. While premarital sex is said to be common, they have a very strong social cohesion. Both men and women wear bright colors.

The *Meo* come from south China and live at high altitudes. Traditionally they have been more extensively engaged in opium production than any other hilltribe. The women wear simple black jackets and trousers with embroided borders and silver jewelry. The group traces kinship through the father. They are Thailand's second largest hilltribe group.

The *Yao* come from central China and live around the 1,000-meters height. Their main agricultural crops are dry rice and corn. The tribes are polygamous and the adoption of children is common. The women wear black jackets and trousers embroidered with patches and red fur collars.

The *H'Tin* and *Khamu* are both found only in the eastern part of north Thailand and are small in number. The H'Tin are slash-and-burn cultivators while the Khamu are part hunters and part cultivators.

The *Lua* are found nowhere else but in northern Thailand but are being rapidly absorbed into general Thai society.

The *Mlabri* are a small group of hunter-gatherers who have no fixed settlements and move camp every few days.

The Thai government, while trying to change agricultural crops and methods, is showing considerable interest in helping to preserve and promote the hilltribes' culture and tradition. As a visitor you can help by following a few simple rules. Please do this so that future visitors will also have a chance to see these fascinating cultures.

    a. Respect the tribes' beliefs and religious symbols and structures.

    b. Be careful about what you touch and point at. Remember that you are a guest in their village.

    c. Dress appropriately. Hilltribe people are generally modest so cover up bare skin to a reasonable degree. It is not appropriate to wear swimsuits or workout gear no matter how hot the weather.

    d. Ask before you take a photograph of someone. Some villages do not permit photography while others will expect to be paid for any photographs.

    e. Do not give or trade Western medicines. Most hilltribe people are not familiar with the use of these medicines and have no regular access to them. At the present time it is better for them to use traditional treatments which have general tribe support.

    f. Do not give or trade clothing to the more remote tribes. This will introduce a new element of dressing and grooming which will have novelty value for the tribes people but will ultimately change their traditional mode of dress for no good reason.

    g. If you want to give something, choose something that will contribute to their welfare. Pens, paper, needles, thread, cloth, and other materials used for handicrafts may be appropriate.

8. Culture

All Thais love celebrations but northerners have a special flair for them. It is not surprising then to find that festivals dot the northern calendar. Even those events which are celebrated nationally are often more enthusiastically embraced here than elsewhere. These are some of the special local festivals that visitors are most welcome to attend.

The Bo Sang Umbrella Fair is held in late January to celebrate this unique craft. The Fair is held over three days on the main street of Bo Sang and features contests, exhibitions, stalls selling umbrellas, and the selection of Miss Bo Sang.

Luang Wiang Lakon at Lampang is held over two days in early February. During the festival five important Buddha images are carried through the streets in a large procession. Evening events include a khantoke dinner, traditional dancing, and a light and sound presentation at the beautiful Wat Lampang Luang.

The Chiang Mai Flower Festival is also held in early February to display the rich variety of temperate-zone plants that are at their best during the cool season. Spectacular floral floats are a dazzling sight together with flower displays, handicraft sales, and beauty contests.

The **Phra Buddha Chanarat Fair** is held in Phitsanulok in mid-February. This fair honors one of Thailand's most sacred Buddha images but it is festive as well as religious. Featured are folk theater and ram-wong dancing as well as stalls selling local products.

Mae Hong Son is the site for the **Poi Sang Long Festival** in early April, which celebrates the ordination of novices belonging to the Thai Yai tribal group. Offerings for monks are carried through the town in a gala procession and there are dances by performers in animal costumes.

The **Songkran Festival** is held nationwide but nowhere with more enthusiasm than in Chiang Mai. On April 13 and for several days later, no one in Chiang Mai is dry. Part of the celebration is religious but part is pure pleasure—throwing water on anybody and everybody being one of the highlights. There are also parades and beauty contests but whatever the event, you seem to end up wet.

May is highlighted by the **Lychee Fair** in Chiang Rai. This fair celebrates the harvest season with sales of fruit, displays of fruit and local handicrafts, and the selection of Miss Lychee.

A similar festival is held in Lamphun in early August to celebrate the harvest of longan (lamyai) fruit. There is the inevitable beauty contest for Miss Lamyai.

A celebration of a different sort is held during the **Phickit Boat Races** in early September. Here the regatta takes place on the Nan River and features numerous low-slung wooden boats racing with great gusto to the cheers of enthusiastic supporters.

Later in the month there is a **Fruit Fair** at Uttaradit for the langsat fruit and a **Banana Festival** at Kamphaeng Phet. Both have entertainment, displays, and beauty contests.

The **Lanna Boat Races** are held in mid-October in Nan. This accompanies the Kathin season when groups present robes to the monks of local temples in merit-making ceremonies. The races are enhanced by the distinctive long hollowed-out logs which are painted with bright colors and adorned with fanciful designs.

The Loi Krathong and Candle Festival originated in Sukhothai and the most impressive celebration is still held in the atmospheric ruins of the ancient city. Highlights include displays of lighted candles and fireworks, folk dancing, and a spectacular light and sound demonstration. A different type of celebration is held in Chiang Mai where, after a day of merit making, the people launch colorful hot-air paper balloons into the sky. In the evening, all homes and shops are decorated with beautiful lanterns. In many towns in the north, the river or stream that runs through the town becomes ablaze with a slowly drifting mass of little candlelit boats, each carrying a wish from the person who launched it.

Northern hilltribe dancers.

The **Days of Roses** in early December is becoming a popular annual celebration in Chiang Mai to honor the world's favorite flower. There are cultural performances and exhibitions.

You don't have to wait for a festival to experience the beauty of northern Thai dance. It can probably best be seen as part of a khantoke dinner (see Section 5). An essential part of classic Thai dance is the mastery of movements and positions of the hands and this is best demonstrated in the famous fingernail dance. Many of the other dances, however, are more relaxed and fun and you can easily participate in some such as the ram-wong circle dance.

9. Sports

Northern Thailand is no world sports center. The tropical weather is not particularly conducive to vigorous exercise so most visitors will not be looking for great facilities. But at least in the October to February period, northern Thailand has weather which is not too hot for most outdoor sports.

Most of the large hotels have **pools.** The largest is at the Rincome (which has two pools) but others are found at the Chiang Inn Hotel, the Chiang Mai Hill Hotel, the Chiang Mai Orchid, the Chiang Mai Plaza, the Chiang Mai President, the Holiday Lodge, the Dusit Inn, the Mae Ping, the Prince, the Poy Luang, the Royal Park, the Scala Palace, the Sri Tokyo, and the Novotel Suriwongse.

Hotel **tennis** courts are hard to come by but the Rincome saves the day with some that are reasonably well used. Public tennis courts are available at **Anantasiri Courts** on Chiang Mai's superhighway opposite the Museum.

Chiang Mai has the par 72 **Lanna Golf Course** (Tel. 221-911), which welcomes visitors. Green fees are B150, caddy fees B100, and club rental B200. The course is moderately difficult with more than twenty lakes and water hazards, plenty of mature trees, and elevated greens. There is also the nine-hole **Yim Khana Golf Course** (known also as the Gymkhana Club), which offers the marvellous setting of a large cricket ground surrounded by mature rain trees and teaks and a pleasant clubhouse. Green fees here are B100, caddy fees B50, and club rental B200. There are several other courses around including the eighteen-hole course at **Bhumipol Dam** (see Section 6) and a course surrounding the **Chiang Rai airport.**

Chiang Mai has a **boxing** stadium on Bongzai Road, another at the Sanpakoy Market, and a smart municipal stadium for **soccer** and other sports just north of the old walled city. **Fishing** can be done at Adisara Farm, on Mae Sa Samerng Road, for B15 a pole and **windsurfing** facilities are at Huey Dterng Tao, Agricultural Development Center, Chotana Road, near Mae Rim. **Horse racing** is held at the racetrack on Chotana Road on Sundays, while bowling is available at the Chiang Mai Bowl at the Chiang Inn.

Hand painting umbrellas.

10. Shopping

Many visitors consider northern Thailand to be the best area in the country for shopping. Certainly no area surpasses it for handicrafts. While some other northern centers specialize in one or two items, around Chiang Mai, you can find examples of all the crafts which are made in the north.

A major change has occurred in Chiang Mai handicraft shopping since the mid-eighties. Because of the huge increase in tourists visiting this area, many shops and factories have relocated from their old premises and are now concentrated along the Chiang Mai-San Kamphaeng Road. I am sorry about this because some of the previous glamor and excitement has gone, but there is no doubt that facilities for shoppers are now much better (even though prices have risen to pay for large airconditioned display rooms).

Silverware. The making of silverware was carried out for centuries along Wualai Road (just south of the walled city) in an area still known as Silver Village. There are still a few shops and factories here producing intricate hilltribe-inspired designs or stories of Buddhism, but the largest outlets have relocated. A number of shops also sell the less refined silverware of the hilltribes, so you should be aware of what type of silver you are buying. Two recommended outlets are **Siam Silverware,** 5 Wualai Road, Soi 3 (Tel. 233-736) and **Chiang Mai Silverware,** 62/10 Chiang Mai-San Kamphaeng Road (Tel. 246-037).

Lacquerware. Farther along Wualai Road was the traditional center for the lacquerware industry but this has also largely relocated. You can, however, both here and on the San Kamphaeng Road, see artisans at work. They shape bamboo strips into a frame, apply layers of lacquer, then polish this with an ash and clay compound to produce a smooth black glossy surface. The final touch is to paint decorations on the surface. Two recommended manufacturers are **Ratana,** 185/3 Wualai Road (Tel. 234-094) and **Boon Lacquerware,** 9/4 Mu 7 Chiang Mai-San Kamphaeng Road (Tel. 331407).

Umbrellas. Bo Sang just east of Chiang Mai is the umbrella-making village. Umbrellas were probably first made in China then later in other parts of the world. Today silk and cotton umbrellas are displayed here but so too are the traditional paper variety. The paper is still made from the bark of mulberry trees which has been mashed flat and put into a vat of water. After a long wait, a piece of wire mesh is dragged through the tank of liquid to catch the fibers, which are then dried. The resulting umbrellas are brightly painted and become a visual delight. Walk around Bo Sang and buy anywhere.

Silk. A few kilometers past Bo Sang is San Kamphaeng, the silk and weaving center. This is Thailand's best-known craft. I am not convinced that prices here are cheaper than elsewhere but there is some value in buying from the region where it is made. There are many outlets for Thai silk and cotton. Be sure you know exactly what you are buying. Try **HM Thai Silk Co. Limited**, 99/3 Chiang Mai-San Kamphaeng Road (Tel. 331-781) or **Shinawatra Panich**, 73 Chiang Mai-San Kamphaeng Road (Tel. 331-187).

Ceramics. This same area is also famous for ceramics. One type of pottery, known by the French name *celadon,* is unique in both process and product. The clay pots are fired, with designs painted on later. The items are then covered in an ancient wood-ash glaze. When fired again, the results are a distinctive cracked surface and subtle colors not made commercially elsewhere. Other varieties of ceramic ware are available. There is stoneware folk pottery with a slightly rough feel and subdued earthy colors. There are blue and white and colorful Bencharong varieties. Two suggested manufacturers are **Siam Celadon**, 40 Mu 6 San Kamphaeng Road (Tel. 331-526) and **Mengrai Kilns**, 31/1 Rat-Util Road (Tel. 241-802).

Woodcarving. This is a well-developed art and the skills of the carvers are amazing. Most carvings are done in teakwood but visitors are warned to be wary of teak items being hawked on the streets and in some of the markets, as the wood is green and will crack within a few months. Two outlets that have a good reputation are **Prapaat**, 206 Mu 3, Bo Sang (Tel. 331-212) and **Tusnaporn**, 123 Mu 3, San Kamphaeng Road (Tel. 242-913).

Antiques. Chiang Mai is also a treasure trove for the antique buyer. Many of the items appear to originate in Burma and have probably been smuggled across the border. You must be aware that Thailand strictly controls what antiques can leave the country so deal with a reputable company and make sure they complete all the necessary paper work. For true antiques which are allowed to be taken out of the country, prior permission must be obtained from the Fine Arts Department of the Thai government. The object in question must be inspected by the Department and two 6 x 9cm photographs left with the Department. You will find some fascinating pieces at **Amarauadi Antiques**, 31/3-4 Nantaram Road (Tel. 232-156) and at **Iyara Art**, 35/4 San Kamphaeng Road.

11. Entertainment and Nightlife

Chiang Mai has no nightlife area to correspond to Patpong in Bangkok. What you will find, however, is a collection of discos, bars, live music, and massage parlors which will keep most people happy.

The major **discotheques** are situated in the big hotels. All have a cover charge of about B100. Some alternate recorded music with a live band. My suggestions are:

Bubbles Disco—Pornping Hotel, Charoen Pra Thet Rd.
Club 77—Chiang Mai Orchid Hotel, Huay Koew Rd.
Music Room—Dusit Inn, Changklan Rd.

Mammoth Discotheque—Iyara Hotel, Chotana Rd.
Plaza Discotheque—Chiang Mai Plaza Hotel, Sri Donchai Rd.

Live music earlier in the evening (but it often also goes late) can be found at several of the hotels and a range of other places in the city. Of the hotels, the following are my pick: **Fah Mui Cocktail Lounge** in the Novotel Hotel, Changklan Road; **La Grillade Piano Bar** in the Chiang Inn Hotel; **Opium Den** in the Chiang Mai Orchid Hotel, Huay Koew Road; and **Rincome Lobby Bar** in the Rincome Hotel, Huay Koew Road.

Away from the hotels the music is often more wild but the atmosphere can be more natural. Several places provide good live music. The **Boot Pub**, 130 Soi Polec, Chotana Road, features rock and blues. The **Hard Rock Cafe**, 6 Kotchasan Road, Soi 1, offers jazz and rock, while the **Marble Bar**, 100/3 Huay Koew Road, has jazz, pop, and blues. Easy listening can be found at **Rinkaew Lounge**, Rinkaew Complex. Another possibility is **Rock** on Chiang Puak Road.

Bars and cocktail lounges with or without dancers and hostesses are scattered throughout the city rather than being concentrated. You should do your own investigation of these.

Chiang Mai is one of the best centers for traditional **massage**. There appear to be quite a few places which provide this facility for about B200 an hour. The following four are recommended for both men and women: **D.K. Massage**, 277/5 Changklan Road (Tel. 234-919); **Petngarm Hat Wail**, Diamond Hotel, Charoen Pra Thet Road (Tel. 234-155); **Rinkaew Pouech**, Rinkaew Complex near Old Cultural Center; and **Wang Come Ancient Massage**, 301/2 Nimmanhomin Road (Tel. 210-960).

12. The Chiang Mai Address List

Airline—Thai Airways International, 840 Phrapokklao Rd. (Tel. 211-044).
Churches—Chiang Mai Community Church, Kaeo Nawarat Rd., Tel. 242-661; Sacred Heart Cathedral, 225 Charoen Pra Thet Rd.
Crisis Center—Tel. 277-8811.
Hash House Harriers—Black Cat Bar (Tel. 216-793)
Hospitals—Lanna Hospital, Superhighway, Tel. 211-037; McCormick Hospital, Kaeo Nawarat Rd., Tel. 241-107.
Immigration—Superhighway near airport (Tel. 213-510).
Language Center—FLC Language Center, 19/43 Singharat Rd.
Mayor's Office—Tel. 235-010.
Medical Center—Huai Kaeo Polyclinic (Tel. 223-060).
Police Station—Tel. 221-040.
Post Office—Jarern Muang Rd. (Tel. 241-070).
Rail Bookings—State Railways (Tel. 223-0341).

Telephone calls (international)—Tel. 245-366.
Theater—Chiang Mai National Theatre, Suriwongse Rd., Soi 5 (Tel. 235-966).
Tourism Authority of Thailand—Tel. 235-334.
Tribal Research Institute—Chiang Mai University (Tel. 221-933).
U.S. Consulate—387 Wichayanon Rd. (Tel. 252-629).

7

Phuket and the South

1. The General Picture

A quick look at a map shows that the south of Thailand is a long narrow stretch of land. It is bordered in part by Burma but mainly by the clear blue waters of the Gulf of Thailand to the east and the Andaman Sea to the west. Finally it reaches Malaysia in the far south.

What the map cannot indicate is that, for the visitor, this is a fabulous area of wild jungles, sharp mountains, and powdery beaches just waiting to be explored. For the local Thais, there are huge rubber plantations, rich tin mines, and a growing tourism industry that ensures the future prosperity of this vast isthmus.

In some ways, the south is quite different from the rest of Thailand. The climate is wetter, the Muslim religion is stronger, rubber plantations become more common than rice paddies, and the cuisine has a distinct Malay influence.

The south has no dominant city such as Chiang Mai in the north, but it certainly has a tourism center. In the 1970s Phuket was an undeveloped island with a tin mining industry, situated off the mainland west coast. In the years since then the island has become a major international destination greatly favored by Europeans chasing the sun, but increasingly it is being visited by many types of travellers from around the world.

Today more than a million visitors enjoy the sun, sand, and surf of Phuket.

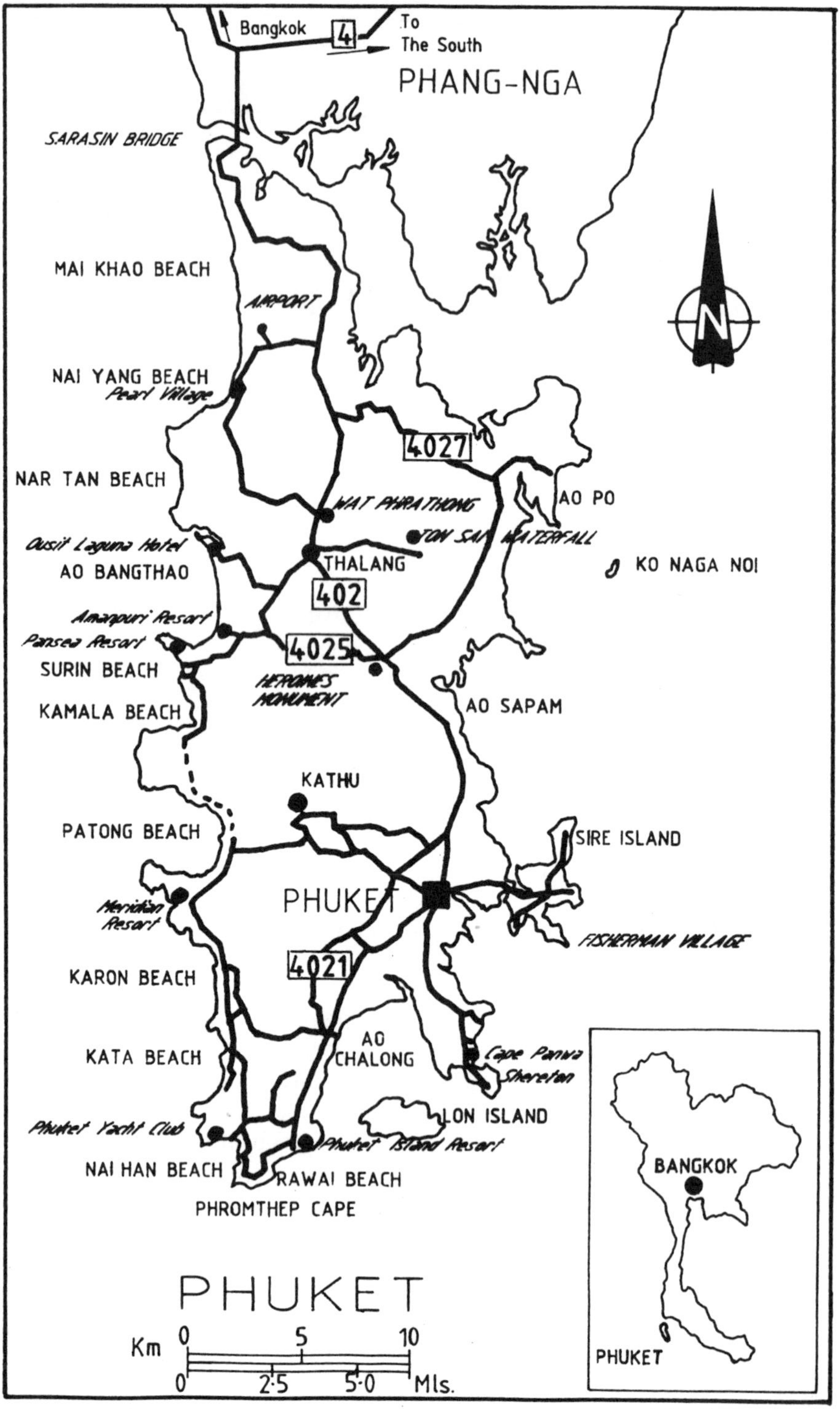
Bangkok
4
To
The South
PHANG-NGA
SARASIN BRIDGE
MAI KHAO BEACH
AIRPORT
NAI YANG BEACH
Pearl Village
4027
NAR TAN BEACH
AO PO
WAT PHRATHONG
TON SAI WATERFALL
Dusit Laguna Hotel
AO BANGTHAO
THALANG
KO NAGA NOI
402
Amanpuri Resort
Pansea Resort
4025
SURIN BEACH
HEROINES MONUMENT
KAMALA BEACH
AO SAPAM
KATHU
PATONG BEACH
SIRE ISLAND
PHUKET
Meridian Resort
FISHERMAN VILLAGE
4021
KARON BEACH
AO CHALONG
KATA BEACH
Cape Panwa Sheraton
LON ISLAND
Phuket Yacht Club
Phuket Island Resort
NAI HAN BEACH
RAWAI BEACH
PHROMTHEP CAPE
PHUKET
Km 0 5 10
0 2·5 5·0 Mls.
N
BANGKOK
PHUKET

Building continues at a frantic pace and new resorts appear on the scene every month. Despite this, most areas of Phuket remain unspoiled by excessive high-rise and trashy development. Yes, there has been dramatic change but it is still relatively easy to find a small cove with no one else on the beach. Patong Beach may no longer be everyone's idea of paradise but its popularity can be judged any day or night by the crowds that throng there, seeking the pleasures that a deserted beach can never offer.

Now a new challenger is emerging. Koh Samui is an island off the mainland east coast. While it is closer to Bangkok, it lacks a major airport at present, so it has not yet experienced Phuket's rocketing success. Koh Samui, however, already has a substantial tourism infrastructure—it started as a backpacker's resort but now the up-market properties are appearing. There is now a small private airport with several flights from Bangkok every day and the ferry transportation from the mainland is rapidly improving. A company has just announced that hydrofoil services will be introduced from Bangkok and from Surat Thani.

Then there is Hat Yai and Songkhla in the deep south, which have developed a large and growing tourism industry, mainly for Malaysians who come across the border for more excitement than they can find at home.

Away from these tourist centers, life goes on much as it did 100 years ago. There are villages among coconut palms, fishermen on white beaches, dramatic coastlines and mountain ranges—just about everything you need for your own "tropical paradise." No wonder more and more visitors are discovering the south and returning for more.

2. Getting There

Phuket has an international airport with an increasing number of direct overseas flights, but most North American and South Pacific visitors will arrive by air from Bangkok.

Thai Airways International operates numerous daily flights from Bangkok and a new terminal on the island provides good facilities. Flights also arrive from other centers in the south—Surat Thani, Trang, and Hat Yai—and from Chiang Mai in the north. The Bangkok-Phuket flight takes one hour and fifteen minutes. In Bangkok phone 280-0070 for bookings and in Phuket phone 211-195.

Non-airconditioned **buses,** normal airconditioned buses, and VIP buses all connect Phuket to Bangkok. They leave the Southern Bus Terminal at Thonburi in Bangkok and, after crossing the causeway to Phuket Island, arrive at the terminal on Phang-Nga Road in Phuket town. There is no advanced booking on the non-airconditioned services. The journey of about 900km (560 miles) takes about 14 hours.

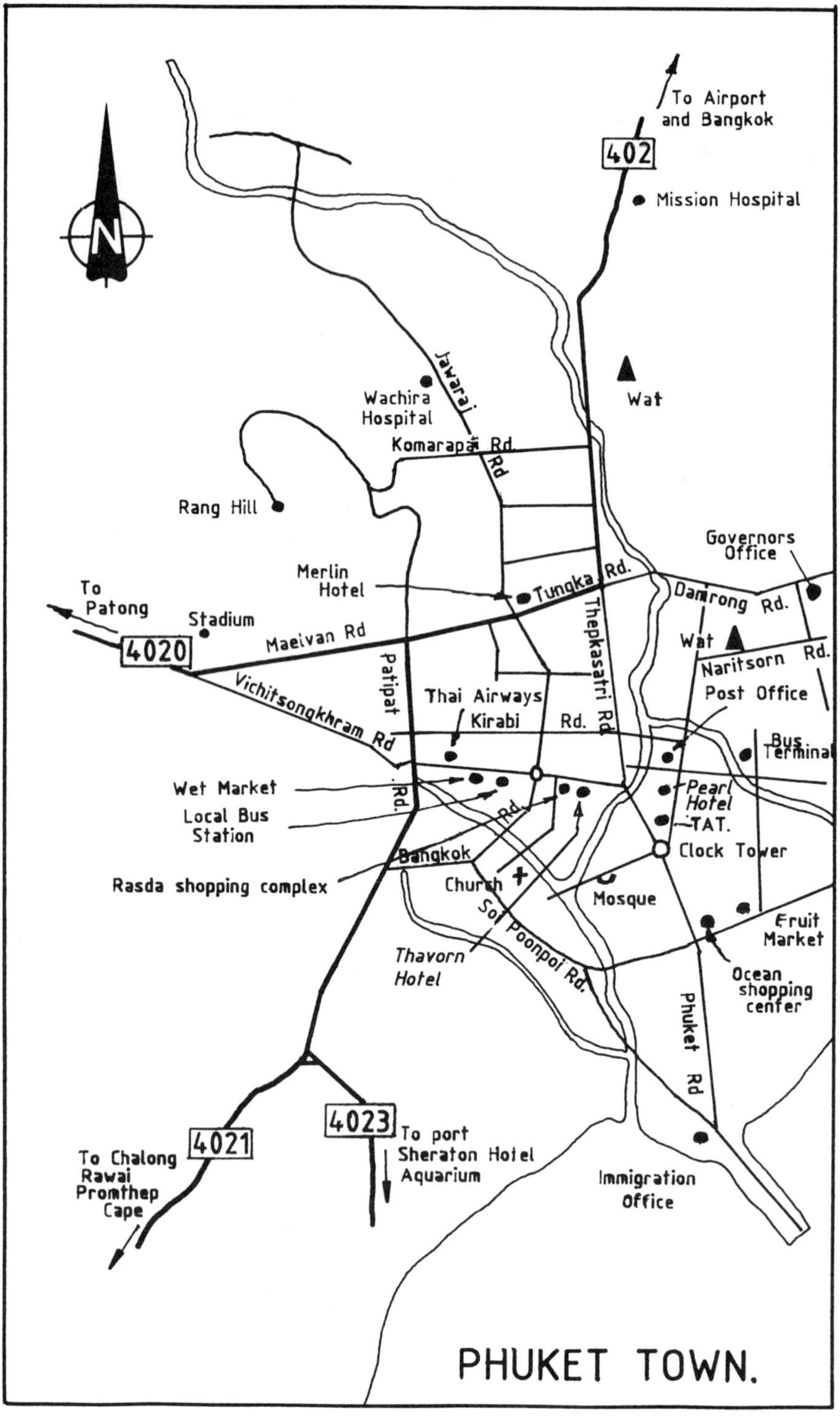
To Airport
and Bangkok
402
Mission Hospital
Wat
Wachira
Hospital
Jawaraj
Komarapai Rd.
Rd
Rang Hill
Governors
Office
Merlin
Hotel
To
Patong
Stadium
4020
Maeivan Rd
Tungka Rd.
Damrong Rd.
Wat
Naritsorn Rd.
Post Office
Thepkasatri Rd
Patipat
Rd.
Vichitsongkhram Rd
Thai Airways
Kirabi Rd.
Bus
Terminal
Wet Market
Local Bus
Station
Pearl
Hotel
TAT.
Clock Tower
Bangkok
Rd.
Rasda shopping complex
Church
Mosque
Soi Poonpoi Rd.
Thavorn
Hotel
Fruit
Market
Ocean
shopping
center
Phuket Rd
4021
To Chalong
Rawai
Promthep
Cape
4023
To port
Sheraton Hotel
Aquarium
Immigration
Office
PHUKET TOWN.

There is no **rail** connection to Phuket but you can catch the overnight train in Bangkok for Surat Thani (11 hours) and connect with an airconditioned bus that transports you to the major hotels in Phuket (4 1/2 hours).

Long-distance **taxis** operate from several centers including Surat Thani, Trang, and Hat Yai. Fares are about double normal bus fares. Taxis leave from central Phuket town for these other centers whenever they have four or five fare-paying passengers.

3. Local Transportation

Phuket is an ideal location to rent a car, jeep, or motorbike. For those not used to driving on the left, this is almost a perfect place to see if you can adapt. The roads are generally good, the traffic is not heavy and travels at a sedate pace, and most direction signs are in English.

International **car rental** agencies such as Avis and Hertz have cars available at the airport, at many of the hotels, and at central locations in Phuket town and Patong Beach. Local operators such as Pure Car Rent provide price and service competition and still offer fully insured vehicles. Watch out for the street bike hustlers. The vehicles they promote are generally not insured.

Some visitors will not wish to rent their own transportation and there are certainly alternatives. Most of the major hotels are quite some distance from the airport (20-45 kilometers) but all provide **minibus** transfers either free or for a reasonable cost. In addition, Thai Airways International has both a **limousine** service and a minibus service from the airport to Phuket town. The cost is around B300 for the limousine and B70 per person for the minibus. A limousine to one of the resort beaches is about B500.

Public buses operate from Phuket town to all beaches. The converted minitrucks (songthaews) depart from the local bus station on Ranong Road every 30 minutes or so from about 8 A.M. to 6 P.M. The level of service depends on demand and the 20 baht fare will provide you with an hour of interest and fun.

Taxis are also readily available but ask a local or your hotel for an indication of the price before you negotiate with the driver. Within Phuket town and at some of the beaches, small pickup taxis operate on more or less fixed routes for a fixed price of B5-10. These vehicles can be hailed anywhere and if business is slow they will chase you for a fare. After dark the price tends to rise.

4. The Hotel Scene

A fundamental decision needs to be made about Phuket accommodation. The choice is between staying in Phuket town, at one of the self-contained isolated beach resorts, or at one of the developed beaches. The decision depends on your reason for visiting Phuket. I have listed the accommodation by area because most will know the type of accommodation they need but will be unsure of which area is best for their needs. Within each area, I have run through the list roughly from most to least expensive. The exception is the Phuket Resorts section, where all the resorts mentioned are in the expensive category.

PHUKET TOWN

Phuket town is attractive and pleasant by Thai standards and the best shopping on the island is still here. Nevertheless, not too many international visitors stay in town because for most, the beaches are the big attraction on the island. If you have arrived on Phuket and the beach is not your thing, you can stay in town and spend a very pleasant day or two just wandering around the shops, markets, wats, and streets.

The two major hotels in town, the **Phuket Merlin** (Tel. 212-866), 180 rooms, and the **Pearl Hotel** (Tel. 211-044), 250 rooms, both have adequate rooms and good facilities. They have a choice of bars and restaurants, shopping facilities, swimming pools, discos, and travel desks. Both hotels have sister properties on the beach with complimentary transfer between the beach and the town, so in some ways you can enjoy the best of both worlds. For beach lovers though, the inconvenience of having to bus to the sand would be a frustration. Prices at both the Pearl and the Merlin start at about B1000 (significantly less than most of the beach resorts). (For reservations write to the following: Phuket Merlin, 158/1 Jawaraj Rd., Phuket 83000; Fax: 6676-216-429. Pearl Hotel, 42 Montri Rd., Phuket 83000; Fax: 6676-212-911.)

Cheaper rooms are available at the **Thavorn Hotel** (Tel. 211-333), 200 rooms, from B550, in a good central location on Rasda Road next to one of the major shopping areas; at the **Siri Hotel** (Tel. 211-307), 42 rooms, from B400, on Jawaraj Road, and at the City Hotel (Tel. 211-383), 168 rooms, from B700, on Krabi Road. This last hotel has a wide range of facilities and is very popular with middle-class Thais. I have not stayed there but it appears to be a good value.

PHUKET RESORTS

Phuket has a multitude of bays and beaches and many remain undeveloped except for a major resort. Sealed road access is available to most of these locations. All can be considered in the up-market category. Many visitors claim that this is what Phuket should be all about—good accommodation, good food, sporting opportunities, private beaches, tranquility, and great service. Certainly some of the best resorts offer all this and even more.

The Pearl Village (Tel. 311-376), 177 rooms, is on Nai Yang Beach relatively close to the airport. The beach is part of Nai Yang National Park and it is a real delight—few people, good sand, lovely casuarina trees. The resort is set amid lawns and palm trees and is very attractive. Guest rooms are excellently appointed—some even include a video player—and there is a very large pool with a waterfall and jacuzzi. There are three restaurants, three bars, two tennis courts, pitch and putt golf, horseriding, and other sporting opportunities. Prices start at about B2500 for a room. (Reservations with the hotel at P.O. Box 93, Phuket 83000; Fax: 6676-311-304.)

The **Dusit Laguna Hotel** (Tel. 311-320), 240 rooms, is on Bang Tao Beach some 15 kilometers to the south. The hotel is reached by driving across several kilometers of uninviting country but when you reach it, the location between two lagoons is attractive and there is a long sandy beach. The low-rise property has good facilities, including two restaurants, coffee shop and disco, nice lawns, and a feeling of seclusion. Sporting facilities include tennis, volleyball, sailing, windsurfing, and water skiing. The specially developed lagoon allows water sports all year. Prices from B2800. (Reservations with the hotel at 390 Sri Soonthorn Rd., Phuket 83000; Fax: 6676-311-174.)

Another 5 kilometers to the south the **Amanpuri Resort** (Tel. 311-394), 40 rooms, provides the most exclusive address in Phuket. Service here is discreet but superb. The resort has no need to advertise—many guests are repeat visitors. They come to enjoy the teakwood suites with the best facilities, the stunning ocean views, and the ultimate exclusivity. (Reservations with the hotel at 18 Sri Soonthorn Rd., Phuket 83000; Fax: 6676-311-100.) Room rates are from B7000.

Close by is the **Pansea Resort** (Tel. 311-249), 100 rooms, with traditional-style bungalows overlooking the sea and a private bay. This French-run resort has attracted a dedicated clientele who enjoy seclusion, peace, and privacy. It is recommended for those wanting some time together in a tropical hillside setting. The site is too steep for the elderly or the infirm. Prices from B2500. (Reservations with the hotel at 118 Mu 3, Choeng Talay, Phuket 83110; Fax: 6676-311-252.)

The **Meridien Phuket** (Tel. 321-480), 470 rooms, is currently the largest hotel on Phuket island with every imaginable facility. The size of the hotel and the type of building (high-rise slab) means that there is no fear of feeling isolated. Facilities include four tennis courts, two airconditioned squash courts, gym and aerobics center, two swimming pools, sauna, archery range, and games room. There are three restaurants, two bars, a disco, and some shops. The hotel has its own private bay but is only a few kilometers from Patong Beach with its after-dark action. Prices from B3000. (Reservations with the hotel at 8/5 Mu 1, Karon, Phuket 83000; Fax: 6676-321-479.)

Much has been written about the **Phuket Yacht Club** (Tel. 214-020), 108 rooms. The hotel is built on a steep hill and spills down through nine levels to a pool, the bars and restaurants, and the beach. Each room features a large private patio and sundeck giving magnificent views over the sea and the offshore islands. This is still one of the nicest resorts on the island. Prices from B3500. (Reservations with the hotel at 23/3 Viset Rd., Nai Harn, Phuket 83130; Fax: 6676-214-028.)

The only major resort on the eastern side of Phuket is the **Cape Panwa Sheraton** (Tel. 391-123), 160 rooms. The main hotel overlooks the sea and out to Phi Phi island. There are lawns, palm trees, and two attractive beaches for swimming and water sports. Two unusual features are an English pub with entertainment, and an authentic Thai mansion housing a restaurant, library, and bar. Prices from B2500. (Reservations with the hotel at 27 Mu 8, Cape Panwa, Phuket 83000; Fax: 6676-391-177.)

RAWAI BEACH

Rawai Beach was Phuket's first developed beach but even today it is not too gaudy or brash. The beach is 17 kilometers south of Phuket town and regular buses service the area. There are good seafood restaurants and nice views towards the offshore islands but the beach itself is unlikely to excite you.

Rawai is home port for many of Phuket's sea gypsies. These independent people appear to be unrelated to most mainland Thais. The young people become expert divers at an early age and can stay underwater for prolonged periods while chasing lobsters or gathering pearl oysters.

This is also the departure point for trips to some of the closer islands. Fresh-fruit vendors will pack you a picnic lunch, and a boat with captain will cost you about B400 for the day. It can be a very pleasant low-key day.

The best hotel at Rawai Beach is the **Phuket Island Resort** (Tel. 215-950), 300 rooms. This is one of Phuket's best-equipped hotels with a wide range of restaurants and sporting activities yet it is losing out now to some of the newer hotels on the west coast. There is a fitness center with a sauna and jacuzzi, tennis courts, badminton courts, two swimming pools, and a shopping center. To add to the hotel's appeal, an offshore island is also owned by the same group and a boat ferries guests across to the private beach and small restaurant. Prices from B1800. (Reservations with the hotel at 73/1 Rasda Rd., Rawai, Phuket 83000; Fax: 6676-215-956.)

Much cheaper accommodation is available at the **Rawai Resort Hotel** (Tel. 212-943), 90 rooms, from B400 and the **Rawai Garden Resort** (Tel. 213-

996), 8 rooms, from B250. Both are well located but naturally they lack many of the resort facilities of the major hotels.

KATA BEACH

Kata Beach is the first of the developing west coast beaches as you head north from Phromthep Cape, the southernmost point on Phuket island. Kata is really two beaches—Kata Noi and Kata Yai—separated by a rocky headland. Both are delightful and each is dominated by a major resort. My favorite spot is the northern end of Kata Yai, where there are beach showers, deck chairs, massage ladies, and windsurfers and catamarans for rent. Po Island is just offshore and the delightful warm water appears safe all year.

The Club Mediterranee (Tel. 214-830), 300 rooms, occupies a large beachfront site in the middle of Kata Yai. The low-rise hotel is surrounded by all the usual resort facilities provided by Club Meds worldwide, and the beach provides a good getaway for those seeking some privacy. The beach fronting the resort has good sand but only sparse vegetation so at midday it can be too glary and hot. Notices warn of dangerous water currents at some times of the year. By wandering down to one end of the beach these problems can be overcome. Prices from B3000. (Reservations through the Club Med organization or at P.O. Box 145, Phuket 83000.)

The **Kata Thani Hotel** (Tel. 381-124), 183 rooms, has an absolute beachfront location at the northern end of Kata Noi. This beach is less developed than Kata Yai but has more trees and more opportunity to be alone. The hotel is modern and low-rise. I have not stayed here and know little about its level of service. The hotel provides a minibus to Kata township for those needing some different action. Prices from B2800. (Reservations with the hotel at 62/4 Rasda Rd., Phuket 83000; Fax: 6676-381-426.)

The **Boathouse Inn** (Tel. 215-185), 36 rooms, is situated on the headland between the two bays. Accent is on service and the opportunity to have privacy in a lovely setting. Prices from B3000. (Reservations through the Bangkok office at Soi 15, Phetchaburi Road, Bangkok 10400; Fax: 662-234-3365.)

Cheaper accommodation is provided by numerous small inns and bungalows. Many of these do not have telephones but most will be clean and some offer basic Thai food. Costs start at about B100. It is best to catch a bus out to the beach then wander along making your own inspection of the places that may have appeal. If you arrive early in the day you will usually find a room because there is a good turnover of guests and few people book this accommodation.

For those staying a week or more, the **Kata Plaza** (Tel. 215-502), 20 rooms, offers very modern self-contained serviced apartments with airconditioning, kitchenette, restaurant facilities, etc. from B5000 per week.

KARON & KATA BEACHES
PHUKET ISLAND

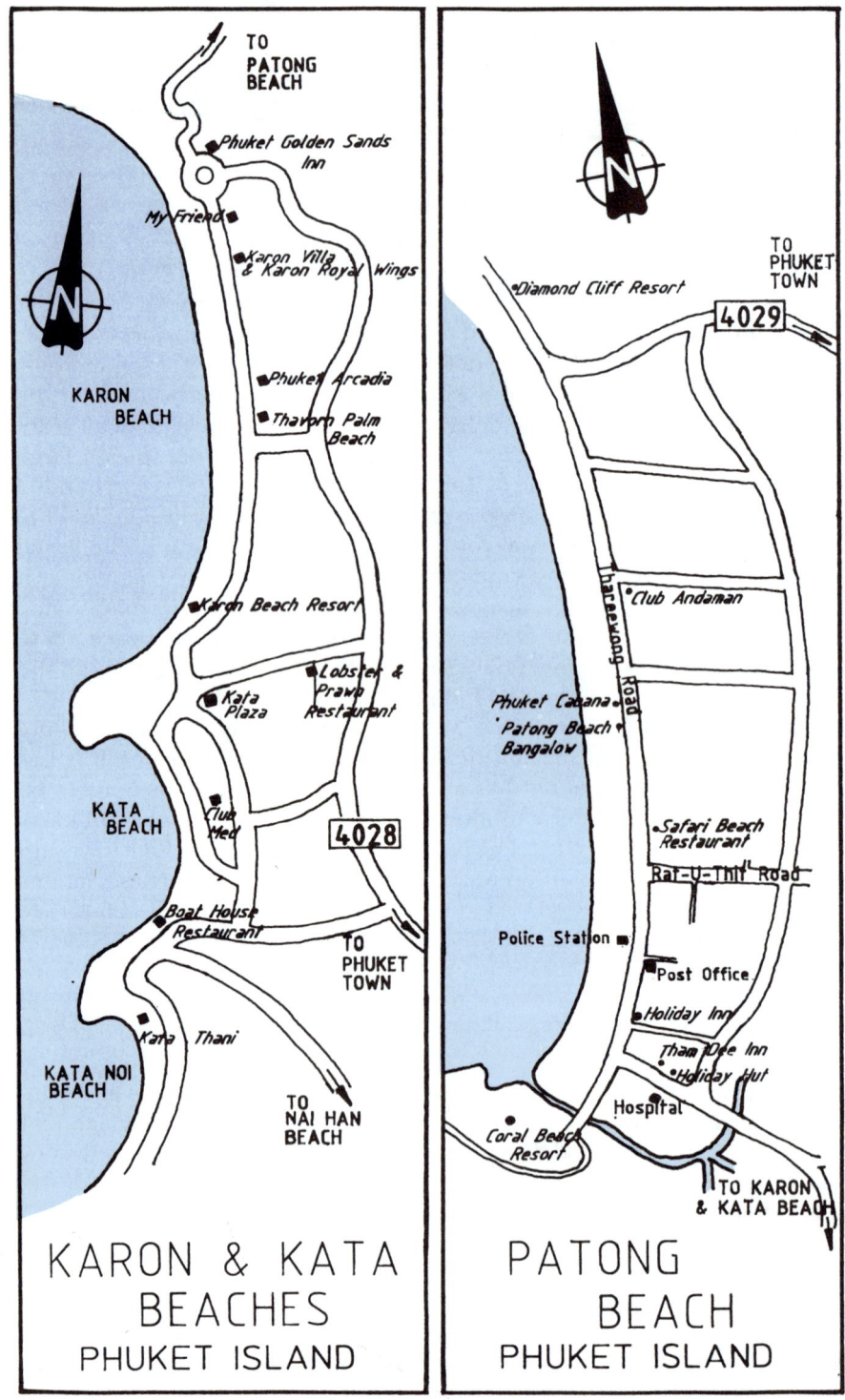

PATONG BEACH
PHUKET ISLAND

L.R. Copyright

KARON BEACH

Karon Beach has recently become a boom area and it lacks the appearance of some of the longer established centers. The beach is long and open with little vegetation. New roads are being pushed through the sand dunes as development proceeds and this is changing the appearance of the area, but a brackish lagoon remains and the general lack of vegetation can be disconcerting in the hotter months. The beach here is dangerous during certain wind and tide conditions so check with your hotel or the locals.

Karon is dominated at present by four major resorts but more are on the way. The **Karon Villa and Karon Royal Wing** (Tel. 214-820), 300 rooms, is the most northerly of the four. The original resort consisted of individual cottages in nice gardens with sauna, squash and tennis courts, and three swimming pools but the new Royal Wing is a seven-story modern concrete building. The rooms are well appointed and there are Thai and Japanese restaurants, a health club, and a discotheque—but you be the judge on whether this beach needs a concrete high-rise. Prices start at about B2200. (Reservations with the hotel at 36/4 Karon Beach, Phuket 83000; Fax: 6676-214-823.)

The **Phuket Arcadia Hotel** (Tel. 214-812), 255 rooms, is slick, modern, and rises to eleven stories. The hotel is complete in itself and almost treats the beach and surrounding area with contempt. The rooms are contemporary with large windows. The hotel has a large, unshaded pool, several restaurants and bars, a discotheque, and all the usual facilities of an international resort. It is affiliated with the Montien group. Prices start at B2500. (Reservations with the hotel at 78/2 Karon Beach, Phuket 83000; Fax: 6676-214-840.)

Right next door is the **Thavorn Palm Beach Hotel** (Tel. 214-835), 210 rooms. The hotel is modern but only rises to four stories and more emphasis seems to be placed on the beach. There are restaurants, bars, fitness center, games room, tennis courts, and jogging track. Prices start at B2200. (Reservations with the hotel at 128/10 Karon Beach, Phuket 83000.)

The **Karon Beach Resort** (Tel. 214-828), 100 rooms, opened in 1989 at the southern end of Karon Beach. The hotel is the only major accommodation situated right on the beach. It would seem to have good potential. Prices from B2200. (Reservations with the hotel at 27 Rasda Rd., Phuket 83000; Fax: 6676-214-828.)

Karon Beach has many budget hotels and bungalows which provide adequate facilities. Most are back from the beach, none are glamorous, and many do not have a telephone. Try **Phuket Golden Sands Inn** (Tel. 214-308), 50 rooms, at about B500 a room or **My Friend** (no telephone), 39 rooms, at about B200. Both are near the roundabout at the northern end of the beach.

The **Karon Inn** (Tel. 214-828), 100 rooms, has resort facilities from B900 a room as does the **Phuket Island View** (Tel. 212-696), 51 rooms, from B1100. I have not, however, personally inspected either property.

PATONG BEACH

Patong Beach was once an idyllic white powder beach backed by coconut groves. The 2-kilometer-long beach is still there but the coconuts have been largely replaced by hotels, bars, shopping centers, roads, and condominiums. Patong Beach will cause some conservationists much heartache but most visitors enjoy the swimming, paragliding, windsurfing, sailing, water skiing, and other facilities on offer and the unequalled shopping, dining, and nightlife attractions.

Despite the amazing development, Patong Beach has not yet been ruined. However, the massive high-rise Paradise Complex goes a long way towards changing Patong's attractiveness forever.

The appeal of Patong today is its great variety. There are low-cost bungalows, open-air bars with leggy hostesses, and motorcycles and long-tail boats to rent. But there are also top-class resorts, excellent restaurants, discos and cultural shows, chaffeur-driven cars and motor cruisers. Here is a selection of accommodation from the huge variety available.

The **Coral Beach Resort** (Tel. 321-106), 200 rooms, is unique in Patong. The low-rise resort is situated at the southern end of the beach on a dramatic headland and is linked to Patong by a private bridge. There are two swimming pools, several restaurants and bars, a sports club, and a private beach. The standard rooms are not as large or modern as some others in Phuket, but the seclusion combined with the proximity to all that Patong offers is a good combination. Because of the hilly site, this is not for the elderly or handicapped but the sprawling layout has much appeal to others. The lobby is a huge open-ended high-roofed Thai-style building which also contains a restaurant, tours desk, and bar. It looks out over one of the pools and then out to the bay. This really is what Phuket is all about. I recently spent two very pleasant days at this resort and will return for a longer stay at the first opportunity. Prices from B2000. (Reservations with the hotel at 104 Mu 4, Patong, Phuket 83000; Fax: 6636-321-114.)

The **Holiday Inn Phuket** (Tel. 321-020), 280 rooms, is near the southern end of the main Phuket development. The modern concrete building provides good facilities in an international style. The private balconies, indoor/outdoor coffee shop, pool, and pool bar are some concessions to the beachfront location. There is also tennis, sauna, and a health club. The hotel is well sited for those seeking an active stay in Phuket. Prices from B2000. (Reservations through the Holiday Inn network or direct with the hotel at 86/11 Taweewongse Rd., Patong, Phuket 83000; Fax: 6676-321-433.)

The **Diamond Cliff Resort** (Tel. 321-501), 220 rooms, is one of the newer resorts developing a good reputation. This hotel is at the extreme north end of Patong Beach about 1 1/2 kilometers from the center of things. It has its own small rocky cove and a delightful beachfront restaurant but it's just a little far to walk downtown comfortably at night. Public transportation is not a problem but if you prefer to be completely independent, you would be better in the center of the beach. Prices from B2400. (Reservations with the hotel at 61/9 Kalm Beach Rd., Patong, Phuket 83000; Fax: 6676-321-507.)

Two low-rise resorts are probably the best value here. The **Phuket Cabana** (Tel. 321-138), 75 rooms, has the best location right on Patong Beach. The individual units are rather close together and lack some of the newest facilities, but the food is excellent. There are three bars and a beachside pool. Prices from B1600. (Reservations with the hotel at 94 Patong Beach Rd., Patong, Phuket 83000; Fax: 6676-321-178.)

The **Club Andaman Beach Resort** (Tel. 321-102), 128 rooms, has bungalows set in spacious, well-manicured grounds and it is very popular with families. Some rooms offer fans rather than airconditioning and start at B900 a night. You need to cross the road to the beach and the main center of Patong is about half a kilometer away, but I still consider this a good location. (Reservations with the hotel at 77/1 Patong Beach Rd., Patong, Phuket 83000; Fax: 6676-321-404.)

Down-market from here there is a wide range. The **Patong Beach Bungalow** (Tel. 321-213), 34 rooms, has a great position right on the beach and prices that start at B500. Cheaper still are the **Tham Dee Inn,** 20 rooms, and the **Holiday Hut,** 20 rooms, side by side on the new road leading to Karon Beach. True budget accommodation is becoming harder to find as Patong land prices rocket upwards, but if you look along the streets back from the beach you may find something suitable.

5. Dining and Restaurants

Phuket is justifiably famous for its seafood, so this should be on everyone's menu at least once during your stay. Good seafood is not cheap but in Phuket you know it is fresh and you have a choice of grilled, fried, sauteed, baked, roasted, or steamed in either Thai, Western, or Eastern style.

Most restaurants sell tiger prawns, king lobsters, oysters, mussels, clams, crabs, and fresh fish by weight. A typical meal for two people will cost B500 in the better restaurants.

SEAFOOD RESTAURANTS

Good seafood restaurants abound. In Phuket town, **Phuket Seafood** (Tel. 212-245), off Phuket Road near the Mine Monument, offers good food in a fine setting. This has become a favorite with tourists but it's good to see that Thais still consider it a good value. On Rasda Road, **Llai-an Seafood** is another which receives good support.

Most people still regard **Kan Eang Restaurant** at Chalong Bay (Tel. 216-

726) as the finest seaside seafood restaurant in Phuket. When a restaurant achieves this reputation I fear that its standards will slip or that it will become complacent. Fortunately there is no indication that this is yet happening. It pays to book on weekends or holidays.

Kata Beach has two seafood restaurants worthy of note. The **Lobster and Prawn** (Tel. 381-619) is part of the Kata commercial center. Prices are reasonable and the food, in either Thai or Chinese style, is good. The restaurant has a good offer of free transportation for anyone within the Kata, Karon, and Kata Noi beach area. The **Boat House Restaurant** (Tel. 381-657) is actually part of the Boathouse Inn, but it is a seafood restaurant with a fine location and great food which is well patronized by the general public. It is also an excellent location to see a spectacular sunset, so arrive early just in case.

As you would expect, Patong Beach, as the most developed tourist beach, has the greatest choice of seafood restaurants. On the beachfront road (Thareewong Road), **Malee Seafood Village** (Tel. 321-204) is excellent for European-prepared seafood. I can thoroughly recommend the **Patong Safari Beach** restaurant (Tel. 321-230) after several delightful meals in the open-air section, surrounded by hundreds of fairy lights. At a cost of B300 for two, it is an excellent value.

Away from the beach, local experts recommend **Oni Seafood**, a seafood palace with a Thai and international menu. That's on my list to try on my next trip. In the same area, **Tum Restaurant** (Tel. 321-260) and **Patong Number 4 Seafood** both have good reputations with the locals.

Mention should also be made of the markets and food stalls that offer seafood in less luxurious surroundings. The menu choice will be small and the facilities bare but don't be put off by that. Some of my most memorable meals have been had in these places and the cost is ridiculously cheap.

OTHER ALTERNATIVES

Of course, most of us can't eat seafood all the time so Phuket offers other alternatives. In common with most of Thailand, good Western food is difficult to find outside the international hotels. One alternative available at Patong is the **Jaegerstube** restaurant (near Oni Seafood), where authentically prepared German and European cuisine is on offer.

Also at Patong the **Shalimar Restaurant** (near the Post Office) offers Indian food with specialties of Tandoori chicken and mutton curry.

THAI FOOD

Southern Thai food has the same basic ingredients as elsewhere in the country but there is a greater emphasis on curries. Phuket itself has some specialties and you should try them while you are there.

Khanom chin is Thai rice noodles normally eaten with a curry soup made from minced fish or shrimp. This dish is available throughout Thailand, but in Phuket it has a richer flavor and is served with a greater variety of fresh and preserved vegetables. It is a typical breakfast for the people in Phuket and is widely available at restaurants, food stalls, and at the market.

Noodles are universally popular in Thailand. In Phuket there are two distinctive styles of fried noodles—*mi hun*, which is fried with fresh shrimp, pork, shellfish, and green cabbage, and *mi sapan*, which has seafood and gravy on top. Noodles are bought mainly at food stalls but Phuket town has a **Thai Fast Noodle** shop on Montri Road which can satisfy every noodle desire.

Namphrik kung siap is Phuket's style of hot shrimp paste sauce with sweetened crisp shrimp, eaten with vegetables. This is one dish that visitors who are not used to Thai food should take care with, but it is well worth a try. I guarantee that most visitors who spend a few weeks in Phuket will love it before they leave.

Curries are universally popular throughout the south but Phuket's *kaeng luang*—a sour curry with fish and vegetables—has a delightfully different taste. I'm somewhat undecided about *kaeng tai pla*, fish viscera curry, so make up your own mind on that.

I have no doubts at all about *ho mok*. This is steamed curried fish with vegetables which is normally served with plain rice. It's delicious.

Thai food is obtainable everywhere. Surprisingly, some of the best dishes are found in the most basic of food stalls. I had a great meal on the Kata Beach sitting on a log in the sand. It cost me B25. Try the night-market food stalls on Phuket Road in Phuket town or the collection of small restaurants between Kata and Karon beaches.

All hotels, no matter how basic their restaurant, will be able to serve you Thai food. The same goes for the seafood restaurants mentioned before. Don't, however, automatically equate quality with price. There is often little relationship between the two.

HOTEL RESTAURANTS

The Tourism Authority of Thailand's small brochure "Hotels and Bungalows in Phuket" lists about 170 alternatives. Almost all have at least one restaurant; some have up to ten. It is probable that there are 500 hotel restaurants in Phuket offering an amazing variety of food to you, the visitor.

Without doubt the best Western-style food is available at some of these restaurants. It's probably reasonable to say also that some provide some of the worst. I have not eaten at all the hotel restaurants, but the best I have found to date is the **Chart Room** at the Phuket Yacht Club. This only opens from 7:30 till 10:00 each evening so you can't really enjoy the magnificent views over the water. The food, however, is superb.

I could do no better than to advise you to try the "Seafood ragout and artichokes poached in white wine" or the brochette of rock lobsters. French, Italian, German, and Australian wines are available to complement the meal.

Many hotels have special dinners on a regular basis. The Coral Beach Resort, for instance, has an Oriental food night each Sunday where there is a buffet with a selection of Chinese, Thai, Korean, and Japanese food and a barbecue dinner on Wednesday night. The Asian food at such dinners is modified for Western tastes but it is a good way for the less adventurous to try something different.

6. Sightseeing

Although Phuket is an island, you really need your own transportation or a selection of organized tours to see all the sights. The exception to this is Phuket town, where you can walk to many of the points of interest.

Phuket has a long history of contact with the Western world. In 1786, the Sultan of Kedah offered Captain Light of the British East India Company the opportunity to establish colonies in Phuket and on the Malaysian island of Penang. After considerable delay, the British finally accepted Penang but decided against Phuket.

That could have been a big mistake because 100 years later, Phuket was a rich and thriving center based on a tin industry. Gangs of Chinese came north from Malaysia to try and seize the mines, and the first foreign bank built in Thailand outside Bangkok was established. That bank, the **Chartered Bank** on Phang Nga Road, is still there today and you should not miss seeing it. It is one of several fine examples of Sino-Portuguese architecture in the town.

The tin industry brought Chinese merchants and you see their influence at the **Put Jaw Chinese temple** on Ranong Road and at other temples throughout the town. The Chinese temples with their glazed ceramic tile roofs and scrolled lattices add an interesting contrast to the Buddhist and Muslim buildings you see elsewhere on the island. Colorful festivals such as fire-walking rituals are held from time to time at these gaudily decorated temples, but you are welcome to visit at any time provided you are clothed conservatively and behave appropriately.

Asian markets fascinate me and the one at Phuket is no exception. It's worth a trip just to see the produce sold from bamboo baskets in a way that has changed little in a hundred years. Flower stalls are across from the market and food stalls are set up all around offering fried bananas, coconut juice, and other local "goodies." The market operates 6 A.M. to 6 P.M. Monday through Saturday.

Just a few kilometers north of Phuket town, on the road to the airport, you will find the **Phuket Orchid Garden and Thai Village.** The attraction is open daily from 11 to 4 and is a mixture of orchid display, handicraft workshops, tin-mining and rubber-making demonstrations, lunch, and an unusual show. If so inclined you can finish the visit with an elephant ride. Admission and lunch is about B180.

Ten kilometers southeast of Phuket town is the **Marine Biological Research Centre and Phuket Aquarium.** This is established in a lovely location at the tip of Panwa Cape. The display tanks which show brilliantly colored fish, corals, and other sea creatures are a great preview for your own snorkeling trip.

If you travel south through Rawai Beach you reach the southern extremity of Phuket island at Phromthep Cape. There is a small park, some food and souvenir stalls, and a path that leads to the tip of the **promontory.** This is a great place for a photograph but take one before the hordes of tourists descend from the buses that include this on the sightseeing tours.

From here it is possible to travel north on the west coast, visiting all the popular beaches and some isolated coves which still have no development. The road from here to Kata, Karon, and Patong beaches is good and there are some magnificent viewing points which are worthy of some time. North of Patong the road deteriorates and there are some very steep sections to **Kamala Beach.** This is undeveloped and most of the beach is fairly open. There is a small fishing village located at the mouth of the small stream.

Surin Beach is a popular picnic spot and there is a 9-hole golf course right beside the beach. This is a dangerous swimming beach for much of the year, so please beware.

The road from here curves right and heads inland to join the airport road at the **Heroines' Monument.** This is a life-size bronze statue of two sisters who led the defense of Phuket during the Burmese invasion of 1785. In reward for their heroism, King Rama I conferred the status of nobility on them.

If you turn left and head north, in about 8 kilometers you reach the small town of Thalang, once the capital of Phuket. Turn right at the traffic lights and travel for about 4 kilometers on a delightful narrow road through rubber plantations to the **Ton Sai Waterfall.** The falls themselves are small but there are some food stalls, a pretty lake, and the surrounding jungle is attractive. It makes a nice change from the beach.

Back at Thalang, if you turn right at the main road, it's only about a kilometer to **Wat Phra Thong**—the Temple of the Golden Buddha. This is a nice Buddhist temple with considerable significance to local people.

Just north of the temple a road to the left leads through rice paddies and rubber plantations to the **Nai Yang National Park.** About halfway along this road, a side road to the left takes you through a pretty valley to Nar Tan and eventually to **Nar Tan Beach.** This is the way Phuket was everywhere, until tourism started in the 1980s. It's a place to enjoy.

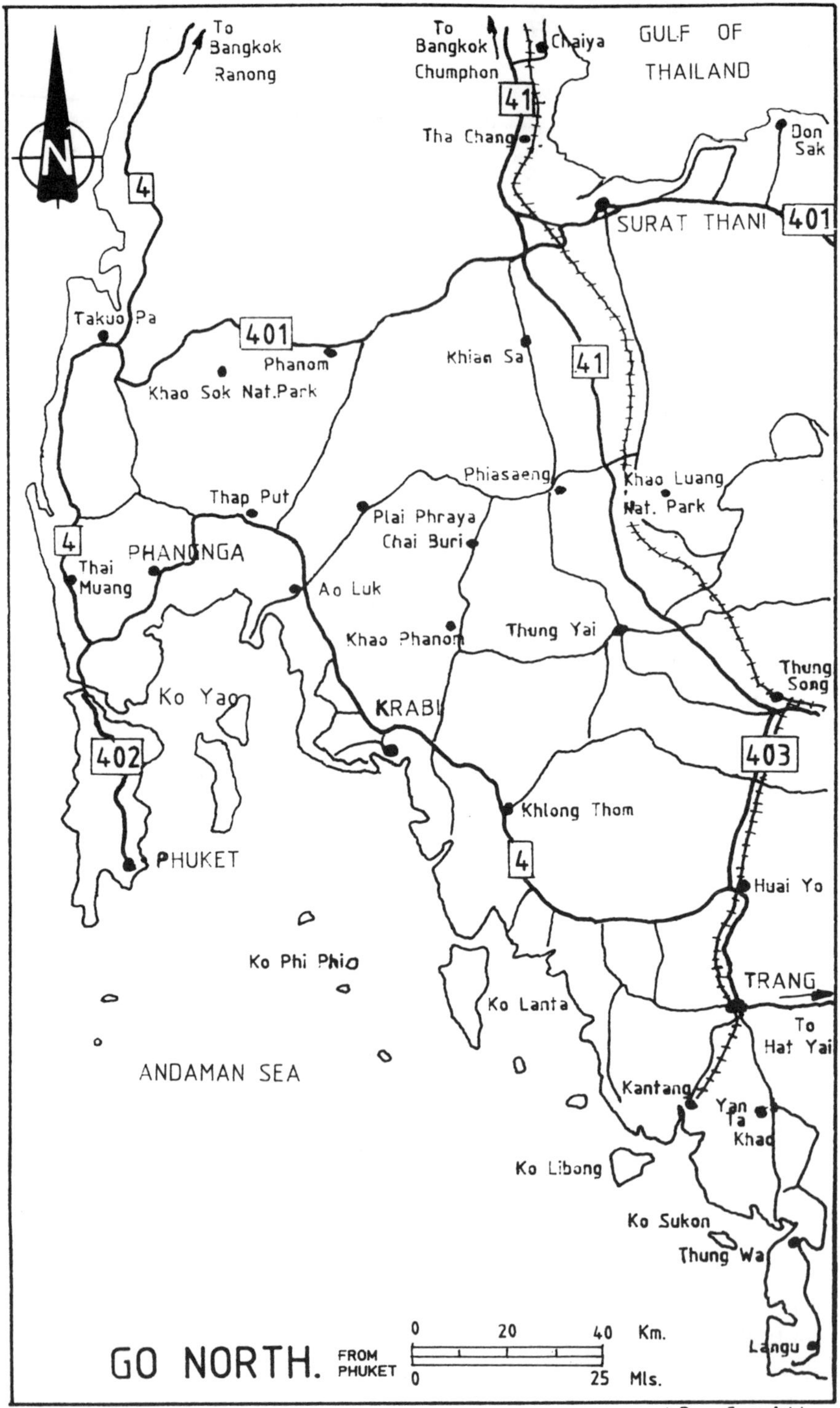

To Bangkok Ranong
To Bangkok Chumphon
Chaiya
GULF OF THAILAND
41
Tha Chang
Don Sak
4
SURAT THANI
401
Takuo Pa
401
Phanom
Khao Sok Nat.Park
Khian Sa
41
Phiasaeng
Khao Luang Nat. Park
Thap Put
Plai Phraya
Chai Buri
4
PHANGNGA
Thai Muang
Ao Luk
Khao Phanom
Thung Yai
Thung Song
Ko Yao
KRABI
402
403
Khlong Thom
4
PHUKET
Huai Yo
Ko Phi Phio
TRANG
To Hat Yai
Ko Lanta
ANDAMAN SEA
Kantang
Yan Ta Khao
Ko Libong
Ko Sukon
Thung Wa
Langu
GO NORTH. FROM PHUKET
0 20 40 Km.
0 25 Mls.

Back at the national park, the waters are crystal clear and teeming with fish. This is a good place to snorkel and beachcomb. Just north of here, **Mai Khao** or Airport Beach is a lovely deserted stretch of sand where you can almost be alone for much of the year. Between November and February, at night you may have to share it with quaint green sea turtles which lumber ashore to lay, then bury, their eggs in the sand.

If you are still keen to sightsee, a road will lead you down the east coast through rubber, cashew, coconut, and pineapple plantations to Ao Po and Pa Klok. Boats leave Ao Po for Phang Nga Bay (see Section 7) and for the pearl farms on Ko Naga Noi. There is another small waterfall at Bang Bee in the **Pa Pra Taew National Park** and you may well see wild orchids and a variety of wildlife. Then it's straight ahead back to Heroines' Monument and your hotel.

GO NORTH

The road journey from Phuket to Bangkok is something that many visitors will wish to avoid (14 hours by bus, several days by private vehicle if you wish to stop and see some of the sights). But the trip north to Surat Thani is a delight and this is a great way to reach Koh Samui.

After crossing the causeway to the mainland, the Phuket road runs north to the small town of Khok Kloi. This brings you to the main southern highway. Turn right and you eventually reach Malaysia. Straight ahead lies Bangkok.

Route 4 heads north for about 90 kilometers to Takua Pa. On the way you pass several places worthy of a stop. Your first stop could be at **Lam Pi Waterfall** (off the highway 2 kilometers to the right). The drive through rubber plantations is interesting and the pool at the base of the falls is ideal for swimming.

Farther north there are some lovely beaches, including Khao Luk Beach and Bang Sak Beach, and a stretch of rugged coastal country which provides lovely views.

Takua Pa has little interest although this has been a port for well over a thousand years and was a trading port for Indian merchants for quite some time. Four kilometers north of the town, Road 401 leads off to the right. The next 130 kilometers to Surat Thani are a delight. You initially travel along the wide Takua Pa River valley, then you enter a world of limestone crags and spectacular mountains. This is dramatic country and the road twists and turns as it avoids impassable obstacles.

With the hills behind you, the last 20 kilometers or so into **Surat Thani** pass through dense rubber plantations. The town has no special interest for tourists but there are important shipbuilding, mining, and fishing industries and tourism is now making its mark. Surat Thani has an airport with several

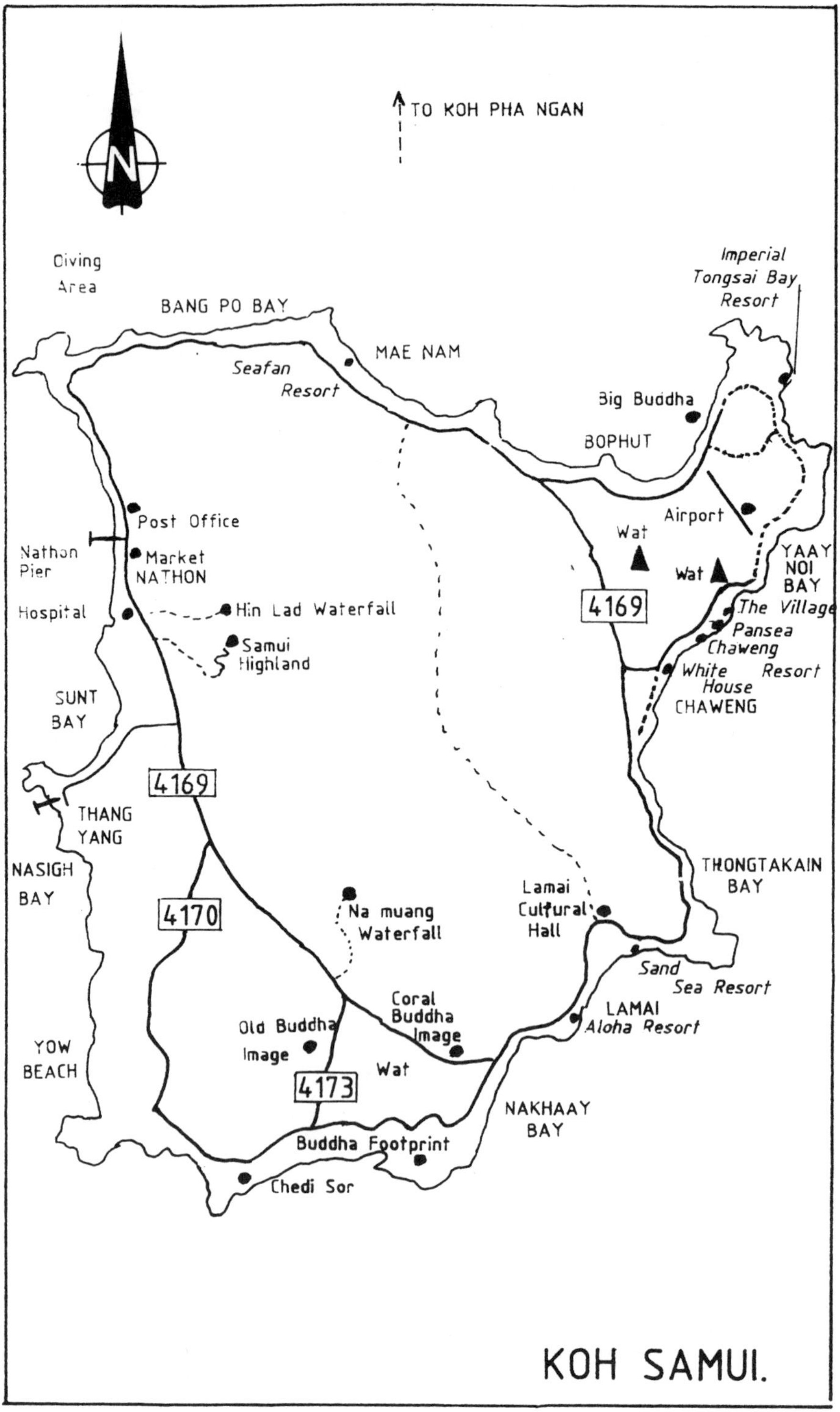

N
TO KOH PHA NGAN
Diving Area
BANG PO BAY
MAE NAM
Seafan Resort
Imperial Tongsai Bay Resort
Big Buddha
BOPHUT
Airport
Wat
Wat
YAAY NOI BAY
4169
The Village
Pansea Chaweng
White House
Resort
CHAWENG
Post Office
Nathon Pier
Market
NATHON
Hospital
Hin Lad Waterfall
Samui Highland
SUNT BAY
4169
THANG YANG
NASIGH BAY
4170
Na muang Waterfall
Lamai Cultural Hall
THONGTAKAIN BAY
Sand Sea Resort
LAMAI
Aloha Resort
Coral Buddha Image
Old Buddha Image
Wat
4173
YOW BEACH
NAKHAAY BAY
Buddha Footprint
Chedi Sor
KOH SAMUI.

jet flights a day to Bangkok and it is an important rail and coach center. Buses leave Thonburi in Bangkok for the 12-hour journey at regular intervals and there are two trains a day from Hua Lampong station with sleeper accommodation. If you decide you would like to stay here, reasonable accommodation is available at the **Siam Thani** (Tel. 273-081; Fax: 6677-282-169), 180 Surat-Phunphin Rd., 170 rooms. The hotel has a restaurant, bar, swimming pool, tennis, and disco. Useful telephone numbers are: Police, Tel. 272-095; Hospital, Tel. 272-231; Thai Airways International, Tel. 272-610; Railway Station, Tel. 211-213; and Bus Station, Tel. 272-524.

Surat Thani is important for visitors because it is the departure point for trips to Koh Samui, Koh Pha Ngan, and the Ang Thong Archipelago.

There are three ways to reach **Koh Samui** from Surat Thani. The most popular is the 2-hour express boat service that departs from Ban Don, a short distance from town. This is operated by Songserm Travel (Tel. 421-228; Fax: 6677-421-544) and departures are three times a day. The company has representatives which meet the trains and airconditioned coaches, and there is a free transfer to the ferry terminal. Cost of the trip is B90. Thai Airways International provides a service from the airport using this express boat at a cost of B170.

There is also a night boat leaving Ban Don for Koh Samui. It takes 5 hours for the crossing but many passengers manage some sleep. The third service operates from Don Sak, which is about 1 hour by road from Koh Samui. Because this is much nearer to Koh Samui, the crossing only takes 1 hour and 15 minutes. For train and coach passengers, the cost from Surat Thani to Koh Samui by this service is the same as the express boat. Also make inquiries to see if the hydrofoil service is operating. This will provide the fastest and most comfortable crossing.

All express and night passenger ferries from Surat arrive at Nathon on Koh Samui and this is the main center for the island. The town has banks, currency exchange booths, travel agencies, an immigration office, a post office, gift shops, pharmacies, bookshops, and all the things you would expect from any thriving beach center.

Few people stay at Nathon, however, because the attraction of Koh Samui is its long uncrowded beaches and its rugged interior. There are good roads on the island, two major beaches and several others where development is now underway. Minibuses serve all areas of the island and jeeps and motorcycles are available for rent. You should note that the car ferries from the mainland arrive at Thang Yang. There is accommodation here for those who need it at the Coco Cabana Beach Club or the Samui Ferry Inn.

Chaweng Beach is the action place on Koh Samui. This is the longest beach on the island, has the best swimming, and is naturally very beautiful. The development which has occurred, however, has done little to enhance what nature provided. There is a vast selection of bungalows and more upmarket accommodation on the beach, and behind these are a growing number of shops, discos, and bars. There is even a restaurant (called Manohra) which features classical Thai dancing with dinner. This is no longer the place for a quiet getaway holiday.

Some of the developments have good facilities and you cannot dispute the beauty of the beach. Some of the better properties are **The Imperial Samui** (Tel. 421-390), 80 rooms with balconies, swimming pool, TV, and in-house movies, towards the south end of the beach (Bangkok reservations, Tel. 254-0111); **The White House** (Tel. 421-382), 10 rooms, a modest friendly place which is a little farther north (Bangkok reservations, Tel. 234-0982); and a collection of properties close together on the central part of the beach— **The Chaweng Cabana** (Tel. 421-377), 25 rooms; the **Chaweng Resort** (Tel. 421-378), 40 rooms with swimming pool, timber deck, and restaurant overlooking the beach; the **Pansea Resort** (Tel. 421-384), 50 rooms, with its open-air, seaview restaurant and bar; and the **Village** (Tel. 421-382), 19 rooms. All these properties have airconditioned rooms, attached bathrooms, sports facilities, and some meal facilities. Some do not have hot water. Prices range from about B1000 to B2000. (Reservations for these properties can be made through the following addresses and numbers. Imperial Samui, Chaweng Beach, Koh Samui 84140; Bangkok Tel. 02-254-0111. The White House and The Village, P.O. Box 25, Koh Samui 84140; Bangkok fax: 662-234-0982. Chaweng Cabana, Chaweng Beach, Koh Samui 84140. Chaweng Resort, Chaweng Beach, Koh Samui 84140; Fax: 6677-421-378. Pansea Resort, Chaweng Beach, Koh Samui 84140; Bangkok Tel. 02-235-6075.)

Many people will be happy with a non-airconditioned room and fewer luxury features—there is usually a breeze and the beach really is the big attraction—and the choice of budget accommodation here is quite immense. There is so much continuous change in these bungalows that it is impossible to give a recommendation. The best idea is to take a bus from the ferry terminal, get out at the beach, and walk until you find something that appeals to you. Prices start at about B100.

A wide variety of visitors seems to enjoy Chaweng. You will find sports enthusiasts, swinging singles, yuppies from Bangkok and abroad, middle-aged hippies, and happy family groups. It's basically its own little world which has become almost self-sufficient, at least for the short term.

Lamai is rapidly becoming a rival to Chaweng and is increasingly being taken over by foreigners. The beach is smaller and the bungalows generally less ambitious than the high-priced ones at Chaweng. Lamai beach faces southeast while Chaweng faces east so there are noticeable differences in weather conditions on a given day. The two beaches are not far apart and the round-island road provides a very pleasant view from the scenic lookout between the two.

A few years ago Lamai was sleepy, quiet, and a great place to "drop out" for awhile. You can still do that but the discos, ice-cream parlors, bars, and general activity are making it increasingly difficult.

There is a good selection of down-market bungalows starting at about B100 a night and several more up-market properties. Two of the better resorts are **Aloha Resort** (Tel. 421-418), 30 rooms, at the south end of the beach and **Sand Sea Resort** (Tel. 421-415), 20 rooms, at the extreme north end. Both have airconditioned rooms or rooms with fans. Prices are about B500-900 depending on the location and facilities you choose. You may be able to do much better than this, however, during the August to November off-season.

Koh Samui has some attractions other than beaches, and visitors who stay more than a few days will be tempted to explore them. At the northern end of the island near Bophut village, a causeway leads to the **Temple of the Big Buddha.** This is a Buddhist monastery and retreat but visitors are most welcome. At the base of the huge modern image there are booths selling incense and Buddha statues and around the edge of the temple grounds there are huts selling food and drinks. Although this is a very casual beach island, you are still expected to be properly dressed to visit the temple.

At the western side of the island, not far from Nathon, there is a hiking trail to **Samui Highland Park.** The 2-hour trek takes you through a rubber plantation to the top of the highest accessible ridge, where you get outstanding views over the Ang Thong Marine National Park. The area is nicely kept and the atmosphere is unexpected on a tourist island. Farther south the **Na Muang Waterfall** is attractive. Water cascades down the mountainside into a sandy pool that is ideal for swimming. A local attraction is the stone carving of initials left by royalty who have visited before you.

Away from the two main beaches, new bungalows and small resorts are appearing every month. On the north coast, **Mae Nam beach** is attracting development with its good shore and snorkeling. Best accommodation here is the **Seafan Resort** (Tel. 421-350), 15 rooms. In the northeast corner of the island the **Imperial Tongsai Bay Resort** (Tel. 421-450), 80 rooms, provides the most luxurious accommodation available on its own private bay and beach. There is a snack bar, a good restaurant, a swimming pool, and water sports facilities. There are enormous luxury rooms and great views. Prices are B2000-2800. (Reservations can be made through the Imperial office, Wirless Road, Bangkok 10330; Tel. 02-254-0023; Fax: 662-253-3190.) Other resorts offering better than average accommodation are **Chaba Samui Resort** (Tel. 421-380), 16 rooms; **Coral Bay Resort** (Tel. 272-222), 36 rooms; **FarnBay Resort** (Tel. 273-920), 30 rooms; and **Nara Lodge** (Tel. 421-364), 45 rooms. All these are located in the Bophut area. All are priced B800-1200.

Good water sports facilities are available on the island. These include windsurfing (Lamai, Chaweng, Mae Nam), catamaran sailing, snorkeling, and diving. Diving trips and instruction can be arranged with Koh Samui Divers (Tel. 421-465).

Recently there has been an improvement in the standard of Koh Samui restaurants but seafood is still the best choice. If you catch your own, the bungalow will be happy to cook it for you. After dark, favorite pastimes are the campfire beach parties which are advertised on banners in front of the hosting bungalow. You invite yourself and pay for drinks. It can be a good way to meet some of your fellow travellers.

If you decide Koh Samui is too developed for your liking, a visit to **Koh Pha Ngan,** an island 15 kilometers to the north, should make you happy. You get there on the interisland express boat which leaves Nathon twice a day for the 40-minute crossing. If you already know Koh Pha Ngan and have decided to stay at Rim Beach, you can catch a boat there from Bophut Bay on Koh Samui.

What you find when you get to Koh Pha Ngan is something quite delightful. Many people say it's like Koh Samui in the 1970s. The daily boat arrives at **Thong Sala** pier near the largest town on the island. Tied up on either side of the pier are long-tail boats heading to various bays around the island. At the end of the pier, small covered pickup trucks wait to take passengers to the bungalows that are accessible by road. There are some bungalows within walking distance of the pier. The town, with its small selection of shops, restaurants, and motorcycle rentals, is worth seeing.

It is immediately obvious that this is not Koh Samui. The pace is much slower, people are positively "laid back," and the facilities generally match this ambience. Many of the bungalows have no proper running water or electricity. Some have small generators which thunder away for part of the time but prices fit the facilities. Bungalows start at an amazing B30 a night and the top price is B300. There are over 90 bungalows from which to choose.

Most bungalows are on the west coast north of Thong Sala or on the south coast and in particular the southeast corner at **Rim Beach.** Rim Beach is reached by boat from Thong Sala or you can go by road to Bann Khany and take a boat from there. Rim Beach is actually two beaches separated by a ridge. The east beach is long, beautiful, and quiet and there is a good choice of bungalows. One of the favorites is **Paradise** for both staying and eating. The west beach has great sunsets but does not appeal to me as much as the east.

Another alternative is **Thong Ta Pan Beach** in the northeast. This is a most impressive beach and it was once a favorite of King Rama V. Land access is possible by four-wheel drive over a very rough road and you can make a side trip to Than Sadel waterfall on the way. Again there is a choice of bungalows with **Panviman Resort** probably one of the best.

The other area of interest in the region is the **Ang Thong Marine National Park,** a collection of twenty or so islands with interesting caves, lagoons, and rock formations. There is an all-day trip from Koh Samui to the Park each day at a cost of B200. **Sleeping Cow Island** is the largest island and headquarters for the Park. There are clean basic bungalows for rent with running water. Attractions are swimming, snorkeling, and diving or just getting away from civilization for awhile. On Koh Mae there is a steep climb to an emerald-green saltwater lake surrounded by steep cliffs.

GO SOUTH

When you cross the causeway from Phuket to the mainland, to head south towards Malaysia you turn right at Khok Kloi onto Highway 4. This is the road to Phang-Nga Bay (see Section 7). The scenery for the next 100 kilometers is absolutely stunning. There are rich valleys, dramatic hills, spectacular limestone monoliths and untamed jungle.

The unbelievable 200-meter-high sheer rocks dominate both on and off shore. The town of **Ao Luk** is a good place to stop and do a little exploring. Take the road from Ao Luk which leads to the coast at **Luem Sak.** Boats leave from here for Tham Lod, a dramatic grotto; Tham Pee Huo To, a cave with prehistoric paintings; and Tham Pra Tur Saksit, a brilliantly colored limestone cave.

On the way back to the main road, stop off at the **Tarn Boke Koranee National Park,** one of the best small parks in Thailand. The park has helpful guides, a photo display with English descriptions, and numerous walks, waterfalls, and caves. The main falls are created by an underground spring which comes to the surface at the mouth of a cave. The spring flows all year and there are several pools in the stream which will entice you to stay and swim. The dramatic rock wall dominates the whole park and it really is a great place to get back to nature. You will find a satisfactory room in the park at the **Waterfall Inn** for between B250 and B700.

When you can drag yourself away from all this tranquility, head back to Route 4 and turn right towards Krabi. As you travel south the beaches to your right are deserted and magical. The difficulty in getting to them is one reason why they have remained in this state. After about 30 kilometers on the highway, there is a road to the right which leads through several small villages and eventually to several of these beaches. It also eventually leads to the **Susan Hoi Shell Cemetery** near the village of Ban Laem Pho.

Here part of an ancient sea floor has worked its way to the surface and the solid slabs reveal millions of seashells compressed together and cemented by time. There is a concerted attempt to push this as a "world-class" tourist attraction. Certainly it is very unusual as such a phenomenon is only known

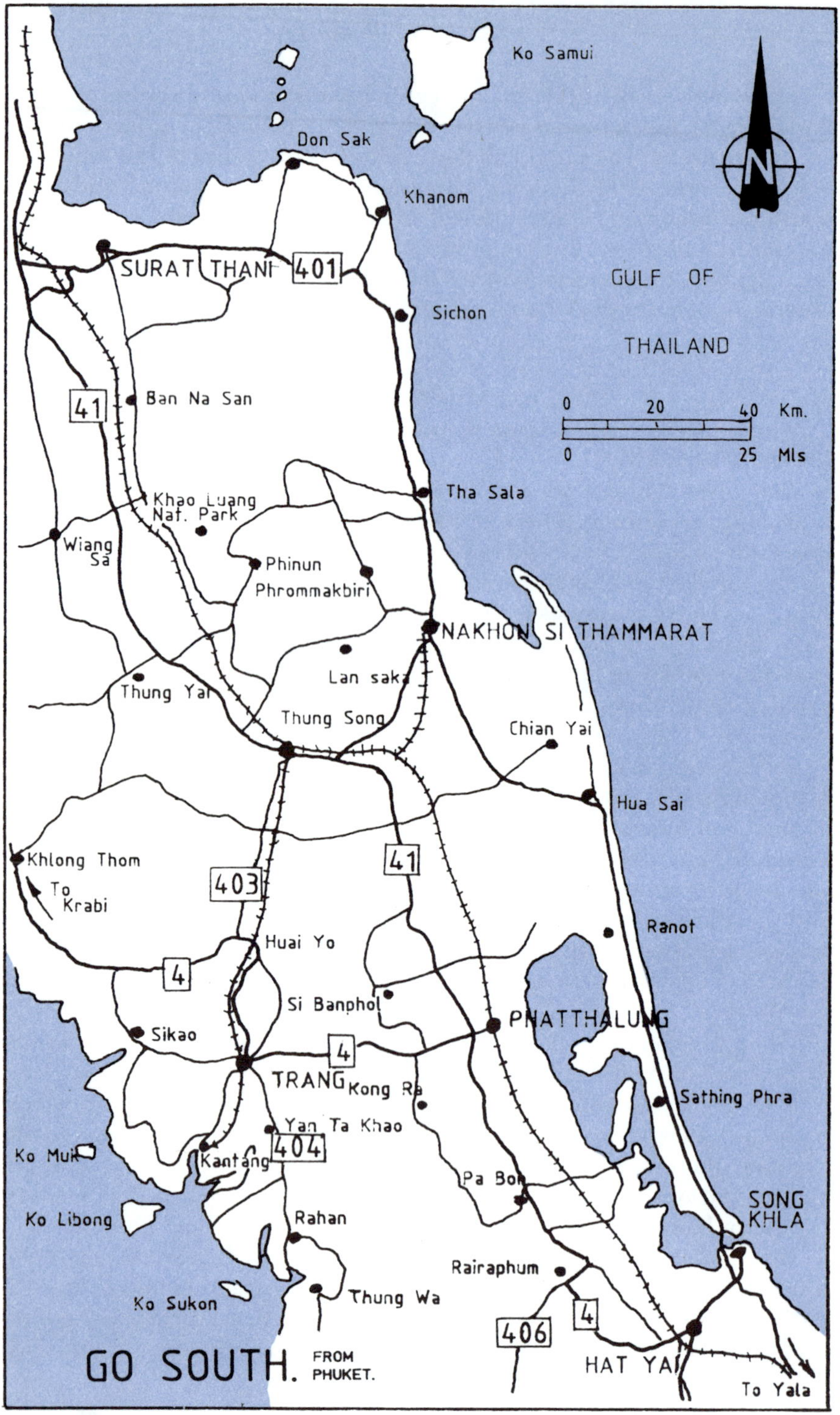
Ko Samui
Don Sak
Khanom
SURAT THANI
401
Sichon
GULF OF
THAILAND
0 20 40 Km.
0 25 Mls
N
41
Ban Na San
Tha Sala
Khao Luang
Nat. Park
Wiang
Sa
Phinun
Phrommakbiri
NAKHON SI THAMMARAT
Lan saka
Thung Yai
Thung Song
Chian Yai
Hua Sai
Khlong Thom
To
Krabi
403
41
Huai Yo
Ranot
4
Si Banphol
PHATTHALUNG
Sikao
4
TRANG
Kong Ra
Sathing Phra
Yan Ta Khao
404
Ko Muk
Kantang
Pa Bon
Ko Libong
Rahan
SONG
KHLA
Rairaphum
Ko Sukon
Thung Wa
4
406
GO SOUTH.
FROM
PHUKET.
HAT YAI
To Yala

to occur in three countries in the world. Despite this, many visitors are disappointed by what they see.

The ideal place to stay in this area is **Phra Nang Beach.** This pink coral beach scattered with untold shells stretches between two limestone headlands. The water is generally clear and calm. The **Krabi Resort** (Tel. 611-389; Fax: 6675-611-914), 44 bungalows and 36 hotel rooms, at 53 Pattana Rd., has the usual facilities of pool, bar, and restaurant plus a lovely position nestled beneath the northern limestone headland. An alternative is the **Phra Nang Inn** (Tel. 612-173; Bangkok Tel. 02-468-0676; Fax: 6675-612-251), at 119 Mu 2, which is decorated in a tropical style using local timber and bamboo. Both have lovely beaches and both offer a range of land and sea tours. There is also a big choice of down-market beach bungalows.

The most popular trip from here is the 20-minute, calm-water trip to **Princess Cave.** At the cave you can climb to the top of the hill and descend into a hidden saltwater lagoon. Fishermen come here before going to sea and believe they are entering the sacred womb of the Princess's spirit. It's all very exciting. The **Phra Nang Place** resort (Bangkok Tel. 02-468-0676; Fax: 6675-612-251), 120 bungalows, is built on a marvellous site at the base of the Princess Cave. It has nice bamboo huts and after the day-trippers have left, it is utterly delightful.

Slightly farther afield is **Poda Island** but this is worth the trip for the exciting snorkeling opportunities it offers. The water is clear, the coral is good, and the shallow waters are swarming with tropical fish. A 5-hour round trip from the mainland will cost about B300.

The largest town in this region is **Krabi,** some 20 kilometers from Phra Nang Beach. The road wanders through jungle, rubber plantations, and around the ever-present limestone monuments. This is almost untouched rural countryside with intricately crafted bamboo houses, the occasional Buddha statue, and tiny villages.

Krabi is a fast-growing, prosperous town built on the banks of a river estuary, but there is little of specific tourist interest. It is, however, a good size to explore by foot and the riverfront park and the tall casurina trees add appeal to this area. There are several reasonable hotels. The **Thai Hotel** (Tel. 611-474) has somewhat overpriced rooms from B300 while the **Vieng Thong** (Tel. 611-188) has been refurbished and now offers large fanned rooms with bath for B300 and airconditioned ones for B400. A real alternative is the **Chao Fah Valley Resort** on Chao Fah Road not far from the center of town and the pier.

Boats leave the Chao Fah jetty in town for Phra Nang Beach, Princess Cave, Phi Phi Island (see Section 7), and other destinations. There are also excellent game fishing prospects offshore. Marlin, sailfish, barracuda, and tuna are all available. See Pee Pee Marine Travel Co. (Tel. 611-496) for boat rentals and general information.

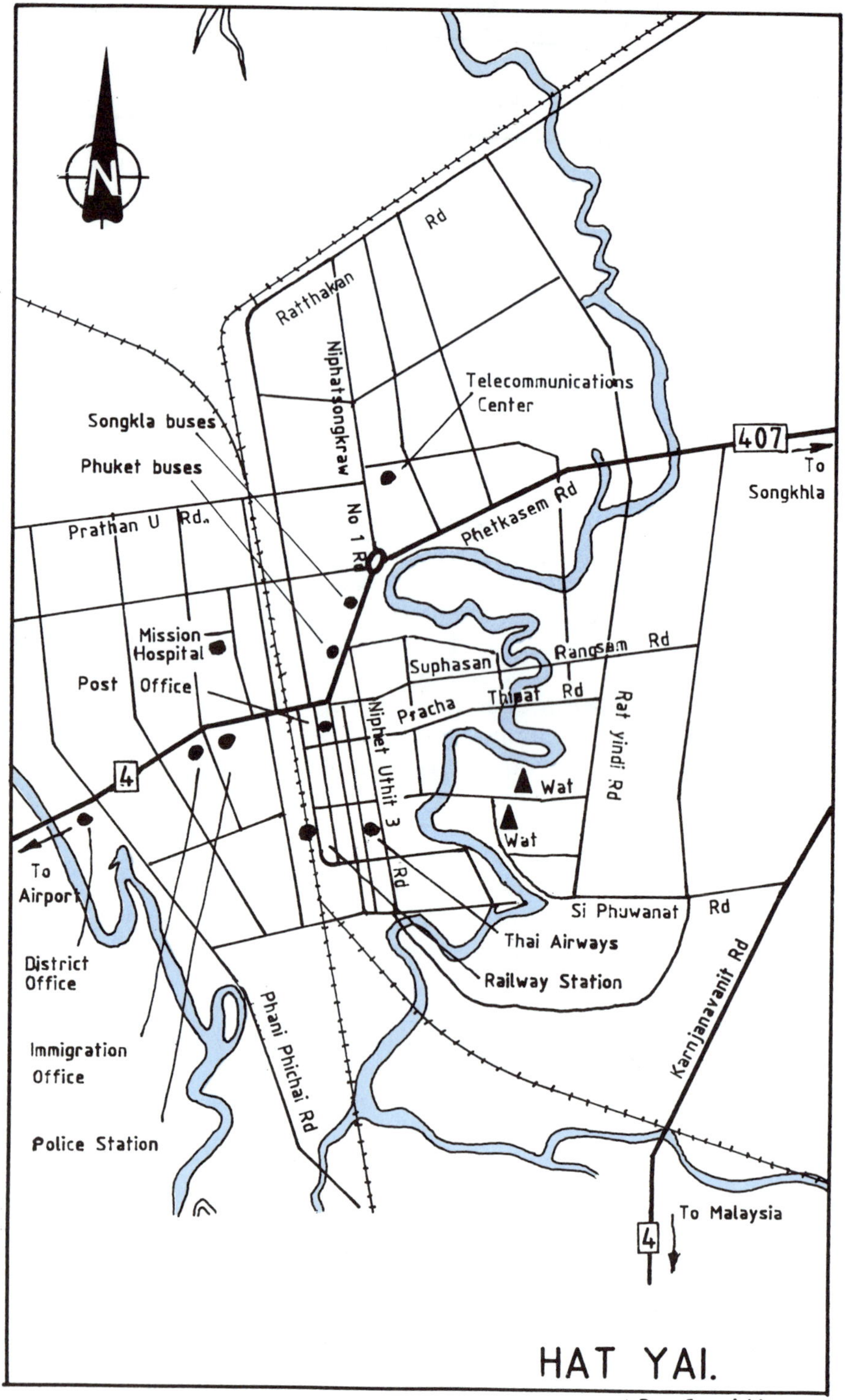
N
Ratthakan
Rd
Niphatsongkraw
Telecommunications
Center
Songkla buses
Phuket buses
407
To
Songkhla
No 1 Rd
Phetkasem Rd
Prathan U Rd.
Mission
Hospital
Post
Office
Suphasan
Rangsam Rd
Pracha Thipat Rd
Niphet Uthit 3 Rd
Rat yindi Rd
Wat
Wat
4
To
Airport
Si Phuwanat Rd
Thai Airways
Railway Station
District
Office
Immigration
Office
Police Station
Phani Phichai Rd
Karnjanavanit Rd
To Malaysia
4

HAT YAI.

To go farther south you have to return to Route 4, which is 5 kilometers north of town. A local bus leaves every hour for the 3-hour journey to Trang (B35) and shared taxis are also available (B60). A few kilometers out, the **Tiger Cave Monastery (Wat Tham Seva)** is worth seeing particularly because of its lovely location. You reach it by following a path through the jungle to the top of a low ridge. The main temple is in a shallow limestone cave, but a walk past the main buildings eventually takes you to a lovely valley of tall trees and limestone caves which will provide many photographic opportunities.

It is now about 140 kilometers to **Trang,** the next provincial capital. As you travel down Route 4, the land gradually flattens and dike-enclosed ricefields appear. This region is largely untouched by tourism so the lovely sandy beaches, the dramatic offshore islands, and the clear water are in pristine condition.

Just before you leave Krabi province, a road heads off to the right to Sikao and **Haat Pak Meng** beach. This 5-kilometer stretch of white sand backed by pine trees looks out to precipitous Koh Meng. It is the takeoff point for the 30-minute long-tail boat trip to **Koh Hai**, which has coral, brilliant clear water, and bungalows for rent.

Trang is a prosperous town with Chinese merchants quite prominent. There is a dragon gate at the edge of the city and several interesting temples and monuments. **Surin Park** just before the city is a worthwhile stop.

Route 4 continues through attractive country to **Phatthalung.** About halfway from Trang, a road to the right leads in to Kachoong Waterfall and the Khao Chong Nature Reserve. Here a small zoo houses a collection of local fauna. At Phatthalung turn right and head for **Hat Yai.**

This bustling city is the commercial capital of southern Thailand and one of the major cities of the kingdom. Since the 1980s it has gained considerable sophistication and a thriving tourism industry from Malaysians and Singaporeans who holiday in the city. Many of these are escaping the more restricted life-style in their own countries so Hat Yai's nightlife has become big business.

Hat Yai is not renowned for its daytime attractions although there are some things of interest. Visit **Wat Hat Yai Nai** on Phetkasem Road to see what is claimed to be the third largest reclining Buddha in the world. Rather strange is the museum-shop within the monument. You can climb some stairs to the inside workings of the heart and organs, have your fortune told, and buy a reminder of your visit.

On the road to Songkhla is the Songkhla Nakharin University on its large campus, and next to it is the **Rubber Research Center.** You can organize a guided tour of the center by telephoning them and arranging a time.

The **Museum of Southern Thailand,** which is open from Wednesday to Sunday, displays artifacts of the south dating back 1,500 years. There are some good full-size replicas of ancient houses. More local information can be obtained from the helpful TAT office (Tel. 243-747), located at 1/1 Soi 2 Niphet Uthit 3 Road.

Sports fans are not forgotten. The **Kho Hong Army Camp Golf Course** is available to the public (Tel. 243-605) and is open daily. The camp also has a shooting range and there is another range called **Ruchirawongsee** (Tel. 243-311). Thai boxing takes place at the **Television Stadium** each Saturday afternoon and bull fighting happens most weekends at either the area near the Nora Hotel or in the Hat Yai Nai district near the airport.

You can take a minibus or drive to **Ton Nga Chang Waterfall** 25 kilometers west of the town. This seven-tiered waterfall tumbles down the mountainside inside a wildlife sanctuary. The first three falls are within reasonable walking distance from the car park and from the third you get a good view of the surrounding countryside. Above here the climb becomes more difficult and hardly seems worthwhile.

Hat Yai has many large, modern hotels with rooms to B1500. The **JB Hotel** (Tel. 234-300), 410 rooms, a short distance from downtown, is considered to be the best with its swimming pool, tennis court, and other facilities. **The Montien** (Tel. 246-968), 180 rooms, is moderate but adequate and its night club is popular with locals. The **Grand Plaza** (Tel. 234-340), 145 rooms, and the **Lee Gardens** (Tel. 234-420), 122 rooms, both have well-established upper mid-market reputations and a regular clietele, while the **Hat Yai International** (Tel. 231-022), 210 rooms, is slightly more basic but still satisfactory. Less expensive, the **King's Hotel** (Tel. 234-966), 88 rooms, is popular while the **Cathay Guest House** has become a favorite center for backpackers.

Useful telephone numbers for Hat Yai are: Police, Tel. 231-644; Hospital, Tel. 246-088; Thai Airways International, Tel. 233-433; Railway Station, Tel. 243-705; and Bus Station, Tel. 244-792.

Thirty kilometers away, the city of **Songkhla** is a good contrast to Hat Yai. This has been a beach resort for many years but is also the largest fishing port in the Gulf of Thailand. The inhabitants are a real mixture of Thais, Malays, and Chinese and some sections of town reflect this combination and past history. Walk down the back streets near the inland sea waterfront and you will find many buildings that show Portuguese influence. The **National Museum,** near the center of town on Rongmuang Road, is an excellent example of nineteenth-century architecture and the display is interesting and extensive. Note that it is not open Monday or Tuesday.

The beach is what originally made Songkhla a tourist center but in reality it is not wonderful, particularly when compared to many of the undeveloped beaches between here and Phuket and Samui. The center point of the beach is a bronze statue of a mermaid which is photographed by everyone who wants to prove they have been to Songkhla.

The harbor on the other side of the city is more interesting with its constant activity of fishing boats coming and going, fish markets being assembled and disassembled, and long-tail boats heading off for commuter runs or tours. The harbor is on **Thape Sap,** a large brackish inlet that has created the **Khun Khat Waterfront Park.** This wildlife park is home for more than 200 bird species and an excursion is available from the harbor for a cost of about B180.

The trip leaves for **Koh Yor Island,** located near the center of the inlet. Here the Koh Yor islanders weave cotton cloth into a distinctive geometric pattern. Apart from the more commercial areas visited by the boats, it is possible to walk around and find households working on rustic looms who are quite prepared to bargain with you to make a sale. Back on the water you then head across shallows, along snaking channels fringed by reedbeds. Early morning and late afternoon are the best times for bird watching but a trip at anytime is a good experience for the idyllic landscape and tranquility.

The **Samila Hotel** (Tel. 311-310), 70 rooms, on the beachfront is the best hotel. There is a pool and other facilities and it is right next to the Thong Yai Golf Course. Prices here start at about B1000. Less expensive, the **Queen Hotel** (Tel. 311-138) has airconditioned rooms from about B350 while the **Songkhla Hotel** has rooms from B150 for budget travellers.

Seafood is the specialty of Songkhla so visit one of the restaurants in town or a food stall on the beach. My experience is that the stalls near the Samila Hotel tend to be overpriced and a bit "touristy" but others say they feel more comfortable here and some English is spoken.

If you now return to Hat Yai, a left turn would take you the 60 kilometers to the Malaysian border while the road back to Bangkok is a long 950 kilometers. Fortunately this distance can be covered in 1 hour and 20 minutes in a Thai Airways International jet (several flights a day) or you can also fly back to Phuket or Surat Thani. There are also the rail (17 hours) or coach (14 hours) options to Bangkok.

7. Guided Tours

I'm not a guided-tour fan but at times this is by far the best way to see the attractions in the shortest time. As well, there are places you can visit only with a tour. Phuket has examples of both.

For an orientation of a new destination, there is nothing better than a half- or full-day tour. Several companies offer these every day. The company you travel with depends to a large extent on where you stay. Most of the major hotels have an arrangement with one or another of the tour companies or they may, in fact, operate their own buses.

Half-day tours usually cover Phuket town, Rawai Beach, and Phromthep

Cape, then they may visit one or more of the other beaches. The full-day trips do these places then include lunch, a visit to some of the other beaches, and the National Park. If your hotel has no tour facilities you could call **Phuket Centre Tour Co.** (Tel. 212-892) in Phuket town, **Phuket Horizon Tours** (Tel. 211-151) also in Phuket town, or **Imex Travel** (Tel. 321-457) at Patong Beach.

An interesting day trip is available to **Naga Noi Pearl Island.** This is Thailand's largest cultured-pearl farm and tours of this unique industry are given daily. The tour consists of a bus trip to Ao Po, a boat trip to the island, a tour of the pearl beds and processing plant, lunch, then a return to your hotel. The cost is about B180.

The most popular day trip from Phuket is to **Phang-Nga Bay.** This spectacular bay is about 75 kilometers from Phuket and should not be missed. This ancient sea is studded with limestone islands of every imaginable shape and size. There are over 100 islands and each is fascinating. The tour starts with a 75-minute coach ride across the causeway to the mainland. Then you board a narrow long-tail boat for several hours on the water.

The boats seat about fourteen people, two abreast. They have wooden seats which become uncomfortable after awhile, a cover to keep off the sun, and a makeshift plastic curtain to keep out some of the water spray. Boats leave from various points around the bay but all travel through creeks and mangrove swamps before bursting out into the open water.

Many of the islands rise sheer from the water to a height of 200 or 300 meters. Many have jungle-clad crowns and sometimes these disappear into cloud. At their narrow bases many have caves and clefts which add to the intrigue. The various tour boats are being forced to visit different places because the tourist volume has grown so dramatically. Some areas within the bay now have a time limit on how long a boat can stop. Most trips, however, visit some or all of these locations.

Tham Lod Cave is a large cavern which passes completely under one of the islands. Huge stalactites hang down halfway to sea level and you feel as if the boat has to twist and turn to avoid them.

Khao Kien is an island which has a cavern containing primitive paintings on the walls depicting humans and animals. It is believed that the drawings could be 5,000 years old.

Koh Pannyi is an island with a Muslim fishing village built completely on stilts out over the shallow water. This is the usual lunch stop. Although you get the feeling that life has been forever changed for the villagers and some may not like that, the village is fascinating and the meal is good. The 150 or so houses, shops, and restaurants are connected with bamboo and timber walkways which the visitor is initially concerned about, but which the locals treat as a regular sidewalk. Visit the school to see its over-the-water playing field and the mosque which clings to a cliff face.

Koh Khao Ping Gun (James Bond Island) was used to film part of the 1970s Bond thriller *Man with the Golden Gun*. There are two small attractive beaches, a network of small caves and several viewpoints where great photographs can be taken looking out to Koh Tapoo, a narrow, vertical island that rises to 200 meters just offshore. The island is a popular spot for hawkers to sell shell jewelry, clothing, drinks, and other miscellaneous "junk."

After spending 4 or 5 hours on the bay, you are returned to your coach. Some trips then proceed to one of the large land caves in the area, while some visit Phang-Nga town. For those wishing to spend more time in the area, the **Phang Nga Bay Resort Hotel** (Tel. 411-057), 88 rooms, offers good accommodation from about B800 a night. Costs for the various day tours range from about B400 to B600.

Another tour which is rapidly gaining in popularity is to **Phi Phi Island.** In fact, these are two islands about 45 kilometers to the southeast of Phuket. Both are quite spectacular. Tours pick up at hotels then take you to Chalong Bay, where express boats take 1 1/2 hours to make the crossing to Phi Phi Don. This island is much like the letter *H*. The two uprights are rugged limestone hills, the cross line is a coconut-covered sand bar 100 meters wide and 1 kilometer long, and the spaces between are the two beautiful bays.

The tour boats land at the fishing village of Tonsai Bay and most of the restaurants, cabins, and hotels are close by. The whole of the coastline of Phi Phi Don is a mixture of cliffs and beaches. Everywhere there is clear water, coral, and an abundance of marine life. All-day trips include meals and snorkeling gear and there is plenty of time to swim or lie on the powder-white beaches.

Phi Phi Ley is the other island—smaller, with one large beach and many sheer cliffs. Day-trip tourists visit to swim and snorkel and locals come to collect the birds' nests which are a Chinese cuisine delicacy. The birds nest in caves, and ropes and long bamboo poles are used to get to the prized nests. Thai collectors clamber up the poles, which appear to be fragile and unsafe. The whole exercise seems bizarre but it obviously pays well.

For those who fall in love with Phi Phi, there is a rapidly growing choice of accommodation. Most is on the sand ridge but the new **P.P. International Resort** (Tel. 214-272 in Phuket) is built on the North Cape. It has airconditioning, TV, telephone, and two restaurants. The **Pee Pee Island Cabana** (Tel. 075-611-496) is a popular hotel with a good restaurant and the **Pee Pee Island Village** is popular with some of the tour operators who now package these islands. There is a choice of budget accommodation at Long Beach. The day tour from Phuket runs at about B900 with hotel pickup. (Book accommodations on Phi Phi by contacting the following. P.P. International, 54/3 Montree Rd., Phuket 83000; Fax: 6676-214-301; Bangkok

Phi Phi Island, south of Phuket.

Tel. 251-8994. Room rates from B1500. Pee Pee Island Cabana c/o 210/3 Uttarakji Rd., Krabi 81000; Fax: 6675-612-196; Bangkok Tel. 252-4945. Room rates from B600 with fan, B1200 with airconditioning.)

For those who enjoy the sea and wish to be among the first to visit a new destination, the day trip to the **Similan Islands** will appeal. This national park in the sea is an uninhabited cluster of nine islands which before too long will be recognized as one of the best dive locations in the world. The Similans have soft white beaches, clear waters, jungle-covered hills, and enormous granite boulders combining to form a spectacular setting.

Off the east coast of the islands, massive coral heads dot the sea floor. Off the western shoreline, giant boulders are piled on top of each other to form twisting tunnels decorated by tropical fish, pastel-tinted corals, and all manner of sea life. A day trip operates from November to April by fast boat from Patong Beach. Travel time is 3 1/2 hours one way and the day costs about B1600.

8. Culture

Phuket is far from being the cultural center of Thailand. The great weather, sparkling beaches, and outdoor living are less conducive to cultural activities than some other areas. Nevertheless, this is not a cultural wilderness and those with strong cultural interest will find something to keep them happy.

The Vegetarian Festival, however, is one event that is well worth catching and, elsewhere throughout the south, there are festivals dotting the calendar. Most are local in nature but as a visitor you will be warmly welcomed to watch and participate.

The first strictly local festival for the year is the **Chao Mai Lim Ko Nieo Fair** held for a week in mid-February in Pattani. This celebrates a goddess believed to possess potent magic powers who is revered in Pattani and other provinces of the far south. This annual fair pays homage to her and features ascetics able to perform extraordinary feats of endurance as well as a lively procession of devotees through the provincial capital.

The Hae Pha Khun That (Homage-Paying Fair) is held about the same time in Nakhon Si Thammarat. During this three-day event, the people pay homage to locally enshrined relics of the Buddha. There are a number of religious ceremonies, among them a traditional merit-making procession which brings a Phra Bott—a cloth painting of the Buddha's life story—to be placed over the relics.

The **Barred Ground Dove Festival** held in Yala in early March is something quite different. Dove lovers from all over Thailand as well as others from Singapore, Malaysia, and Indonesia come to Yala for this event. The highlight is a dove-cooing contest involving more than 1,500 competitors. Young prize doves are on sale along with local products, and other events such as sports contests are held.

A major **Food and Thai Handicraft Fair** is held in mid-May in Hat Yai and Songkhla. All sorts of delectable Thai foods and fruits are feasted on at this popular annual event. There are cooking demonstrations, sales of local handicrafts, and a beauty contest to select Miss Southern Thailand.

The **Rambutan Fair** is held in Surat Thani during the first week of August. The first rambutan tree was planted in this region in 1926 and this fair celebrates the delicious fruit which now grows widely. Highlights include exhibitions of local products and ornamental plants, floats adorned with rambutan and other fruits, and demonstrations of trained monkeys who harvest coconuts in this area.

There are two major festivals in late September-early October. The **Festival of the Tenth Lunar Month** is celebrated at Nakhon Si Thammarat during the fifteen nights of the waning moon period in the tenth Lunar month. It aims to bring merit to the souls of ancestors. Buddhists offer a variety of food and other gifts to monks and there are numerous cultural performances, exhibitions, contests, and other entertainment.

Then there are **Vegetarian Festivals** in both Phuket and Trang. These annual festivals originated among immigrant workers in the nineteenth century and they are now major events at both places. Residents of Chinese ancestry go on a nine-day vegetarian diet and there are ceremonies at local Chinese temples as well as parades that feature remarkable feats by ascetic believers. You can see fire walkers, others who drive nails through their bodies without apparent ill effect, and others with hundreds of fish hooks through their skin. It is all rather bizarre and very difficult to explain but some visitors will find it fascinating. Side by side with all this are the elements that are present in all Thai festivals—music, parades, stalls selling all manner of goods, open-air movies, beauty contests, and so on. If you are in Phuket at this time, go to one of the Chinese temples and join in the fun.

The **Chak Phra Festival** at Surat Thani in mid-October is much more conventional. In this week-long festival, Buddha images are placed on elaborately decorated carriages which are pulled by local people in ceremonial procession through the streets of the provincial capital. Other processions are held on water and there are buffalo races and the usual evening entertainment.

In Phuket, the **Kings Cup Regatta** has become an annual sailing event held in early December. The races are sponsored by the Phuket Yacht Club and other companies. Competitors come from Thailand, Malaysia, Singapore, and some other places to compete for trophies in several different categories.

9. Sports

Phuket is a water sports mecca and the facilities to enjoy every conceivable watersport are excellent. There are also good land-based sporting opportunities so no visitor should be disappointed. Here is a rundown on some of the possibilities.

Swimming is great from November to April at practically all the beaches on the island. The water is warm and calm and the beaches never become overcrowded. My favorite swimming beaches are Nai Yang, Patong, and the north part of Kata. For the rest of the year it is advisable to ask the locals about the conditions at some of the beaches. I would not advise swimming at Surin, Karon, or the south end of Kata during this period unless it is clear that there is no current.

All the major resort hotels and most of the mid-range hotels have pools. Some of these are large enough for even the expert swimmer. They provide a variation from the salt water and are also good for people watching.

Catamarans and **sailing** dinghies are available for rent at Patong and Kata beaches and some of the resorts have their own catamarans for the use of guests. Rental fees for one hour are about B350-600, for half a day B600-900, and for a full-day B1200-1800. You can also rent by the week. For those unsure of sailing techniques, most rentals will give you free lessons to get you started. Captains can be rented if you think learning is beyond you.

Larger sail and power charter vessels with captain and crew can be rented from several operators. Try **The Travel Company** (Tel. 321-292) at Patong or the **Yacht Charter Company** (Tel. 216-556).

All the main beaches have **windsurfing** schools with boards for rent and expert teachers who have a reasonable command of English. Rental costs are B100-140 for an hour and B250-500 for a day.

Water skiing is available at Patong Beach and at some of the resort hotels which have their private bays. The cost for a half-hour is B600-800. For those who need some variation, **parasailing** is also available from the same operators at Patong Beach. Costs seem to vary considerably depending on the number of customers.

Fishing is one of the most popular sports with organized trips heading out into the Andaman Sea every day. Sailfish, marlin, barracuda, and king mackerel are just some of the fish to be found. Equipment can be hired from many of the dive shops. A rod and reel will cost about B600 for the day.

Fishing boats for deep-sea and sport fishing are available at Chalong Bay. Prices vary depending on the type of craft and provision for bait, food, and drink. A long-tail boat will cost about B500 for the day and a fishing boat between B1500 and B4000 a day. Most travel agents offer organized fishing tours for those who want everything provided.

Masks, fins, and **snorkels** can be rented at all the popular beaches around the island. Unfortunately the inshore coral is not as good as it once was due to the damage done by divers but there is still plenty to see. A real experience is the night snorkeling which is offered by a number of sports shops in Patong and Kata. It's a marvellous first-time experience. Snorkel equipment rental is about B100 a day.

This is one of the better places in the world to learn to **scuba dive**. Many of the instructors are Europeans or Americans and most provide NAUI courses which are universally recognized. The sea temperature is 22-24 degrees Celsius (75 F) and all dive shops have all the modern equipment. Most shops offer introductory lessons to beginners and these inevitably start with experience in one of the hotel swimming pools. The following are indicative prices of NAUI courses:

Introductory Dive. Half-day B1000. Full day B1800-2000.
Refresher Dive. 1 day and 2 dives. B1400.
Experienced Diver. 2 days and 3 dives. B2600-B3000.
Open-Water Diver. 4/5 days and 5 dives. B6000.
Open-Water Diver. 3 days and 6 dives. B4000-4500.
Advanced Open Water. 5 days and 8 dives. B7000.

Dive shops are located throughout the island. Some of the more well known operators are **Phuket International Diving Centre** (Tel. 321-106) at the Coral Beach Hotel and at Le Meridien, **Andaman Divers** (Tel. 321-322) at Patong, **Phuket Aquatic Safaris** (Tel. 216-562) in Phuket town, and **Siam Diving Centre** (Tel. 212-901) at Kata.

Phuket has seen **golf** played for fifty years but recently there has been an upsurge in interest because of a new international championship course.

The original course is at Surin beside the sea. The challenging 9-hole layout is attractive and costs are reasonable. Green fees B150, club rental B150.

The new **Phuket Golf and Country Club** (Tel. 321-547) is situated midway between Phuket town and Patong. The par 72 course is surrounded by limestone cliffs and spectacular views and the course, though new, is in excellent condition. There is a driving range with 32 tee-off platforms. Green fees B600, club rental B300.

No resort has full golf facilities but some, including the Dusit Laguna, Pearl Village, Club Mediterranee, and Le Meridien, have putting greens, driving ranges, or short courses.

Almost all the major resorts have **tennis** courts and some have other facilities. Some, including the Coral Sea Resort, Le Meridien, and the Phuket Island Resort, have tennis, squash, and fitness centers.

10. Shopping

Phuket town has excellent shopping facilities at prices generally slightly below those in Bangkok. Of course the range is not as good, but there are some specialty items which you will find almost unobtainable in the capital.

Phuket is known as the "Pearl of the South" so it is no surprise to find that natural pearls, cultured pearls, Mobe pearls, and imitation pearls are all widely available. One of the better outlets is **Phuket International Lapidary** (Tel. 215-876) in Phuket town. They will provide free transportation so you can inspect their wares.

Phuket's artificial pearls are made from pearl dust and are cemented together into a perfect sphere by a well-guarded process. Their lustre and beauty make them difficult to tell from the natural pearl so take care when buying any pearl jewelry. The best guarantee is to shop at a reputable outlet.

Phuket is Thailand's main tin-producing center and pewterware (a combination of lead and tin) is readily available. Pewterware comes as tankards, vases, trays, goblets, clocks, and other products. It is claimed that these days the items are tarnish-free. The products are elegantly styled and crafted by local metalsmiths, rivaling any other pewterware for design and quality. Try **Supremo Gift Shop** (Tel. 216-870) in Phuket town for a good range.

Wood carvings are another specialty of the region and you can visit several places where these items are manufactured. The better pieces are made from teakwood and some are amazing for their detail. The Thai government has stopped the export of raw teak and this has encouraged the talents of Thai craftsmen. Try the **Cheewa Thaicraft Centre** (Tel. 311-124) or the **Native Handicraft Centre** (Tel. 214-113), both on the road between Phuket town and the airport.

Genuine leather goods can be excellent buys and they make good gifts because many are small and easy to carry. Apart from crocodile and the other more common leathers, Phuket produces armadillo and stingray leathers which are made into wallets and purses. A good place to see this is at **Thai Phuket** (Tel. 215-890) in Phuket town.

Tailoring is a service well known throughout Thailand and Phuket has many places that will make dresses, suits, shirts, and other garments both quickly and cheaply. There has been a marked increase in quality in both the materials and workmanship in recent years, so now getting something made while you relax is something that all visitors should contemplate. All the beaches and Phuket town have tailors that will produce good-looking articles. I can recommend **Creative Tailoring** (Tel. 211-993) in Phuket town, and **Alex Fashion** (Tel. 321-469) and **Exclusive Custom Tailors** (Tel. 321-294), both at Patong, for reliability and workmanship.

Some Thai shopping delights.

Thailand's Queen Sirikit has been very active in encouraging the continuation and promotion of Thai crafts. The Queen initiated her SUPPORT program back in 1976 by setting up centers to help craftsmen and to provide financial and other support for small industry. One of the crafts that had been almost lost was the making of bags from lipao fiber. Now it has been revived and it is flourishing. The process is elaborate and involves the weaving of the lipao vine into handbags of a classic Thai form. The clasp, hinges, and accessories are made of gold nielloware—another ancient craft.

The area of Phuket town around **Rasda Road, Rasda Mall,** and **Phuket Shopping Center** offers untold opportunities for shoppers to browse and compare quality and price. You are almost assured of finding something to suit your needs in this area.

Phuket has an important cashew industry that is not readily visible to the visitor, and in Phuket town you can visit a cashew nut factory. The industry is labor-intensive and somewhat primitive but the final product is delicious. At **Eastern Orchid Co.** (Tel. 213-215) you can see the cooking, shelling, and packing process and you can buy fresh cashew nuts and delicious cashew nut candy, and see a wide variety of Thai sweets. I doubt if you can resist the temptation to buy.

Finally a few words on seashells. It seems that seashells can be made into just about every conceivable shape for just about any souvenir imaginable. There are boxes, lamps, flower settings, and much more. The shells themselves are attractive and sometimes the craftsmanship can be clever, but experience has led me to the conclusion that these souvenirs have limited value once they are transported thousands of miles to a totally different environment. You will be tempted to buy something right up until you leave the departure lounge of the airport, but my advice is to resist the temptation. You will find some better way to spend that money.

11. Entertainment and Nightlife

Visitors expecting Phuket nightlife to be as wild as Bangkok or Pattaya will be disappointed, although Patong is rapidly gaining a collection of bars and discos. In short, you don't visit Phuket for the nightlife.

For a leisurely evening in Phuket town, a stroll up **Khao Rang** (Phuket Hill) will give you a lovely view, a nice sea breeze, and the opportunity to join hundreds of Phuket locals who do this every night. If this seems a bit mundane you can try one of four **movie** theaters. Each will rent headphones so that you can hear the English version of the movie, if it originally had an English soundtrack.

For a bit of sporting action the **Pearl Bowling Alley** next to the Pearl Hotel can be fun and you will certainly be mixing with the locals. The same can be said of a visit to the Thai **kick-boxing stadium** in the Saphan Hin sector of town on a Sunday evening.

Action of a different kind can be found at two Thai traditional massage parlors—the **Greenleaf Coffee Shop** and the **Imperial Hotel**—both on Phuket Road, and at the less traditional massage parlor at the Pearl Hotel.

Phuket town has several disco lounges. The **Marina Club** in the Phuket Merlin Hotel is probably the most up-market, but **The Ware** at the Pearl Hotel, the **Diamond Disco and Nightclub** at the Thavorn Hotel, and the **Mayfair Cocktail Lounge** are all suitable for international visitors. At Patong Beach, the **Banana Disco** is popular, as is **My Way** night club. Several resort hotels have discos that are open to the general public. These include the Phuket Arcadia and Karon Villa, both at Karon Beach, the Dusit Laguna, Club Mediterranee, Phuket Island Resort, and Le Meridien.

Many hotels also have live music lounges where Thai or Filipino groups entertain drinkers and diners. With a little careful planning you can visit several of these in a few hours without breaking the bank.

The more down-market bars will cost you even less. At Patong Beach there are twenty or thirty mainly open-sided bars which have music videos, or loud rock and roll, or both, and a collection of young Thai ladies who will happily drink and talk with you. These bars are not just for males as it is quite common to see couples or groups of Western women enjoying the music and friendship within. As Kata and Karon beaches become more developed, bars are appearing at these locations also. At present they tend to be quieter than their Patong cousins but no doubt this will change in time.

12. The Phuket Address List

Airline—Thai International, Nong Rd. (domestic), Tel. 211-195; (international), Tel. 212-400.
Bus Terminal—off Phang-Nga Rd. (Tel. 211-480).
Hospitals—Mission Hospital (medical, dental), Thepkasatri Rd., Tel. 211-173; Wachira Hospital, Jawaraj Rd., Tel. 211-114.
Immigration Office—Phuket Rd. (Tel. 212-108).
Pharmacy—Chao O Sot, Montri Rd., Tel. 212-043
Police Station—Phuket town, Choomporn Rd., Tel. 212-115; tourist, Tel. 212-213.
Post Office—Bangkok Rd. (Tel. 211-020).
Telephone Centre—Phang-Nga Rd. (Tel. 211-199).
Tourism Authority of Thailand—Phuket Rd. (Tel. 212-213).

8

Pattaya and the East

1. The General Picture

Pattaya is the most Westernized place in all of Thailand. Your judgment as to whether this is good or bad will determine your attitude towards this most commercial and successful seaside resort.

If you want to see traditional Thailand, don't go to Pattaya. If you enjoy luxury hotels, sun, after-dark activities, and water sports, you will love it. There are more foreigners than locals in Pattaya—or so it seems. Take a walk down the main street just after dark and it is easy to believe you are on the French Riviera. Westerners of all nationalities are disappearing into British and German pubs, Swiss and French restaurants, and Australian and American bars. Signs, in English, offer all sorts of distractions.

Twenty kilometers or so down the coast, though, the picture is entirely different. Here a small group of Thais sit on a sandy beach listening to a youth strumming a guitar while they watch the gentle waves washing the shore. The air is soft, the water clean, and commercialism almost unknown.

These two activities occur almost side by side and they are one reason why this region is so interesting. Of course the lovely beaches, the offshore islands, the inland mountains, the forests, the waterfalls, the gemfields, and the national parks also do their bit to help.

Pattaya was developed in the 1960s and it prospered in the 1970s and 1980s. The 1990s have brought a new maturity to the city and a new

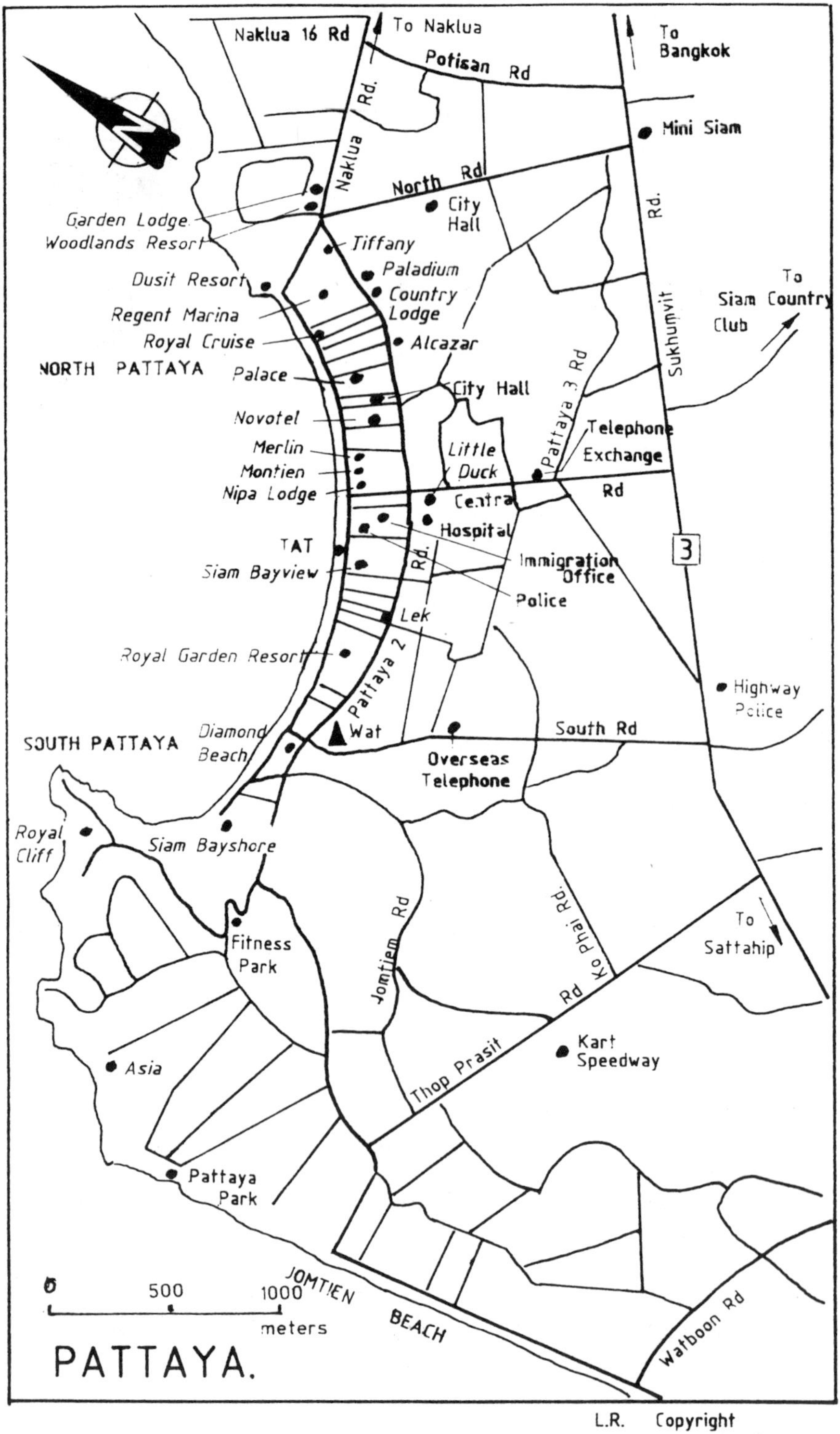

L.R. Copyright

popularity to the area immediately to the south. Farther afield, the cities of Rayong, Chantaburi, and Trat all continue to grow and show signs of tourism appeal. Offshore, Ko Samet has entered the mainstream of tourism after being a backpacker's retreat for years, while Ko Chang and some other islands remain virtually undiscovered.

2. Getting There

There are an increasing number of air services scheduled to **U-Tapao Airport** (30 kilometers south of Pattaya) but more than 90 percent of Pattaya's visitors arrive by road. Most foreign tourists will travel by coach from Bangkok (2 hours) or direct from Bangkok International Airport (2 to 3 hours). **Airconditioned buses** leave for Pattaya from Bangkok's Eastern Bus Terminal on Sukhumvit Road about every half-hour from early morning until mid-evening. The fare is about B60 and the service is efficient and reliable. The Pattaya terminal is at Regent Marina Square at the extreme northern end of the main Pattaya Beach. Similar airconditioned buses leave on the hour from Bangkok's Northern Bus Terminal on Phahon Yothin Road. The fare is only slightly more.

An **airport bus** service runs from Bangkok International Airport to Pattaya on the hour from 7 A.M. until 7 P.M. The fare is about B100. Thai Airways International also operates a coach service several times a day at a fare of B180. This will drop you off at most hotels.

Several private companies have regular Bangkok to Pattaya coach services. Most pick up from Bangkok hotels and deliver to Pattaya hotels. Two well-known services are **Diamond Coach,** which has a Bangkok terminal on Phetchaburi Road, and **Erawan Coach,** which has a terminal in Gaysorn Road. A typical charge is B110-120 one way.

Limousine transfers are also available. Thai Airways International offers a 24-hour service from Bangkok International Airport at a cost of B1500 a trip. Avis has a 24-hour service from either the airport or central Bangkok by Volvo car for B1800 a trip.

Coach services to other points in the east (Sattahip, Rayong, Chantaburi, and Trat) are less frequent, but there are good services from the Eastern Bus Terminal in Bangkok and other services from Pattaya.

3. Local Transportation

Pattaya has grown to the extent that it is no longer easy to walk around and take in all the sights. The main beach is about 3 kilometers long but hotels are appearing to the north of here. Off to the south there is dramatic development, particularly along Jomtien Beach.

The result is that there are a huge number of **songthaews** (converted pickup trucks) cruising the main Beach Road and the inland Pattaya 2 Road, looking for fares. Show the slightest interest in them and they will stop. If you wish to go somewhere, hop onboard then knock on the metal roof to get the driver to stop where you wish to get off. You pay at the end of your journey. Vehicles rotate around town in a counterclockwise direction. The basic fare is B5.

Some songthaews run to Naklua market (a few kilometers north) for a fare of B10 and some go to the hotels between South Pattaya and Jomtien (Royal Cliff, Asia, Pattaya Beach, and others) for a fare of B10-15. The system to Jomtien is still evolving but there are regular services for about B15, and some vehicles are interested in a "special hire" for two people of about B50-60.

For destinations a little farther out, orange **buses** (non-airconditioned) run eastwards on Highway 3 to Sattahip, Rayong, and beyond. The fare to Sattahip is B12. Airconditioned minibuses operate from Pattaya to Ban Phe for those wishing to visit Ko Samet. The one-way fare is around B120. **Boats** take passengers from Pattaya to Ko Karn (about 20 minutes) for a fare of B100 return.

Car rental firms offer cars and jeeps for rent. **Avis** has depots at the Dusit Resort and Royal Cliff Beach Resort while **Hertz** is based at the Royal Garden Resort. Jeeps can also be rented on the streets. The rates will be cheaper than the major companies but be warned—there is no insurance on these vehicles and sometimes the maintenance is less than great.

Finally there are **motorcycles.** Small 90cc models rent at around B150 a day. Larger models go up to B500.

4. The Hotel Scene

Pattaya is Thailand's ultimate resort for package tourists. There are excellent Western-style hotels, a vibrant waterfront, good eating opportunities, and plenty of day and nighttime activities.

While there are over 150 choices of accommodation in Pattaya and along Jomtien Road, the majority of rooms are in the expensive category.

EXPENSIVE HOTELS

Rates are rising rapidly and these days this category will cost you B1600 and upwards. There are few "international" chain hotels in Pattaya but nevertheless all the expensive hotels have the usual amenities like color televisions, airconditioning, a room refrigerator, bars and restaurants, pools, and sporting facilities.

It is generally conceded that the **Royal Cliff Beach Resort** (Tel. 421-421) offers the most luxurious setting in Pattaya. The 670-room hotel is really a self-contained resort within a resort. The hotel offers several different wings, two beaches, three pools, six restaurants, a 24-hour coffee shop, four bars, massage parlor, bowling alley, six tennis courts, airline office, supper club, extensive gardens, and so forth. The lobby of the main resort is not stunning but as you walk to your room you get the impression that there is much to do and see. The rooms are large, well furnished, and all have good views. While the whole resort is obviously stylish, there is an even more up-market section called the Royal Wing which has its own check-in, restaurants, pool, and so forth, although most of these can be used by other guests as well. The whole complex is delightfully landscaped and it is a perfect place to forget the outside world.

For those who like crowds, shopping, and nightlife, the location of the Royal Cliff is somewhat of a problem. It is a hilly 2 kilometers from the main Pattaya beach and although the hotel has its own regular shuttle bus service, the need to be somewhat regimented when visiting downtown is still unattractive to some people. Room rates start at about B3000. (Reservations with the hotel at 378 Pratamnak Rd., Pattaya 20260; Fax: 6638-428-511.)

While the Royal Cliff dominates the area immediately south of Pattaya, the **Dusit Resort** (Tel. 429-901) equally dominates north Pattaya. This 500-room hotel is set in superb grounds on a point at the extreme northern end of the beach. It has the attraction of beach and cliff frontage and this allows spectacular views and brilliant settings for restaurants, pools, and outdoor areas.

The hotel has recently been extensively refurbished. This shows to good effect in the lobby and adjacent glass-roofed, landscaped court where a waterfall, pool, and tropical plants combine to present an atmosphere of tranquility, sophistication, and glamor. About half the rooms have a water view, but even the ones that do not look out over interesting gardens and each has a balcony. The hotel has attractive bars and eating areas—one particularly recommended is an indoor-outdoor affair adjacent to the point swimming pool. The hotel has a nice feel and there is a good mix of Thais and foreign guests. Room rates start at about B2000 and rise to B7000. (Reservations with the hotel at 240 Pattaya Beach Rd., Pattaya 20260; Fax: 6638-428-239.)

A property which I particularly enjoy is the **Siam Bayshore** (Tel. 428-678), 270 rooms. The hotel is situated in what some people consider the "wrong end" of Pattaya between the restaurants and girlie bars of south Pattaya and the "gay" sector of town. This may be the case for some people, but for me, the compensations are the closeness to shops, restaurants, nighttime excitement, the beachfront location, and the interesting low-rise structure itself, which is set in spacious gardens.

A rather unimposing entrance leads past an elevator to the reception lobby on the right and two of the restaurants on the left. Straight ahead is a sunken lounge where there is evening entertainment. Way off to the right, past the French restaurant, a door opens to an outdoor garden walkway which leads to an attractive wing surrounding one of the two swimming pools. If you can get a ground-floor poolside room, you will not be sorry. The rest of Pattaya could be a thousand miles away. The hotel has a night club with some excellent jazz, a small beach which no one uses, a beachside pool, and several restaurants. I can recommend this property without reservation. Room rates are about B2000. (Reservations with the hotel at 559 Mu 10, South Pattaya 20260; Fax: 6638-428-730.)

It is not difficult to go on about Pattaya hotels for many pages—the difficulty is to know where to stop. The following are some other luxury properties which you could consider.

A-one The Royal Cruise (Tel. 424-8749), north Pattaya, 200 rooms, recently opened on Beach Road and is built in the shape of a cruise liner. Prices from B1800.

Asia Pattaya (Tel. 428-6026), south Pattaya, almost to Jomtien Beach, 310 rooms, is somewhat isolated and consequently fully self-contained with all sporting facilities, shops, disco, health club, etc. Prices from B1750.

Montien Pattaya (Tel. 428-155), mid Pattaya, 300 rooms, is a very popular medium-rise hotel, with three restaurants and three bars, centrally situated within large gardens. Higher-level rooms have lovely views over the nice pool area to the beach beyond. Prices from B1750.

Four hotels that are almost side by side are **Merlin Pattaya** (Tel. 428-755), mid Pattaya, 360 rooms, prices from B1500; **Nipa Lodge** (Tel. 428-195), mid Pattaya, 360 rooms, prices from B1500; **Novotel Tropicana** (Tel. 428-645), mid/north Pattaya, 190 rooms, prices from B1500; and **Pattaya Palace** (Tel. 428-487), north Pattaya, 260 rooms, prices from B1600. All have large landscaped grounds, are centrally located, and generally have a similar ambience.

Royal Garden Resort (Tel. 428-126), south Pattaya, 150 rooms, is a low-rise property with two restaurants, three bars, and good sporting facilities close to the shopping and nightlife area. Prices from B1900.

Siam Bayview (Tel. 428-678), mid Pattaya, 260 rooms, is a sister property to the Siam Bayshore with similar facilities. Prices from B2100.

Woodlands Resort (Tel. 421-707), north Pattaya, 120 rooms, is low rise a few hundred meters from the beach. Prices from B1400.

It is appropriate to also consider Jomtien Beach hotels at this point. The nearest hotels to Pattaya are only 2 kilometers from the shops and nightlife of south Pattaya while some others are up to 15 kilometers away. Jomtien is far less developed than the main Pattaya beach area but it is undergoing massive building construction at the moment. Unfortunately poor planning has condemned the area to future problems of overcrowding, traffic chaos, and narrow beaches. This area, which could have been a delightful resort with wide boulevards and lovely beach, will never achieve that now. However, this is not likely to stop development in the near future and many of the small down-market guesthouses, restaurants, and bars are now disappearing. In their places are appearing twenty-story-high condos and apartment blocks with their huge "for sale" billboards.

The Ambassador Resort Jomtien (Tel. 231-501) largely escapes these problems because of its size and relative isolation. This complex is by far the largest hotel in Thailand. In fact, it is several hotels together in one compound which has absolute beach frontage to south Jomtien Beach. The 2,500 rooms provide a wide choice of accommodation and there are restaurants, bars, shops, and other facilities by the bucketful. The resort has several pools and a nice beach which, unlike Pattaya, can actually be used for swimming.

The Ambassador was opened in 1988 and is still developing. It suffers somewhat from its newness and frankly I find it all too big, but there are many Thais and foreigners who would go nowhere else. You need to sort out your preferences with the receptionist when you are booking because you will find that almost every request can be met. Room rates vary between about B1400 and B13000. (Reservations with the hotel at 21/10 Sukhumvit Rd., Jomtien, Sattahip 20250; Fax: 6638-231-731.)

Three other Jomtien properties, all much closer to Pattaya, which you could consider are the **Natural Park Beach Resort** (Tel. 231-561), a low-rise resort across the road from the beach, 116 rooms, prices from B1500; **Pattaya Park Beach** (Tel. 423-000), a fairly stark high rise adjacent to the water funpark, 240 rooms, prices from B1700; and **Jomtien Hill Resort** (Tel. 422-378), a low rise, 64 rooms, prices from B1600.

MEDIUM-PRICE HOTELS

There is considerable choice in this category but no outstanding property that combines great location, great facilities, and great price. The following is an alphabetical guide to some of the better alternatives. Prices range from B500 to B1200.

Beach View (Tel. 422-6604) is well positioned next to the Royal Cruise Hotel. The 135-room, six-floor property has a nice pool and dining and bar facilities. Prices from B850.

Coral Inn (Tel. 231-283) is a small property on Jomtien Beach Road. The 36-room hotel has a pool and dining and bar facilities. Prices from B800.

The **Diamond Beach Hotel** (Tel. 429-885) would command a much higher price if it were on a larger site opposite the beach. The 149-room hotel is hidden away in south Pattaya but it has a good range of facilities. Prices from B800.

Golden Beach (Tel. 429-969), 240 rooms, suffers because it is not on the beach, yet the one-block walk can save you B500 a night. Prices from B800.

The **Island View Hotel** (Tel. 428-818) is across the street from the Royal Cliff. The 210-room hotel has good facilities but is remote from the center of town. Prices from B900.

The **Little Duck Pattaya Resort** (Tel. 428-104) is very popular with young travellers. There is a good pool, a crowded disco, and plenty of action. The rooms are small but well appointed. Prices from B600.

Pattaya Inn Beach Resort (Tel. 428-718) is behind the Royal Cruise Hotel. The 120-room hotel has excellent facilities including tennis, pool, disco, shopping, and hair dressing. Prices from B600.

The **Regent Marina** (Tel. 428-015) is at the top end of this mid-range. The 220-room hotel has a good position close to the beach and next to the airconditioned-bus terminal. Prices from B1250.

BUDGET ACCOMMODATIONS

Within this category you can still get some reasonable accommodation. Because Pattaya is an outdoor place, I prefer a hotel with space and nice grounds. If the rooms are not super I can put up with that because I want to be out in the action for most of the time.

Three recommendations with nice settings are the **Sunshine Garden** (Tel. 428-629), the **Palm Garden Hotel** (Tel. 429-386), and the **Garden Lodge** (Tel. 429-109). These are situated on Naklua Road near the Dusit Resort, a short distance from the beach. All are low-rise properties with 80-110 rooms. All have swimming pools and rooms in the B350-500 price range.

There are several properties which offer both airconditioned rooms and rooms with fans. If you can live without airconditioning, you can save further money without necessarily sacrificing other facilities. The **Country Lodge** (Tel. 428-484) in north Pattaya and the **Diana Inn** (Tel. 429-675) in south Pattaya both offer fan rooms at B200 while still providing pools and restaurant facilities in reasonably modern buildings. For anyone on a budget, either property would be quite suitable. Diana Inn has particular appeal to young people. Both hotels are on Pattaya 2 Road, one block back from the beach.

It is not so easy to find reasonable budget accommodation at Jomtien Beach but I am told that the **Sunlight Guest House** (Tel. 429-108) at the north end of the beach (and thus nearest to Pattaya) has 14 airconditioned rooms at B250, while the **Kitti Guest House** (Tel. 423-034) has 10 fan-cooled rooms from B100. If you wish to be in a larger hotel with pool, restaurant, and so on, the **Sea Breeze** (Tel. 231-056) at B400 a room is a good value.

5. Dining and Restaurants

I am a firm believer in the principle that you should eat local food, if possible, while you are in a foreign country. However, I am well aware that many travellers do not agree with me.

In Pattaya, it seems easier to find Western food than Thai food. This has led to prices which make dining in Pattaya more expensive than just about anywhere else in Thailand. There are, however, several groups of restaurants that should be on every visitor's list. Here are some of the best.

SEAFOOD RESTAURANTS

The so-called specialty of Pattaya is seafood and there are a cluster of **seafood supermarket restaurants** on Beach Road in south Pattaya. Several of these offer open-air dining over the water and on a calm night the atmosphere is lovely. Service is fast and waiters attentive. You finally realize that the object of the exercise is to get customers served and out again in the shortest possible time.

You can select the creatures that you like and specify how you want them cooked. You pay by the weight, and prices are high. If all this is too much trouble, you can order one of the set menus which will give you three or four dishes for B500.

As well as these supermarkets, there are a few conventional restaurants that specialize in seafood. At the top of my list is the **Villa Seafood Restaurant** (Tel. 422-523) on Soi 7. Here chefs prepare seafood using original Chinese recipes and present them in a most appealing manner. Some particular recommendations are the five-flavored Broiled King Lobster, the Peking Duck, and the Stir-fried Black Pepper Crabs. All major credit cards are accepted.

While not strictly just a seafood restaurant, the **Buccaneer Terrace** (Tel. 428-195), in front of the Nipa Lodge Hotel, serves a great seafood platter for B280 while at the same time this roof-top open-air restaurant provides a beautiful view of the bay. Strolling guitarists provide a romantic atmosphere.

The **Green Bottle** (Tel. 429-675) within the Diana Inn is a favorite among the local expatriates. It serves a Lobster or Crab Thermidor with white wine cream sauce and buttered rice for B140 and throws in a vocalist to help with the atmosphere. Excellent for good Western-style home cooking.

The **Kruatalay** (Tel. 423-000) within the Pattaya Park Beach Hotel complex at Jomtien Beach serves the same purpose with Thai-style cooking.

There is a good range of seafood dishes at reasonable prices. This is a place for young couples or the whole family.

THAI FOOD

The food in Thai garden restaurants is often not very special. A great setting and classical dancing can take the place of quality. But the **Reun Thai Restaurant** manages to achieve everything. The setting for the restaurant is classic Thai—four pavilions set in palm trees and gardens.

There are over 250 selections on a menu covering both Thai and Western choices. Minced Shrimp and Pork with Chinese Cabbage is B55, Steamed Mussels B45, and spicy Thai soups B50-70. The restaurant is open 11 A.M. till midnight, seven days, and there is traditional Thai dancing from 7:30 till 11. The children have a playground and there is ample parking if you have a vehicle. The restaurant is just off Pattaya 2 Road in south Pattaya.

The **PIC Kitchen** (Tel. 428-387) at Soi 5, north Pattaya, is another place where you can dine in a Thai classical environment. There is seating for 300 diners in four pavilions set in a tropical garden. Excellent menu choices are Grilled Kingfish in Tamarind Sauce for B120, or Stuffed Beef Rolls with Mashed Potatoes for B130. Entertainment includes a Wednesday evening Thai classical dance show from 7:30, or nightly listening to recorded jazz favorites in the Jazz Pit starting at 7. The restaurant is open from 8 A.M. until midnight for breakfast, lunch, dinner, and snacks.

Visitors will find that some of the best Thai food is obtained in the luxury hotels. To some, it has the added advantage of being less spicy than that enjoyed by the Thais and so it is more attuned to the Western palate. One of the best venues is the **Thai Food Market** restaurant at the Royal Cliff Hotel. The decor and atmosphere are of a traditional Thai market. Small stalls serve up food. You wander around and decide what you want and a waiter delivers the dishes to your table. You can order individually or share dishes, Thai style. It's fun to tour the stalls, see how the dishes are prepared, then ask the cooks to tone down (or up) the spice level. This is not strictly authentic Thai food as the rural Thais would eat it but, for most visitors, it is delicious.

If wandering around and ordering from individual stalls is not your scene, you can sample Thai food at a Thai buffet at many of the major hotels. The **Dusit Resort** has an excellent buffet served under the stars each Thursday night, while you can sample something similar at the **Siam Bayview** on a Monday or Friday night for B200 per person.

OTHER ASIAN RESTAURANTS

Japanese food fanatics have a choice of two good outlets. **Akamon** (Tel. 423-727) on Pattaya 2 Road, north Pattaya, is hard to miss with its large Tori sign. Kimono-clad waitresses lead you to one of two dining areas—Western or classical Japanese. The Japanese section has low tables and rice mats for sitting. All the traditional favorites are available—teppanyaki, sukiyaki, tempura, and so on. There is also a sushi bar.

The **Yamato** (Tel. 429-685) in Soi 13, south Pattaya, started as a sushi bar but has expanded into a full restaurant. The bar is still a meeting place for casual dining but families and couples may prefer the cubicles where you sit on mats and dine in true Japanese style. This is a clean, well-designed restaurant, as close as you will come to a Tokyo eatery without the high price tag.

The **Narissa** restaurant (Tel. 428-678) at the Siam Bayview Hotel offers the right ambience and food for a great night out. Peking Duck is the specialty here. Two sizes at B300 or B350 are available. The chef requires 30 minutes to prepare it, so order before you relax over a drink. Other favorites are Shark's Fin Soup and Roast Pigeon in Casserole, as well as a full range of Cantonese and Thai dishes and sushi from the Japanese corner.

The Siam Bayshore's **Bali Hai** restaurant (Tel. 428-678), on the beach in south Pattaya, offers the option of an airconditioned section which is ideal for small parties or for visitors escaping the heat, or an open-air section which fills the bill perfectly for intimate dining under the stars. There is a good selection of Chinese, Thai, and Indian dishes.

INTERNATIONAL CUISINE

It is generally conceded that **Dolf Riks** restaurant (Tel. 428-269) is outstanding for gourmet continental cuisine. Located behind the Regent Marina Hotel and run by noted food columnist and artist Dolf Riks, the restaurant has a friendly and intimate atmosphere. There is a daily Indonesian "Rijsttafel" with its eighteen small dishes prepared by the owner himself. Or for dinner try a Seafood Casserole at B175 or Medallions of Beef at B160.

Good steaks are found at the **El Toro Steakhouse** (Tel. 426-238) on Pattaya 2 Road near the Royal Palace Hotel. The fully airconditioned restaurant offers Fillet Steak at B170, Pepper Steak Flambe at B190, and Steak Tartare at B160. There are also soups, salads, grilled dishes, and desserts. It is open from 3 till 11.

The **Mai Kai Supper Club** (Tel. 428-645), on Beach Road at the Novotel Tropicana, is the only uniquely Polynesian restaurant in Pattaya. Seafood, Polynesian dishes, and cocktails combine to create a great evening while a Haiti band entertains. Open from 7 to 11 P.M.

The **Orient Express** (Tel. 428-195), on Beach Road at the Nipa Lodge Hotel, is a restaurant extraordinaire. Two classic Thai railway carriages have come to a halt to create a specialty restaurant serving French cuisine and premier wines. Some of the better selections are Veal Fillet Medallions on an exotic walnut sauce for B240, or Sole Fillets with fresh oysters in a light herb sauce for B190. You can finish off with an Irish coffee.

The **Blue Parrot** (Tel. 424-885) on Pattaya 2 Road has what many consider to be the best Mexican food in Thailand. The Enchiladas, tacos, and burrito combo plate costs B90, while Tacos Con Carne will cost you B75.

EUROPEAN FARE

Alt Heidelberg (Tel. 421-258) is a cheap and lively bar/restaurant that opens from 9 A.M. until 2 A.M. Perhaps this is not the best place to bring your grandmother, but the beer is cold, the German sausages hot, and the country-style sandwiches justifiably famous.

Angus Steakhouse (Tel. 426-193) on Pattaya 2 Road has tender meat, good wine, and a nice ambience. Norwegian salmon and some chicken dishes are also served for those who like the company of steak lovers but do not share their eating habits.

The **Cherry Tree Pub** (Tel. 422-385) on Siam Country Club Road is as close to an English country pub as you will find in Thailand. It is some way out of town so it helps if you have your own transportation. A Ploughman's Lunch will cost B45 and traditional Shepherd's Pie B55. There is cold draft beer on tap. If you arrive early you can play croquet or have a few holes of golf.

La Gritta (Tel. 428-161), on the extreme north end of Beach Road, is perhaps the most authentic Italian restaurant in town. You will find Spaghetti Bolognese or Neopolitana at B65; special La Gritta Pasta with homemade sauce, clams, herbs, and white wine sauce at B75; and Rock Lobster Italian at B140. A pianist entertains during dinner.

Oslo Restaurant (Tel. 426-425), on Pattaya Road Soi 2 in south Pattaya, is a recently opened Scandinavian restaurant which serves breakfasts, lunches, and dinners. Prices are reasonable and the food is prepared by a chef who has shipped in his own supply of Scandinavian herbs, spices, and condiments to give a "true Viking taste."

The Rhine Grill (Tel. 428-755) at the Merlin Hotel has fine food, wines, and atmosphere. Open only for dinner.

Savai Swiss Restaurant (Tel. 421-089) on Pattaya 2 Road is newly opened but is already doing well. Homemade pâté is available at B90, while chicken breast oven-baked with ginger and Swiss cheese and served with hash brown potatoes and vegetables costs B160. Beef fondue, cheese fondue, and Swiss coffee are all excellent.

For a real splurge, you could consider a romantic dinner at the Royal Cliff Beach Resort Royal Wing's **La Ronde Pavillion** (Tel. 421-421). Each Wednesday and Saturday there is a seven-course menu served in this idyllic island retreat restaurant surrounded by the pool of the Royal Wing. The food is served in style with flowers, candlelight, and soft music.

6. Sightseeing

Few people come to Pattaya for sightseeing. It is the beach, the resort atmosphere, the sun, and the nightlife that is appealing. Nevertheless, most people tire of spending all day in the sun so some man-made sightseeing attractions have appeared.

Possibilities for sightseeing include the remarkable **Wat Yannasangwararam** (what a mouthful), which is built behind Jomtien Beach. The temple is a fascinating mix of architectural styles with each building given different treatment. The main temple is a delightful modern interpretation of classic Thai design while other shrines use Western and Oriental style. The temple is situated in extensive landscaped gardens which provide a tranquil atmosphere for visitors.

Another outdoor delight is **Mini Siam.** This is southeast Asia's version of Holland's Madurodam. On show are eighty miniature models of interesting places in Thailand. The park is open from 7 A.M. to 10 P.M. and there is a restaurant for those who need sustenance. In my opinion the best time to visit is late afternoon or early evening when the sun has lost most of its punch. Then you can happily wander around for several hours. Mini Siam is on the Sukhumvit Highway adjacent to north Pattaya. Entrance fee is B200.

The **Pattaya Elephant Village** is something quite different. Frankly if you have seen a similar performance in the north of Thailand, the setting here will be a disappointment to you. However, for those visitors who will not get that opportunity, this visit will show you more about elephants than you ever knew. The village is along the Siam Country Club Road, 20 minutes from Pattaya. About fifteen elephants roll timber logs, play football, and present a stately parade. There are good photo opportunities. The daily show is at 2:30 and entrance is B160.

A little way offshore from Pattaya, there are several small islands which are worth visiting. By far the most popular is **Ko Larn (Coral Island).** There is a public ferry from Pattaya which takes about 50 minutes. It cannot berth at the island so passengers are transferred to shore by long-tail boat. The main beach on the island is backed by a continuous line of restaurants and souvenir stalls but the pleasant surprise is that the beaches are clean and the water ideal for swimming. The commercial activity on the beach is frantic because visitors usually only stay for a few hours. In that time, you will be expected to eat lunch, buy some souvenirs, take a ride in a glass-bottomed boat to see some poor coral, try a water scooter, and either water ski or parasail. The ferry fare is B50. Accommodation is available at the 60-room **Ko Larn Island Resort** (Tel. 420-422) for B700 a night.

Nong Nooch Village is a recreational park located about 20 minutes by road from Pattaya, south on the Sukhumvit Highway. The area has Thai-style houses, orchards, orchid and cactus gardens, and a large artificial lake. The park has a cultural show (somewhat similar to that at the Rose Garden near

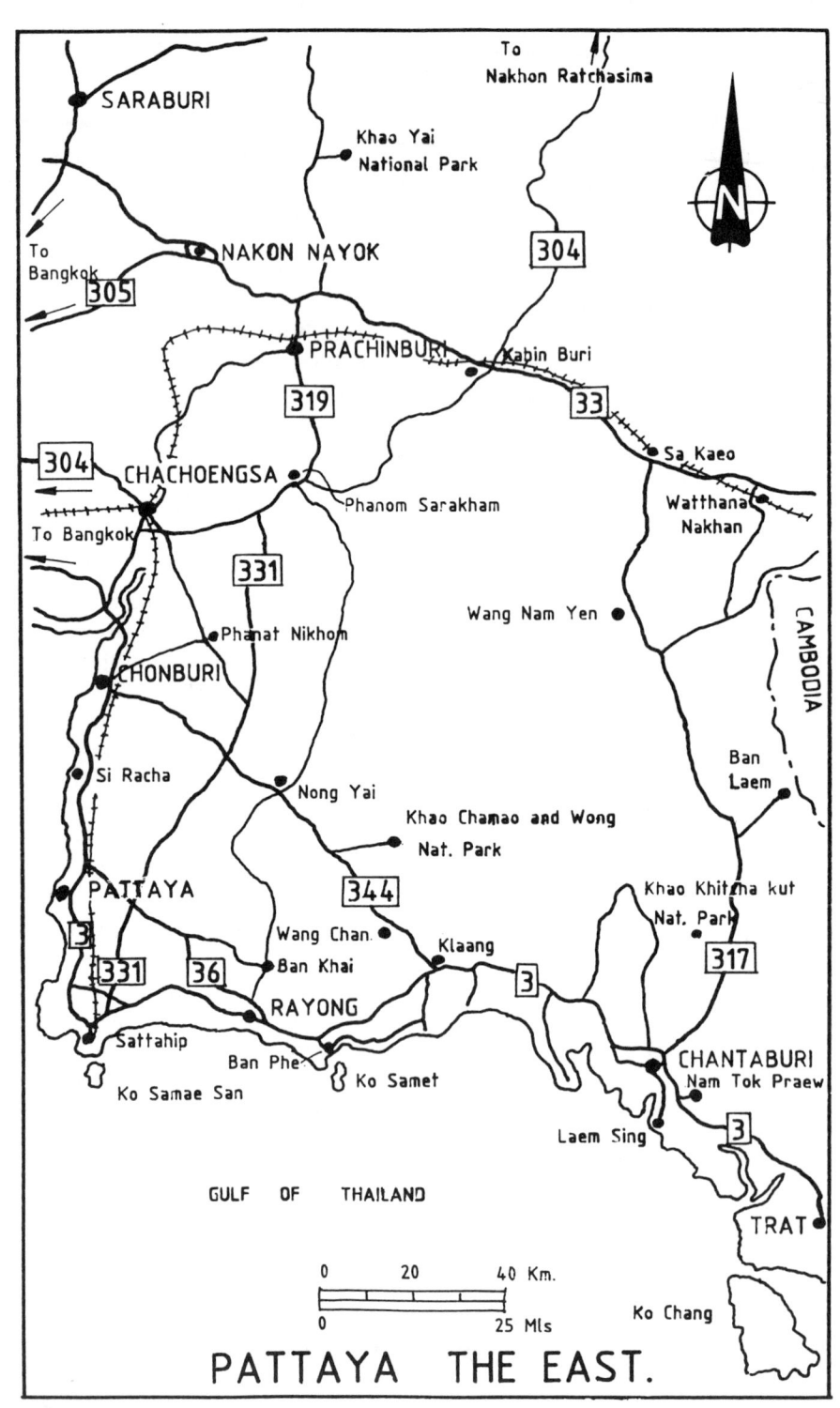

PATTAYA THE EAST.

Bangkok) each morning at 10 and each afternoon at 3. There is a miniature zoo and aviary where you can see monkeys pick coconuts and there are two restaurants. Overnight accommodation is available (Tel. 429-342) starting at B300 a night.

BETWEEN BANGKOK AND PATTAYA

If you get onto the Bangkok elevated freeway and head south, you won't immediately find any signs which say Pattaya. This is very disconcerting for a visitor, but if you first follow markers to Bang Phi, then Chonburi, you will be heading in the right direction. As the high-rise and crowded conditions of central Bangkok give way to more sedate surroundings, you will see examples of strange modern Thai architecture that to Western ideas is like something gone very wrong. Also lining the roads are huge billboards advertising the new "good life" as represented by housing estates and high-rise condos.

The road to Pattaya is a toll road. You pay B10 in Bangkok then another B3 some 50 kilometers down the road. Hopefully the toll will be used to make improvements to the road, which is heavily trafficked by trucks and buses. The first major center southeast of Bangkok is **Chonburi**, a bustling commercial city of several hundred thousand people. The 110-room **Likhit Hotel** (Tel. 271-996) on Chetchamnong Road has rooms from B130 and the **Done Nightclub** provides after-hours entertainment. In the center of town, **Wat Dhamma Nimitr** contains a huge Buddha image and other interesting items. The shore has been extensively developed. There is little beach but there are lakes, slides, swimming enclosures, and ponds for public enjoyment. South of the town, there are extensive filled areas which presently sit vacant and forlorn. In case of emergency you should telephone the following while you are in the Chonburi region: Police, Tel. 428-223; Chittapharan College Hospital, Tel. 428-379.

South from here is the little village of **Ang Sila.** This was once favored as a royal sea resort but its claim to fame today is the rock carvers that work here. You see the results of their work in roadside displays. There are mortars and pestles in their thousands, enormous stone balls, and gigantic rock carvings that would be almost impossible to move. I cannot imagine who buys all the items that are produced. There is no good beach in this area but there are restaurants along the coast and little piers for fishermen and others. The area has many prawn farms with their own restaurants so seafood at these is fresh, good, and relatively cheap.

The first major beach south of Bangkok is **Bang Saen.** Here you see the development of a typical Thai beachfront: umbrellas by the thousands, deck chairs, small mobile restaurants, inner tubes for rent, boats, bicycles, water scooters, and a general carnival atmosphere. Just at the northern end of the

A low-rise modern resort in Bang Saen.

beach is the **Bang Saen Beach Hotel** and farther along is the **Bang Saen Beach Resort** (Tel. 376-675). Both offer medium-price accommodations. There are plenty of eating places right along the beach. If you prefer a restaurant to the beach side stalls, the **Seaview Restaurant** will provide a good meal. Bang Saen is the site for a large amusement park called **Ocean World** on the main road opposite the beach. I have never visited here but some Thai friends say it is a great place. This whole area is extremely popular with Thais from Bangkok and there is a general aura of prosperity. Few foreign visitors come here but it is well worth a visit. For those on a strict budget, there are many low-cost bungalows for rent right along the beach road.

Between Bang Saen and Si Racha the popular Bang Phra Golf Course and the Panya Resort are off to your left. **Si Racha** town is a beach resort with a small offshore island called **Ko Loi,** fishing piers, some cheap accommodation, and some good restaurants. This is quite a pretty place. Ko Loi is connected to the mainland by a causeway. There is a Thai-Chinese temple on the island which is a good photo subject from the mainland. Farther offshore is a larger island called **Ko Si Chang** which has a town, a few beaches, and some sparsely settled areas. There are regular ferry connections from Si Racha town.

Five or ten kilometers south of Si Racha you pass a huge new industrial complex which includes a large oil refinery and new port called Laem Chabung. This is the new face of Thailand—that of an emerging industrial nation. It is in total contrast to the village of **Naklua** just north of Pattaya, which still has a traditional market, some small shore restaurants, a fishing pier, and a nostalgic feel.

Inland from Bang Saen is the well-known **Khiao Open Zoo.** Here 1,200 acres (500 hectares) of forest and open hillside provide a home for fifty species of animals. There is also a huge aviary which enables you to walk around inside with the birds, and bungalows are available if you wish to spend the night. The Chanta Then waterfall, 7 kilometers down the road from the zoo's entrance, is worth seeing.

EAST FROM PATTAYA

The Sukhumvit Highway (Route 3) goes south from Pattaya then turns east through Rayong and Chantaburi to Trat. This is close to the Cambodian border and there is much of interest in the area.

To see this area, head from Pattaya or Jomtien to Route 3, then turn right. The divided highway that extended all the way from Bangkok has now finished and the volume of traffic is appreciably less. This makes it much more practical to explore the area and some interesting sightseeing possibilities emerge. At the 165 kilometer marker (20 kilometers south of Pattaya) a road leads off to the right to the fishing village of **Bang Saray.**

This is a delightful little spot that should have appeal to just about everyone. Windsurfers, dinghy sailors, swimmers, and sunbathers should head for the **Sea Sand Club** (Tel. 01-211-0632), 40 rooms, just north of the village. You can stay at the resort for B650 a night. Game fishermen will head for the **Fisherman's Inn,** which is home to the Bang Saray Fish Club and has spacious grounds with a swimming pool and beach area, small marina, restaurant, and bar. Alternatively they will stop at the **Fisherman's Lodge,** where the Thailand Game Fishing Association has its headquarters and the weigh-in equipment graces the hotel's jetty. Accommodation at both hotels is available at B550 a night. Casual visitors might head for the **Seafood Restaurant** or the **Ruan Talay Restaurant** sitting on a spacious jetty. There are shops, a market, and a temple, **Wat Kong Kara.**

The next point of interest is **Sattahip,** home of the Thai navy. This very attractive town has a nice beach, some interesting fishing piers, and an air of prosperity. There are many naval and air force compounds in the region and much of the payroll finds its way into the local community. There is also a commercial port which welcomes cruise ships and cargo carriers and a rail connection to Bangkok. There is some good accommodation too. Try **Ocean Marina** (Tel. 423-686), 40 rooms, for rooms at B800, or the **Aqua Marina Cabana** (Tel. 231-290), 29 rooms, for rooms at B600. Cheaper rooms are available at **Swan Lake** (Tel. 436-114), 120 rooms.

Route 3 now heads east. An interesting side trip to the village of **Samae San** is available by turning right at the intersection with Route 331. This is an undeveloped fishing village which will appeal to many visitors. When the catch is brought in the jetties are alive with activity, but for the rest of the time it is very slow. As you wander around you see lines of squid drying in the sun and nets waiting to be repaired. There are five islands close to Samae San, so island hopping is a great activity. Finding a boat can be somewhat of a problem but a visit to the **Larn Samae San Seafood Restaurant** will often solve that worry. You should be able to visit all islands for B300 on your own charter.

If you just wish to see Ko Samae San, there is a regular ferry for B10 each way. Bungalows are available on the island for B500-B800 a day including Thai meals. On the mainland, **Sakol Bungalow** has 16 rooms at B600 a night, while **Samae San Villa** has 16 rooms from B150.

Twenty-five kilometers before Rayong, you pass by a huge new industrial complex on the right with a petrochemical plant and industrial port. This obviously has an effect on **Rayong** because the town is bustling and prosperous. The town itself is of little interest but the surrounding province produces fine fruit and a famous fish sauce much loved by Thais. There are at least three hotels in town worth considering—the airconditioned **Otani Hotel** on the main street; the **Rayong Hotel** (Tel. 611-073), 50 rooms, which has accommodation from B150; and the 80-room **Burapha Inn** (Tel. 612-

482), which has double rooms from B600. Useful telephone numbers in this region are: Police, Tel. 611-111; Hospital, Tel. 612-002; Bus Station, Tel. 611-006.

The main interests here are the beaches to the south which start at **Ban Phe,** 20 kilometers east of the provincial capital. At the turnoff to Ban Phe, there is a lovely Thai house museum and garden well worth a stop. To describe Ban Phe as a fishing village gives a wrong impression but, until a few years ago, that was its main preoccupation. Fishing is still important but tourism has assumed the top position and hence the town is rapidly changing. It is finding it all a bit difficult and sometimes just cannot cope with the crowds.

The main cause of the problem is the offshore island of **Ko Samet,** which has been "discovered" by both local and foreign visitors. The trip to the island is by motorized wooden boat (there are twenty or thirty of them), which takes about 30 minutes and costs B20 each way. Boats are leaving all the time so you rarely have more than 15 minutes to wait for a trip. On busy days thousands of people travel to the island. Frankly, I am appalled at what is happening to Ko Samet. Until the early 1980s it was almost unknown. Now it is practically overrun by tourists yet the roads, the water supply, and the transportation system have had great difficulty in keeping up and are all terrible. The whole island is supposed to be a national park yet commercial development has rampaged through the nicest beaches, leaving any semblance of "natural conditions" in total disarray. The best that can be hoped for now is that more controls are put on bungalow construction, the main road is totally reconstructed, and environmental efforts are directed towards preserving the clean sand and clear water that still exists on the eastern side of the island.

The boat from Ban Phe will arrive at the pier at Na Daan, a cluster of shabby shops, restaurants, and huts overwhelmed by visitors and pickups. No one wants to stop here, so you can either walk the 1 kilometer to the beach at Hat Sai Kaea or take a pickup to one of the other beaches. The beach at **Hat Sai Kaea** is probably the best on the island for shade, deck chairs to rent, restaurants for drinks and snacks, and even a money changer who also rents out masks and snorkels for B40 a day. Unfortunately there are very few Thais to be seen.

This is also the beach which has much of the accommodation. At the northern end, **Diamond Bungalows** (Tel. 321-0814) is forever expanding and this has a good restaurant. Near the center of the beach, **Sai Kaew Villas** (Tel. 321-0975) offers the best accommodation in this sector of the island, while at the southern end, **White Sand Bungalow** has a large number of reasonable bungalows with prices starting at B500 then falling as you move back from the beach.

The other major beaches which are served by the goat track that is called

CHANTABURI

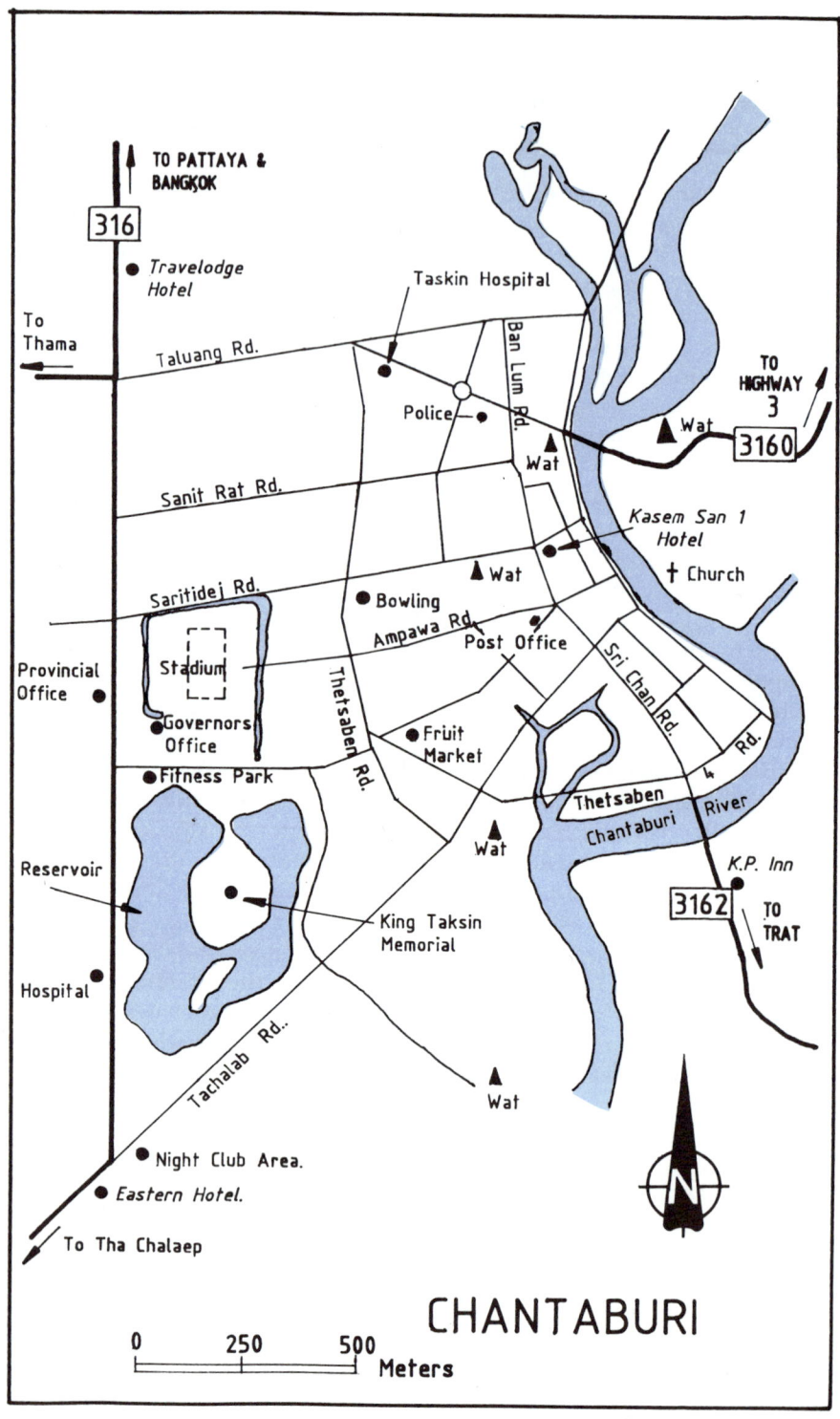

a road are **Ao Phai** and **Ao Wong Duan.** Both beaches are attractive but facilities are patchy. The best bungalows at Ao Phai are probably those at **Seabreeze** (Tel. 321-0975), where 36 bungalows rent for between B100 and B350 a night. Also on this bay is **Naga Bungalows** (Tel. 211-2968), which has bungalows scattered over a low hillside. Many of these establishments advertise video movies in the evening as their form of entertainment.

On the next bay, **Tub Tim Bungalow** is a friendly place with very basic bungalows from B70 and others up to B300. It is on Wong Duan beach that you find the up-market sector of Ko Samet. **Malibu Bungalows** start at B400 for fan-cooled and top B1000 for airconditioned units. For what you get, the prices seem high, yet by Western standards I guess they are not. Here you will find that there are more man-made activities, the restaurants are better, and they even have a disco. Perhaps this is a sign of where Ko Samet will ultimately head. If you don't like lying in the sun you wouldn't be on Ko Samet but for those who seek a break from this activity, there are two **boat trips**—around the island for half a day, and a whole-day coral island trip—which will help vary the routine. Then you can always go to **Roger's Fun Bar Disco** near Na Daan pier for some nighttime entertainment.

Note that malaria is still present on Ko Samet. It is necessary to take medication while visiting and after leaving the island. If you plan to stay in this area you should talk to your doctor before you leave home and get his or her advice on the right medication for you.

Back at Ban Phe, I recommend that you head east along the coast. This is a lovely drive through palm trees, then a pine forest national park. For several kilometers you parallel the white sand beach, passing several small resorts on your left. Many of these are of very average standard but good accommodation can be obtained at **Amornphan Villa** (Tel. 612-918) with 40 rooms from B400, the **Coral Reef Resort,** 35 rooms, from B600, the **Phe Villa,** 30 rooms, from B400-2500, and the 45-room **Rayong Resort,** which has double rooms from B1600. All of these properties are close to the beach and all have some restaurant facilities.

Seventeen kilometers along this road brings you to the lovely **Suam Wang Kaew Beach Resort,** where seaside gardens contain a variety of accommodation (much of it self-contained). This is a wonderful place which would be ideal for a couple wishing to unwind after several weeks of travel. The best accommodation is excellent and the waterfront location a delight. Realistically you need your own transportation to reach and enjoy this area. Further details are available from Bangkok Tel. 02-252-5053. Nearby the **Bang Sai Resort** has a pool, tennis courts, and other good sporting facilities.

East of here you enter Chantaburi province and it is worth stopping in **Chantaburi** town. This region is famous for its fruit and you pass through orchards along almost any road you travel. The area is also a gem-mining center, and on Siam Gem Street in the center of the city, you can see dozens of shops trading in sapphires and rubies. The town has much evidence of prosperity. Vehicles clog the narrow streets of the central city while wide divided boulevards are a feature of the newer areas. The town is dominated by a large lake which has an island and monument to King Taksin in its center. There are boats to rent, a fitness park to try, and many restaurants around the shore. Of interest to visitors is the French-style **Church of the Immaculate Conception,** the largest in Thailand, built in the nineteenth century by members of the Thai-Vietnamese Christian community.

The city has several reasonable hotels with the 140-room **Eastern Hotel** (Tel. 312-218) on Tachalab Road considered to be the best. Rooms are from B330. (Reservations with the hotel at 899 Tachalab Rd., Chantaburi 22000.) A reasonable and larger property on the north side of town is the 212-room **Travelodge Hotel** (Tel. 311-531) with rooms from B300. Across the river, the **K.P. Inn** (Tel. 311-756) is a modern building with a good bar, restaurant, and massage facilities. For something cheap, the **Kasem San 1 Hotel** (Tel. 311-100) has rooms from B120. Much of the nightlife is clustered around the Eastern Hotel. There are cocktail lounges, bars, massage establishments, and whatever else. Useful local telephone numbers are: Police, Tel. 311-111; Phra Pok Kao Hospital, Tel. 311-611; and Bus Station, Tel. 311-187.

A few kilometers south of Chantaburi is **Noen Wong,** a ruined fortress that was used by King Taksin when he retreated from Ayutthaya, and later by King Rama III. There are a few ancient cannon. To the southeast of the city lies the **Pliew Waterfall and National Park.** Buses leave the provincial market for the Park each day or, if you have your own vehicle, it is about a 15-minute trip. You turn left at the K364 marker on the Sukhumvit Highway and go inland for 2 kilometers. The approach to the falls is lined with makeshift shacks and restaurants selling basic food and souvenirs but the Park is quite peaceful. The falls are not great but the setting is attractive and the pool at the bottom is a good place for a swim. Rest houses are available.

It is about 70 kilometers from here to the town of **Trat.** The small center is about 2 kilometers from the Trat River, only 20 kilometers from the Cambodian border. This, in some ways, is still frontier country, particularly around Bo Rai some 45 kilometers to the north of town.

Bo Rai is a gem-mining area and you can see petty miners selling their week's work to dealers at the Bo Rai Gem Market each morning. South of Trat town, a road leads out to **Laem Ngop,** which is the setting-out point for trips to several islands, including **Ko Chang,** Thailand's third largest island. There are camping facilities on pristine beaches and the opportunity to visit the Than Sanuk waterfall in the Chang Isles National Park.

Recommended accommodation in Trat town is at the 125-room **Muang Trat Hotel** (Tel. 511-091), where rooms cost from B200, or at the **Thai Roong Roj Hotel** (Tel. 511-141) in the center of town. At Bo Rai the choice is between the **Vartadise Hotel** (Tel. 512-801) near the post office or the

Honey Inn near the gem market. Useful telephone numbers in this region are: Police, Tel. 511-239; Hospital, Tel. 511-040; and Bus Station, Tel. 511-577.

7. Guided Tours

Because most people arrive in Pattaya on package holidays which include few sightseeing tours, there is a thriving industry of local operators who offer a wide range of alternatives. I suggest you contact **Diethel Travel** (Tel. 425-283), **Malibu Travel** (Tel. 423-180), or **Resort Travel** (Tel. 421-452) for further information.

Half-day tours are offered daily around Pattaya (B300), to the Elephant Village (B160) in the afternoon, to Nong Nooch Village Wonderland (B200 morning and B250 afternoon), and to Khao Khiao Open Zoo (B400) in the morning.

Day trips extend farther afield. There is a daily trip to Bangkok which visits many of the capital's best sights and costs about B950. Many operators offer a full day to the Coral Island at prices between B250 and B300. At least two companies have day trips to Ko Samet which include minibus transfer to Ban Phe, ferry to the island, and lunch at the Malibu Beach Resort. Cost is about B600 for the day. The minibus fare only is B200 return if you wish to do the island part by yourself.

Then there are the more unusual tours which go less regularly and require a minimum of about four people before they will operate. These include a day trip to Chantaburi to see the actual sites where miners dig the stones out of open pits and a subsequent visit to the gem cutters, then a visit to some of the scenic attractions in the area. The cost is about B800 per person. Another interesting tour gives a glimpse of several activities north of Pattaya. You visit Bang Saen, Ang Sila, the caves of giant bats, and a village where brick making is the prime occupation. This trip operates Wednesdays and costs about B700.

For those interested in the water, daily, weekend, and longer sailing charters are available through several operators. For information on tours try telephoning 423-686, 421-211, or 423-630. Rates average at B1500 per person per day. Sleeping accommodation onboard is available and equipment such as snorkel gear, fishing equipment, and windsurfing boards are available on request.

8. Culture

There are few cultural events or activities which distinguish the east of Thailand except perhaps the remarkable way the population has adapted to the influx of tourism and learned how to benefit from the visitor and his money. A good example is the painting industry which produces copies of the works of the great masters for sale to tourists, or portraits of tourists from photographs or real life. Then there are the tourist attractions which use elephants, dancing, and so on as ways of bringing visitors' dollars their way.

Apart from these activities though, there are still genuine cultural events in which the local population actively participate during the year. These are best illustrated by the festivals which occur in each province.

The **Tap Tim Siam Fair** is held in Trat in March. Rubies are among the natural treasures found in this province and at this fair you can see many specimens, as well as buy semiprecious stones. There are also demonstrations of the techniques used to excavate rubies, and stalls selling other local products such as preserved durian and straw hats.

The **Pattaya Festival** is held in the first week of April and the whole resort puts on its most festive face for this annual event. Food and floral floats, beauty contests, stalls selling local delicacies, and a spectacular display of fireworks on the beach are a few of the events which attract merrymakers.

The **Paet Riu Mango Festival** is held a week later in the city of Chachoengsa, just one hour to the east of Bangkok. Thai mangoes are regarded among the finest in the world and some of the best come from Chachoengsa. Many varieties can be sampled at this festival and there are also cultural displays, sales of local produce, and a competition to select Miss Mango.

Both Chantaburi and Trat hold fruit fairs in the first week of June. The **Chantaburi Fruit Fair** celebrates the abundance of such local fruits as rambutan, durian, jackfruit, and pomelo. Besides stalls selling the produce of surrounding orchards, there are cultural shows and exhibitions of provincial handicrafts. The Trat **Rakham Fair** is similar but also has a competition for a special breed of Thai dog.

One week later a similar fair is held in Rayong. Fruit is on sale, together with the shrimp paste and fish sauce for which the province is noted and a wide variety of local handicrafts.

The **Chonburi Buffalo Races** held in October are events worth seeing. The water buffalo is one of the mainstays in the life of the Thai farmer but in this annual event it is put to more amusing use than ploughing the local fields. There are races, tests of strength, beauty contests, and displays.

9. Sports

Pattaya is a sportsperson's paradise. As well as the expected water sports facilities, there is a wide range of other land-based sporting activities. All the major hotels have swimming pools, most have tennis courts, and some have other facilities such as bowling, table tennis, darts, badminton, and golf driving ranges. Outside the hotels there are vast alternatives and I will attempt to list some of them.

Archery is available on the outdoor range at Nong Nooch Village, 18 kilometers south of Pattaya. The fee is B30. The Sea Sand Club at Bang Saray has facilities for hotel guests only.

Badminton is an extremely popular sport with Thais, so it is no surprise to learn that the Pattaya Badminton Courts on Soi 17 in south Pattaya are open 24 hours a day. Rates are B35 per game, rackets B10, and shuttlecocks B16. The Siam Bayshore Hotel and Siam Bayview Hotel also have facilities for hotel guests.

Bowling is a popular sport served by four bowling alleys. **Pattaya Bowl** (Tel. 429-466) on Pattaya 2 Road has 20 computerized lanes in an airconditioned complex. There is a lounge, coffee shop, and pro shop. Prices are B25 a game during weekdays, B30 in the evenings, and B30 all day on weekends and holidays. Other alleys are the Palace Bowl at the Pattaya Palace Hotel, the OD Bowl in south Pattaya, and the 18-lane Royal Cliff Beach Bowl adjacent to the hotel.

Fishing is available at several locations but the best action will be found at Panarak Park on the road to the Siam Country Club. Rods and bait cost B40 while entrance to non-anglers is B30. There is an hourly fishing fee of B25. For those who fail to catch anything, there is a restaurant on hand. About 5 kilometers north of Pattaya, on the coast, is Banglamung Shrimp Farm which has a reservoir, rods, and bait and an hourly fee of B20. The restaurant here will cook your catch. If larger action is more your style the Pattaya Game Fishing Club has biweekly trips for groups of four to six. You normally need to be a member but a call to 429-645 will give you more information. Boat charter is available from Dieter Floeth (Tel. 428-725) at B6000 a day. He also occasionally has full-day deep-sea fishing trips for B600 per angler.

Golf is another sport with good facilities here. The **Siam Country Club** (Tel. 428-002) is one of the better courses in Thailand and it is only a 20-minute drive from the beach. This is a private club but visitors can make arrangements to play through the major hotels. Green and caddy fees are B650 while on the driving range 40 balls will cost B20. There is a nice clubhouse, restaurant, and pro shop, and even accommodation is available. The **Royal Thai Navy Course** (Tel. 428-422), known as Phu Ta Luang, is near Sattahip. Green fees are B100 weekdays, B150 weekends, and B100 for a caddy. The **Pattaya Sports Club** holds Thursday tournaments where visitors are welcome. The cost is B200 plus green fees and clubs are available for rental. Call 429-845 for current details. Golfers and nongolfers are welcome at the Asia Pattaya Hotel's par three nine-hole course behind the hotel. The green fee is B50 a round.

Go-carts for both children and adults are available at the Pattaya Kart Speedway behind Jomtien Beach. The 400-meter track is open daily with a choice of 80cc or 120cc carts. Rates are from B50 to 200 for 12 minutes of racing. A new 1,080-meter track is available for professional racers at the Bira International circuit.

Horse riding is an experience to remember at the **Reo Ranch** (Tel. 421-188) on the road to the Siam Country Club. Experienced riders are charged B300-400 per hour while lessons are available for the new rider.

Miniature golf is hardly a serious sport but the kids will love the nine tricky holes at the Novotel Tropicana's course or the layout at the course near Naklua Road opposite Garden Lodge. Rates are B20 a round.

Motor racing is the newest spectator sport in the region. Races are held on weekends at the 2.4-kilometer track on Highway 36 some 20 kilometers from Pattaya. Admission is B80-150 for regular meetings with motorcycles, production cars, and formula 3 racing cars but there is a surcharge for international events.

Parasailing achieved instant popularity in Pattaya and now there are at least three locations on Pattaya Beach where boat boys hawk their trade. The sport is also offered at the Royal Cliff and at the northern end of Jomtien Beach. Rates are B200-250 for a 5-minute flight.

There are eight **scuba** shops in Pattaya but the **Seafari Sports Center** (Tel. 429-060) at the Royal Garden Resort is the only top-class training facility in the region. A basic resort course is available at B2000 per person which offers one day's tuition in the pool and an offshore island dive with full instruction. Full PADI-recognized courses are also available.

Sailing dinghies are available on most beaches. The most popular are the single-handed fiberglass Lasers which rent at B300 an hour. Also available are Hobie Cats and Prindles at B500-600 per hour. The Olympic Sailing Team at the Sigma Resort in Jomtien offers a 2-hour sailing trip at B500 per person. Departures are at 10 A.M. and 2 P.M. A full-day trip is offered every Saturday and Sunday at B1500, including lunch and soft drinks.

Shooting is centered at **Tiffany's** (Tel. 429-642) on Pattaya 2 Road. Here there is an airconditioned range with 19 galleries which is open from 9 A.M. until 9 P.M. There is a wide selection of handguns and field rifles. Rates are B120 for the range, and bullets and targets are charged by the number used.

Snooker is available on ten professional tables at the Pattaya Bowl (B100 per hour), on four tables at the Palace Bowl, and on four tables at the J.B. Snooker Club at the Jomtien Bayview Hotel (B60 per hour).

Tennis courts are at fourteen major hotels. They are available to guests and nonguests and rentals vary among facilities. Several hotels have resident professionals with instruction fees of B100-200 per hour. A B100 surcharge is added to cover lighting at night.

Weights and lots of other gear are available at the Pattaya Fitness Center near the Regent Marina in north Pattaya. The center has a full range of workout equipment as well as sauna, changing rooms, and health drinks. Gym rates are B80 daily and B350 weekly.

Windsurfing is best from October to June and there are twenty schools to choose from along the various beaches. The Pattaya Windsurf Club on Jomtien Beach holds regular competitions throughout the year and a major event in December.

10. Shopping

Forget shopping in Pattaya if you are spending time in Bangkok, Chiang Mai, or any other major city. Pattaya is for fun and outdoor activities, not shopping. If you just cannot resist that urge, however, here are a few suggestions that may save you some heartache afterwards.

Some of the most beautiful arts and crafts that you will ever see are on display at **Chetralada** (Tel. 428-462) at the P.K. Villa in south Pattaya. This is a branch of the well-known Bangkok-based company that now has outlets at Chiang Mai, Phuket and the Rose Garden.

Sak's Gallery in the Siam Bayview Hotel will satisfy your urge for a self-portrait. A 30 x 40 cm original sells for about B700.

Tailors are available everywhere throughout Pattaya but two of the better ones are located at the Royal Cliff Beach Resort. **Boss International** has three outlets at the Royal Cliff and one at the Siam Bayshore. All offer free transportation if you phone 421-421 or 423-871. Styles tend to be modern, cloth expensive. The other is **William Lee Master Tailor,** who specializes in men's suits. He has a shop in the Royal Wing.

The **Joe Sephine Batik Shop** on Naklua Road has some items not found in other stores in Pattaya. A batik wall hanging or swimsuit may still have appeal once you get it home. So too may teak furniture which is available from the **House of Teak** on Soi 6 opposite City Hall or from **Northern Thai Handicrafts,** 2nd Road, south Pattaya. Both have a good selection and nice designs.

Thai silk is available from many outlets. I have found **Reun Thai Silk** (Tel. 426-191), on Pattaya Soi 2, helpful in the past. I'm told that **Da Thai Silk** (Tel. 429-056) is good for ready-made ladies' silk clothes. The **Beach Bum Boutique** on Beach Road (near the TAT office) has interesting wooden work, good handicrafts, and stunning swimwear.

Finally there are several jewelry shops on Beach Road in south Pattaya which have obtained the seal of approval from TAT. These are **World Gems** (Tel. 428-742), **Best Gems** (Tel. 429-115), **Pattaya Lapidary** (Tel. 429-142), and **Pan-Chinese Gems** (Tel. 429-092). It will be good for your peace of mind to use these listed establishments.

11. Entertainment and Nightlife

Pattaya has variously been described as sin city, brash, glittering, boisterous, outrageous, and fun. The descriptions are usually applied because of the entertainment and nightlife scene which is a very visible part of Pattaya life. They are all accurate.

The entertainment scene starts in the daytime. As well as the sporting activities already covered in the sports section, there are places such as **Pattaya Park,** which is a world of slides, whirlpools, and lagoons beside Jomtien Beach. Social fitness enthusiasts can meet Monday afternoon at 4 at Nyhaun Rest, 24 Soi 13, for a run with the **Pattaya Hash House Harriers.** You will be transported to an out-of-town starting line by minibus for a 45-minute run. Visitors pay B100 if they are female and B150 if male, and this includes a free beer and snacks. You can only assume that the men eat more!

By sunset, most visitors are in need of a cool drink, and the hotel bars and those in south Pattaya will welcome you with open arms. Many of these have early evening happy hours with two drinks for the price of one offers. Many visitors find it difficult to refuse.

As the evening moves on, the scene quickens. Pattaya has a big reputation for high-quality transvestite shows. **Tiffany's** (Tel. 429-642) was the first and 60 cabaret dancers perform in its 700-seat theater, seven nights a week. Shows are at 7:00, 8:30, and 10:00 each evening with an 11:30 show on Saturdays. Not far down Pattaya 2 Road, **Alcazar** (Tel. 429-746) offers 70 dancers performing song and dance acts in a similar performance. Showtimes and prices are similar to Tiffany's. Cost is B200 a performance which includes a soft drink. Both operations are very slick, well done, but rather cold. It is certainly hard to believe you are not seeing professional female performers. The cast lines up for photographs afterwards.

Simon Cabaret (Tel. 429-647), in south Pattaya, is another similar show but it skips the cover charge and asks B95 for a drink. The different variety shows are staged nightly by 40 cabaret dancers. The **Marine Bar,** on Beach Road in south Pattaya, is not specifically for transvestites but you will find some there, along with plenty of straight girls and guys. The place is huge, open on the sides, and it screens movies on a full-size screen. It also has a boxing ring for Thai boxing matches and go-go dancers to add some glamor.

Across the road is the **Plaza Disco** (Tel. 429-568), one of several such establishments in town. The largest and most lavish of these is the **Palladium** (Tel. 424-922) on Pattaya 2 Road in north Pattaya. This huge complex contains a massage parlor, lounge, and high-tech disco with smoke machines, huge video screens, strobe lights, and so on. For nondisco regulars it is an eye opener; for disco freaks it is heaven.

Several hotels also have discos and the best of these are at the Dusit Resort (Tel. 429-901), the Novotel Tropicana (Tel. 428-645), the Regent Marina (Tel. 429-977), the Little Duck Pattaya Resort (Tel. 428-104), and the Ambassador City between Jomtien and Sattahip (Tel. 231-501). Many hotels have night clubs with live or recorded music, drinks, and dance floors. Most do not have hostesses or single ladies. The standard varies considerably and the following are considered to be the best: the Asia Pattaya Hotel (Tel. 428-602), the Montien (Tel. 428-155), the Royal Cliff (Tel. 421-421), the Siam Bayshore Telephone Club, which has excellent jazz six nights a week (Tel. 428-678), the Diamond Beach (Tel. 428-071), and the Ambassador City (Tel. 231-501).

Outside the hotels there is some choice. The **Jazz'n Blues Pub** (Tel. 426-258), Pattaya 2 Road, has a nice atmosphere. The **Club V** on Soi 4 is Japanese-style with hostesses.

Then there are the go-go clubs. These are mainly clustered in south Pattaya near Pattayaland and between Soi 15 and Soi 16. Class and discretion are not too much in evidence at these establishments, but there is no doubt that some of the women are extremely pretty and most will not hassle you if you only want a drink and a look at the scenery. As with many Bangkok bars, a bar fine system exists if you wish to go elsewhere with one of the ladies.

Finally there is massage. Modern massage appears to be more popular than ancient massage in Pattaya, even within the hotels. Some of the top hotels such as the Royal Cliff, the Montien, and the Ambassador provide in-house massage facilities which are well organized and well run. Outside the hotel, the standard and facilities vary from excellent to extremely basic. The prices reflect fairly well the standard you will get. The more popular facilities are at the **Palladium Massage** on Pattaya 2 Road; **Rainbow Massage,** second floor of the Palace Bowl; and **Sabailand** on Soi 3. All of these estabishments cater to women as well as men. Prices start at about B100 and go way up.

Information on many aspects of the nightlife and entertainment scene can be found in two free publications which circulate within Pattaya—"Pattaya Tourist Guide" and "Explore Pattaya."

12. The Pattaya Address List

Banks—Bangkok Bank, Naklua Rd., Tel. 429-347; Bangkok Metro Bank, 464 Beach Rd., Tel. 428-768.

Buses—Bangkok Bus Terminal (A/C), Beach Rd., Tel. 429-378; Diamond Coach, Nipa Lodge, Tel. 428-321; Erawan Coach, Tel. 428-729.

Churches—Pattaya Christ Church, Soi 13, Tel. 429-004; Roman Catholic Church, Sukhumvit Rd., Tel. 428-932.

City Hall—Soi Yodsak (Tel. 429-124).

Hospitals—Banglamuing Hospital, Sawangroh Rd., Tel. 429-244; Pattaya Memorial Hospital, Klang Rd., Tel. 429-422.

Immigration Office—Soi 8 (Tel. 429-409).

Limousine—Thai Limousine, Royal Cliff Beach Resort (Tel. 428-513).

Lions Club (third Thursday of month)—Tel. 428-015.

Medical Clinic—International Clinic, Soi 4 (Tel. 428-374).
Police—Pattaya, Beach Rd., Tel. 428-223; Tourist Police, Beach Rd., Tel. 429-371.
Post Office—Pattaya, Soi Chalyasit (Tel. 429-341).
Radio Station—Tel. 429-281.
Rotary Clubs—Pattaya Rotary Club (every Thursday at 6:30 P.M.), Tel. 428-487; Jomtien Rotary Club (every Friday at 6:30 P.M.), Tel. 425-515.
Sea Rescue—Tel. 423-752.
Tourism Authority of Thailand—Beach Rd. (Tel. 429-113).

9

The Northeast

1. The General Picture

Thailand's sprawling northeast plateau contains a quarter of the kingdom's provinces and a third of its population. Despite this, I-san, as it is known to the Thais, receives few tourists and most foreigners would be hard pressed to name a city or major attraction in the region.

I-san has traditionally been Thailand's problem area, where nature has provided thin soil and too little rain and where successive Bangkok administrators have neglected development and channelled much needed resources to other areas. This is the poorest section of the country, its agriculture-based economy lagging behind other regions.

Despite this, or perhaps because of this, the Northeast's cultural traditions are better preserved and more a part of everyday life than those in other parts of the country. This, together with the gentle-natured and genuinely hospitable people, makes I-san a most unusual and attractive destination for visitors who don't need, or want, mass tourism.

The Northeast is bordered to the north and east by the Mekong River and Laos, and to the south largely by Cambodia (Kampuchea). The area is generally flat, although it is not low lying like the Central Plains. Rivers flow north or east towards the Mekong rather than south towards the sea. Roads radiate from Nakhon Ratchasima (Korat) and Khon Kaen, two of the region's largest cities.

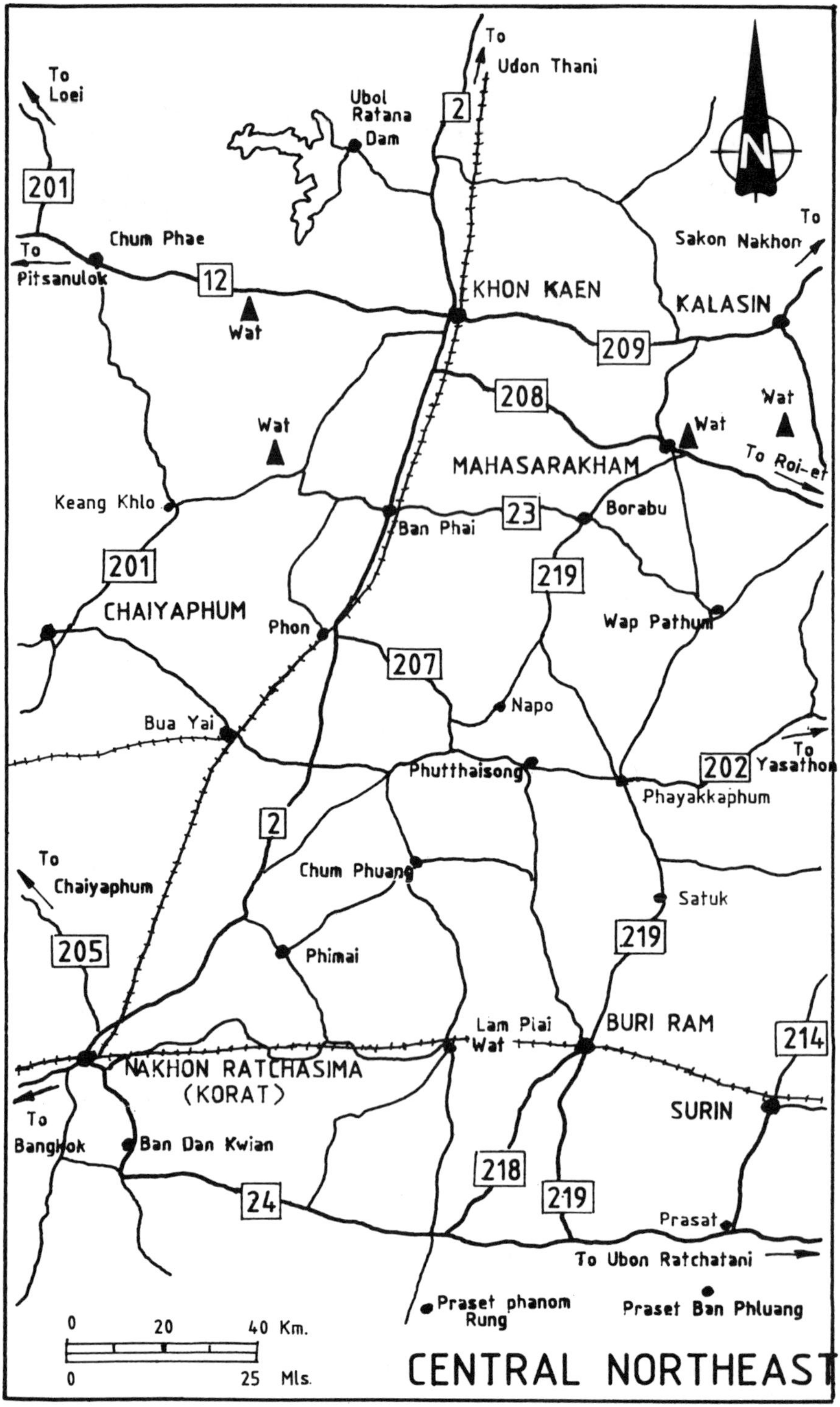

CENTRAL NORTHEAST

I-san has no single major tourist center so it is more difficult to tour than most other regions. There are, however, a number of natural and man-made attractions that rival the best available elsewhere. No one should miss the massive Khmer temples, the delightful national parks in Loei Province, the ancient center of Ban Chiang, or the many unique festivals that dot the calendar.

On top of all this is the attraction of a traditional way of life that, outside the cities, has so far sacrificed little to the modern world. Despite roads, electricity, and television, local attitudes are still governed largely by family, village, and religious influences.

I don't recommend I-san to the tourist looking for the glamorous, the picturesque, or the romantic. It is for those who wish to see a different aspect of Thai life—to understand the internal influences on Thai civilization rather than the external influences of international tourism.

For the thinking traveller, some time in I-san will be well rewarded. It will certainly give you a different perspective on the taxi drivers, the bar girls, and the laborers in Bangkok.

The Northeast is now receiving priority from the Thai government when resources are allocated. It will inevitably change. The Tourism Authority of Thailand is, for the first time, promoting the region as a "unique experience." Transition is already occurring. Yet visitors should be aware that, outside the major hotels and tourist attractions, English is seldom spoken or understood. The general population, however, is friendly and helpful and every effort will be made to comprehend the wants and needs of the visitor.

2. Getting There

The Northeast is well served by road, rail, and air links with Bangkok and there are road and air links with the northern region.

Buses leave Bangkok's Northern bus terminal (Tel. 271-0100) for the Northeast at frequent intervals throughout the day. Both airconditioned and non-airconditioned services operate to most centers throughout the region. Most foreign visitors will be amazed at the frequency. Buses leave for Korat, for instance, about every 15 minutes during the busy periods of the day. Most other major centers have at least an hourly service.

Distances and travel times from Bangkok to some of the major centers are:

Nakhon Ratchasima (Korat)	250km	4-5 hours
Khon Kaen	450km	6-7 hours
Udon Thani	560km	8-9 hours
Nong Khai	610km	9-10 hours
Sakon Nakhon	590km	9-10 hours

Surin	450km	6-7 hours
Ubon Ratchathani	670km	10-11 hours

Two main **rail** lines serve I-san. The southern line goes via Korat then through the provincial capitals of Buri Ram, Surin, and Si Sa Ket to Ubon Ratchathani. The northern line also passes through Korat then to Khon Kaen, Udon Thani, and to the Mekong River at Nong Khai. A secondary line bypasses Korat and rejoins the main line at Bua Yai, south of Khon Kaen. The trains have sleepers in first and second class and although the travel time is longer than the coach, many people prefer the space afforded by the train. Trains leave from Bangkok's Hualamphong Station (Tel. 223-7461).

The major **air** link is Bangkok to Khon Kaen. There are at least two direct flights a day and some days there is a flight via Korat. Udon Thani, Sakon Nakhon, and Ubon Ratchathani also receive some flights. Khon Kaen is also linked with Chiang Mai in the north while flights to Loei link with Bangkok and Chiang Mai flights at Phitsanulok.

The Northeast is an ideal place to have a **rental car** either self-driven or with a chauffeur. Distances between points of interest are longer than in most other parts of Thailand, the roads are good, and there is much less opportunity to join organized tours.

3. Local Transportation

The local long-distance **bus** network is excellent. All major centers and many minor ones are linked by non-airconditioned buses at regular intervals. The major centers have well-organized bus terminals and you will usually find someone who can speak some English.

From the major towns, local buses or **songthaews** operate to almost all villages. At worst, you will be dropped on the main road at the village turnoff and will have to walk or travel the last few kilometers by motorized samlor.

Most major cities have pedal **samlors** and songthaews offering an inner city service. Some have motorized samlors which operate as taxis. Regular **taxis** are rare. A few places offer **motorcycle rental.**

4. The Hotel Scene

The Northeast does not have the five-star luxury hotels or the small bungalows that cater to the opposite ends of the Western visitor scale. It does have, however, a number of adequate mid-range hotels and a good variety of inexpensive hotels which mainly serve Thai visitors, government officials, and salesmen. These are what tourists will also use and you will find that in most cases they will be clean and friendly. Western tourists are still a novelty in some areas of the Northeast and at times you will be treated as such. People you meet may be keen to try out their limited English on you so be prepared to answer the many questions you will be asked. The following are some hotel suggestions throughout the northeast.

KHAO YAI NATIONAL PARK

The **Khao Yai Resort** (Bangkok Tel. 02-255-2480), 56 rooms, has good restaurant and sporting facilities and rooms from B1600 a night. The **Khao Yai Motor Lodge** (Tel. BK 02 281-3041) has rooms and bungalows to rent. Rooms from B400, bungalows from B600.

NAKHON RATCHASIMA (KORAT)

The **Chom Surang Hotel** (Tel. 257-088), 120 rooms, 2701 Mahat Thai Road, has a pool and good facilities. A double room is about B600, high by I-san standards. Similar facilities can be found at **Sri Pattana Hotel** (Tel. 246-323), 180 rooms, 346 Suranati Road, the largest hotel in the city. Rooms go for about B400. For something much cheaper, the **Siri Hotel** (Tel. 242-831), 60 rooms, 167 Pho Klang Road, has been recommended as a friendly place. Rooms with fans begin at B130.

KHON KAEN

This city has some of the best accommodation in the region. The **Roserkon Hotel** (Tel. 237-797), 80 rooms, at 1/11 Klang Muang Rd., is the newest hotel and the most Western-oriented. There is a good restaurant and bar. Rooms about B500.

The **Kosa Hotel** (Tel. 225-014), 120 rooms, at 250 Sri Chan Rd., has a pool, disco, restaurant, and massage parlor, and is situated near a department store and supermarket. Rooms about B450. The **Khon Kaen Hotel** (Tel. 237-711), 140 rooms, at 43/2 Phimphasut Rd., has an extremely popular Thai/Chinese night club and probably the city's best disco. Rooms are good, costing B450. The **Khon Kaen Bungalow** (Tel. 236-220), 48 rooms, has been recommended as a good value in the cheaper range.

NAKON PHANOM

The **Nakon Phanom Hotel** (Tel. 511-455), 60 rooms, at 403 Aphiban Bancha Rd., has a good reputation for reliability and service. Rooms cost about B350. The **River Inn** (Tel. 511-305), 16 rooms, has a great position and recent improvements have made it reasonable. You can breakfast on a river terrace. Costs from B150. For those on a budget, the **First Hotel** (Tel. 511-253), 60 rooms, at 370 Si Thep Rd., is recommended. From B100 up.

SAKON NAKHON

The **Dusit Hotel** (Tel. 711-198), 120 rooms, at 1784 Yuwa-Phattana Rd., has rates from B250. The **Imperial Hotel** (Tel. 711-887), 100 rooms, offers accommodations from B200 at 1892 Sukkasaem Rd.

UDON THANI

The **Charoen Hotel** (Tel. 221-331), 120 rooms, at 549 Phosri Rd., has reasonable rooms, a restaurant, and a night club. Rooms are from B350. The **Chaiyaporn Hotel** (Tel. 221-913), 80 rooms, has both airconditioned and non-airconditioned rooms at 209 Mak Khaong Rd. Prices start at B180. The **Charoensi Palace** (Tel. 222-601), 110 rooms, at 60 Pho Si Rd., has rooms available with rates from B280.

NONG KHAI

The **Prajak Bungalows** (Tel. 411-116), 27 rooms, have reasonable rooms from B100 at 1178 Prajak Rd. The **Pongwichit Hotel** (Tel. 411-583), 39 rooms, on Banthoengit Road, has been recommended as being clean and cheap. A room with a fan will run B120, airconditioning will mean B200. The **Sukaphan Hotel** (Tel. 411-894), 25 rooms, has a bar, coffee shop, hairdresser, and rooms from B150.

LOEI

The **Sam-O-Hotel** (Tel. 812-353), 30 rooms, offers good clean rooms. Near the market, at 55 Charoen Rat Rd., the **Phu Luang Hotel** (Tel. 811-532), 90 rooms, is a lively place. There is a night club and airconditioned and non-airconditioned rooms, with prices from B150.

The **Sarai Thong** (Tel. 811-582), 60 rooms, on Ruamjit Road, is recommended for budget travellers. The **Phu Kradung** (Bangkok Tel. 02-579-0529), 16 rooms, in the National Park, can give you lodging from B500 to 1200. The **Pru Rua Chalet** (Tel. Bangkok 01 433-5396), 5 bungalows, at the National Park, can do this from B120 to 1000.

UBON RATCHATHANI

Probably the best hotel in town is the **Patumrat Hotel** (Tel. 241-501), 145 rooms, at 173 Chayang Kun Rd. It includes a restaurant, pool, and night club. Rooms about B450. The **Ratchathani Hotel** (Tel. 254-599) has both airconditioned and non-airconditioned rooms and a nice atmosphere at 229 Khuan Thani Rd. Rooms from B250.

SURIN

The **Petchkasem Hotel** (Tel. 511-274), 160 rooms, at 104 Jit Banrung Rd., has a restaurant, bar, shopping facilities, and pool. Rooms go for about

B500. For those seeking cheaper accommodation, the **New Hotel** (Tel. 511-341), 100 rooms, at 22 Thanasan Rd., is recommended. Fan-cooled rooms from B130.

ELSEWHERE IN THE NORTHEAST

In **Mahasarakham,** at 20 Sarmut Sakdarak Rd., the **Wasu Hotel** (Tel. 711-046), 100 rooms, has good accommodation from B400 a night. The **Hua Nam Hotel** (Tel. 611-137), 30 rooms, in **Mukdahan,** has a choice of fanned or airconditioned rooms. The **Mukdahan Hotel** (Tel. 611-619), 55 rooms, is similar.

You can stay in **Si Sa Ket** at the **Phromphiman Hotel** (Tel. 611-141), 125 rooms, with rates from B150 (fan) or B300 (airconditioned). In **Roi-Et,** the **Mai Thai Hotel** (Tel. 511-038), 110 rooms, at 99 Halsok Rd., has a restaurant, bar, disco, massage, and airconditioned rooms from B400. The **Si Chumphon** (Tel. 511-741), 100 rooms, is a slightly cheaper alternative there just across the road.

The **Suphak Hotel** (Tel. 811-315), 50 rooms, in **Kalasin,** charges from B120 a night for a fan-cooled room, B220 for airconditioning. In **Yasothon,** the **Yothnakhorn Hotel** (Tel. 711-122), 50 rooms, at 141/1 Uthairamrit Rd., has fanned rooms from B120 and airconditioned ones from B240. If you wish to overnight in **Chaiyaphum,** the **Lert Nimit Hotel** (Tel. 811-522), 90 rooms, has a restaurant and disco. Rooms cost about B300 for airconditioning, B150 for a fan. The **Sirichai Hotel** (Tel. 811-543), 100 rooms, has good facilities and rooms from B200.

5. Dining and Restaurants

I-san Thais love food cooked in their own distinct way. With this, they eat glutinous rice which they squeeze into balls with their hands. Much of the food is spicy and some of it is quite unusual.

At the market food stalls you will see dishes such as fried grasshoppers, ant eggs, and snail curry, but don't be put off by this. Many of the other dishes are much more ordinary and most of them are delicious.

All visitors to the Northeast should try at least three local dishes. These are *gai yung,* a barbecued spiced chicken; *larp,* a spicy minced chicken with mint, shallots, and green peppers; and *som tum,* a salad of green papaya mixed with sliced tomatoes, chopped garlic, chillies, dried shrimp, and some lemon juice.

It should be said that while Northeastern food is distinctive and varied, it is probably not immediately as popular with visitors as the food from the central Thailand area. It is also much more difficult to find a restaurant with an English-language menu than in most other parts of Thailand. The first-

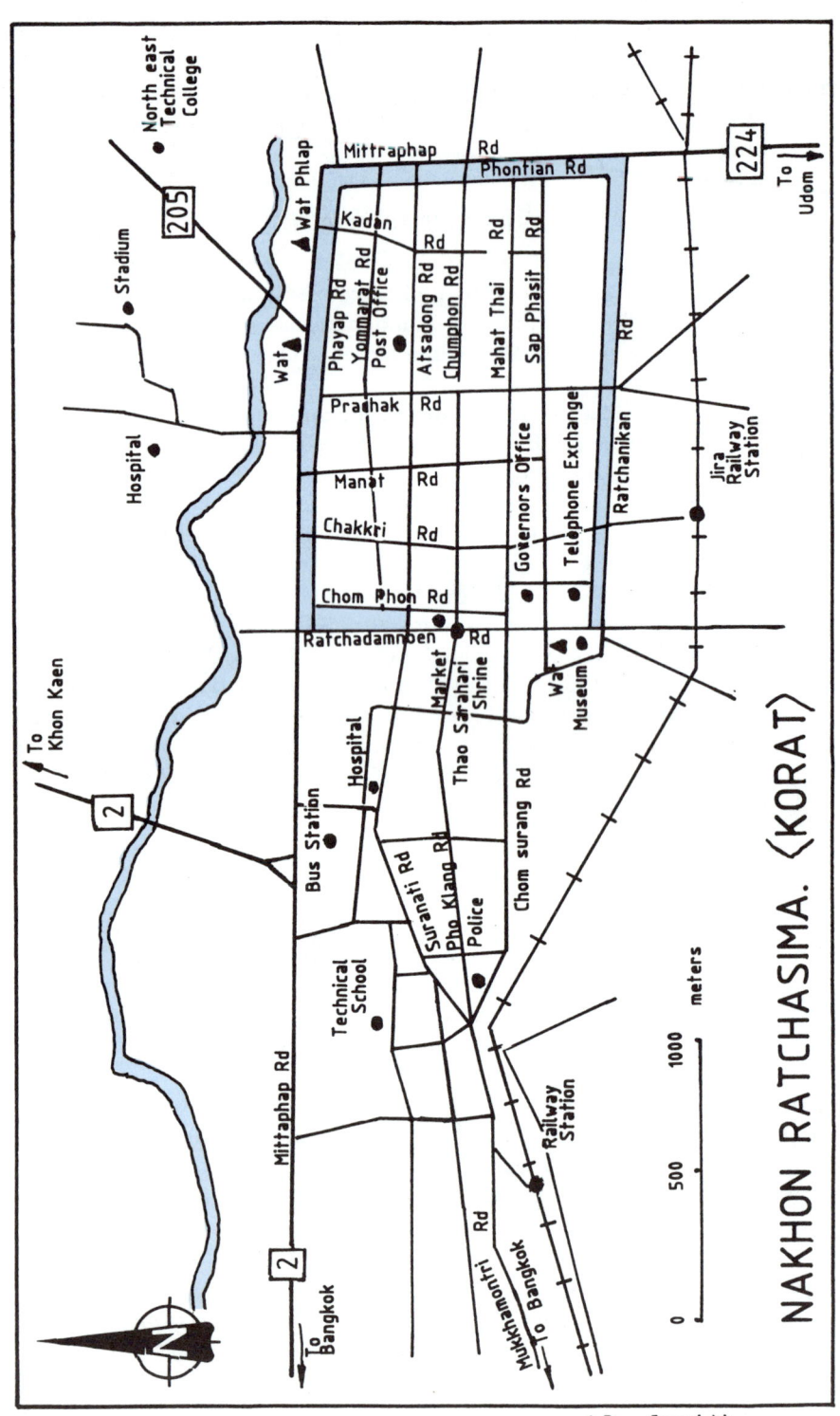

NAKHON RATCHASIMA. (KORAT)

time visitor is thus likely to find dining in I-san somewhat bewildering. Some people will stick with the hotels. The bold will walk the streets until they see something that appeals.

Most I-san cities and towns have sections where you find the best restaurants or best food value. The following guide should help in locating these sections:

Nakhon Ratchasima—the area close to Thao Sarahari Shrine.

Khon Kaen—on the road circling Lake Kaen Nakhon.

Udon Thani—on Prachak Road northwest of the clock tower.

Nong Khai—on Rimkong Road overlooking the river. Also try Prajuk Road.

Loei—on Charoen Rat Road. Try the **Green Garden Restaurant** or **Tip Cafe** for Thai food.

Nakon Phanom—along Bamrung Muang Road.

Mukdahan—on the road fronting the Mekong River.

Ubon Ratchathani—in the area around the provincial office.

6. Sightseeing

The Northeast is large and distances between major attractions are long. The major roads are good and traffic is lighter than in most other parts of the country. All this means that I-san is an ideal area to explore by car.

The natural access to the Northeast from Bangkok is Route 2, which branches from Route 1 (to the north) at Saraburi. At about the 45 kilometer mark, a sign points to a majestic white Buddha which sits on a green mountain. You will not miss it.

Another 15 kilometers along this road, a turnoff to the right leads to **Khao Yai National Park.** This 760-square-mile (2,000 sq. km) park offers a good forest, cool nights, excellent walks, a golf course, interesting wildlife (monkeys, gibbons, elephants, deer, tigers, and pigs), and a variety of accommodation including hostels, bungalows, and a motel. There is a good restaurant, and night flashlight hunting for deer, and perhaps tiger, is popular.

Back on Route 2, the road continues climbing the Korat Plateau. You see **Larn Takong Reservoir** on your left and now the vegetation changes to the typical dry Northeast scrub. The first major city you reach is **Nakhon Ratchasima (Korat).** Korat is a major business and commercial center that has rapidly grown since the 1970s. The initial impetus came from a buildup of the Royal Thai air base during the Indochina war but now the growth is in industry, government, and commerce.

In town, there are several things to see. Start at the **Thao Sarahari Shrine,** which commemorates the brave deed of Khunying Alo (a national heroine), who rallied the women of Korat into enticing many invading Laotian

Phimai's stone castle.

soldiers to a drunken party and then killing them. The memorial looks out over the town square and the old city wall. **Wat Sala Loi** is interesting mainly because the *bot* (chapel) is built in the shape of an ancient boat. The **Somdet Mahawirawong Museum** is situated in the compound of Wat Suthachinda opposite city hall. There is a good display of art objects and relics from the Khmer and Ayutthaya periods.

Korat has a TAT office (Tel. 243-427) which has some further information on the city and the northeast region. Other useful telephone numbers are: Police, Tel. 242-011; Maharat Hospital, Tel. 246-369; Railway Station, Tel. 242-044; Bus Station, Tel. 242-777; and Thai Airways International, Tel. 257-211.

One of the major attractions of this area is 60 kilometers northeast of Korat at the small town of **Phimai.** Here you will find the largest and best Khmer stone castle outside Cambodia. From an archaeological standpoint, this is one of the most significant sites in southeast Asia. From a tourist viewpoint it is most impressive. The temple was probably built in the eleventh century and even today it projects a strange majesty. Much of the structure has been recently restored by the Fine Arts Department so it's possible to see how magnificent the original structure must have been.

The Khmer empire was originally based at Angkor in Cambodia but it held influence over a large area. Exactly why this massive castle was built by the Khmers at Phimai is unknown, but it is thought that Phimai was a rare fertile oasis in an otherwise dry and inhospitable area. The stone structures that remain today are just the remnants of a center built mainly in timber. The shops, pilgrims' shelters, and houses have since disappeared but perhaps they were something like the scattered new town of today.

The old Victory Gate entrance to the sanctuary still remains in the main street while at the other end of town there is an outdoor museum and some more ruins. About 2 kilometers away is a huge banyan tree, the largest in Thailand, known locally as Sai Ngam.

Back on Route 2 it is 150 kilometers north to the city of **Khon Kaen.** This thriving center is at the junction of the major north-south and east-west roads of northeast Thailand. Here is also the major airport for the region and the town is becoming the most important education and government center. Khon Kaen is a manageable city because of its grid layout and relative spaciousness. The main highway bypasses the main business district so heavy trucks are not a problem. It is a good city for walking and shopping.

The city has a branch of the **National Museum** with some ancient objects particularly from Ban Chiang and Kalasin. It's open Wednesday to Sunday. Admission is B10. The public is welcome to drive through the extensive grounds of **Khon Kaen University** to see the various faculty buildings and sports areas. There is also a pleasant drive around the shores of Lake Kaen

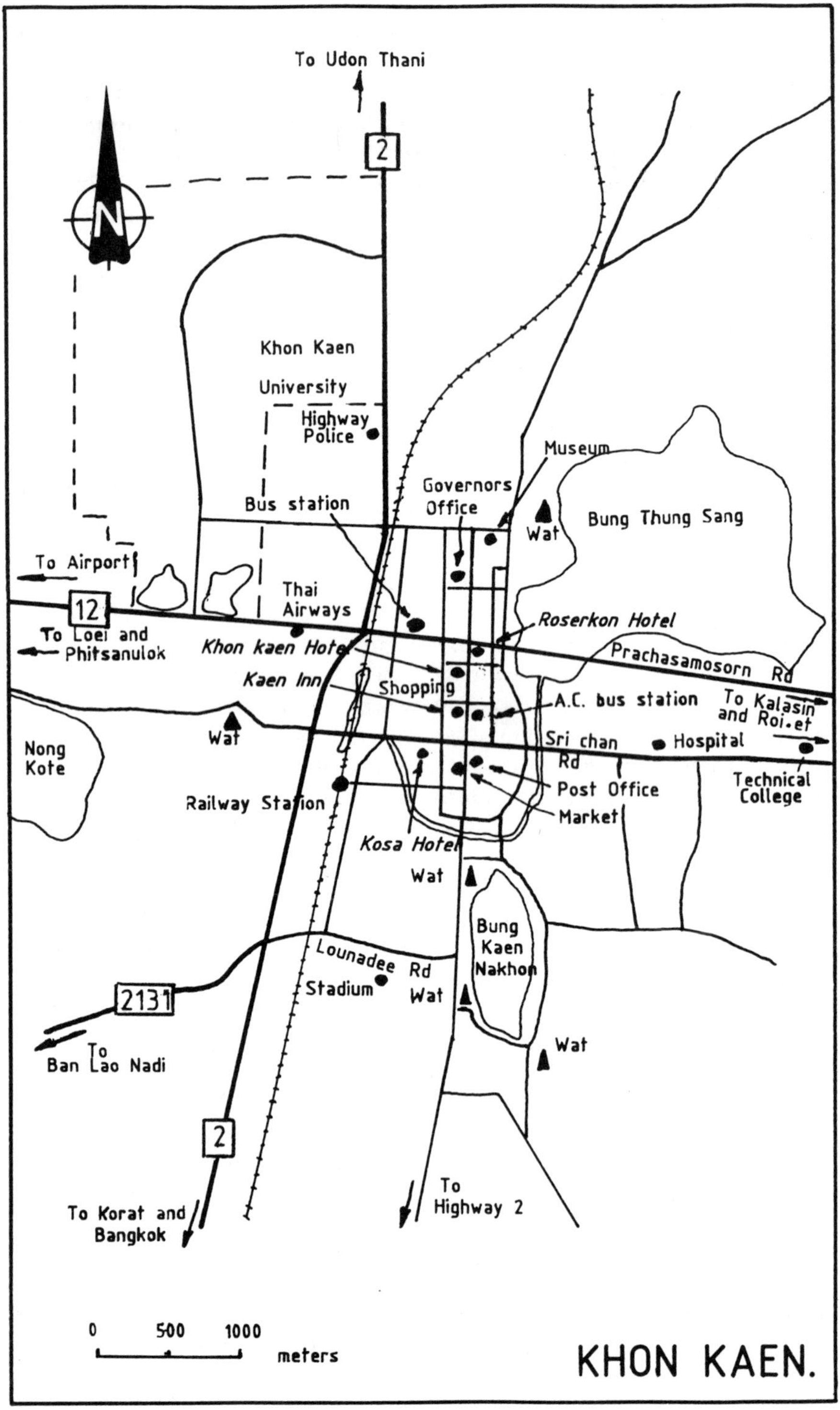

To Udon Thani
2
N
Khon Kaen
University
Highway
Police
Museum
Governors
Office
Bus station
Wat
Bung Thung Sang
To Airport
12
Thai
Airways
Roserkon Hotel
To Loei and
Phitsanulok
Khon kaen Hotel
Prachasamosorn Rd
Kaen Inn
Shopping
A.C. bus station
To Kalasin
and Roi.et
Wat
Sri chan
Rd
Hospital
Nong
Kote
Technical
College
Post Office
Railway Station
Market
Kosa Hotel
Wat
Bung
Kaen
Nakhon
Lounadee Rd
Stadium
Wat
2131
Wat
To
Ban Lao Nadi
2
To
Highway 2
To Korat and
Bangkok
0
500
1000
meters
KHON KAEN.

Nakhon, just south of the main business district. Here there are restaurants, a park modelled on one in Australia, some new up-market housing developments, and a Northeastern-style wat.

Useful telephone numbers for Khon Kaen are: Police, Tel. 221-162; Hospital, Tel. 236-005; Railway Station, Tel. 221-112; Bus Station, Tel. 239-472; and Thai Airways International, Tel. 236-523.

Route 2 continues north of the city. After about 30 kilometers, a road to the left goes west to the **Ubol Ratana Dam.** This is an impressive structure and a good picnic or lunch spot. There is a restaurant, a hilltop wat, boat rides on the reservoir, a golf course, and cabins for those who want to stop for the night. It is well worth the trip.

From Khon Kaen, Route 12 heads west to **Chum Phae** and eventually across the mountains to Pitsanulok and North Thailand (see Chapter 6). Southwest of Chum Phae is Chulaborn Dam, where there are bush walks, chalets, and a challenging golf course. A few kilometers west of Chum Phae, a road branches north to the province of Loei. This is one of the most picturesque areas in I-san.

A major attraction along this road is the **Phu Kradung National Park.** The park embraces the highest mountain in Loei (about 1,500 meters) and this is high enough to lower the temperature considerably at night. In fact in February and March it has been known to fall nearly to freezing. That may not be cold to you, but it's certainly cold for the tropics. The park is generally closed during the rainy season from mid-July to mid-October.

The attraction of the park is the cool, invigorating air and the wilderness on top of the plateau. There is no road to the top so there is an unspoiled atmosphere after you brave the 5-kilometer climb up the mountain. The walk takes about 4 hours and is very scenic. Once you reach the top there are clear, level paths crisscrossing the plateau and a park headquarters with cabins and tents. There are some waterfalls, and you may see some wildlife. Try and catch the sunrise at Liem Pha Nok Hain cliff and generally soak up the tranquility.

Back at ground level, it's almost 70 kilometers on to the town of **Loei.** This is one of the Thai provincial towns least changed by modern development. That's not to say it is backward; in fact, there are good hotels, restaurants, shopping facilities, markets, and so on. It is more a feeling that you are a long way from central government here and not many locals are complaining. They just go about living and enjoying themselves as best they can.

The area surrounding Loei is full of attractions. To the west on Route 203 is the Phu Rua National Park (50km), set in fine forest and offering lovely views. To the northwest is **Tha Li** (50km), surrounded by mountains and close to the Lao border. This is one area where the Mekong River is not the border between Thailand and Laos. The much smaller Mae Herang is the

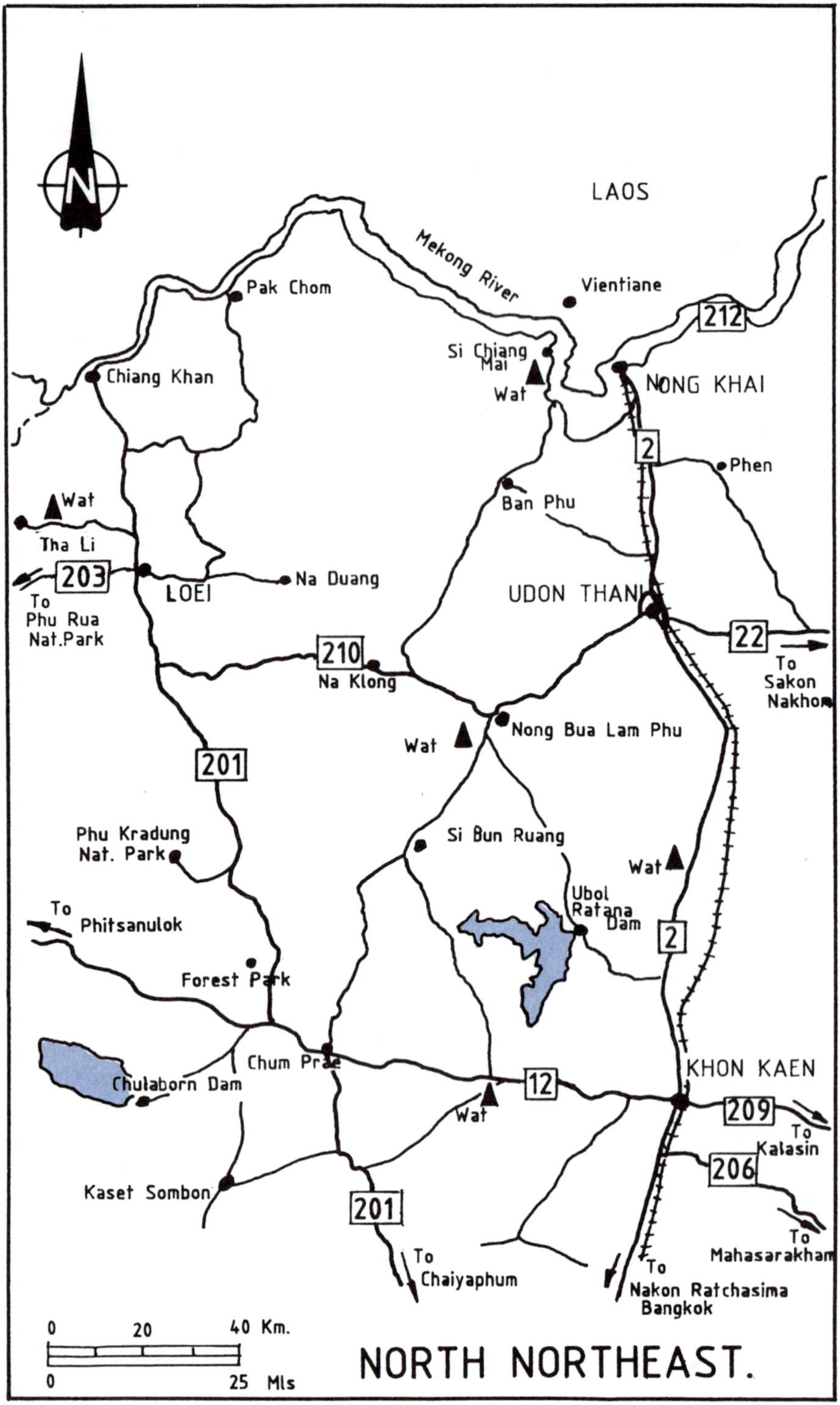

L.R. Copyright

barrier here and because it is much easier to cross, black market border trade thrives. The popular drink in this region is *lao khao,* or Lao whiskey, a clear firewater that tastes terrible.

Chiang Khan is 50 kilometers north of Loei, on the Mekong River. The town is surrounded by mountains and so it spreads along the river. This is one of several towns where there are restaurants right on the riverbank. Eat in one of these and you have a great view of the river, the valley, and the activity on the water. They are delightful spots. Just downstream from here the Kaeng Khut Ku rapids are worth visiting. There is a 700-year-old wat just outside town.

The road from Chiang Khan downstream beside the river is a delight. It is possible to follow the river for almost a thousand kilometers as it winds between mountains then widens into a broad plain. One of the best sections of this drive is from Chiang Khan to Nong Khai. With one or two stops it will take 4-5 hours. You pass through small areas of natural jungle, other areas where reforestation is underway, many vegetable gardens close to the river, irrigated ricefields, cotton, bamboo, peanuts, and various other vegetation. There are several waterfalls, some small towns with riverside restaurants, and a view across the river to the Laotian capital of Vientiane as you get close to **Nong Khai.** About 15 kilometers before you reach Nong Khai you will pass a wat which is believed to be about 2,000 years old. Nothing remains of the original structure but there is a restored sixteenth-century chedi and some other buildings.

Nong Khai Province is long and narrow and the town is similar. Both sprawl along the Mekong River. It is both a barrier and a lifeline. Relationships with Laos are improving but at the time of writing foreigners were still unable to cross the river. That will change shortly and plans are being prepared for a major bridge across the river at this point.

There is evidence of French influence here. The town has some French-Chinese architecture and you can buy long bread loaves and even some French wine. There are several good restaurants by the river.

Just a few kilometers east of the town, **Wat Khaek** is a temple like you have never seen. It was established around 1975 by Luang Pu, a "priest" who combines Buddhism, Hinduism, mythology, and other "isms" to produce a philosophy that is difficult for a foreigner to grasp. The temple has a large collection of bizarre cement statues and there is a small museum-shrine with an amazing collection of photographs, carvings, and sculpture.

You can continue following the river but an alternative is to travel the 50 kilometers south on Route 2 to **Udon Thani.** This city of about 100,000 is one of the big-four northeast cities—Korat, Khon Kaen, Udon Thani, and Ubon Ratchathani. All except Khon Kaen were major military bases during the Vietnam War of the 1960s-1970s. The war was a major development factor

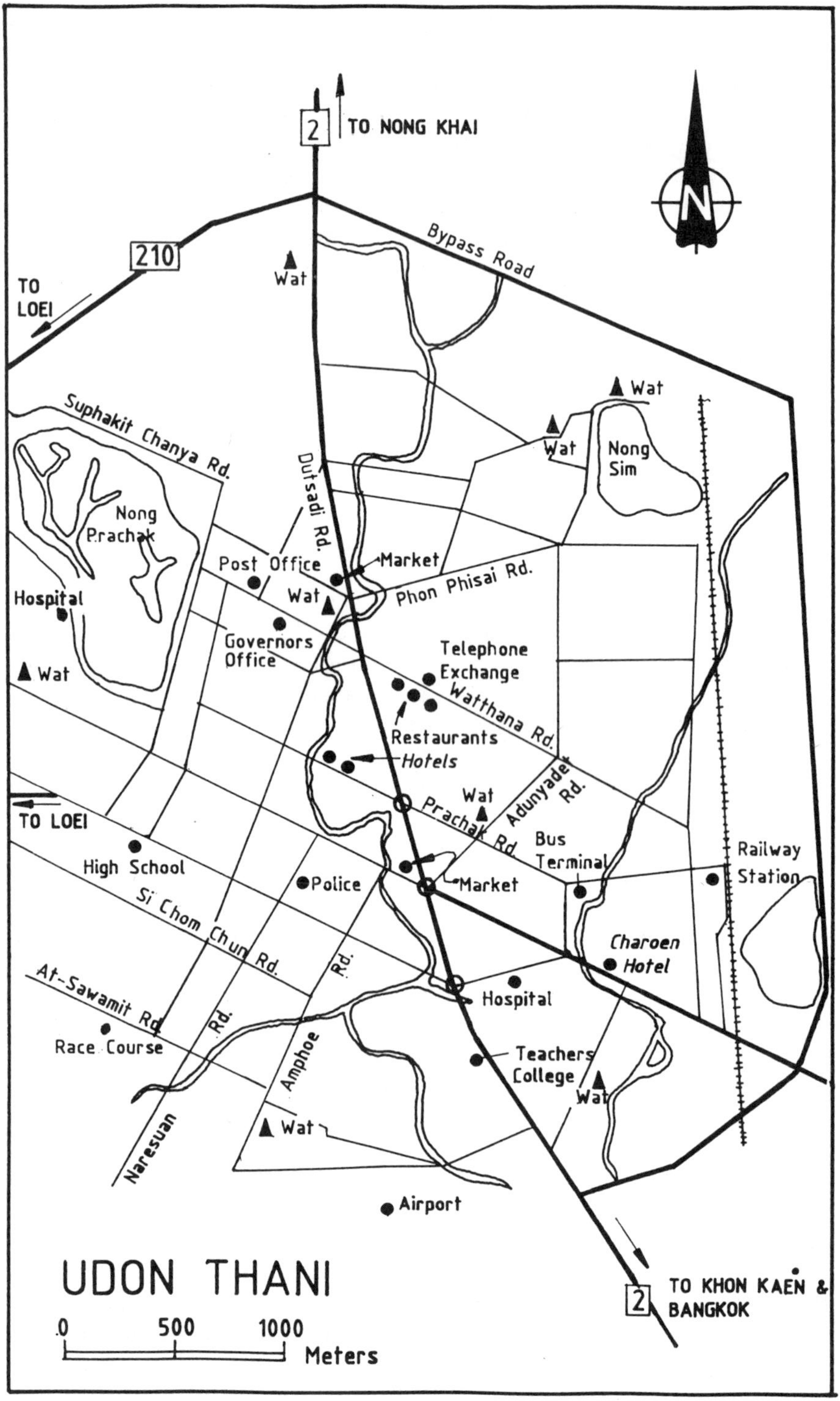

TO NONG KHAI
2
210
TO LOEI
Bypass Road
Wat
Wat
Wat
Nong Sim
Suphakit Chanya Rd.
Dutsadi Rd.
Nong Prachak
Post Office
Market
Wat
Phon Phisai Rd.
Hospital
Governors Office
Telephone Exchange
Wat
Watthana Rd.
Restaurants
Hotels
Wat
Adunyadet Rd.
TO LOEI
Prachak Rd.
Bus Terminal
Railway Station
High School
Police
Market
Si Chom Chun Rd.
Charoen Hotel
Rd.
At-Sawamit Rd.
Hospital
Rd.
Race Course
Amphoe
Teachers College
Wat
Naresuan
Wat
Airport
UDON THANI
0
500
1000
Meters
2
TO KHON KAEN & BANGKOK

for Udon and there are still remnants to be seen—airconditioned coffee shops, ice-cream parlors, massage parlors, and Western cafes. Useful telephone numbers in town are: Police, Tel. 222-285; Hospital, Tel. 222-572; Railway Station, Tel. 222-061; Bus Station, Tel. 222-915; and Thai Airways International, Tel. 221-004.

The major interest in this area is a small village called **Ban Chiang,** about 50 kilometers to the east. The village is about 6 kilometers off Route 22 but it is well signposted. Archaeological discoveries made in the 1970s uncovered evidence of a Bronze Age civilization that flourished here over 5,000 years ago. Although not yet conclusive, this would make this civilization older than those in China and Mesopotamia which are presently the earliest known agrarian, bronze-making civilizations. The find has thrown the archaeological world into disarray.

One of the pits that was opened during the massive controlled "dig" of 1974-75 remains today. In it you can see human skeletons, distinctive patterned pottery, and other objects. I visited at a time when there was no one else around. It was fascinating and I could not suppress my excitement. A short distance away in the center of the village, there is a small museum which is well worth visiting. It is closed Monday and Tuesday. Admission is B10. Be very careful if you plan to buy anything from the locals—much of it is fake. Genuine pieces will not be allowed out of the country.

From Ban Chiang, Route 22 takes you to the town of **Sakon Nakhon.** The town has some charm but few real features. It spreads out onto the plain which surrounds Lake Nong Han and you see evidence of the rich agricultural activity in this region. In town, Wat Phra That Choemg Chum is worth visiting.

Route 22 continues east towards Nakon Phanom. You immediately see evidence of French, Lao, and Vietnamese influence. The village of **Tha Rae** has a sizable Catholic population which supports a large seminary. Signposts on the main road show the direction of refugee settlements that seem to have become almost a permanent feature of this area. There seem to be as many Christian crosses here as there are Buddha images.

Nakon Phanom is a strange town. For many foreigners the major charm of the place would be the old-style French-Chinese river shop/houses, but the local authority in its wisdom is in the process of pulling them all down and replacing them with a Western-style promenade. The river is wide and attractive at this point but seeing it from a restaurant balcony would be far more interesting than what is proposed. Fortunately there are some other examples of French-influenced architecture in town which are safe for the moment. The old administrative offices and the jail are good examples.

I used to think that Nakon Phanom had the making of a fascinating tourist town but in some ways that chance has been lost. It is still nice along

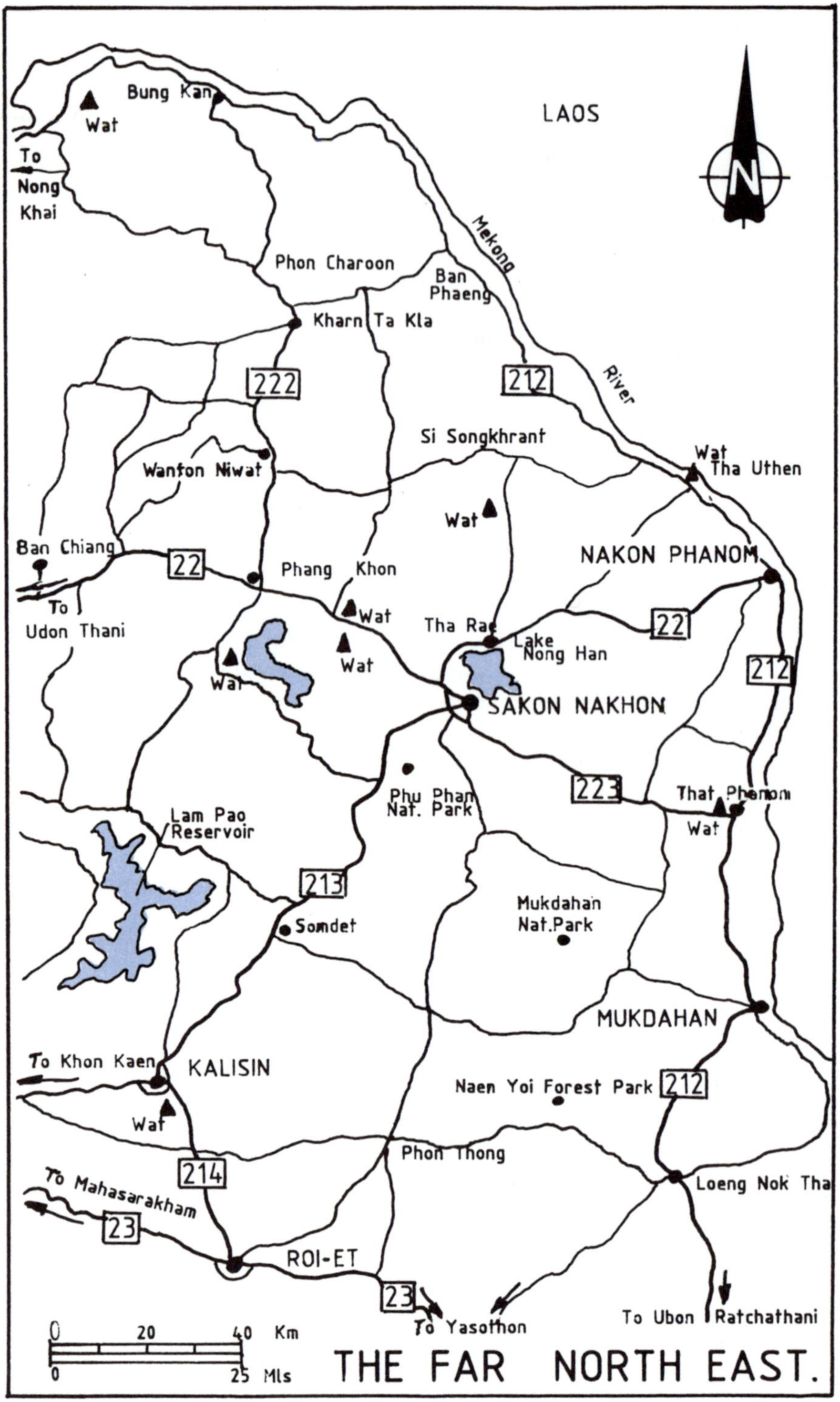

THE FAR NORTH EAST.

the river though, particularly early in the morning when you can see the rugged mountains in Laos.

For Thais the most important center in these parts is 50 kilometers south of Nakon Phanom. It is to **Wat That Phanom** that thousands of worshipers come each year to make offerings at a temple that was probably built almost 1,500 years ago. Very little of the original remains and the main chedi has been restored several times—the most recent being in 1979. The original wat was built by Laotians and is very similar to another that exists in Vientiane. Around the chedi there are various buildings and Buddha images. The wat always seems crowded and full of life but the town itself is often quiet. There is an interesting archway over the road leading to the river and the architecture here has much French influence. You could convince yourself you were in Laos or Vietnam. There are a couple of old hotels in town (rooms about B100) and several reasonable restaurants. It's an appropriate place for lunch after you have looked around the wat.

The road south from here generally follows the river but is several kilometers inland, so it is not until the town of **Mukdahan** that you get back to the water. This province was only created in the early 1980s so Mukdahan does not have the feel of an established provincial town. Its big asset is the road alongside the river. There are good views across the water to the Lao city of Savannakhet and you can buy a variety of Lao goods in the riverside market area. This road has a number of local restaurants which are casual and friendly.

From Mukdahan there are several roads west to Khon Kaen. One is via **Kalasin** and another passes through **Roi-Et** and **Mahasarakham**. These three towns are all provincial capitals but each is different in style. Roi-Et is the most developed and there is a nice lake, a huge Buddha image, a well-organized park, and some good hotels, restaurants, and nightlife. The country around all three is slightly rolling to flat and there are ricefields in all directions. Water buffalo are still the farmers' prize possessions and communities have changed little in this century.

South from Mukdahan, Route 212 brings you to **Ubon Ratchathani.** This is Thailand's most easterly province and the largest in I-san. The provincial capital is a vibrant city with good accommodation and restaurants, due in part to the Vietnam War. There are also a couple of interesting wats. The city has a bus service that makes it easy to travel around once you understand which bus goes where. If you plan to be around during the city's July Candle Festival, prebooking of accommodation is necessary. Useful telephone numbers are: Police, Tel. 321-215; Phra Si Mahapha Hospital, Tel. 254-462; Railway Station, Tel. 321-004; Bus Station, Tel. 254-564; Thai Airways International, Tel. 254-005.

There is an interesting excursion east of Ubon Ratchathani city to the point where the Mun River joins the Mekong at the Thai-Lao border. On the

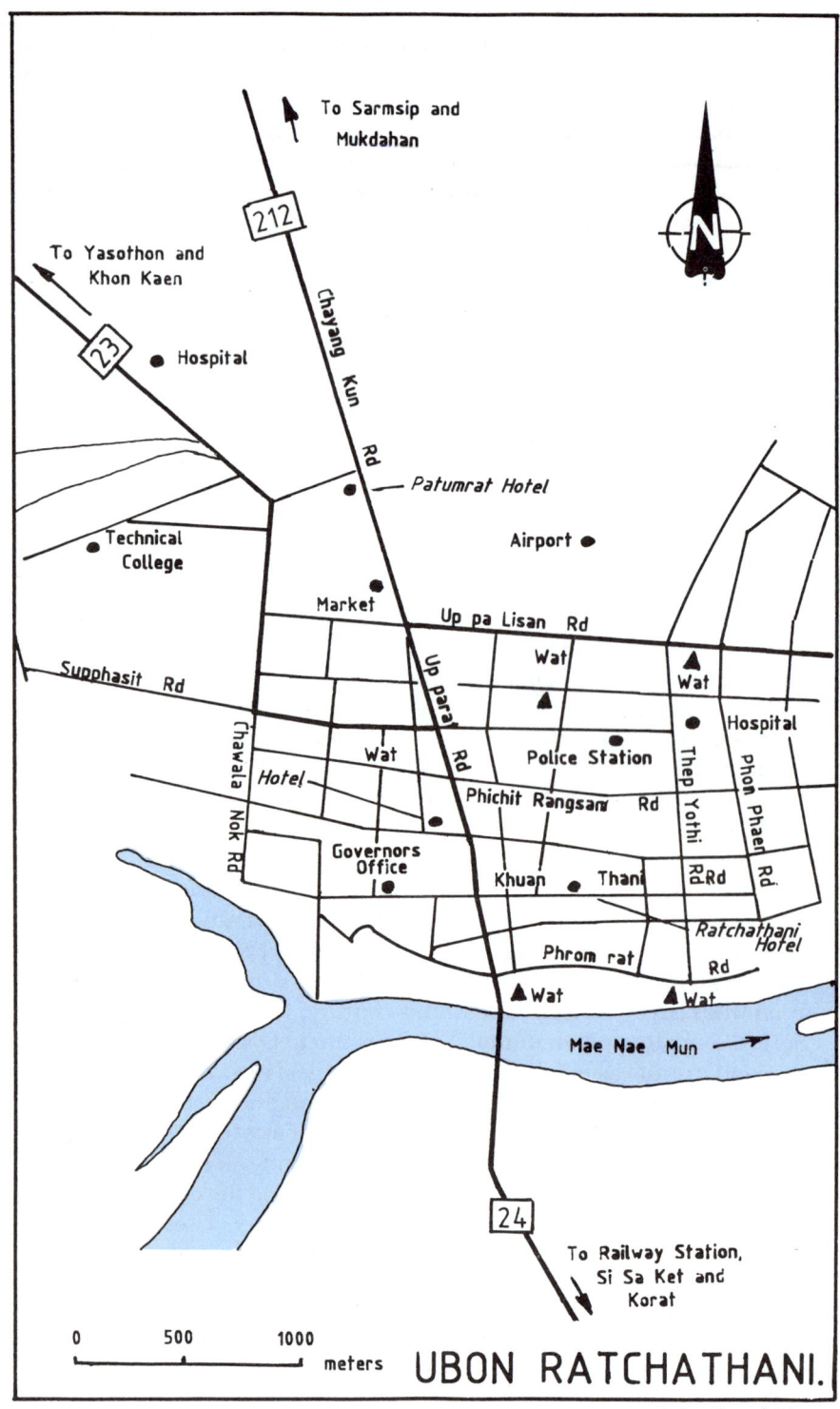

UBON RATCHATHANI.

way visit Kaeng Sapu rapids, about 45 kilometers east of Ubon. Then continue past the Sirindhorn Dam to the **Kaeng Tana National Park** to see the series of rapids where the Mun River flows over multitiered rock formations between high banks. From here it is not far to the prehistoric rock paintings at Pha Taem which extend for over 1 1/2 kilometers along the valley.

To complete your sightseeing in I-san you can travel west from Ubon, heading for Korat. You will pass through the small provincial capital of Si Sa Ket, then via a roundabout route you reach **Surin.** This town has been "put on the map" by the Elephant Roundup held each November. The town itself has little of particular interest, but at Sikoraphum some 35 kilometers to the east, **Wat Ra Ngeng,** an eleventh-century Khmer temple, is worth seeing. In fact there are numerous small Khmer sites in this region, several close to routes 24 and 214. Some like **Praset Ban Phluang** have been carefully restored while others lie in ruined splendor.

For those wishing to see elephants at a non-Roundup time, a visit to Tha Thum district's **Ban Tha Klang** elephant village will be interesting. This is where the first-ever Roundups were held and you can see massive shelters attached to dwellings, beneath which elephants have a home.

You should now return to Route 24 and visit two fine Khmer temples in the province of Buri Ram. **Praset Phanom Rung** stands on a wooded hill not far from the Cambodian border. The temple is approached by a magnificent 200-meter avenue, a bridge, and a five-level staircase. It is believed the temple dates from the beginning of the Angkor period and took over 200 years to complete. It was situated on the road that linked Angkor with Phimai. The whole complex is most impressive and has been nicely restored.

Nearby **Muang Tham** is quite a contrast. This was also on the Angkor-to-Phimai road but it dates from the tenth century. Unfortunately it is in a very poor state of repair and while parts of the laterite wall that enclosed the complex are still in reasonable condition, other buildings have collapsed. This temple is situated on the plain and its setting in open fields adds to its feeling of desolation. Both temples are well worthy of a visit.

Close to Korat, the villagers at **Ban Dan Kwian** have created decorative ceramics which are on display in roadside stalls. The village also has a collection of traditional farming implements and carts.

7. Guided Tours

Very few tours operate to the Northeast, and within the region the opportunity to pick up a local tour is almost nonexistent. The best approach is to ask the TAT offices in Bangkok (Tel. 282-1143), Korat (Tel. 243-427), or Ubon Ratchathani (Tel. 255-603) for advice.

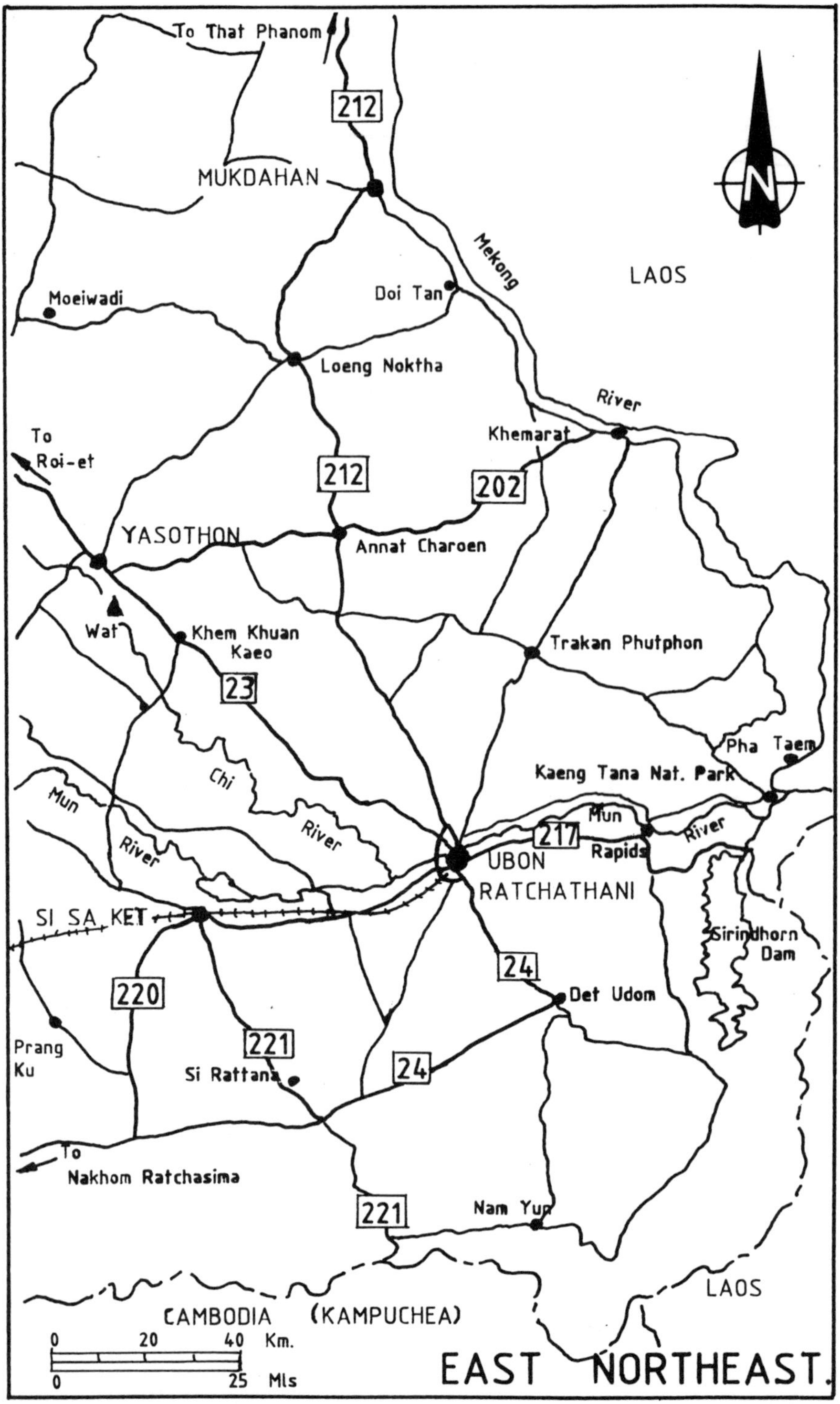

L.R. Copyright

8. Culture

The economy of the Northeast is based almost entirely on agriculture. Consequently the people pursue agrarian life-styles in countless small villages, largely unchanged over time and still ruled by the annual cycle of the farming seasons. Because of this, cultural traditions in music, folk dances, festivals, and legends are better preserved here than elsewhere in Thailand.

What the visitor sees today are genuine cultural traditions, not something for the benefit of the visitor. They may not be as organized and sophisticated as in some other places but they are particularly colorful and boisterous affairs designed to punctuate an otherwise arduous agricultural cycle. Here are some of the more important events to be seen during the year. Visitors will be welcomed by the locals, to all these events.

The Chaiyaphum Elephant Round-up is held in mid-January in this town which is 120 kilometers north of Korat. Although this is smaller than the Surin Roundup, it is nevertheless a colorful event that brings together numerous elephants from nearby areas to demonstrate their prowess. There is a spectacular re-enactment of medieval warfare.

The Phra That Phanom Fair in mid-February, at the famous wat in Nakhon Phanom Province, attracts thousands of devotees who pay homage at the shrine and also enjoy the numerous entertainments of this five-day event.

The Panom Rung Fair in mid-April is held at the impressive Khmer hillside temple in Buri Ram Province. The temple is the centerpiece of activities but there are also various exhibits, dancing, and singing.

The Rocket Festivals of I-san are spectacular events which originated a thousand years ago or more, when the Brahmanist Khmers who ruled the Northeast launched rockets into the air to remind the gods that rain was needed down below. The most spectacular festival is held in Yasothon. Months ahead of time, various villages start work on their rockets and their dance troupes. On the eve of the event, dancers and musicians give dress rehearsals in their own villages, then they parade the next day through Yasothon. High-spirited revelry accompanies the event with beauty parades, folk dancing, and stage shows. On the last day, the rockets are taken to a big field and launched one by one. The highest trajectory wins a prize and much honor for its village.

Loei has the **Phi Ta Khon** festival in mid-June. This unusual event derives from a local legend of two lovers who were sealed in a cave. Residents in ghostly costumes re-enact this colorful drama.

The Candle Festival is held at the beginning of the Buddhist Rains Retreat in mid-July at Ubon Ratchathani. It displays artistic skill as well as piety as beautifully carved beeswax candles, some several meters tall, are taken

Surin Elephant Roundup.

Thai folk dancing.

around the city in a colorful procession before being presented to local temples.

The **Wax Castle Festival** is an event to mark the end of the Rains Retreat. It is held in Sakon Nakhon in mid-October. Splendidly embellished beeswax creations in the form of miniature Buddhist temples and shrines are carried in procession through the town before being offered at temples to make merit for ancestors.

The **Illuminated Boat Procession** at Nakon Phanom is held at a similar time. Intricately decorated little boats, each containing a lighted candle, are set adrift on the river at night. Various entertainments are also provided in the town during the four days of the festival.

Boat races are also traditionally held at this time. The major events are at Nakon Phanom and Nong Khai, both on the Mekong River. Dates are usually in early November. Races are also held on the Mun River near Korat in November. Here there is a competition of boats decorated to resemble the famous Royal Barges.

The **Surin Elephant Roundup** is held mid-November. This event is now internationally famous and it brings crowds to Surin, where over 100 trained elephants are assembled. Among the spectacular features are wild elephant hunts, tugs-of-war, demonstrations of log-pulling skills, and a parade of elephants outfitted for medieval war.

The **Khon Kaen Silk Fair** is the last major event for the year in the Northeast. This event is held over about ten days at the very beginning of December. This is one of the major centers of silk production and much fabric is offered at the Fair. Various festive processions and cultural shows add to the atmosphere.

Traditional hand-woven **textiles** are common in rural communities and this handicraft flourishes in the Northeast. The most famous fabric of the region is *matini silk*. Unlike other kinds of Thai silk, matini is made from tie-dyed yarn which permits the weaver to work distinctive, multicolored patterns into the design. There are several places where you can see matini being made. The village of Chonnabut, a few kilometers off the Korat-to-Khon Kaen highway, is one of the best.

Cotton weaving is also a handicraft practiced throughout I-san. A style known as *phakhit* is practiced particularly in the Nong Khai area. The distinctive patterns are commonly used on the colorful decorative cushions and pillows that you see everywhere.

Folk dancing is an integral part of a vibrant folk culture within the region. You can see dancing at several restaurants in Korat, Khon Kaen, Udon Thani, Nakon Phanom, and Ubon Ratchathani. Most of the Northeastern dances are more vigorous than the sensual or static dances from other regions. Most concern farming rituals, courtship, or welcoming ceremonies.

Painting and sculpture concentrates mainly on religious subjects—particularly Buddha images and episodes from Buddha's life. Some local organizations exist to promote specific cultural activities. For instance the Buri Ram Local Art Promotion Center employs a dozen or so skilled masons to turn out quality reproductions of ancient Khmer artifacts carved in the distinctive sandstone of the Lahamsai district.

Northeastern **music** is quite distinctive and very popular. It is a vibrant syncopated, boisterous music that, depending on its tempo, can be exciting or sentimental. Locally called *maw larn,* it originally was a verbal "courting" contest, a fascinating play on words, between a male singer and a female singer backed by the nasal, reedy sound of a versatile *khaen,* a bamboo wind instrument with vertical organlike pipes.

Nowadays, troupes of *maw larn* singers and musicians roam the Northeast, playing in villages and towns at temple fairs, village festivals, and all manner of social celebrations. You can also hear it played regularly on regional radio stations throughout I-san.

9. Sports

Sports facilities are less developed in the Northeast than in other regions of the country. This is probably because the population is predominantly rural, the average income is less than elsewhere, and the region receives less visitors. Despite this, most of the major centers have some sports facilities. Khon Kaen, Korat, and some other cities have **horse-racing tracks.** Korat, Ubon, Udon, and Khon Kaen have **golf courses** (although none match the standard of the Bangkok, Chiang Mai, Pattaya, or Phuket courses). Most centers have outdoor basketball courts, public swimming pools, public tennis courts, indoor badminton complexes, and bowling alleys. Even small villages sometimes have pool halls and table tennis tables which serve as local meeting spots.

10. Shopping

When compared with other parts of Thailand, the Northeast is no shopping paradise. Shops cater primarily to locals so there is limited choice for foreign visitors. The other difficulty is that most shopkeepers do not speak English so unless you can see what you want, it can be hard to get your needs across to the shop assistant.

There are, however, a few items which are better buys in the Northeast than elsewhere. **Matini silk** is manufactured throughout I-san but the best variety is found in Khon Kaen. If you want to buy it directly from the manufacturer I suggest a visit to Chonnabut. The price is unlikely to be less but you can buy from the factory where it was made. **Phakhit**-covered pillows are also good buys. Again these are available throughout I-san but Nong Khai and Udon Thani traditionally have the best selection.

Lao materials, jewelry, and antiques are available at towns right along the Mekong River. Chiang Khan, Nong Khai, Bung Kan, and Mukdahan are the best places to buy in my experience.

There is a small village south of Nakon Phanom called Renu Nakhon which is famous throughout the Northeast for its **embroidered handicrafts**—cloth, shirts, sarongs, and similar items. If you visit the important temple at That Phanum, it is worth detouring to see what is available at Renu Nakhon.

There are several centers which make **pottery.** The village of Lan Kwian near Korat is one where there is always a good selection from which to choose.

11. Entertainment and Nightlife

When Korat, Udon, and Ubon were major United States bases during the Vietnam War, each developed a hectic and thriving nightlife industry. Now most of that has disappeared and these cities offer the more traditional local entertainment and nightlife enjoyed by the Thais.

That is not to say that it is boring, however, and most visitors will find plenty to do in the evenings. Throughout the Northeast there are many open-air **restaurants/bars** that have recorded music. Some have hostesses, some have small live bands, and some have a collection of singers.

Each of the major cities has at least one airconditioned restaurant that has classical or traditional **dancing** accompanied by a traditional "orchestra." Some are even venturing into short dramas or re-enactments of wedding ceremonies, etc. These are not directed just at foreign tourists—this culture is almost as foreign to Thais from Bangkok and the south as it is to visitors from other countries.

Discos have become as popular in the Northeast cities as elsewhere around the world. All the major cities have discos within the major hotels and one or more local discos in town. Most of these have unofficial "partners" who will drink, dance, and talk with you. Often other suggestions will be made.

All the cities also have **"coffeehouses"** which are often down-market establishments offering music, drinks, hostesses, and more. These are patronized by Thais and are safe for Western visitors who cannot resist the urge to take a look.

Massage parlors appear to be a local initiative because even some of the smaller centers have "shops" with half a dozen ladies. Apart from the initial drink, which will not be expensive, what you get depends to a large extent on what you want and how much you are prepared to pay. A traditional massage will cost about B200 for 1 1/2 hours.

Here are a few nighttime selections:

Korat—Chom Surang Hotel (cocktail lounge).
—Sri Pattana Hotel (cocktail lounge and coffee shop).
—Mukkhamontri Road (I-san music and theater).
—Korat Hotel (disco).

Khon Kaen—Kosa Hotel (disco and massage parlor).
—Khon Kaen Hotel (disco and cocktail lounge/night club).
—Kaen Inn (live band and cocktail lounge).
—PJ's Disco (local crowd, sometimes has a show).

Udon Thani—Charoen Hotel (night club).
—Tibet Club (local crowd, sometimes has a show).

Nong Khai—Paehani Coffee House (singers, show, hostesses).

Ubon Ratchathani—Patumrat Hotel (night club).

Nakhom Phanom—Tatiya Club (Thai singers, hostesses).

Roi-et—Mai Thai Hotel (disco and massage palor).

Surin—Petchkasem Hotel (disco).

12. The Northeast Address List

Airlines—Thai Airways International, Prachasamosorn Rd., Tel. 043-236-523 (Khon Kaen); Charoenrat Rd., Tel. 042-812-344 (Loei); 14 Manat Rd., Tel. 044-257-211 (Nakhon Ratchasima); Yuvaputana Rd., Tel. 042-712-259 (Sakon Nakhon); Chayang Kun Rd., Tel. 045-254-431 (Ubon); 60 Makkang Rd., Tel. 042-243-222 (Udon).

Khon Kaen University—Tel. 043-239-755

Tourism Authority of Thailand—2102 Mittraphap Rd., Tel. 044-243-427 (Nakhon Ratchasima); Si Narong Rd., Tel. 054-255-603 (Ubon Ratchathani)

Index

Accommodation, 18, 19, 41, 54, 106, 112, 151, 178, 201, 271. *See also* Hotels
Address lists: Bangkok, 171-72; Chiang Mai, 221-22; Northeast Pattaya, 293-94; Phuket, 264
AIDS, 43, 96-97
Air New Zealand, 27
Airfares, 20, 22, 50
Airlines: domestic, 23, 221, 298; international, 23, 25, 51
Airport and Departure Tax, 43
Airports: 43, 52; Bangkok, 40, 106, 171, 267; Chiang Mai, 175; Khon Kaen, 298; Pattaya, 267; Phuket, 225
Akha people, 211, 213
Alphabet, 64, 93, 201
Ambulance (Bangkok), 171
American, 40, 41, 54, 73, 92, 265
American Express, 41
American University (Bangkok), 171
Amporn Gardens (Bangkok), 133
Amulets, 59, 88, 129
Ancestor worship, 60
Ancient City (Bangkok), 135
Andaman Princess, 35
Andaman Sea, 35, 36, 57, 223, 259
Ang Sila (East), 279, 287

Ang Thong Marine National Park (South), 245, 247
Angkor Wat, 18, 92, 93, 97, 305, 315
Anna, 100
Antiques, 55, 125, 165, 166, 185, 195, 220, 320
Anusan Market (Chiang Mai), 183
Ao Luk (South), 247
Ao Phai (East), 285
Ao Po (Phuket), 241
Ao Wong Duan (East), 285
Archery, 289
Art forms, 58, 98
Art galleries, 14, 86
Artifacts, 14, 86
Arts and crafts, 54, 291
Asalaha Puja, 38
Asia, 14, 16, 52, 54, 58, 145, 164
Asia Pacific Orchid Conference, 69
Asian, 16, 25, 27, 42, 100, 238
Asian Wall Street Journal, 45
Australia, 19, 25, 38, 42, 46, 48, 68, 83, 106, 120, 153, 307
Australian, 40, 41, 51, 61, 265
Ayutthaya, 14, 18, 38, 62, 63, 64, 95, 97, 98, 99, 129, 135, 137, 139, 141, 156, 157, 160, 161, 182, 200, 286, 305
Ayutthaya Princess, 156

Backpackers, 18, 188, 225, 267
Badminton, 289
Baggage, 37, 50, 51
Baht, 21, 51
Bali, 54
Ban Chiang (Northeast), 18, 91, 92, 131, 297, 305, 311
Ban Chiang Museum (Northeast), 311
Ban Dan Kwian (Northeast), 315
Ban Don (South), 243
Ban Hmong Mae Sa Mai (Chiang Mai), 185
Ban Nong Pru (Kanchanaburi), 153
Ban Tha Klang (Northeast), 315
Banana Festival (North), 215
Bang Klang Tao, 93
Bang Pa-in Palace, 63, 141, 156, 157
Bang Phe (East), 268, 283, 285, 287
Bang Saen (East), 279, 287
Bang Sai, 160
Bang Saray (East), 281, 289
Bangkok, 14, 16, 18, 19, 22, 27, 29, 31, 32, 33, 35, 36, 38, 40, 41, 42, 44, 45, 48, 52, 57, 58, 61, 63, 74, 82, 83, 85, 86, 87, 90, 92, 99, 100, 105-172, 173, 175, 178, 181, 191, 199, 220, 225, 238, 241, 243, 244, 267, 279, 281, 291, 293, 297, 298, 320, 321
Bangkok Airways, 29
Bangkok driving, 33
Bangkok Flowers Centre Company, 68
Bangkok *Post*, 45
Bangkok post office, 38, 172
Banglampoo (Bangkok), 168
Banks, 51
Bargaining, 109, 164, 166, 183
Barred Ground Dove Festival (South), 257
BBC, 46
Beach resorts, 18
Beaches, 14, 37, 52, 55, 228, 253, 255, 257, 265, 269, 271, 277, 281, 282, 283, 285
Beer bars, 170
Beliefs, 14
Bhubing Palace (Chiang Mai), 184
Bhumibol Dam (North), 191, 199, 207, 217
Birds' nests (South), 255
Blue Pass, 31
Bo Rai (East), 286
Bo Sang (Chiang Mai), 185, 214
Bo Sang Umbrella Fair (North), 214
Boat races (Northeast), 319
Bophut Bay (Koh Samui), 246
Boston, 42
Bowling, 263, 269, 288, 289, 320
Bridge Over the River Kwai, The, 151
British, 46, 54, 100, 238, 265
British Council (Bangkok), 172
British Embassy, 49, 127
Bronze-age civilization, 18, 92
Bua Yai (Northeast), 298

Buddhas, 14, 38, 47, 59, 88, 99, 133, 137, 141, 144, 157, 158, 159, 183, 193, 196, 201, 207, 257, 258, 303, 309, 311, 313
Buddhist, 16, 38, 47, 58, 59, 60, 67, 78, 83, 87, 88, 95, 99, 106, 127, 131, 149, 157, 159, 184, 199, 213, 219, 238, 317, 319
Buffalo races, 258
Bull fighting, 252
Bullet train (Japan), 55
Buri Ram (Northeast), 39, 298, 315, 317
Burma, 52, 54, 57, 92, 93, 95, 97, 98, 99, 133, 149, 151, 165, 173, 182, 187, 190, 196, 197, 199, 210, 213, 220, 223
Bus, 21, 32, 36, 41, 42, 59, 106, 108, 109, 175, 187, 193, 225, 243, 244, 267, 293, 297
Bus safety, 33
Bus terminals, 32, 52, 67, 172, 225, 264
Business class, 23, 51
Business hours, 44
Business travellers, 37

Cambodia, 18, 57, 92, 95, 103, 133, 281, 286, 295, 305, 315
Camping, 14
Canada, 25, 38, 42, 46, 49, 68, 83
Canadian, 40, 41, 51
Canadian International Airways, 27
Canals, 42
Candle Festival (Northeast), 317
Captain Light, 238
Car rental, 33, 196, 227, 268, 298
Castles, 13, 14
Ceramics, 220
Ceylon, 93, 95
Cha-am, 83, 144, 145
Chachoengsa (East), 288
Chaiyaphum (Northeast), 39, 301
Chaiyaphum Elephant Roundup (Northeast), 317
Chak Phra Festival (South), 258
Chakri Day, 38, 158
Chakri dynasty, 38, 99, 158
Chalong Bay (Phuket), 255, 259
Chama Devi, 207
Chandrakasem Palace (Ayutthaya), 141
Chang Isles National Park (East), 286
Chantaburi (East), 39, 99, 267, 281, 285, 286, 287
Chantaburi Fruit Fair (East), 288
Chanut Piyaoui (Mrs.), 82
Chao Mai Lim Ko Nieo Fair (South), 257
Chao Phya Vijayen (Lopburi), 139
Chao Phraya River, 35, 57, 62, 70, 92, 95, 99, 100, 110, 124, 133, 143, 156, 159, 160, 167
Chao Sam and Phya National Museum (Ayutthaya), 141

INDEX

Charlie Amatyakul, 70
Chatichai Choonhaven, 103
Chaweng Beach (Koh Samui), 243, 244
Chiang Dao (North), 193, 210
Chiang Dao Cave (North), 193
Chiang Khan (Northeast), 309, 321
Chiang Khong (North), 196, 197
Chiang Mai, 18, 19, 27, 29, 31, 40, 44, 63, 69, 82, 90, 93, 99, 157, 158, 172-222, 223, 225, 291, 298, 320
Chiang Mai Airport, 175
Chiang Mai Arboretum, 184
Chiang Mai Flower Festival, 214
Chiang Mai Museum, 183, 184
Chiang Mai National Theater, 222
Chiang Mai University, 184, 211
Chiang Mai Zoo, 184
Chiang Mai-San Kamphaeng Road, 181, 185, 219, 220
Chiang Rai, 29, 39, 83, 93, 175, 193, 197, 199, 209, 210, 215, 217
Chiang Saen (North), 196, 197
Chicago, 42
Chillies, 71, 72, 73
China, 54, 69, 91, 93, 98, 101, 133, 213, 219
Chinatown, 110, 112, 122, 164, 166
Chinese, 14, 52, 54, 55, 72, 87, 93, 95, 97, 165, 180, 236, 238, 249, 252, 258
Chinese New Year, 38
Chinese restaurants, 180, 196, 205
Chitralada Villa or Chitladda Palace (Bangkok), 63, 112, 128
Chom Thong (North), 191, 209
Chonburi (East), 39, 279
Chonburi Buffalo Races, 288
Chong-Kai War Cemetery (Kanchanaburi), 151
Chonnabut (Northeast), 319, 320
Christians, 60, 98, 213, 311
Chulaborn Dam (Northeast), 307
Chulalongkorn Day, 38, 159
Chulalongkorn University (Bangkok), 70, 100
Chum Phae (Northeast), 307
Chumphon (South), 39
Church of the Immaculate Conception (East), 286
Churches: Bangkok, 172; Chiang Mai, 221
Classical dance, 13, 88, 122, 126, 135, 156, 161, 181, 217
Climate, 57
Clubs, 16
Coach. *See* Bus
Cocktail lounges, 170
Communism, 103, 196
Confucianism, 60
Conrad, Joseph, 16
Constantine Pharlkon, 98

Consulates, 50
Cool season, 36, 37
Coral Island (Pattaya), 157
Coronation Day, 38
Costs, 18, 23
Cotton weaving (Northeast), 319
Council of Elders, 79
Country village, 59
Credit cards, 40, 50, 51, 52, 273
Crocodile Farm (Bangkok), 135
Cruise ships, 27, 282
Cruises, 35
Cuisine, 14
Cultural traditions, 295, 317
Culture, 13, 14, 18, 19, 20, 21, 46, 55, 58, 59, 87, 128, 157, 173, 175, 201, 214-217, 257-258, 287-288, 317
Culture show, 135, 234, 258, 277, 319
Custom tailoring, 164
Customs, 14, 43, 46, 48, 58, 106, 164
Customs and courtesies, 46

Dallas/Fort Worth, 25
Damnern Saduak, 155, 156, 158
Dance, 54, 217
Dancers, 95, 181, 288
Days of Roses (Chiang Mai), 217
Death Railway (Kanchanaburi), 32, 151, 155
Delta Airlines, 27
Democracy Monument (Bangkok), 112, 122
Department stores, 144, 166
Departure tax, 43
Detroit, 42
Dining and restaurants, 20, 122-27, 180-82, 235-38, 273-76
Discos, 16, 168, 205, 220, 228, 229, 234, 243, 264, 285, 292, 299, 321
Discover Thailand, 29
Dive shops, 246, 259, 260
Diving, 246, 257, 260, 290
Do Musu (North), 205
Doi Inthanon National Park (North), 191, 209
Doi Suthep (Chiang Mai) 182, 184, 209
Doi Tao (North), 191
Doi Tung (North), 199
Don Muang Airport, 106, 137. *See also* Airports
Don Sak (South), 243
Drama, 18
Duang Prateep Foundation, 77
Dusit Zoo (Bangkok), 112, 133
Dutch, 54, 97
Duty free, 43
Dvaravati Kingdom, 92

Early settlers, 92
East, 13
Eastern Bus Terminal (Bangkok), 168, 267
Eastern Rail Line, 29
Economy, 83, 85, 86, 101, 105
Economy class, 23, 25, 51
El Paso, 42
Electric current, 40
Elephant riding, 14, 200, 209, 210, 239, 277, 303
Elephant Training School, 199, 209
Embassies and consulates, 48, 172
Embroidered handicrafts, 321
Emerald Buddha, 63, 99, 128, 129, 155, 200
English, 14, 19, 21, 31, 33, 42, 45, 46, 64, 65, 67, 82, 87, 97, 98, 99, 100, 106, 109, 110, 122, 131, 168, 171, 176, 188, 263, 274, 297, 298, 301, 320
Entertainment and nightlife, 20, 168-71, 220-21, 263-64, 291-93, 321-22
Erawan Falls (Kanchanaburi), 153
Erawan Shrine (Bangkok), 161
Europe, 23, 45, 68, 98, 106, 120
European, 14, 18, 23, 25, 40, 42, 44, 63, 97, 100, 128, 137, 139, 223, 276
European domination, 14
European writers, 13
Excess baggage charges, 51
Exchange rates, 40
Express train, 31

Family Planning Service, 96
Fang (North), 193, 210
Ferries, 41, 243, 244, 277, 281, 287
Festival of the Tenth Lunar Month (South), 258
Festivals, 18, 54, 79, 106, 157, 173, 238, 258, 288, 317
Filipinos, 54
Film industry, 45
Fine Arts Department, 165, 201, 220, 305
Firearms, 43
First class, 23
Fish Cave (North), 189
Fishing, 253, 259, 282, 287, 289
Floating Market (Damnern Saduak), 155, 156, 158
Flying Vegetables, 205
Folk arts, 88, 90, 158, 160
Folk dancing, 317, 319
Folk music, 158, 317
Food and Thai Handicraft Fair (South), 258
Food stalls, 18, 131, 145, 236, 237, 238, 253, 301
Foreign exchange, 85, 86
France, 57, 70, 99

Freedom From Drug Abuse Campaign, 77
French, 54, 97, 98, 100, 265, 309, 311, 313
French Riviera, 265
Fruit Fair (North), 215

Game fishing, 249, 282
Gasoline, 40
Gems, 85, 205, 265, 285, 286, 287
Gems and jewelry, 164
Georgetown, 108
Getting there, 20, 106, 175, 225-27, 267, 297-98
Go-carts, 289
Go-go bars, 170, 171, 292, 293
Gold, 166
Gold and silver, 164
Golden Triangle (North), 18, 173, 193, 197, 209
Golf, 87, 145, 161, 207, 217, 252, 260, 288, 289, 303, 307, 320
Government offices, 37, 38, 44
Governmental fiddle-faddle, 41
Grand Palace (Bangkok), 63, 87, 110, 112, 127, 128, 129, 141, 155, 158, 160
Guided tours, 20, 155-57, 209-14, 287, 315
Gulf of Thailand, 35, 36, 57, 85, 143, 223, 252

Haat Pak Meng Beach (South), 251
Hae Pha Khua That (South), 257
Handicrafts, 18, 219
Hash House Harriers, 292
Hat Sai Kaea (East), 283
Hat Yai, 27, 38, 44, 225, 227, 251, 252, 253, 258
Health, 42
Hell Fire Project, 153
Heroines' Monument (Phuket), 239, 241
Hilltribes, 14, 18, 63, 92, 173, 175, 184, 190, 193, 195, 196, 197, 199, 211, 213, 214, 219
Hilltribes Center (North), 196
Himalaya Mountains, 54
Hindus, 60, 309
History, 14, 18, 54, 101
Hmong Hilltribe Village, 197
Ho Chi Minh City, 54
Holland, 153
Hong Kong, 54
Honolulu, 42
Horse riding, 290
Hospital (Bangkok), 172
Hospitals, 42, 59, 60, 67, 221, 264, 293
Hot (North), 191
Hot season, 36, 37
Hotel restaurants, 123
Hotel taxis, 109. *See also* Taxis

INDEX 327

Hotels: 14, 16, 18, 19, 20, 21, 33, 40, 41, 43, 44, 45, 51, 52, 54, 55, 59, 67, 68, 74, 106, 109, 137, 145, 155, 170, 176, 181-82, 1 95, 203, 220, 227, 234, 252, 313; Bangkok, 82, 110-122; Chiang Mai, 178-80; Northeast, 298-301; Pattaya, 268-73; Phuket, 228-35
Houses, 79
How to get there, 23
HRH Prince Vajiralongkorn, 63
HRH Princess Chulabhorn, 63
HRH Princess Sirindhorn, 63
H'tin people, 211, 213
Hua Hin, 18, 35, 38, 63, 143, 145, 149
Huai Khrai (North), 199
Hualamphong Railroad Station (Bangkok), 31, 298
Hydrofoils, 35, 225, 243

I-san (Northeast), 205, 295, 297, 298, 303, 307, 317, 320, 321
Illuminated Boat Procession (Northeast), 319
Immigration offices: Bangkok, 172; Chiang Mai, 221; Koh Samui, 243; Pattaya, 293; Phuket, 264
India, 69, 93, 95
Indochina, 103
Indonesia, 54, 69, 257, 275
International Herald Tribune, 45
Islands, 14, 18, 55, 67, 265, 281, 282, 285

Jakarta, 52
Japan, 55, 68, 106, 153
Japanese, 54, 85, 95, 97, 153
Japanese food, 233, 238, 274
Java, 52
Jazz, 125, 170, 221, 270, 274, 293
Jeath Museum (Kanchanaburi), 153
Jet lag, 25
Jomtien Beach (Pattaya), 167, 268, 270, 281, 289
July Candle Festival (Northeast), 313

Kachoong Waterfall (South), 251
Kaeng Kra Chan National Park (Patchaburi), 144, 147
Kaeng Song Waterfall (North), 205
Kaeng Tana National Park (Northeast), 315
Kalasin (Northeast), 39, 301, 305, 313
Kamala Beach (Phuket), 239
Kamphaeng Phet (North), 39, 205, 215
Kamsingh Srinawk (writer), 88
Kanchanaburi, 32, 38, 44, 92, 149, 151, 153, 157, 160

Kanchanaburi War Cemetery, 32, 151
Kansas City, 42
Karen people, 147, 191, 209, 211, 213
Karma, 58
Karon Beach (Phuket), 233, 236, 239, 259, 264
Kasetsart University, 68
Kata Beach (Phuket), 61, 231, 236, 239, 259, 260, 264
Khamu people, 211, 213
Khantoke dinners, 180, 181, 209, 214, 217
Khao Chong Nature Reserve (South), 251
Khao Kien (South), 254
Khao Luang Caves (Phetchaburi), 147
Khao Rang (Phuket), 263
Khao Sam Roi Yod National Park (Hua Hin), 147
Khao Yai National Park (Northeast), 299, 303
Khiao Open Zoo (East), 281, 287
Khmer temples, 297, 315
Khmers, 14, 18, 91, 93, 97, 137, 139, 144, 305, 317, 320
Khon Kaen (Northeast), 27, 29, 39, 175, 295, 297, 298, 299, 303, 309, 313, 319, 320, 322
Khon Kaen National Museum, 309
Khon Kaen Silk Fair, 319
Khon Kaen University, 305, 322
Khun Khat Waterfront Park (South), 253
Khunying Alo, 303
Kilogram, 40
Kilometer, 39
King Ananda, 63, 102
King Bhumipol, 38, 47, 60, 62, 63, 64
King Boromokot, 98
King Chulalongkorn, 100, 131, 133, 159, 160
King Ekatotsarot, 98
King and I, The, 100
King Mengrai, 182, 183, 193, 196
King Mongkut, 99, 100, 141, 144. *See also* King Rama IV
King Narai, 98, 137
King Narai's Palace (Lopburi), 137
King Pha Yu, 182
King Prajadhipok, 100
King Rama I, 63, 64, 99, 105, 129, 151, 239
King Rama III, 186
King Rama IV, 99, 196
King Rama V, 128, 159, 246
King Rama VI, 100
King Rama VII, 102. *See also* King Ananda
King Rama IX, 63, 99. *See also* King Bhumipol
King Ramathibodi, 95, 97
King Ramkamhaeng, 200
King Sri Intratit, 93
King Taksin, 99, 182, 286

King Vajiravudh. *See* King Rama VI
King's Birthday, 38, 160
Kings Cup Regatta (Phuket), 258
Kite flying, 131, 163
Klong Toey (Bangkok), 76, 77
Ko Chang (East), 267, 286
Ko Karn (Pattaya), 282
Ko Loi (East), 281
Ko Naga Noi (Phuket), 241
Ko Samae San (East), 282
Ko Samet (East), 39, 267, 268, 283, 285, 287
Ko Si Chang (East), 281
Koh Hai (South), 251
Koh Khao Ping Gun (James Bond Island) (South), 255
Koh Panayi (South), 254
Koh Pha Ngan (South), 246
Koh Samui (South), 18, 29, 35, 39, 157, 225, 241, 243, 244, 245, 246, 247
Koh Tapoo (South), 255
Koh Yor (South), 253
Korat (or Khorat or Nakhon Ratchasima) (Northeast), 22, 297, 298, 303, 309, 315, 319, 320, 321, 322
Korea, 55, 238
Krabi (South), 39, 247
Krasae Cave Bridge (Kanchanaburi), 32
Krung Thep (Bangkok), 105
Kuala Lumpur, 52, 106

Laem Chabung (East), 281
Laem Ngop (East), 286
Lahu people, 211, 213
Lam Pi Waterfall (South), 241
Lamai (Koh Samui), 244, 245
Lampang (North), 39, 199, 200, 207
Lamphun (North), 39, 207, 215
Lan Kwian (Northeast), 321
Land of the Free, 14
Land of Smiles, 13, 16
Langkawi, 35, 52
Language, 14, 58, 64, 65, 175, 211
Lanna (North), 173, 182
Lanna Boat Races (North), 215
Lansang National Park (North), 205
Lao Khao, 309
Laos, 52, 57, 99, 103, 173, 193, 196, 213, 295, 307, 311, 321
Laotians, 14, 93, 95, 303, 309, 313
Larn Takong Reservoir (Northeast), 303
Leather goods, 165, 261
Leisure time, 86
Limousines, 227, 267, 293
Lisu people, 211, 213
Literature, 18, 87, 98, 129
Litres, 40
Lo Thai, 95

Local transportation, 20, 36, 108, 176-77, 227, 267-68
Loei (Northeast), 39, 297, 298, 300, 303, 307, 309, 317
Loi Krathong, 81, 159, 215
Long distance trains, 29
Long distance travel, 32, 298
Long-tail boats, 36, 157, 253, 254, 259, 277
Lop Buri, 39, 92, 137, 207
Lop Buri National Museum, 137
Los Angeles, 27, 42, 45
Louisiana, 101, 102
Lu Thai, 95
Lua people, 211, 213
Luang Pu, 309
Luang Wiang Lakon (North), 214
Luem Sok (South), 247
Lumpini Park (Bangkok), 86, 87, 161
Lungshan culture, 92
Lychee Fair (North), 215

M. L. Tritosyuth Devakul, 61
Mae Chan (North), 196, 210
Mae Herang (Northeast), 307
Mae Hong Son (North), 18, 39, 175, 187, 188, 189, 190, 193, 209, 293, 209, 210, 215
Mae Klang Falls (North), 191
Mae Nam beach (South), 245
Mae Ping (Chiang Mai), 182
Mae Rim (Chiang Mai), 188, 193
Mae Sa Falls (Chiang Mai), 185
Mae Sai (North), 196, 197
Mae Salong (North), 196
Mae Sariang (North), 187, 190, 191
Mae Sot (North), 175, 191, 205, 207
Mae Suai (North), 193
Mae Taeng (North), 193
Magic Land (Bangkok), 168
Mahasarakham (Northeast), 39, 301, 313
Mai Khao (Phuket), 241
Mail and telephone service, 38
Makha Puja, 38, 157
Malaria, 42, 43, 100, 285
Malay, 52, 54, 95
Malays, 14, 93, 252
Malaysia, 27, 35, 52, 57, 60, 69, 93, 101, 108, 133, 223, 225, 238, 241, 247, 251, 253, 257, 258
Man with the Golden Gun, 255
Mandalay, 54
Manufactured goods, 85
Marble Temple (Bangkok). *See* Wat Benchamabopit
Markets, 13, 18, 41, 67, 69, 71, 106, 139, 183, 220, 236, 238, 301
Martial law, 103
Massage, 129, 147, 168, 171, 205, 221, 231,

INDEX

264, 269, 286, 292, 293, 299, 311, 321
Matini silk (Northeast), 319, 320
Maugham, Somerset, 16
Maw Larn singers (Northeast), 320
Mealtimes, 71
Mechai Vivavaidya, 96, 97
Medical facilities, 42
Medical insurance, 50
Mekhala, 156, 157
Mekong River, 57, 196, 197, 295, 298, 307, 309, 319, 321
Meo people/village, 184, 190, 209, 211, 213
Mermaid Statue (South), 252
Metrics and electrics, 39
Mi pen ri, 66, 79
Mini Siam (Pattaya), 277
Miniature golf, 290
Mr. Orchid, 68
Mlabri people, 211, 213
Money exchange booth, 41
Money and prices, 40
Monks, 13, 47, 59, 60, 63, 79, 81, 95, 157, 159, 258
Mons, 14, 92, 93, 158
Montgomery, 42
Montreal, 42
Mosques, 52
Motor racing, 290
Motorcycle rental, 33, 190, 234, 243, 246, 298
Movie industry, 87
Muang Tham (Northeast), 315
Mukdahan (Northeast), 301, 303, 313, 321
Mun River (Northeast), 313, 319
Museum of Southern Thailand (South), 251
Museums, 14, 86, 131, 141, 251, 283, 305, 311
Music, 18, 45, 258, 264, 317, 320, 321
Muslim, 47, 60
Muslim festivals, 60
Muslim fishing village (South), 254

Na Daan (East), 283
Na Muang Waterfall (Koh Samui), 245
Naga Noi Pearl Island (Phuket), 254
Nai Yang Beach (Phuket), 229, 259
Nai Yang National Park (Phuket), 229, 239
Nakhon Pathom (Central), 32, 39, 58, 149, 155, 156, 160
Nakhon Ratchasima (Northeast), 31, 38, 44, 295, 297, 299, 303
Nakhon Sawan (North), 39
Nakhon Si Thammarat (South), 39, 90, 257, 258
Naklua (East), 281
Nakon Phanom (Northeast), 39, 299, 303, 311, 313, 313, 317, 319, 321, 322
Namtok (Kanchanburi), 151, 155
Nan (North), 175, 199, 215
Narathirat (South), 63
Narcotics, 43
Naresuan the Great, 97
Nathon (Ko Samui), 243, 246
Nation newspaper, 45
National Assembly (Bangkok), 112, 131
National Museum (Bangkok), 112, 129, 160
National Palace Museum (Taipei), 55
National Parks, 13, 14, 253, 257, 265, 283, 285, 297
National Parks Department, 189
National Stadium, 87
National Theater, 160
Nepal, 54
New Life Project, 77
New Orleans, 42
New York, 42, 45, 88
New Zealand, 25, 40, 42, 49
News media, 45
Newspapers, 45, 172
Nielloware, 263
Night Bazaar (Chiang Mai), 178, 179, 181, 182, 183
Nightlife, 14, 19, 37, 106, 110, 168, 220, 234, 251, 263, 277, 286, 291, 313, 321
Nirvana, 58, 59
Noen Wong (East), 286
Non-immigrant visa, 42
Nong Khai (Northeast), 39, 297, 298, 300, 303, 309, 319, 321, 322
Nong Nooch Village (Pattaya), 277, 287, 289
Nonthaburi (Bangkok), 110
North America, 23, 51
North American, 23, 25, 27, 42, 45, 225
North Thailand, 18, 36, 90, 91, 93, 99, 158, 164, 173-222, 307
Northeast Thailand, 18, 36, 72, 91, 131, 295-322
Northwest Airlines, 27
Northern Bus Terminal (Bangkok), 175, 267, 297

Ob Luang Gorge (North), 191
Obscene literature, 43
Ocean World (East), 281
OK Phansa, 159
Opium, 63, 191, 196, 211
Orchid Queen, 156
Orchid World, 68
Orchids, 25, 68, 185, 209, 238, 277
Oriental Queen, 143, 156
Ottawa, 42

Pa Dawn people, 190
Pa Muang, 93
Pa Peung Waterfall (North), 205
Pa Pra Taew National Park (Phuket), 241
Package tours, 20, 21
Packing and wearing, 37
Paet Riv Mango Festival (East), 288
Pagen, 54
Pai (North), 187, 188, 189, 193
Painters, 95
Painting and sculpture (Northeast), 319
Pala Waterfall (Hua Hin), 147
Palaces, 16, 88, 98, 106, 127, 131, 155, 157
Panom Rung Fair (Northeast), 317
Panwa Cape (Phuket), 238
Parasailing, 259, 277, 290
Parks, 14
Passport, 41
Patong Beach (Phuket), 225, 227, 230, 234, 235, 239, 254, 257, 259, 260, 263, 264
Patpong (Bangkok), 118, 125, 166, 171, 220
Pattani (South), 39, 257
Pattaya, 18, 19, 27, 29, 35, 38, 40, 44, 45, 82, 145, 157, 175, 263, 267-94, 320
Pattaya churches, 293
Pattaya Elephant Village, 277
Pattaya Festival, 288
Pattaya hospitals, 293
Pattaya Immigration Office, 293
Pattaya Lions Club, 293
Pattya Rotary Clubs, 294
P'ayao, 93
Pearl Farm (Phuket), 254
Pearl of the South, 261
Pearls, 261
Penang, 52, 108, 238
Persia, 95
Pewterware, 261
Pha Taem (Northeast), 315
Pha Thai Cave (North), 199
Phakhit (Northeast), 320
Phang Nga Bay (South), 39, 241, 247, 254, 255
Phatthalung (South), 251
Phayao (North), 199
Phetchaburi, 38, 144, 149, 157
Phi Phi Don (South), 255
Phi Phi Island (South), 230, 249, 255
Phi Phi Ley (South), 255
Phi Ta Koh Festival (Northeast), 317
Phichit (North), 39
Phichit Boat Races, 215
Philadelphia, 42
Phimai (Northeast), 18, 305, 315
Phitsanulok (North), 27, 39, 45, 95, 199, 203, 215, 298
Phnom Penh, 97
Phra Buddha Bat Fair (Saraburi), 158

Phra Buddha Chanerat Fair (North), 215
Phra Nakon Khiri Fair (Petchaburi), 157
Phra Nakon Khiri Palace (Petchaburi), 144, 157
Phra Nang Beach (South), 249
Phra Pathom Chedi (Nakhon Pathom), 32, 149, 160
Phra Phuttabaht, 137, 158
Phra That Phanom Fair (Northeast), 317
Phrae (North), 39, 210
Phraya Nakhon Cave (Hua Hin), 147
Phromthep Cape (Phuket), 231, 239, 253
Phu Kradung National Park (Northeast), 307
Phu Rua National Park (Northeast), 307
Phuket, 18, 27, 29, 35, 38, 40, 45, 61, 82, 145, 157, 175, 223-64, 320
Phuket Aquarium, 239
Phuket Hospital, 264
Phuket Immigration Office, 264
Phuket International Airport (South), 225
Phuket Police, 264
Phuket Town, 225, 228, 237, 238, 253, 254, 260, 261, 263
Phuket Yacht Club, 61, 230, 237, 258
Phya Chakri, 99
Phya National Museum (Ayutthaya), 141
Phya Taksin, 98
Pibulsongkhram, Lt. Luang, 102, 103
Pierce, Gerald, 101
Planetarium (Bangkok), 168
Planning your trip, 20, 21, 36
Pliew Waterfall and National Park (East), 286
Poda Island (South), 249
Poi Sang Long Fest (North), 215
Poi Waterfall (North), 205
Police, 52, 67, 172, 221, 264, 294
Pollution, 16, 18
Population and Community Development Association, 96
Population growth, 96
Portuguese, 54, 60, 97
Post Office, 41, 67, 172, 221, 243, 264, 294
Poste Restante Bangkok, 38
Prachinburi (Central), 39
Prang Khack (Lopburi), 139
Prang Sam Yod (Lopburi), 139
Prasat Muang Singh Ruin, 32
Praset Ban Phluang (Northeast), 315
Praset Phanom Rung (Northeast), 18, 315
Prateep Ungsongtham, 76, 77, 78
Pratu Chiang Mai Market, 183
Pratunam Market (Bangkok), 167
Prem Tinsulanonda, 103
Press, 45
Prices, 21
Pridi Phanomyong, 102
Prince Amanda Mukidol, 102
Prince Piya, 98

INDEX

Princess Cave (South), 249
Pub, 125
Public holidays, 37
Put Jaw Chinese Temple (Phuket), 238

Qantas Airways, 27
Queen Sirikit, 47, 46, 82, 294
Queen's Birthday, 46

Radio, 45, 46, 82, 294, 320
Raft trips, 188, 190, 209, 210
Rafting, 14, 190
Rai, 40
Rail, 27, 29, 227
Rail fares, 29
Railroads, 21, 27, 155, 177, 178, 253, 298
Railway station, 50, 52, 67, 172, 221, 243
Rains Retreat, 38, 59, 60, 81, 159, 317, 319
Rainy season, 36, 37
Rakham Fair (East), 288
Rama I Road (Bangkok), 112, 133, 161, 165
Rama IV Road (Bangkok), 31, 35, 120, 161, 170, 172
Ramathibodi II, 97
Rambutan Fair (South), 258
Ramkamhaeng the Great, 93, 95
Ramkamhaeng National Museum (Sukhothai), 201
Ramkamhaeng National Park, 203
Rangoon, 54
Ranong (South), 39
Rapee Sagarik, Dr., 68, 69
Rapid train, 31
Ratchaburi, 38, 149
Ratchadamnoen Nok Road (Bangkok), 112, 131, 160, 172
Rawai Beach (Phuket), 230, 239, 253
Rayong (East), 39, 83, 267, 268, 281, 282, 288
Ready-to-wear clothes, 164
Reclining Buddha (Bangkok), 129
Reclining Buddha (Hat Yai), 251
Red Pass, 31
Religion, 47, 48, 58, 92, 95, 213, 214, 257
Rental cars, 33, 177, 187, 196, 227, 268
Restaurants, 14, 16, 18, 19, 37, 41, 44, 51, 54, 67, 68, 69, 71, 72, 73, 74, 81, 112, 123, 137, 145, 147, 151, 156, 179, 180-82, 188, 195, 203, 233, 235, 236, 237, 246, 269, 309, 313, 321
Rice, 65, 67, 69, 72, 78, 81, 85, 92, 93, 125, 143, 158, 174, 223, 237, 239, 257, 301, 309, 313
Richmond, 42
Rim Beach (South), 246
River City (Bangkok), 110, 116, 124, 167

River Kwai (Kanchanaburi), 32, 149, 151, 153
River Kwai Bridge, 32, 155, 157, 160
River Kwai Bridge Week, 151, 160
River Kwai Jungle House, 32
Rock carvers, 279
Rock paintings, 315
Rocket festivals (Northeast), 317
Roi-Et (Northeast), 39, 301, 313, 322
Roong Aroon Hot Springs (Chiang Mai), 187
Rose Garden, 135, 149, 156, 277, 291
Royal barges, 64, 133, 319
Royal ceremonies, 63
Royal family, 47, 62, 99
Royal Ploughing Ceremony (Bangkok), 63, 158
Royal Thai cuisine, 125
Royal titles, 64
Rubber, 223, 238, 239, 241, 245
Rubber Research Center (South), 251
Rubies, 286, 288. *See also* Gems
Ruins, 13
Rural life, 74, 81

Safety, 43
Safety deposit boxes, 51
Saigon, 54
Sailing, 258, 259, 287, 290
St. Joseph's Catholic Cathedral (Ayutthaya), 141
Sakon Nakhon (Northeast), 39, 63, 297, 298, 299, 311, 319
Sakunothayan Forest Park (North), 205
Samae San (East), 282
Samlors, 36, 108, 141, 176, 298
Samoeng (Chiang Mai), 185
Sampans, 16
Samui Highland Park (Koh Samui), 245
Samut Sakhon (Central), 38, 143, 144
Samut Songkhram, 144
San Francisco, 27
San Kamphaeng (Chiang Mai), 185, 219
Sanam Luang (Bangkok), 87, 128, 131, 163
Sangkhlaburi (Kanchanaburi), 153
Sanuk, 73, 79, 81, 82, 86, 168
Saraburi (Central), 39, 137, 158, 159, 303
Sarit Thanarat, 103
Sattahip (East), 267, 268, 282, 289
Savannakhet (Laos), 313
Sawardee, 22, 25, 66
Scandinavian Airlines System, 25
Schools, 60, 62, 76, 79, 97
Science Museum (Bangkok), 168
Sculptors, 88, 95
Sea gypsies (Phuket), 230
Seashells 263
Seafood restaurants, 235, 236, 246, 273-74

Seatran Queen, 36
Seatran Travel, 36
Seattle, 25
Security boxes, 43
See-lor, 176
Seri Snowapong (writer), 88
Shooting, 290
Shopping, 14, 20, 51, 106, 110, 112, 120, 164-68, 209, 219, 220, 228, 261-63, 291, 320
Shops, 16, 19, 68, 155, 228, 246
Shuttle bus service, 269
Si Racha (East), 281
Si Sa Ket (Northeast), 39, 298, 301, 315
Si Satchanalai (North), 260, 201
Si Satchanalai National Park (North), 203
Si Sawat (Kanchanaburi), 153
Siam, 98, 105, 200
Siam Country Club (East), 289
Siam Park (Bangkok), 168
Siam Society, 160
Siam Square (Bangkok), 119, 165,.166
Sightseeing, 18, 20, 127-55, 238-53, 277-87, 303-15
Sikoraphum (Northeast), 315
Silk, 101, 133, 164, 165, 175, 181, 185, 187, 217, 219, 291, 309
Silom Road (Bangkok), 112, 119, 120, 121, 123, 125, 126, 127, 166
Silom Village (Bangkok), 126
Silver, 175, 185, 197, 219
Similan Islands (South), 257
Sing Buri (Central), 39, 139
Singapore, 27, 52, 93, 108, 251, 257, 258
Sleeping Cow Island (South), 247
Snake Farm (Bangkok), 135
Snooker, 290
Snorkeling, 245, 255, 260, 287
Somdet Mahawirawong Museum (Northeast), 305
Sompet Market (Chiang Mai), 183
Songkhla (South), 35, 39, 225, 252, 258
Songkhla National Museum (South), 252
Songkran festival, 38, 81, 158, 215
Songthaew, 36, 184, 267, 268, 298
Sop Ruak River (North), 197
South China Sea, 57
South Pacific, 23, 27, 45
South Thailand, 36, 90, 92, 108, 223-64
Southeast Asia, 14, 21, 25, 35, 46, 52, 100, 105, 131, 305
Spanish, 54, 60, 97
Special express train, 31
Spice Islands, 52
Spices, 69, 72
Spirit houses, 16, 79
Sports, 20, 86, 87, 161-63, 217, 252, 259, 260, 288-91, 320
Sri Nakharin Dam (Kanchanaburi), 153

Stang, 40
State Railway of Thailand, 29, 175
Street stalls, 42, 69, 72, 122, 157, 166
Suam Wang Kaew Beach Resort (East), 285
Sukhothai, 14, 18, 39, 93, 137, 159, 199, 200, 201-3, 205
Sukhumvit Highway (East), 277, 281, 286
Sukhumvit Road (Bankok), 35, 44, 48, 49, 50, 118, 120, 121, 122, 123, 124, 125, 126, 127, 160, 167, 168, 170, 171, 172, 267
Suphanburi (Central), 38
SUPPORT Program, 263
Surat Thani (South), 27, 35, 39, 45, 225, 227, 241, 243, 253, 258
Surin (Northeast), 39, 298, 300, 315, 319, 322
Surin Beach (Phuket), 239, 259, 260
Surin Elephant Roundup, 315, 317, 319
Susan Hoi Shell Cemetery (South), 247
Suwance Sukhontha (writer), 87
Swimming, 87, 259

T-bird, 96, 97
Taiwan, 54
Tak (North), 39, 175, 199, 207
Tak Bat Dok Mai (Saraburi), 159
Takraw, 163
Takua Pa (South), 241
Tap Tim Siam Fair (East), 288
Tarn Boke Koranee National Park (South), 247
TAT Duty Free Shop, 168
Taxis, 36, 41, 44, 50, 51, 106, 108, 109, 124, 125, 176, 227, 298
Telephone charges, 112
Telephone system, 38
Television, 19, 45, 46, 68, 82
Temperature, 36, 39, 57, 260, 307
Temple of the Big Buddha (South), 245
Temple of Dawn (Bangkok), 129, 155, 156
Temple of the Emerald Buddha, 128
Temple fairs, 81, 86
Temple of the Golden Mount (Bangkok), 160
Temples, 13, 14, 16, 18, 47, 54, 59, 60, 78, 87, 88, 99, 127, 129, 133, 139, 144, 155, 159, 173, 191, 196, 209, 228, 277, 281, 305, 309, 315, 317
Tennis, 87, 161, 163, 207, 217, 229, 230, 243, 260, 269, 288, 290, 320
Tha Kilen, 32
Tha Li (Northeast), 307
Tha Rae (Northeast), 311
Tha Thon (North), 193
Thai Airways Company, 25
Thai Airways International, 21, 23, 27, 29, 52, 68, 108, 193, 243, 253, 264, 267, 322
Thai architecture, 61

INDEX

Thai boxing, 161, 252, 264, 292
Thai calendar, 18
Thai character, 58
Thai Cooking School (Bangkok), 70
Thai cotton, 165
Thai currency, 21, 40, 43
Thai customs, 46, 60
Thai dancing, 13, 88, 126
Thai drama, 88
Thai embassies, 42
Thai family, 76
Thai food, 18, 69, 70, 71, 180, 195, 231, 236, 258, 273, 274
Thai food centers, 122-23
Thai government, 29, 297
Thai Intertransport Company, 35
Thai life, 21, 46, 58, 131, 156, 297
Thai life-style, 58, 60, 74, 101
Thai lunar calendar, 37
Thai military, 64
Thai monarchy, 62
Thai navy, 282
Thai New Year, 37
Thai painting, 88
Thai people, 21
Thai Population and Community Development Association, 127
Thai restaurants, 69, 124-25, 233
Thai village, 60
Thailand Game Fishing Association, 282
Thais, 14, 18, 21, 32, 37, 40, 42, 47, 48, 58, 59, 60, 62, 64, 65, 69, 73, 74, 79, 81, 82, 86, 90, 92, 93, 95, 97, 102, 106, 144, 160, 168, 171, 187, 203, 223, 235, 252, 269, 271, 274, 281, 301, 313, 321
Thalang (Phuket), 239
Tham Lod Cave (South), 254
Thammasat University (Bangkok), 82, 131
Than Sanuk Waterfall (East), 286
Than Tarn-lod National Park (Kanchanaburi), 153
Thao Sarahari Shrine (Northeast), 303
Thape Sap (South), 253
Thoen (North), 207
Thompson, Jim: 101, 133; House (Bangkok), 133; Jim Thompson Thai Silk, 101, 102, 166
Thonburi, 64, 99, 102, 110, 129, 133, 143, 156, 158, 163, 225, 243
Thong Phraphum (Kanchanaburi), 153
Thong Sala (South), 246
Thong Ta Pan Beach (South), 146
Thung Sa Laeng Luang National Park (North), 205
Tiger Cave Monastery (South), 251
Tipping, 44
Tokyo, 55
Ton Nga Chang Waterfall (South), 252
Ton Tai Waterfall (Phuket), 239

Tonsai Bay (South), 255
Topography, 57
Toronto, 25, 88
Tour buses, 32
Tourism, 85, 223, 241, 251
Tourism Authority of Thailand, 13, 19, 21, 35, 44, 45, 106, 112, 122, 127, 151, 161, 164, 172, 195, 203, 222, 227, 237, 252, 264, 294, 297, 305, 322
Tourist assistance center (Bangkok), 44
Tourist information, 21, 44
Tourist police, 211
Tourist Thailand, 16
Tourist visa, 42
Traditions, 14
Traffic, 16, 18
Trang (South), 39, 225, 227, 249, 251, 258
Transportation, 16, 18, 32, 33, 52, 54, 55
Transportation within Thailand, 27
Transvestite shows, 292
Trat (East), 39, 267, 281, 286, 288
Travel agents, 20, 23, 25, 27, 31, 33, 41, 177, 243, 259
Travel facts and figures, 36
Travel insurance, 50
Travel tips, 50
Traveller's checks, 41, 50
Travellers' aid counter (Bangkok), 32
Travellers' guide, 43
Trekking, 14, 18, 42, 188, 191, 207, 209, 210
Trekking companies, 210, 211
Tribal Research Institute (Chiang Mai), 184, 211, 222
Trooping of the Colors (Bangkok), 160
Tuk-tuks, 36, 108, 125

U-drives. *See* Rental cars
U-Tapao Airport (East), 29, 267
Ubol Ratana Dam (Northeast), 307
Ubon Ratchathani (Northeast), 39, 45, 298, 300, 303, 309, 313, 317, 319, 320, 321, 322
Udon Thani (Northeast), 39, 297, 298, 300, 303, 309, 319, 320, 321, 322
Umbrellas, 185, 214, 219
United Airlines, 27
United Kingdom, 49
U.S. Consulate (Chiang Mai), 222
U.S. Embassy, 49, 126
United States, 25, 38, 42, 44, 51, 57, 61, 68, 70, 82, 83, 99, 103
Uthai Thani (North), 39
Uttaradit (North), 39, 215

Vancouver, 27
Vegetarian Festival (Phuket), 257, 258

Victory Monument (Bangkok), 127, 168
Vientiane (Laos), 309, 313
Vietnam, 54, 103, 313
Vietnam tourism, 54
Vietnam War, 39, 313, 321
Vietnamese, 14, 95
Village headman, 78
Village life, 82, 86
Villages, 63, 64, 67, 79, 81, 91, 106, 156, 193
Vimanmek Mansion (Bangkok), 133
Visas, 41, 42, 52, 54
Visakhaa Bucha, 38, 159
Visit the region, 52
Visit Thailand Rail Pass, 31
Voice of America, 46

Wai, 46, 47
Warowot Market (Chiang Mai), 183
Washington, 42, 61
Wat Arun. *See* Temple of Dawn
Wat Benchamabopit (Bangkok), 112, 133, 155
Wat Chang Lom (North), 200
Wat Chao Chan (North), 200
Wat Chedi Chet Thaew (North), 200
Wat Chedi Luang (Chiang Mai), 182
Wat Chiang Man (Chiang Mai), 182
Wat Dhamma Nimitr (East), 279
Wat Hat Yai Nai, 251
Wat Jed Jod (Chiang Mai), 182
Wat Kamphaeng Laeng (Petchaburi), 144
Wat Khaek (Northeast), 309
Wat Khao Suwan Khiri (North), 200
Wat Kong Kara (East), 282
Wat Koo Tao (Chiang Mai), 183
Wat Kukut (North), 207
Wat Lampang Luang (North), 207, 214
Wat Mahathat (Ayutthaya), 141
Wat Mahathat (Bangkok), 131
Wat Mahathat (Phitsanulok), 203
Wat Mahathat (Sukhothai), 201
Wat Na Phra Meru (Ayutthaya), 141
Wat OO-Mong (Chiang Mai), 183
Wat Phanon Choeng (Ayutthaya), 141
Wat Phra Keo (Bangkok), 127-28
Wat Phra Keo (Chiang Rai), 195
Wat Phra Keo Don Tao (North), 200
Wat Phra Phai Luang (Sukhothai), 203
Wat Phra Ram, 141
Wat Phra Saeng (North), 200
Wat Phra Si Rattaremahathat Chaliang (North), 200
Wat Phra Si Sanphet (Ayutthaya), 139
Wat Phra Sing (Chiang Mai), 182
Wat Phra Sri Ratana Mahathat (Lopburi), 197

Wat Phra Thai Pukhao (North), 197
Wat Phra That Doi Wao (North), 197
Wat Phra That Si Chom Thong (North), 191
Wat Phra Thong (Phuket), 239
Wat Phrae (North), 205
Wat Phrathat Doi Suthep (Chiang Mai), 184
Wat Phrathat Haripoonchai (North), 207
Wat Po (Bangkok), 112, 129, 155
Wat Ra Ngeng (Northeast), 315
Wat Raajanadda (Bangkok), 155
Wat Raj Burana (Ayutthaya), 141
Wat Sakhet, 112, 131, 155. *See also* Temple of the Golden Mount
Wat Sala Loi (Northeast), 305
Wat Saphan Hin (Sukhothai), 203
Wat Si Chum (Sukhothai), 203
Wat Sibunruang (North), 205
Wat Sra Sri (Sukhothai), 201
Wat Sri Sawai (Sukhothai), 201
Wat Suwan Davavam (Ayutthaya), 141
Wat Suwannaraur (Petchaburi), 144
Wat That Phanom (Northeast), 313
Wat Traimit (Bangkok), 155
Wat Trapang Ngoen (Sukhothai), 201
Wat Yannasangwararam (Pattaya), 277
Water, 42
Water skiing, 259, 277
Water sports, 259, 265
Wats, 16, 78, 79, 127, 176, 182, 190, 228, 307, 313
Wax Castle Festival (Northeast), 319
Weather, 211
Weather and climate, 36
Weekend Market (Bangkok), 86, 131, 135
Western, 42, 45, 48, 60, 69, 72, 83, 88, 98, 99, 103, 105, 125, 137, 143, 168, 181, 238, 274, 298, 311, 321
Western meals, 41, 180, 181, 195, 236
Western restaurants, 125-26, 273
Westerners, 14, 37, 48, 67, 71, 79, 101, 128, 159, 171, 265
While you are away, 51
Wiharn Phra Monkol Bopit (Ayutthaya), 141
Windsurfing, 245, 287, 291
Woodcarving, 220, 261
World War II, 82
Writers, 95

Yao hilltribe village, 197, 211, 213
Yala (South), 39, 257
Yasothon (Northeast), 39, 301, 317
Young, Stephen, 91

Zoos, 279, 281

Please tell us about your trip to Thailand below.
(You may use this page as an envelope. See over.)

Cut along this line.

Cut along this line.

Fold here. Fasten lip on front with clear tape.

Cut along this line.

Fold along dotted lines to make an envelope.

```
_____

_____

_____
```

re: 1st edition Thailand

Place first class postage here

The Maverick Guides
Pelican Publishing Company
P.O. Box 189
Gretna, Louisiana 70054

Cut along this line.